Wine

by
THE EDITORS OF TIME-LIFE BOOKS

TIME-LIFE BOOKS·AMSTERDAM

TIME-LIFE BOOKS
EUROPEAN EDITOR: John Paul Porter
Design Director: Louis Klein
Photography Director: Pamela Marke
Planning Director: Alan Lothian
Chief of Research: Jackie Matthews
Chief Sub-Editor: Ilse Gray

THE GOOD COOK
Series Editor: Ellen Galford
Series Co-ordinators: Debbie Litton, Liz Timothy

Editorial Staff for *Wine*
Text Editor: Margot Levy, Deborah Thompson
Anthology Editor: Tokunbo Williams
Staff Writers: Alexandra Carlier (principal),
Tim Fraser, Thom Henvey
Researcher: Krystyna Mayer
Designer: Mary Staples
Sub-Editors: Sally Rowland, Charles Boyle,
Kate Cann, Frances Dixon
Anthology Researchers: Debra Raad, Stephanie Lee
Anthology Assistant: Aquila Kegan
Design Assistant: David Mackersey
Proofreader: Judith Heaton
Editorial Assistant: Molly Sutherland

EDITORIAL PRODUCTION FOR THE SERIES
Chief: Ellen Brush
Quality Control: Douglas Whitworth
Traffic Co-ordinators: Jane Lillicrap, Linda Mallett
Picture Co-ordinator: Ros Smith
Art Department: Janet Matthew
Editorial Department: Lesley Kinahan, Debra
Lelliott, Sylvia Osborne

ISBN 7054 0614 8
TIME-LIFE is a trademark of Time Incorporated U.S.A.

Cover: A fine Bordeaux—a Domaine de Chevalier 1969—
is poured into a wine glass. The glass has a wide bowl
narrowing towards the top in order to trap the wine's
bouquet in the space between the surface of the wine and
the rim. Thus the bouquet can be savoured fully before the
wine is tasted (*page 34*).

THE CHIEF CONSULTANT:
Richard Olney, an American, has lived and worked since 1951
in France, where he is a highly regarded authority on food and
wine. He is the author of *The French Menu Cookbook* and the
award-winning *Simple French Food,* and has contributed to
numerous gastronomic magazines in France and the United
States, including the influential journals *Cuisine et Vins de
France* and *La Revue du Vin de France.* He has directed
cooking courses in France and the United States and is a
member of several distinguished gastronomic and oenological societies, including *L'Académie Internationale du Vin, La
Confrérie des Chevaliers du Tastevin* and *La Commanderie
du Bontemps de Médoc et des Graves.*

SPECIAL CONSULTANT:
Sybille Bedford, O.B.E., planned and wrote the section of this book that serves as a
guide to the wines of the world. Mrs. Bedford, who lives in London, is the biographer of
Aldous Huxley, and the author of many distinguished novels and works of non-fiction.
She is a dedicated amateur of wine, with a particular interest in the wines of France and
Germany.

THE PHOTOGRAPHER:
Alan Duns was born in 1943 in the north of England and studied at the Ealing School of
Photography. He specializes in food photography and has undertaken many advertis-
ing assignments. His work has appeared in major British publications.

THE INTERNATIONAL CONSULTANTS:
Great Britain: *Jane Grigson* was born in Gloucester and brought up in the north of
England. She is a graduate of Cambridge University. Her first book on food, *Charcu-
terie and French Pork Cookery,* was published in 1967; since then, she has published a
number of cookery books, including *Good Things, English Food* and *Jane Grigson's
Vegetable Book.* She became cookery correspondent for the colour magazine of the
London *Observer* in 1968. *Alan Davidson* is the author of *Fish and Fish Dishes of Laos,
Mediterranean Seafood* and *North Atlantic Seafood.* He is the founder of Prospect
Books, which specializes in scholarly publications on food and cookery. *Russell Hone*
has worked for many years in the wine trade in France, Germany, Great Britain and the
United States. **France:** *Michel Lemonnier* was born in Normandy. He began contributing to the magazine *Cuisine et Vins de France* in 1960, and also writes for several other
important French food and wine periodicals. The co-founder and vice-president of the
society *Les Amitiés Gastronomiques Internationales,* he is a frequent lecturer on wine
and a member of most of the vinicultural confraternities and academies in France.
Germany: *Jochen Kuchenbecker* trained as a chef, but worked for 10 years as a food
photographer in many European countries before opening his own restaurant in
Hamburg. *Anne Brakemeier,* who also lives in Hamburg, has published articles on food
and cooking in many German periodicals. She is the co-author of three cookery books.
Italy: *Massimo Alberini* divides his time between Milan and Venice. He is a well-known
food writer and journalist, with a particular interest in culinary history. Among his 14
books are *Storia del Pranzo all'Italiana, 4000 Anni a Tavola* and *100 Ricette Storiche.*
The Netherlands: *Hugh Jans,* a resident of Amsterdam, has been translating cookery
books and articles for more than 25 years. He has also published several books of his
own, including *Bistro Koken* and *Sla, Slaatjes, Snacks,* and his recipes are published in
many Dutch magazines. **The United States:** *Carol Cutler,* who lives in Washington,
DC, is the author of three cookery books, including the award-winning *The Six-Minute
Soufflé and Other Culinary Delights. Judith Olney* received her culinary training in
England and France and has written two cookery books.

Valuable help was given in the preparation of this volume by the following members of
Time-Life Books: *Maria Vincenza Aloisi, Joséphine du Brusle* (Paris); *Janny Hovinga*
(Amsterdam); *Elisabeth Kraemer* (Bonn); *Ann Natanson, Mimi Murphy* (Rome); *Bona
Schmid* (Milan).

CONTENTS

The Gift of the Vine

The miracle of wine has always been associated with divine alchemy. And why not? A sweet, turbid, sticky mash or juice of fresh grapes is roiled into an angry, frothing boil by a powerful, invisible force that then subsides to reveal limpid nectar, bearing the gift of euphoria. Today, we prefer to divest miracles of their mystery, and the mechanics of this marvellous force, called alcoholic fermentation, can be explained in scientific terms. Wine's diversity and complexity, however, remain inexplicable.

It is an extraordinary phenomenon that grapes from neighbouring vines of the same variety and age, apparently growing in twin soils and sharing the same favours of the sun, treated identically by the same grower, should produce wines of delicately but noticeably different character; and it is an astounding verity that laboratory analyses can disclose identical components but are unable to distinguish a banal, industrially produced wine from one that has a rare prestige.

The role of wine is to give pleasure; but it imparts something more than that. Wine brings with it a message so elemental that it must be embraced or mutely comprehended without being understood. Like the Parthenon, Michelangelo and the changing seasons, it is woven into the fabric of universal order. Wine is subtly altered in relation to food, revealing special qualities at table, and it expresses itself most fully when intimately appreciated and shared with friends in an atmosphere of serenity and expansive well-being. This book is about the care and the service of wine—how to treat it to make it respond in depth, unveiling nuances that less respectful handling would obscure or destroy. The following words of introduction are dedicated to explaining what wine is and how it is made, to deepen the pleasure and the understanding of its gifts when it is poured into our glasses. Subsequent chapters discuss the choosing and storing of wine, the serving of wine, wine's function in a menu, and its role in cooking (or in the kitchen); and specific wines from different vine-producing countries and from the different regions within those countries are discussed in detail on pages 90-138.

Grapes into wine

The two arts, or sciences, on which the qualities of wine depend are viticulture—the culture of the vine, or grape farming—and oenology—the science of wine, from the Greek *oinos*, meaning wine. Oenology encompasses vinification (wine-making)—the controlled transformation by fermentation of grape juice into wine—and the subsequent attentions that are requisite to the stability of the wine.

Millions of micro-organisms, among them a variety of yeasts, attach themselves to the wax-like surface, or pruina, of a grape skin, creating the frosty effect known as the bloom. When the grapes are crushed, alcoholic fermentation is made possible by the presence of these yeasts, which feed on the grape sugars. The yeast's own digestive enzymes break down the grape sugars to provide energy; as a by-product of this process, alcohol and carbon dioxide are also produced.

All grapes will ferment; but of all the world's many species only one, the European wine grape, *Vitis vinifera*, contains enough natural, fermentable sugars and a sufficiently low acidity for its juices to be transformed into balanced and stable wine without massive additions of sugar to raise the level of alcohol and an accompanying dilution with water to lower the acidity. That grape, in its several thousand varieties, provides the world with most of its wine (*pages 18-21*).

The wines produced from *Vitis vinifera* can be divided into four broad categories: dry wines, unfortified sweet wines, sparkling wines and fortified wines.

Dry wines are those in which all the grape sugars have been fermented into alcohol. The usual method of describing the sugar content of grapes or their unfermented juices—a liquid also known as must—is expressed in terms of the potential percentage of alcohol the grape sugars might yield through fermentation. In the case of dry wines, a potential of, say, 12 per cent (normally written as 12°, would also represent the real alcohol content of the finished wine.

In unfortified sweet wines, only a portion of the sugars is fermented out. These rich, sweet white wines, characterized as "luscious", are made either from partially dried grapes or from grapes that have been dehydrated by the action of the mould *Botrytis cinerea*, known, because of its exquisite effects, as noble rot. In each case, the result is a high concentration of grape sugars and an incomplete fermentation: the yeasts are made inoperative either by the alcohol they produce or by the action of the mould. The juice of partially dried grapes, for example, might have a potential alcohol content of 24°. If fermentation ends at 18°, that figure will represent the wine's real alcohol content, while the other 6° will remain in the wine in the form of untransformed grape sugars. Italian *vini santi* wines, from the Muscat grape, and the *vins de paille* of France's Jura region are among the wines produced by this method.

To produce sparkling wines, a second fermentation is induced, inside hermetically sealed vessels, by the additions of refined sugar and yeasts to the finished wine. The carbon dioxide generated by the second fermentation is forced into solution in the wine, making it effervescent. The best sparkling wines are made by a system that, having originated in the Champagne region of France, is known as the *méthode champenoise* (*page 102*).

Fortified wines, as the name implies, have been strengthened by the addition of distilled spirits. Such wines can be dry or sweet, depending on whether the spirits are added early, thus muting the fermentation and retaining grape sugars in the wine, or later, thus increasing the alcoholic strength of a dry wine. Sherry, port and Madeira are fortified wines (*page 108*).

A brief history

Wine is almost as old as agriculture. According to Genesis, a vineyard was the first thing Noah planted after the flood. Evidence exists that wine was made in Mesopotamia several millennia before that, but prehistoric fossil remains of the wild *vinifera* vine have been uncovered throughout Europe. The Greeks were making wine long before Homer wrote of it; when the Phocaeans—Greeks from Asia Minor—founded the city of Marseilles in the sixth century B.C., they introduced their own varieties to the south of France and to Spain. The vine was well established by the time of the Roman Empire; although the Romans instructed the tribes they conquered in the arts of viniculture, such distinctive grape varieties as Riesling, Pinot Noir, Chardonnay and the two Cabernets (*pages 18-21*) probably evolved from plants already native to the Rhine, Burgundy and Bordeaux.

In the ancient world, wine was made to last. Sealed in earthenware jars—amphorae—and buried in the cool ground, many Greek and Roman wines were kept for 15 to 25 years before they were considered ready for drinking. Wooden casks were introduced by the Gauls, and the Romans adopted them for shipping wine, but, for storage, they remained faithful to amphorae and used corks and sealing wax to protect the wine from air.

With the collapse of the Roman Empire, the use of the cork was lost, and with it the whole concept of ageing wine. Throughout the Middle Ages, most wines were stored in casks that were never topped up; as a result, contact with air made them progressively more vinegary, and most were consumed by the time the next year's vintage was ready. The wines were very different from their modern counterpart. Descriptions are rare, but we know that the Bordeaux wines were rosé, not red; that Volnay, among

Stones absorb and reflect the sun's heat at Châteauneuf-du-Pape.

The terrain at Château Loudenne in the Médoc slopes gently.

the most elegant of today's red Burgundies, remained a rosé until the late 18th century; and that in Champagne, no one knew from one year to the next what colour the wine would be.

It was in Champagne, though, that the next step forward came. As in many cold climates, the wines of Champagne have always had a natural inclination to sparkle lightly. This effervescence is the result of low temperatures slowing down the rate at which the natural grape sugars are transformed into alcohol; these remaining traces of sugar continue to ferment very slowly, producing carbon dioxide. Around 1690, Dom Pierre Pérignon, cellar master of Hautvillers Abbey, in his search for a way to imprison this effervescence in the wine, rediscovered the cork and combined it with newly developed, strong glass bottles. For over a thousand years, the only stoppers had been wooden plugs, wrapped with hemp and dipped in olive oil to minimize the passage of air. Within a few years, the use of glass bottles and corks would revolutionize the conservation of all wine.

Another ancient secret was rediscovered at about the same time: the magical properties of Botrytis. An inadvertently delayed harvest in the Tokay district of Hungary obliged growers to make wine from alarmingly shrivelled grapes; the result was beautiful wine with a new taste, a wondrous elixir that was soon honoured with a place at the table of Louis XIV of France.

As Europeans spread throughout the world, so did their vines. In the mid-16th century, the Spanish planted vines in Mexico and soon afterwards in Peru, Chile and Argentina; South Africa had vineyards by the mid-17th century; California and Australia were planted at the end of the 18th century and New Zealand received its first vines a few decades later. In Europe itself, by the 18th century the British were well established in the wine centres that they were to render famous for the production of fortified wines. At that time, port, Madeira and sherry were all dry table wines; the addition of brandy to suit the spirituous British taste—originally a somewhat fraudulent practice—became a respectable tradition, and, within a century, port, sherry and Madeira had acquired the high reputations they retain today.

By the middle of the 19th century, the viticultural world had at last regained most of the lost arts; steady evolution, it seemed, guaranteed slow but continuous improvement. But then disaster struck, the most relentless destruction, the greatest calamity recorded in the history of viticulture. In 1863, not far from the southernmost Rhône Valley vineyards, there appeared the root louse, *Phylloxera vastatrix*—loosely translated as "the devastating leaf-witherer". The creatures had arrived from America, probably on vine cuttings to be used for experimental purposes. Phylloxera, in its most dangerous phase, lives and feeds in the roots of the vine. Native American vines had developed a natural resistance to it, but their European cousins had no such immunity. The louse sucked the life from them, leaving unhealable wounds; the leaves fell off and the vines died.

The plague spread with appalling speed. By the end of the 1860s, all of the Rhône Valley and the Bordeaux region were infected and, by a circuitous route, Phylloxera had arrived in Portugal. Many Bordeaux wine makers fled to Rioja, in Spain; the blight caught up with them five years later. Other growers, from all over the southern half of France, moved to Algeria to plant that country's first vines; Phylloxera followed them in 1887.

During the 1870s, Madeira, most of Spain, Burgundy, Austria, Germany and Hungary joined the victims. The insidious and irrevocable nature of the infestation was not immediately understood, and, during those years, infected cuttings from Europe were carried to Australia, California and, by the early 1880s, to South Africa. Phylloxera reached Italy in 1888, Tokay in 1890, Champagne in 1891 and Jerez in Spain in 1894.

Many treatments were essayed, some of them quite fanciful. In the plains, vineyards were flooded in a vain attempt to drown the creatures. It was discovered that Phylloxera did not like sand: growers who could do so abandoned their vines and replanted in sandy places. The majority, though, faced utter ruin.

In the end, the solution was simple. Indigenous, wild American vines were resistant to Phylloxera, but the wine their grapes yielded was of poor quality. However, by grafting European *vinifera* vines on to American rootstock, growers discovered that they could have the best of both worlds. At first, however, even in the face of catastrophe, there was considerable resistance to what conservative-minded growers held to be the revolting concept of grafting Europe's noble vines on to vulgar roots. Necessity, though, triumphed over nicety; once begun, the lightning reconstitution of Europe's vineyards was miraculous.

During the painful years of recovery, French scientists in search of a less laborious method of repopulating European vineyards created a number of Phylloxera-resistant hybrid vines—crosses between varieties of *vinifera* vines and the commonest of American wild vines, *Vitis labrusca*. These vines, known as French hybrids or, because they are not grafted, as direct producers, had a brief and inglorious existence in Europe. The island of Madeira was planted with them, but the wine they produced was found unacceptable and they had to be torn out and replaced with grafted vines. The use of such hybrids in European countries today is illegal for regions whose wine receives official appellations or denominations. However, they are widely planted in the eastern United States, and new hybrids have been developed which have lost the distinctive taste—described as "foxy"—that is peculiar to American vines. One, at least, called Seyve

Vines on a steep Swiss hillside are planted in terraces.

Villard, produces a crisp, clean and refreshing white wine.

Nevertheless, the world's greatest wines are all made from *vinifera* vines and almost all are grafted. Phylloxera has never been eradicated; except for a few places that have been miraculously spared contact or whose sandy soils repel the parasite—Cyprus, Chile, South Australia, corners of Hungary and Austria and the recently planted north-western states of the U.S.A.—the soil, wherever vines are grown, is hopelessly infested. Thus, without the grafted American roots, there would be no wine as we know it. The art of grafting has progressed enormously since its early days. The first rootstocks used were ill-adapted to the soils that had produced the finest wines, and for many years it was claimed, with some justice, that pre-Phylloxera wines had been finer and longer-lived than their successors. Now, there are many rootstocks, developed from a whole range of American Phylloxera-resistant species; each is particularly suited to certain grape varieties, soil structures and climates in different combinations. The rootstocks thus match the vines that produce today's most celebrated wines, which themselves have evolved out of millennia of mutations and shifting adaptations to particular climates, microclimates, soil structures and sub-structures. In emulation of these wines, the vines that produce them have been transplanted to different climates and soils, sometimes with great success, but never with the same results.

The art of viticulture

To give of its best, a vine must be made to suffer: the finest wine is the result of growing conditions and techniques of cultivation that combine to restrict the plant's yield to a few clusters of exquisitely concentrated grapes. The greatest vineyards are found in the most difficult climates and soils, so poor and barren that little else can take root in them. During winter, radical pruning frustrates the vine's natural inclination to wander, limiting the number of grapes it can produce; during the growing season, to concentrate further the gifts of the soil and the sun in a few selected grapes, other grapes are removed from the vine and discarded. Crowding the vines together also limits production and heightens quality: by doubling the number of vines to each half hectare (acre), a grower will produce no more grapes, but he will make better wine. The exigencies of tractor cultivation today impose a practical limit on overcrowding; but dense, nearly impenetrable vineyards were a feature of pre-Phylloxera viticulture in the most respected areas of Burgundy and Champagne.

The age of a vine is another important factor in the quality of the wine it will produce. A vine may produce fruit as early as its second year, but it will not give its best for a few years more, not until the roots have had time to take strength in the permeable surface soil and have begun their patient, progressive penetration of sub-structures, fissuring solid rock and crumbling packed gravels to an eventual depth of many yards. There, they can feed from underground resources of mineral elements that will, years later, be reflected in the matching depth of a great wine's body and bouquet. (The classified first growths of Bordeaux relegate the harvest from vines less than 10 years old to the production of lesser wines that are sold under their own labels.)

Once established, a vine has a long life: in pre-Phylloxera days, a hundred years was not uncommon. Grafted vines do not

A 50-year-old vine and a three-year-old vine.

enjoy quite the same longevity, and they are often torn out before they reach the age of 40, when their productivity begins to decline. But some growers never remove a healthy, living vine: although the yield falls off, the quality continues to improve. Château Latour of Bordeaux in France is an example: until the property changed hands in the early 1960s, its proprietors had failed to replace even dead vines and the average age of the plants was easily 50 years—a partial explanation of the wine's astonishing complexity and long life.

Yet the vines themselves are not the only source of a great wine's unique character. The situation of the vineyard also contributes. Old or young, vines must have well-drained soil; that, and the need for the protection and warmth provided by particular locations, have always limited the production of better wines to hillsides—some with steep terraces, others more gentle slopes. Another valued feature is gravelly or stony soil: the stones absorb heat from the sun during the day and radiate it on to the vines at night, protecting them from spring frosts and improving the grapes' potential for autumn ripening.

However, it is in their microclimates that vineyards attain most individuality. A microclimate is a climate within a climate—a limited area within a larger region in which specially favourable conditions are created as a result of eccentric natural formations. Typical examples are valleys, which funnel warm breezes to privileged hillsides in cool climates—or cool breezes in hot climates—and natural amphitheatres that receive the maximum of the sun's goodness while shielding vines from winds and frost. An amphitheatre microclimate may be created by no more than a hollow in a hillside, bestowing upon a few vines an advantage over their neighbours; on a larger scale, an amphitheatre may be provided by a structure of mountain ranges, controlling weather conditions within a huge, natural basin.

Different grape varieties demand different soils: chalk and the Palomino grape are associated with quality in Jerez in Spain, for example, and in France in the chalky soils of Champagne and in Burgundy's Côte d'Or, the Chardonnay and Pinot Noir grapes give their most sublime wines. The Gamay grape produces poor wine from the Côte d'Or chalk, but the same grape, growing on the granitic hillsides of Beaujolais, yields wines of great charm. The remarkably adaptable Cabernet Sauvignon, grown so successfully throughout the world, still likes no earth so well as the gravelly quartz, the ferruginous sandstone and the sandy clays of the Bordeaux region of France.

Whatever its variety, a vine should be healthy and disease-resistant, without being over-vigorous: an exuberant vitality would disperse the plant's energies, producing excessive vegetation and too many grapes. To ensure healthy vines of controlled vigour, and to maintain the qualities inherent in particular strains or local variations of a grape variety, many growers practise clonal selection—the reproduction, by cuttings, of genetically identical vines. This means, that an entire vineyard could be populated by thousands of clones of a single vine.

To lend more complexity to their wine, though, growers more often use a selection of several different vines, based on years of experiment to match individual vines to the slight variations in soil structure and exposure in different areas of a vineyard. At Château Haut-Brion in Bordeaux, France, for instance, clones taken from selected Cabernet Sauvignon, Cabernet Franc and Merlot vines are planted singly in different places, and marked; the grapes from each vine on the property are treated separately in laboratory micro-vinifications, to be analysed for structure and aroma before major planting decisions are made.

For the most part, the annual cycle of a vineyard follows an ancient routine. The dormant vines are pruned in late winter, when the harshest cold is past but well before the sap begins to rise with the coming spring. The precise way in which a vine is pruned and trained depends on the particular grape variety and the climate; whatever the style, most of the previous year's growth is removed and the few canes retained are cut back to four or five unformed buds, or eyes. The grape clusters will form on new shoots that grow from each eye. During the growing season, unproductive shoots that issue from old wood are removed. As the season advances, the extremities of the new branches may be lopped off to redirect the plant's energy to the grapes; leaves that crowd the grapes, depriving them of free air circulation, are removed, while leaves that shade them from the direct sun are retained. The removal of mature and healthy leaves, though, is kept to a minimum: as the grapes ripen, the leaves provide them with much of their sugar. The plants flower in early summer; approximately 100 days later, the grapes are ripe and wine-making can begin.

Making red wine

The making of any wine depends on the work of the yeasts, whose microscopic world contains a great variety of organisms of differing shapes, sizes and aptitudes. In vineyards and cellars where

"Noble rot" attacks Semillon grapes at Château d'Yquem in Sauternes.

A machine crushes and stems red grapes at Château Latour.

of noble rot, affecting the first phase of the fermentation.)

Except for *teinturier* (dyer) grapes with red flesh, used to deepen the colour of high-production, undistinguished wines from the plains, the colour of all red wine grapes is in the skins; the flesh and the juice are colourless. To release the maximum colour, as well as the aromatic elements and tannin imprisoned in the skins, the skins' cellular structure must be destroyed—the living cells killed. In a traditional red wine vinification, the ripe grapes are brought directly from the vineyard, lightly crushed and transferred to vats; the fermentation sets in within a few hours—sooner or later, depending on the ambient temperature.

The transformation of the grape sugars into alcohol and carbon dioxide generates heat; the heat and alcohol break down the cells of the skins, and the must turns a dense purple while escaping gas churns the vat's contents, simulating a foaming boil. The heat usually reaches its greatest intensity on the third or fourth day; sometimes it must be restrained by cooling devices, or it will halt the yeasts' activity. As the quantity of alcohol increases and the sugar decreases, the multiplication of the yeasts diminishes rapidly and, with it, the heat and the turbulence.

The alcoholic fermentation is practically finished in six to eight days, but a continued maceration (up to an additional week or two for many Bordeaux wines and the greatest Burgundies) may be felt necessary to absorb the maximum tannin from the pomace—the mass of skins and pulp. Tannin is fundamental to the structure of wines that develop slowly and live long; but if the object is to make a supple, fruity wine with a lovely colour but no

wine has long been made, a natural environmental selection of yeast cultures slowly evolves; such a selection can be unique to a particular growth and is an essential element in the definition of a wine's personality.

Some growers do not believe in tampering with the ecological balance of naturally evolved yeasts, native to their vineyards and cellars, but many others use laboratory-propagated yeasts to influence a fermentation, usually strains taken from the vineyard itself, intended to reinforce the yeast population already present on the grapes, either in case the grapes have been washed by recent rains or for the preparation of a *pied de cuve*—a preliminary batch of fermenting must that is used to inseminate the first vat in a cold year when the beginning of a fermentation may be stubborn. Outside Europe the inclination is to develop yeasts by laboratory selection of strains taken from celebrated European vineyards; since Riesling, Chardonnay, Gewürztraminer, Pinot Noir and Cabernet Sauvignon grapes, among others, are often vinified in the same winery, a number of different yeast cultures are kept on hand.

But although there are dozens of yeasts and many strains of each, three general categories control the beginning, middle and end of the alcoholic fermentation that creates wine. A first set of yeasts launches the fermentation; these are extremely sensitive to the alcohol they produce, and perish at levels as low as 3° or 4°. As the activating yeasts begin to disappear, another type, able to support the levels of alcohol achieved by most dry wines—around 12°—begins to multiply. Finally, the yeasts of a third phase take over. These do not propagate well in the presence of the preceding yeasts, but can withstand alcohol levels as high as 18° to 20°, and are responsible for fermenting out the last traces of sugar in many dry wines and for the last phase of vinification in sweet wines. (A still different yeast develops only in the presence

Red grapes are hand-stemmed at Château Palmer.

hard tannin, seductive in youth but with limited ageing potential, the must can be drawn off into another vat at the height of the fermentation—as soon as it is sufficiently coloured—to complete its fermentation out of contact with the tannic skins.

When the free-run juice has been drawn off, the pomace receives several pressings until there is no more juice. The next pressings may be lower in alcohol but the concentration of acids, tannins and colour will be higher; one or more of the pressings may be added to the wine, depending on its structural needs.

Grape stems are another source of tannin, more acerbic than that of the skins; whether they are separated from the grapes before fermentation—all, partially, or not at all—depends on the grape variety, the vintage, the regional tradition and the desired result. The stems lend a deceptively thin and acrid hardness to the young wine, temporarily masking its other qualities and imposing longer ageing. In Bordeaux and wherever wines are made from the tannic, densely coloured and thick-skinned Cabernet Sauvignon grapes, they are stemmed; in Hermitage in the Rhône Valley of France, the Syrah grapes are not stemmed. In Burgundy, opinions are more divided: many growers stem the grapes so that their wines will have more immediacy in their youth, while others believe that the additional tannin from the stems will permit the wines to evolve with greater depth and longevity, although their virtues will be less apparent when they are young.

Traditionally, grapes were stemmed by rubbing them by hand through wooden grills, leaving the stems behind; mechanical stemmer-crushers, which fling the stems aside and pump the grapes and their juices into the vats, are more common now.

The vats may be of wood, concrete or other materials with inert linings, or they may be of stainless steel. The steel is easy to keep clean, and metal's conductivity allows precise temperature control by means of a system of water flowing down the outside of the vats—hot to launch the fermentation, if necessary, or cold to prevent the temperature from reaching the danger point. Vats may be open or closed; the latter have trapdoors to receive the grapes and permit the gas to escape, and are more practical for large-scale vinification. Where holdings are small or, as in Burgundy, where a grower may own fragments of a dozen different appellations, each to be vinified apart, open vats are traditional.

The head or *chapeau*—a spongy mass of skins and pulp that swells over the must's surface from the pressure of the escaping gas—may be left floating, in which case it is regularly punched down, or it may be immersed, held beneath the liquid's surface by a wooden grid. The choice of method depends largely on tradition, the arguments in favour of the one or the other being tenuous in the extreme. During the first part of the fermentation, must is regularly pumped out of the base of the vat, up and over the surface to aerate the mass, invigorating the yeasts, dispersing the heat and, in the case of a floating head, keeping it moist. After the tumultuous phase of the fermentation is over, the head sinks into the must to macerate of its own accord. The vats are then covered or closed up to retain a blanket of carbon dioxide, protecting the incompletely fermented must from contact with air.

Supple red wines with an attractive colour can be made by heating the crushed grapes to release their colour, cooling them and pressing them immediately, then adding cultured yeasts and

Black and white grapes are crushed in a special Champagne press.

fermenting the juice, out of contact with the skins. Neither the wine nor the colour ages well. A more interesting red wine vinification, known as carbonic maceration, is widely used for the production of wines meant to be drunk very young, called *primeur* in a number of tongues and *vino nuovo* in Italy. In this method, whole, unbruised bunches of grapes are placed in airtight vats under the pressure of carbon dioxide, either pumped in or naturally created by a small amount of fermenting must in the vat; the grapes are kept under pressure for from two to three weeks, during which time an intracellular fermentation takes place in the berries, partially transforming the sugars into alcohol and diminishing their malic acid content by as much as half. (Malic acid, also found in apples, and tartaric acid, unique to grapes, are the two basic acids in a must.) The free juices are run off, then the grapes and pulp remaining are pressed and their juices added to the others in a vat. There, the fermentation is finished, usually in a couple of days. This method produces especially tender and fruity wines, with great charm when drunk young and cool.

Among the micro-organisms clinging, with the yeasts, to the pruina of grape skins are lactic bacteria, the same bacteria that break milk into curds and whey. These bacteria bring about a secondary, malolactic, fermentation by means of which the wine's malic acid is broken down into lactic acid and carbon dioxide. This natural deacidification is essential to the quality of all red wines. Not only is the quantity of acid diminished by half but lactic acid is less aggressive than malic acid, and, as a side effect of the fermentation, the wine's bouquet is rendered more complex by the creation of new elements in its structure. Because the ideal temperature for malolactic fermentation is lower than that of

Steel vats often now replace wooden ones.

the alcoholic fermentation, it rarely begins until the latter is complete or at least on the decline. In those vinifications in which the wine and the pomace remain in the fermenting vats for prolonged maceration, malolactic fermentation often takes place unnoticed before the new wine is drawn off. At other times, it is capricious; like the yeasts, lactic bacteria eventually inhabit the cellars as well as the vineyards, and the fermentation is always particularly difficult to launch in new buildings.

Not all fermentations are welcome, however, and one can be disastrous: acetic bacteria, present in the air, can turn wine to vinegar. The chief weapon against them is sulphur dioxide, the wine maker's universal disinfectant and sterilizing agent. Empty casks are sterilized by burning sulphur wicks, suspended from their bung-holes, and in the vinification itself sulphur tablets, dissolved in wine, are often added to the crushed grapes as they go into the vats and after the termination of the malolactic fermentation. Such practices, though general, are controversial, at least in the making of red wine. Sulphur dioxide has an equally devastating effect on both acetic and lactic bacteria, easily compromising the malolactic fermentation, and it can destroy the more fragile yeasts, diminishing the complexity of the yeast population. Intuition and a fine discretion are necessary, but proponents of the use of sulphur in red wine vinification believe that imperceptible traces of sulphur in a wine are vital to its finesse, helping to define other odours and flavours.

Another controversial process is chaptalization: the addition of sugar to unfermented must to raise the degree of alcohol in a

Fermentation in an open vat, Vieux Château Certan.

wine. The argument has continued since the beginning of the 19th century, when the technique was recommended by the French Minister of the Interior under Napoleon I, Comte J.-A Chaptal, from whom the practice takes its name. Today, for instance, Germany permits the chaptalization of "table" wines but not the more exalted appellations; however, the sweetening of all wines by the addition of sterilized, unfermented grape juice is permitted. Legislation in France permits chaptalization in specific regions in deficient years. It is illegal in Italy and California—but the addition of grape concentrate, an alternative method of increasing fermentable sugars in a must, is permitted in both places. Thus legislation and oenological commonsense are often at odds: when grape concentrate is added to a must, its sugars are fermented out, leaving its concentration of acids and other constituents behind. The effect is to throw the wine out of balance and destroy any character related to its origins. However, a judicious addition of sugar, first dissolved in some must, leaves only an extra degree of alcohol in its place, thereby giving the wine a fuller fruit and better balance in a difficult year, without affecting the wine's basic nature. A heavy hand will destroy the balance, of course, and chaptalization is only acceptable if employed with considerable discretion.

Making white wine

In principle, the vinification of white wine differs from that of red in that the white grapes are pressed immediately after picking and the juice is fermented out of contact with the skins. When red grapes are vinified like white wine, the result is pink or rosé wine. White wine is nearly always made from white grapes but, because the colour of red grapes resides only in the skins, these too may produce white wine on condition that they are picked when only just ripe and pressed quickly without an initial crushing—beyond a certain degree of ripeness, the pigmentation of the skins begins to taint the colour of the juice. Making white wine from red grapes is traditional in—and almost unique to—Champagne, where huge, wide presses extract the colourless juice from a shallow depth of grapes in the shortest possible time.

The refreshing liveliness of a dry white wine depends on a higher level of acidity than that of red wine. The grape variety, the climate and the degree of ripeness are important factors that affect a grape's acidity. As grapes ripen, the sugar content increases and the acidity decreases; they are ripe when they attain maximum size and juice content, the sugar level remaining momentarily stable. Weather permitting, they then move into various stages of advanced ripeness, with sugar again increasing while both acidity and weight decrease.

Grapes ripen differently in different climates. In northern zones they may, in good years, reach high sugar contents in states of advanced ripeness while retaining sufficient acidity to make wine that is perfectly balanced. But the same grape variety, grown in a hot climate, will have a low content in acid when only just ripe. To garner the acid indispensable to the wine's vitality, grapes can be picked at the stage when the flavours of the fresh fruit have fully developed, but before ripeness has reduced their acidity; to heighten the acidity further, the secondary malolactic

The first year cellar at Château Mouton Rothschild, Pauillac.

fermentation may be partially or even completely averted.

White grapes are usually crushed without being stemmed; the brief contact with the stems as the juice is being pressed out does not perceptibly affect it, but the presence of the stems facilitates pressing, preventing the pomace from becoming too compact. Whereas red grapes are propelled into the vats the instant they are crushed, the juices of white grapes are exposed to air for a much longer period, not only in the crushing but throughout the pressing. As a result, they have more need than red wines of protection from harmful bacteria. The sulphur dioxide used for this purpose also temporarily paralyses the yeasts, thus postponing the onset of fermentation and permitting the solids in suspension to precipitate; the relatively clear liquid is decanted into casks or vats for fermentation.

To retain the maximum fruit and freshness of aroma, white wines are fermented at lower temperatures than reds. This has never posed a problem in traditional, small-cask vinifications; at ambient autumn temperatures, there is sufficient loss of heat from a small vessel to prevent the must from rising above 20°C (68°F). The casks are, at first, filled only three-quarters full to nourish the yeasts with oxygen and to prevent the fermenting must from foaming out over the top of the barrel; after the most active phase of fermentation has passed, the casks are topped up to keep the wine from contact with air. Low temperatures prolong the fermentation period and, with the approach of winter weather, it may be necessary to heat the vinification cellars in order to encourage the malolactic fermentation that is essential to the quality and stability of complex white wines.

The larger the container in which fermentation takes place, the higher the temperature will rise and the more difficult it is to control. Cooling systems and refrigerated installations have recently made it possible to ferment white wines in large vats at strictly controlled temperatures, usually about 15°C (59°F) but, in special instances and over a compensatingly lengthy period, temperatures may be held as low as those of a domestic refrigerator. A rapid succession of clarifying treatments—centrifuging, subjection to near-freezing temperatures and filtering—often stabilize these wines for immediate bottling.

Raising wine in wood

Wines with a potential for evolution and longevity, whatever their colour, do not take kindly to the violent treatments that may successfully prepare lesser wines for early marketing. These wines are allowed to mature in wooden vessels. They may be the traditional Bordelaise or Burgundian casks of 225 or 228

Maturing wine is racked to free it of sediment. In the inset picture the wine is tested for clarity.

litres, whose use is now spread throughout the world, or they may be huge tuns containing up to 10,000 litres; the larger the vessel, the smaller the proportion of wine that is in contact with the wood and the slower its evolution.

Depending on the size of the container and the nature of the wine, it may remain in the wood for from six months to several years, progressively purifying. Throughout this period, the wine breathes very slowly through the wood. Because of evaporation, a concentration of all the wine's constituents takes place, the loss of water being greater than that of alcohol. (Although alcohol is more volatile than water, its molecules are larger, hindering its escape.) Oxygen is absorbed through the wood, causing chemical changes in the wine that are also part of the maturing process.

During its time in barrels the wine is regularly racked: decanted from one vessel to another, leaving behind the lees—deposits of dead yeasts, tartar crystals, infinitesimal cellular fragments of grapes and other solids that have fallen out of suspension. As the last of the clear wine is drawn off, it is repeatedly tested for clarity, a glass of it held to a candle flame or dim electric torch, and, at the first sign of cloudiness, the decanting is arrested to prevent the lees getting mixed into the clear wine. As well as being racked, wines are often clarified by a process known as fining. A clarifying agent is whisked into the wine, where it coagulates upon contact with acids and tannins, drawing out of suspension microscopic solids that, clinging to the coagulated fining particles, then fall out of the wine, which is again racked free of the fining lees. Egg white is a typical red wine fining agent and, for white wines, isinglass (a form of gelatine) or bentonite (a clay) are often used. Both racking and fining incorporate air into the wine, supplementing the breathing of the wood.

Wines settle clear in small kegs better than in large tuns and, because fining can be impractical in large quantities, these wines may be filtered in preference to being fined. However, there are purists the world over who do not rack, fine or filter on the grounds that a wine suffers a loss of nuance and complexity through these particular treatments.

Although the absorption of oxygen is useful to the development of a wine, its still surface is never left exposed to the air. Acetic bacteria, always present to transform wine into vinegar, can work only in contact with air and the vessels must be frequently ullaged—topped up. Different sizes of small casks and bottles of the same wine are kept filled in readiness so that no wine is ever left vulnerable. Yet even the most painstakingly cared-for wine can never be 100 per cent free of acetic acid, and imperceptible traces of this volatile substance, known as volatile acidity, can reinforce and help to release a wine's bouquet.

In the earlier part of a wine's development, the shocks of seasonal changes in temperature are useful in bringing about the precipitation of the heavier lees; later, the wine clarifies more sedately and more gracefully at lower and more constant temperatures. Wines that require more than a year's care before bottling are moved from ground level first year cellars to cooler, subterranean second year cellars and, in some instances, to a still cooler, lower level third year cellar, to finish their pre-bottle formation. Throughout this slow process of clarification and maturation, the wine is repeatedly examined and tasted by the

Testing first-year wine at Château d'Yquem.

grower to check its health, its limpidity and its evolution.

The phrase "the taste of wood" is a common conversational crutch when wine is being discussed; it appears to mean different things to different people. Most aged wines are raised in well-seasoned wood that is used year after year. This wood lends no flavour to the wine. When a wine is said to have a taste of the wood, the taste usually has nothing to do with the wood itself, but is the combination of a naturally high tannic content and a long sojourn in casks during which time oxidation, often in excess, alters the wine, making it old before its time; freshness and fruit are lost and volatile acidity may be high. The flavour of new oak in a young wine is unmistakable, but it disappears as the wine ages: and a few of the world's most distinguished wines are raised only in new oak. The top growths of Bordeaux and Burgundy, for instance, begin their careers each year in new oak barrels and are raised in the same wood, racked back and forth among the casks of their vintage until, two to two and a half years later, the wines are put into bottles and the casks are sold off to other vineyards. Other wine growers judiciously use a mixture of new and used oak barrels to avoid overpowering their wines, because new oak is a violent seasoning agent. To absorb new oak's harsh tannins, different from those of the grapes, and the oak's characteristic dry-sweet, vanilla-like flavour, and to still remain in balance, a wine must have a powerful structure and a determined personality. Only the concourse of a privileged microclimate, a privileged soil, selected strains of noble grape varieties, old vines, limited production and a rigid elimination of imperfect grapes, can produce a wine with the stuff to absorb the extra tannins and the flavour of the new oak and come out on top; such a wine may be dense, hard, uningratiating, jealous of its qualities in youth, but, in time, it will open out in beauty and it will live long.

Special vinifications

An undisturbed veil of alcohol-resistant yeasts—called *flor* in Spanish—forming on the surface of certain wines, deliberately kept on ullage in barrels that are neither racked nor topped up, defying the laws that govern the vinification of other wines, creates the typical flavours of fino and amontillado sherries and of the *vins jaunes*, literally, "yellow wines", from the French Jura, the sumptuous, bronze-hued Château-Chalon being the best-known example. The Sardinian Vernaccia di Oristano is also made in this way and the veil of flor has been induced with some success in countries producing imitation sherries.

Like acetic bacteria, the flor yeasts need air, but the two are enemies and only one can dominate. The wines must be strong—a level of about 15° alcohol is necessary to permit the formation of flor while discouraging the attack of acetic bacteria. To attain this alcohol content, sherry grapes are dried briefly on straw mats in the sun to concentrate their sugar, and those of Château-Chalon are picked in a withered state of advanced ripeness. Once flor is firmly established, it seals the wine off from the air, repels the bacteria and, by breaking down any acetic acid present in the wine, diminishes volatile acidity. The wines become concentrated with the passage of time (Château-Chalon must remain beneath its blanket of flor for a minimum of six years before being bottled). Because of the greater evaporation of water, the alcohol content steadily increases; and oxidation over the years is partially responsible for the typical flavour, depth and texture of these extraordinarily dry, nutty wines. Not all of the conditions favourable to the development of flor have been fully

Sediment is ejected from a champagne bottle.

understood, but a dense environmental population of the appropriate yeasts, acclimatized over the centuries, heads the list.

Noble rot

Surely the most implausible of wines, honey-hued or burnished gold, luscious without cloying, vibrant and pervasive, are those made from rotten grapes—or so they appear to be and so they are called. To distinguish their state of alteration from that of pernicious decomposition, the ashen fungus *Botrytis cinerea* (from the Greek *botrys*: bunch of grapes, and the Latin *ciner*: ashes), is termed noble rot when it attacks healthy, perfectly ripened white grapes, withering them within unbroken skins to a concentrated essence. When the fungus attacks unripened grapes damaged by insect punctures or heavy rains, rupturing the skins further and letting destructive bacteria penetrate the flesh, it is called grey rot and can seriously compromise the harvest. It also destroys the pigmentation of red grapes, making a dull, greyish wine.

Botrytis wines, which include French Sauternes, Hungarian Tokay, and the great sweet German wines, cannot be produced every year, for the development of noble rot depends on a combination of warmth and humidity after the grapes have ripened. In a good year, early ripening, tough-skinned varieties will permit the Botrytis to do its work before the bad weather; at the same time, their skins will remain intact under the disintegrating action of the mould, protecting the pulp from contact with the air.

Botrytis invades a vineyard in irregular stages and even on individual bunches the action is progressive. A single cluster may contain withered, fungus-coated berries, others still plump, with skins turned brown and softened by the initial action of the mould, and a portion of ripe, firm, unaffected berries. To attain a plenitude of the Botrytis character in a wine, individual grape berries must be removed from the bunches as they shrivel to the right degree, without completely drying out. This necessitates repeated pickings among the same vine—often as many as five, six, seven or more over a period that in some years may extend for a couple of months. Each batch of grapes is fermented separately.

Two qualities, specific to Botrytis, are responsible for the differences in structure and flavour between these wines and sweet

Champagne bottles are twisted daily to shift sediment gradually.

wines made from grapes withered by simple desiccation. With the latter, the acids and sugars are merely concentrated through loss of water without any alteration in their composition whereas, by feeding on the sugars and the acids, Botrytis effects a chemical alteration in the structure of the grape, creating new elements that will modify the wine's bouquet and, because the fungus consumes more acid than sugar, the acidity of the must is lowered. Secondly, Botrytis secretes an antibody that inhibits alcoholic fermentation. From musts of partially dried but chemically unchanged grapes, alcohol-resistant yeasts are capable of fermenting out the sugars to alcohol levels as high as 18° to 20°; but a high concentration of sugar in Botrytis grapes means a correspondingly high concentration of the mould, which arrests the fermentation sooner. For example, in the wines of Sauternes a perfect balance is derived from sugar capable of being converted into about 20° of alcohol; but because of the inhibiting power of the mould, the wine stops fermenting at 13.5° to 14° alcohol. If the grapes were picked with a higher sugar content, the fermentation would be arrested even sooner and the wine would be sweeter with a lower alcohol content. If the grape is picked at much less than a 20° potential, the wine would be thrown out of balance by excessive alcohol and too little sweetness.

Vinifications vary considerably; the sweet Hungarian Tokays, for instance, are not pure noble rot wines—they are made by adding a paste of noble rot grape to the must of other white grapes. In Sauternes, the only difference in vinification from that of other white wines lies in the impossibility of precipitating solids from the thick, viscous musts before fermentation; the cloudy juices are run directly into the kegs to ferment, the fermentation is very slow and so is the clarification—at Château d'Yquem, three and a half years is considered necessary for the wine to clarify before being bottled and, once in the bottle, it is not unusual for it to reach its centenary with perfect equanimity.

It may be drunk much sooner, of course, but whether it is tasted early or only after decades of slow evolution in the dark, cool stillness of a cellar, it is the pleasure that the wine will give that is the true end of its makers' skill and art. Few wines can match Yquem in greatness; but all wines can give pleasure—and the pursuit of that pleasure is the purpose of this book.

Richard Olney

In a cellar in Burgundy, thousands of bottles wait to be enjoyed.

A Guide to the World's Leading Grapes

All wine begins with the grape. Many wines are vinified from one grape variety alone, and they reflect its distinctive character. Other wines are made from a combination of grape varieties, each grape contributing its special quality, such as aroma, colour, alcoholic strength, acidity and body. It is the balance of these interrelating elements that produces the character of the wine.

More than 3,000 varieties of the European *Vitis vinifera* grape are under cultivation throughout the world, but certain varieties yield the finest wines. Some of the leading white varieties are shown here, and a number of the principal red grapes on pages 20-21. Only the most important regions where these grapes grow are mentioned here; many of the grapes are also grown elsewhere. Other grape varieties are discussed on pages 140-142.

Many European grape varieties have been successfully transplanted to other parts of the world, but in a hotter climate a specific variety will produce perceptibly different results than when it is grown in a mild climate. And the nature of the soil—whether sandy, gravelly, chalky or granitic, for instance—will also alter significantly the character of the wine produced by any grape variety (*page 9*).

Among the noble varieties, the Cabernet Sauvignon is the most adaptable: it has been successfully transplanted from the Bordeaux region to other soils and climates, and lends its character to fine wines in California, South Africa and Australia. By way of contrast, the Pinot Noir from Burgundy adapts to other climates with more difficulty, and outside Burgundy its white mutations—Pinot Blanc and Pinot Gris—often do better.

Other grape varieties have thrived in new terrain—the Zinfandel, for example, is grown in southern Italy, where it is known as the Primitivo, and used largely as a powerful blending wine. This grape flourishes in the cooler, northern parts of California, producing distinctively fruity, slightly herbal wines.

The Chardonnay. This grape produces the great white Burgundies of the Côte de Beaune and Chablis, the white wines of the Côte Chalonnaise, and Pouilly Fuissé and other Macon wines. It is the white grape used in making Champagne. Chardonnay also produces California's finest white wines.

The Semillon. When affected by Botrytis (*page 16*), this grape produces the sweet white wines of Bordeaux, such as Barsac, Sauternes and Loupiac; it is combined with lesser proportions of Sauvignon Blanc (*opposite page, above, right*) and Muscadelle. The Semillon also grows in California, Australia and South Africa, where it is known as green grape.

The Gewürztraminer. Taking its name from the German *gewürz*, meaning spice, this grape produces the highly scented, spicy wines that bear its name in Alsace and Germany. In the French Jura, it is called *savignin*, and produces *vin jaune*—yellow wine. The grape is also grown in Austria, Italy, California, South Africa and Australia.

The Sauvignon Blanc. In the Bordeaux region, this variety is combined with the Semillon (*opposite page, below*) in the sweet wines of Sauternes and Barsac, and in dry white Graves. In the Loire Valley, it is called *blanc fumé* and yields the flinty wines of Sancerre and, in Pouilly sur-Loire, the crisp, fruity Pouilly-Fumé. It also grows in California and Australia.

The Chenin Blanc. This is the leading white grape in the Touraine and Anjou districts of the Loire Valley. The wines of Anjou, Touraine, Saumur, Layon and Vouvray range from dry to sweet; some are made sparkling by the Champagne method. The Chenin Blanc is also grown in South America, California, Australia and South Africa, where it is called Steen.

The Riesling. This is the noble variety grown in Germany, and it is cultivated in many other places—Alsace, Austria, Italy, Switzerland, Yugoslavia and all wine-growing regions outside Europe. The wines are generally fresh, crisp and dry or medium dry, but when affected by Botrytis the Riesling grape produces the most distinguished sweet German wines.

The Merlot. In the Bordeaux region, the Merlot is dominant in Pomerol and St. Emilion, yielding robust, long-lived wines. In the stonier soils of the Médoc and Graves, it is combined with the Cabernet Sauvignon (*right*), to lend the wines softness and roundness. It is also grown in Italy, Switzerland, Yugoslavia, California, Australia and South Africa.

The Cabernet Sauvignon. The most important red grape of Graves and Médoc, this variety is high in acid and tannin, and it produces the long-lived, slow-maturing wines of Bordeaux. Its strong fruit flavour is commonly likened to blackcurrants. This grape also produces high quality wines in California, Chile, Australia and South Africa.

The Mourvèdre. This grape thrives in warm, dry climates, such as south and south-west France, and gives the Bandol wines of Provence—which contain at least 50 per cent of Mourvèdre—their depth of colour and typical fruitiness, often associated with wild berries. The Mourvèdre is also used in the making of Châteauneuf-du-Pape and Palette.

The Gamay. In the Beaujolais district of Burgundy, this variety produces supple red wines distinguished by their fresh, fruity bouquet. The Gamay grape is the origin both of the light Beaujolais wines and the more distinguished village appellations of the area.

The Cabernet Franc. This grape is more productive and less tannic than Cabernet Sauvignon (*left*); in Bordeaux, the two are often combined. In the Loire Valley, this variety produces the wines of Chinon, Bourgueil, St. Nicolas de Bourgueil and Saumur Champigny. It also grows in South America and California.

The Pinot Noir. In the Côte d'Or, this grape yields the finest red Burgundies, which often have great potential for ageing. Blended with white Chardonnay grapes, the Pinot Noir contributes body, strength and long life to Champagne. It is cultivated in other mild climates—Austria, Switzerland, Germany, Hungary and California.

The Syrah. The foundation of many deeply coloured, robust wines, this grape yields some of the finest wines of the Côtes du Rhône, such as Hermitage, St. Joseph, Cornas and, when blended with other grapes, Châteauneuf-du-Pape. It grows well in other warm climates: California, South Africa and Australia, where it is known as the Shiraz or Hermitage grape.

The Grenache. A grape which flourishes in hot climates, the Grenache is grown in the South of France, Spain, North Africa and California. In the Rhône Valley it is an important component of Châteauneuf-du-Pape; it also produces the rosé wines of Tavel and Lirac, and in the Roussillon area of south-west France, the sweet fortified wine, Banyuls.

1
Selecting Wine
The Art of Intelligent Choice

s an important prelude to tasting a wine, a
lass is held by its stem and gently rotated.
hus swirled, the aromatic elements of the wine
re released and held in the bowl of the glass
bove the wine's surface. The taster will smell
e bouquet to perceive its mingled scents
efore drawing a small amount of wine into the
outh to analyse its taste (*page 34*).

Knowing what to expect from a bottle of wine adds tenfold to the pleasure of choosing and serving it. The range of wines available may seem daunting, but the very shape of a bottle often provides a clue to its contents, since certain designs are traditional in the world's major wine-growing areas (*page 26*). The language of the label reveals much more. Most labels will give a country of origin and the name of a specific vineyard, a community of wine growers, a region or a grape variety. This information may be enough to predict the wine's general character, because certain dominant features—such as whether a wine is light or full-bodied, for instance, or fine and complex—typify the wines of particular regions (*page 28*).

Unless the bottle contains a blend of wines from different years, the label will also carry a vintage year. The vintage can be an important guide to a wine's quality because the weather, particularly in temperate climates, can drastically affect the wines produced in a given year (*page 39*); a guide to vintages since 1945 is included with this volume.

A knowledge of vintages is particularly useful if the wine has been aged. Good wines of all types are made every year, most of them everyday wines intended for drinking when young. But the life of a fine wine can range from 10 years to more than a century, and as these wines mature they undergo a fascinating metamorphosis, changing colour (*page 32*) and developing in complexity. A fine wine produced in a so-called light year—a Château Latour 1963, for example—will mature more rapidly than the same wine produced in a great year, such as 1961; after 20 years the 1961 Latour will still be progressing towards its peak.

Although labels give clues to a wine's identity, only the wine itself can reveal its personality. It does so in several ways. First, its colour, which can always be appreciated for its intrinsic beauty, may reveal not only the wine's age, but also how it was made (*page 30*). Then the aroma, released by swirling (*opposite page*) will give advance information about the wine's qualities. With practice at wine-tasting (*page 34*), you will learn to relate impressions of colour and odour to the palate, and to evaluate the wine systematically. Your personal vocabulary will help to define these fleeting sensations, but some of the terms generally used to describe wine are explained on page 24. Recorded in a wine log (*page 36*), your past impressions serve as the best possible guide to choosing wine in the future.

A Lexicon of Wine-Tasting Terms

Wine has its own vocabulary, with good reason. The complicated sensory impressions that come into play when you taste wine would be almost impossible to describe were it not for the terms defined here. Because they make it easier to express and compare nuances of taste, smell and other sensations, these words have become part of the universal language of wine. They are used throughout this volume, and are likely to arise whenever wine is tasted or discussed.

Some of these terms—such as acidity or tannin—apply to the composition of the wine; others—for example, elegant or muscular—are familiar adjectives that make it easier to give a simple, graphic description of any wine's special features.

Acidity. One of the basic savours in wine, providing crispness, vitality and sharpness.

Aftertaste. An impression left on the palate after tasting that differs from, and is often less pleasant than, the original taste of the wine.

Alcohol. One of the principal elements in wine, providing strength and character. See also *Balance*.

Amber. The deep yellow colour present, for example, in a fine, aged Sauternes.

Aroma. Smell of a wine.

Aromatic. Possessing a clearly identifiable fragrance, which is very often related to fruits and spices.

Astringent. High in tannin, causing the mouth to dry and pucker. See also *Tannin*.

Austere. Somewhat hard, without revealing any other conspicuous characteristics. Some great wines that seem austere when they are young may soften and display a more distinctive personality as they age.

Autumnal. Various aromas and tastes in wine reminiscent of dead leaves, humus, truffles, mushrooms, hay and the barnyard.

Balance. Relationship between the basic elements of acidity, tannin and alcohol. If these elements are all in harmony, a wine is said to be well balanced.

Big. Powerful, alcoholic, but well balanced and usually with a potential for further development.

Body. The solidity of a wine, contributed by its basic components: acid, tannin and alcohol.

Bouquet. Smell that develops in a wine during its evolution in bottle. The term is also generally applied to a pleasant smell in any wine. Often used in the same way as the term *Aroma*.

Brick red. The brownish-red colour characteristic of old red wine.

Burning. Fiery sensation due to an excessive proportion of alcohol in a wine. See also *Balance*.

Buttery. A smell, taste and smoothness on the palate—all reminiscent of butter—encountered in some red wines.

Caramel. Rich, slightly burnt and fudge-like smell and taste present in some wines, such as Madeira.

Clean. Devoid of defects, free of any anomaly or foreign taste.

Closed. Not revealing its character. Many fine wines go through a closed period in youth. See also *Austere*.

Coarse. Rough and of poor quality, often due to excess acidity and poor vinification. Coarseness is also characteristic of a wine made from inferior grape varieties, cultivated for their high yield, or grapes that are grown in inappropriate soil.

Complex. Characteristic of great wines with many facets of smell and taste.

Cooked. Heavy, often caramel-like smell and taste sometimes due to heating the must before vinification. The term is also used to describe the jam or prune-like flavour of a wine made from excessively ripe grapes grown in an unusually hot summer.

Corked. A rare fault, causing the affected wine to emit a very disagreeable smell.

Crisp. Refreshing and relatively acidic. Crispness is a desirable quality in light, flinty white wines that are drunk young.

Crystalline. Perfectly limpid and bright.

Crystals. Natural, harmless flakes of tartaric acid found in some white wines.

Deep. Intensely full, with many nuances of flavour, all smoothly interlaced.

Delicate. Fragile quality of a good wine which may just be on the verge of decline. The term is also used to describe a good, well-balanced light wine, with a pleasant but not very assertive smell and taste.

Developed. State of a wine expressed in terms of its maturity. A well-developed wine is one that has matured to the right degree and in the correct way; an undeveloped wine is one that needs ageing.

Distinguished. Fine, with distinctive character, elegance and refinement.

Dried out. Without any fresh fruit flavour. See also *Oxidized*.

Dry. Lacking sweetness. A wine in which the sugar content has been fermented out.

Dull. With uninteresting odour and taste, or lacking limpidity and brightness.

Earthy. Smell or taste reminiscent of earth.

Elegant. Of exceptionally high quality and distinction, harmoniously balanced and with all its virtues intact, possessing a certain lightness and flair.

Exuberant. Lively, vital. The description is often applied to young, fruity wines that are very easy to drink.

Fat. Full of flavour. See also *Full-bodied*.

Feminine. Fine, intricate and delicate.

Fine. Of good quality, distinguished, a term applicable to a wine of any type.

Finesse. Distinction and grace in a wine.

Finish. The final taste of a wine, the last impression.

Firm. Strong and well balanced, but still with a perceptible degree of tannin and acidity. See also *Balance*.

Flabby. Weak, lacking in acidity and character, and with no potential for development.

Flat. Lacking acidity, character and any distinctive flavour; in sparkling wine, signifying a loss of sparkle.

Flavour. Smell and taste combined.

Flinty. A metallic smell and taste associated with wines vinified from Sauvignon Blanc grapes that have been grown on particular soils, such as Pouilly-Fumé.

Flowery. Displaying the fragrance of a flower, such as honeysuckle, jasmine, lilac, orange blossom, rose or violet. However, the smell of geraniums in a wine is considered to be a fault.

Foxy. An aggressive flavour attributed to wines, such as Lambrusca, that are made from native American vines.

Fresh. Young and vital—often applied to well-balanced light wines, low in tannin, that are drunk young.

Fruity. Recalling fruits in flavour. A variety of fruit odours and tastes, apart from the obvious one of grapes, may be discerned in wine— apple, apricot, bilberry, blackcurrant, bramble, cherry, citrus fruit and peel, peach, pear, plum, raspberry or strawberry, as well as the heavy smell of cooked fruit. Young, uncomplicated red wines often display an immediate, open fruity quality.

Full-bodied. Fat, with all elements strongly defined.

Gamey. Recalling the odour of the flesh of game birds, small furred game or venison, usually found in the bouquet of older wines.

Generous. Big, open and rich, usually high in alcohol.

Great. Noble.

Green. Sharp, acidic. Indicates either a wine that is very young, or one that has been made from under-ripened grapes. Can be a pleasant, refreshing quality. The term can also be used to suggest a herbal or grassy quality in a wine.

Hard. Young, undeveloped, with an excessive amount of tannin still masking its qualities.

Harmonious. Perfectly balanced.

Harsh. Rough, tannic and acidic, often a quality of youth.

Heady. High in alcohol.

Herbaceous. Grassy, smelling of fresh herbs and hay.

Herbal. Smelling of herbs, such as lemon balm, savory, thyme, rosemary, sage, lavender, mint, lime blossom and verbena.

Honest. Decent, without flaws or defects, but having no great qualities.

Honeyed. Sweet smell and taste often found in fine Botrytis wines, such as Sauternes (*page 129*).

Insipid. Lacking in taste.

Intense. Deep and complicated.

Intricate. Subtly complex and with many elusive nuances.

Iodine. Taste resembling that of sea urchins.

Iron. Hard, strong structure in a fine wine which will take many years to mellow and soften. A metallic taste, reminiscent of iron, also appears as a nuance in some wines.

Lacy. Intricate, full of subtle, harmonious smells and flavours, delicately bound together.

Legs. Name given to the long rivulets which run slowly down the inside of a glass after a wine has been swirled.

Length. See *Persistence*.

Light. Without much body, usually indicating a young wine that is ready to drink. Lightness is also a derogatory term applied to a wine that does not live up to expectations.

Limpid. Clear and bright.

Loyal. Term that is applied to a simple and honest wine.

Luscious. Rich, smooth, sweet and opulent, with all elements in harmony.

Maderized. Flat, stale-smelling. This fault, to be found in white wine, is caused by oxidation. A maderized wine often darkens to a dull brown colour. See also *Oxidized*.

Masculine. Description applied to a wine that is characteristically big and assertive.

Mature. Ready for drinking, aged to the right degree.

Meaty. Rich, chewable, full-bodied and firm.

Mellow. Mature and soft, with no edge of harshness.

Mouldy. Tasting of mould or rot. This fault occurs in wine that has been made from grapes attacked by grey rot, or in wine kept in casks that have been allowed to deteriorate.

Muscular. Big, robust and full-bodied, with an assertive flavour.

Noble. Of perfect structure, high quality and breeding. The term is applicable to great wines at any stage of their development.

Nose. The sum total of all odours in a wine.

Nutty. Recalling nuts in flavour. The smell and taste of hazelnuts and walnuts is often associated with wines affected by flor (*page 16*). The flavour of almonds may be found in fresh young white wines.

Oak. Smell and taste of a wine that has been aged in new oak barrels.

Opaque. Dense-looking, lacking clarity and transparency.

Open. Yielding all its qualities, extrovert. A fine wine, aged to the right degree, may be said to have "opened-out".

Oxidized. Applied to wine with a flat, stale taste, caused by excessive exposure to air.

Perlant. A French term that describes a slight, tingling prickle, a light sparkle. The German adjective *spritzig* is often used to mean the same thing.

Persistence. Length of time that a wine remains on the palate after tasting.

Pungent. Strong, distinctive and assertive smell characteristic of some wine types, such as the burnt odour typical of Madeira.

Raw. Young and undeveloped, somewhat harsh, with rough edges.

Refreshing. Thirst-slaking—often applicable to acidic light wines drunk young.

Rich. Full, usually harmonious.

Ripe. Fully mature, rich and full of fruit flavour.

Robust. Strong, concentrated and full-bodied, well balanced.

Rough. Hard, acrid and ungiving.

Round. Well developed, with no sharp edges. Usually applicable to mellow, full-bodied, ample wines.

Scented. Agreeably reminiscent of the aroma of flowers, spices or herbs.

Sharp. With a bite, because of a somewhat excessive amount of acidity.

Short. Persisting only briefly on the palate after tasting.

Silky. Delicately smooth and harmonious.

Smoked. Recalling smoked foods, the smell of burning leaves, or other smoky odours.

Soft. Gentle and well balanced, without being flabby or insipid.

Solid. Firm and well structured, with a good potential for improving as it ages.

Sour. Over-acidic, often vinegary. Sourness is an undesirable quality that will not disappear with ageing.

Sparkling. Name given to wines that have been specially treated to imprison carbon dioxide in the wine. It is released slowly, in the form of tiny bubbles, when the bottle is uncorked.

Spicy. Characteristic spice-like smell and taste encountered in many wines, sometimes due to a certain grape variety, such as Gewürztraminer. Some wines have flavours reminiscent of allspice, pepper, cloves, cinnamon or other spices.

Stalky. Smell of green wood occurring in some young wines.

Steely. High in acidity, fairly hard and uncompromising.

Strong. Big and powerful, usually with high alcoholic content.

Structure. A wine's composition.

Sturdy. Strong and assertive.

Sulphur. Sulphur dioxide is used quite commonly in vinification. However, an excess of it—detectable by a prickly sensation in the nose and back of the throat, as well as by its smell—is undesirable.

Supple. With many different characteristics and nuances, some easily discernible, others less obvious, but easy to drink, soft and seductive

with no sharp edges and a good balance.

Sweet. Term applicable to wines in which the sugar content is either naturally high or has been brought up by artificial sweetening.

Syrupy. Excessively sweet, cloying, lacking in acidity.

Tannin. One of the major elements in red wine, identifiable in tasting by the mouth-puckering effect it produces. Tannin is particularly obvious in fine wines that require ageing, such as claret and port; it serves as a preservative during their ageing process, gradually softening as the wines mature and allowing the fruit flavour to emerge. Tannin forms most of the sediment present in red wines that have aged for a number of years.

Tart. Sharp, over-acidic.

Tartar. See *Crystals*.

Thick. Excessively heavy and dense, usually a negative judgement.

Thin. Light and without body, watery.

Tired. Worn out, past its prime, describing a wine that is fading. Wines can also be tired from travelling or being subjected to treatments such as racking and fining—these wines recover with a rest.

Tough. Big and overpoweringly tannic and therefore difficult to drink.

Tuile. A French term describing the colour of an old red wine that has lightened and is veering towards orange.

Unbalanced. Unharmonious—wine in which one or more of the basic elements is too weak or too overbearing. See also *Balance*.

Vanilla. Scent of vanilla which is imparted to some wines by new oak during ageing in cask (*page 16*).

Velvety. Smooth, subtle, rich and harmonious, with no edge of harshness.

Vigorous. Lively and strong wine, usually still developing in a healthy way.

Vinegary. Sour, acetic flavour in a wine that has been spoilt by prolonged exposure to air.

Watery. Lacking in taste and colour.

Weak. Lacking in character, low in fruit, acidity, tannin and alcohol.

Weighty (*puissant*). Heavy, powerful, high in alcohol and tannin.

Yeasty. Smelling of bread, sometimes thought to be an indication that the wine has been exposed to secondary fermentation in bottle.

Young. Immature, light and fresh—the latter if applied to a wine drunk young.

Bottle Shapes that Give Clues to Their Contents

The very shape of a bottle is often the first indication of the character of a wine. Certain classic shapes are traditional in the principal wine-growing regions of Europe, and have been adopted for similar wines in other parts of the world. There are also many unusual designs, some of them the hallmark of a particular region, others unique to a single vineyard.

The cylindrical shape of most wine bottles has the practical advantage of permitting them to be stacked horizontally when the wine is laid down to mature in a cellar (*page 15*). This position ensures that the corks remain moist so that air cannot enter the wine. Green or brown glass protects wine from the harm-ful effects of light during its long period of ageing in the bottle; clear glass is reserved for certain white wines.

Among the classic styles, a Burgundy bottle may be identified by its sloping shoulders. Bottles of this shape are also used throughout the Côtes du Rhône and the Loire Valley, and have been adopted elsewhere for other wines made from the Chardonnay and Pinot Noir grape (*pages 18 and 21*). A similar shape is generally used for Champagne and sparkling wines, but the bottles are much heavier and slightly larger; they are usually made of thick glass, to prevent the bottles exploding due to the pressure of gas inside.

The classic Bordeaux bottle is narrow and high-shouldered, usually green glass for red wines, clear glass for white. This style has been adopted for other red wines made from Cabernet Sauvignon grapes in various parts of the world. A port bottle is also high-shouldered, but the neck bulges

Port

Tokay

Verdicchio

Côtes de Provence

Champagne

Burgundy

slightly. A similar shape is sometimes used for other fortified wines.

Most German wines are bottled in long slender flutes. Brown flutes are traditional in the Rhineland, green flutes in the Mosel-Saar-Ruwer region. A more elongated flute is characteristic of Alsace, the region of France bordering on Germany. Flutes are also used for wines made from Riesling, Sylvaner and Gewürztraminer grapes in other countries.

Certain more unusual shapes may signal particular wines. In central Italy, a curved bottle, like a Roman amphora, is unique to white Verdicchio wine. Tuscany is the home of the straw-covered Chianti flask, but this design is being used less frequently and a Bordeaux-style bottle is generally chosen for Chianti Classico, which is laid down to mature.

A half-litre bottle with a long neck and sloping shoulders is unique to Hungarian Tokay. An undulating shape is sometimes employed in the Côtes de Provence, while Château-Chalon, in the Jura region of France, has a broad-shouldered design for its distinctive yellow wine. A squat flask, known as a *Bocksbeutel*, is traditional in the Franconian region of Germany; a similar but rounder shape is used for some other wines such as Portuguese rosé and some Chilean wines.

The capacity of a standard bottle is usually between 70 and 75 cl, although larger sizes and half bottles are available. The size of a bottle will affect the speed at which a wine matures. In a magnum—1½ litres—wine will mature more slowly than in a standard-sized bottle, and therefore age better; in a half bottle, wine will mature more rapidly.

Bordeaux

Château-Chalon

Chianti flask

Franconian Bocksbeutel

Rhine flute

Alsace flute

A Key to Colour and Character

Every wine has a personality of its own, reflecting the grapes from which it originated and the soil and climate in which they grew, as well as its age and how it was vinified (*pages 8-17*). For example, some white wines are crisp and dry, whereas others are rich and sweet; some red wines are light-bodied, while others are muscular and robust. The charts on the right provide a simple means of finding wines that are likely to have these characteristics. You can also use the charts to find the general character of a particular wine; more detailed information will be found on pages 90-138.

In some cases, wines of different types may bear a single name—one white Vouvray from the Loire Valley may be crisp and light, another complex and full bodied, and a third rich and sweet. Such variations may be due to the weather—a single vineyard can produce very different wines from year to year—or they may arise from the different vinification methods used by each grower. A wine merchant could advise you on the character of a particular bottle of wine.

In the charts, wines are grouped by their country of origin. The systems of naming wines differ. In France, most wines are classified by geographical region, such as Bordeaux, and usually take their specific name from a district—for instance, Graves. Another system is used in Alsace, where wines are named after a grape variety, such as Riesling.

German wines are graded according to their natural richness and intensity of flavour. Kabinett is the least rich of the graded wines whilst Trockenbeerenauslese, being the fullest and richest wine, claims the highest rank.

Some Italian wines are named after places, such as Chianti; others are named after grapes, such as Pinot Nero. In California, Australia, South Africa and South America, wines usually take their names from grape varieties (*pages 18-21*).

The word *primeur*, linked to some red wines—Pinot Noir *primeur*, for instance—indicates a wine that is specially vinified to be drunk young (*page 11*). These light-bodied, fruity red wines are best drunk before they are six months old.

White Wine Categories

Categories (left to right):
1 = CRISP WHITE WINES
2 = HIGHLY SCENTED WHITE WINES WITH AN EDGE OF SWEETNESS
3 = SOFT WHITE WINES
4 = MUSCULAR, VIGOROUS WHITE WINES
5 = COMPLEX, FULL-BODIED WHITE WINES
6 = RICH, SWEET WHITE WINES

Country	Region	Wine	1	2	3	4	5	6
FRANCE	Alsace	Riesling	●				●	
		Gewürztraminer					●	
		Muscat					●	
		Pinot Blanc, Pinot Gris				●		
		Sylvaner, Edelzwicker						●
	Bordeaux	Graves			●	●		●
		Sauternes, Barsac	●	●				
		Loupiac, Cérons	●					
		Ste. Croix du Mont	●					
		Entre-Deux-Mers					●	●
		Bordeaux					●	●
	Burgundy	Chablis Grand Cru and Premier Cru			●			
		Chablis, Petit Chablis						●
		Côte de Beaune			●			
		Côte Chalonnaise			●			
		Mâconnais			●			●
		Bourgogne Aligoté						
	Champagne	Still white wine (Coteaux Champenois)			●			
	Côtes du Rhône	Condrieu			●			
		Crozes Hermitage				●		
		Hermitage			●			
		St. Joseph				●		
		Châteauneuf-du-Pape			●	●		
	Jura	Château-Chalon			●			
		Vin Jaune			●			
		Vin de Paille	●	●				
	Loire Valley	Muscadet, Gros Plant						●
		Coteaux du Layon	●					
		Quarts de Chaume	●					
		Savennières			●			
		Vouvray	●	●			●	●
		Sancerre, Pouilly-Fumé			●			●
		Pouilly-sur-Loire						●
		Quincy, Reuilly (Cher Valley)						●
	Provence	Côtes de Provence				●	●	
		Bellet, Cassis, Palette				●		
ITALY		Soave					●	
		Frascati, Vernaccia				●		
		Verdicchio						●
		Pinot Bianco, Pinot Grigio					●	
GERMANY		Kabinett						●
		Spätlese, Auslese	●					●
		Beerenauslese, Eiswein	●	●				
		Trockenbeerenauslese	●	●				
AUSTRIA			●				●	●
SWITZERLAND		Fendant						●
HUNGARY		Balaton, Badacsony, Somto						●
		Tokay Aszu and Aszu Eszencia	●	●				
OTHER COUNTRIES		Chardonnay: *California, Idaho*				●	●	
		Oregon, Washington				●	●	
		White Riesling: *U.S.A., Australia, South Africa*						●
		Sauvignon Blanc: *California*						●
		Gewürztraminer: *California, South Africa, Australia*	●					●
		Semillon: *Australia*					●	
		Chenin Blanc: *California*					●	●

Red Wine Categories

The five category bands (left to right across the dot columns):

1. **LIGHT-BODIED, NON-TANNIC RED WINES, DRUNK YOUNG AND COOL**
2. **GOOD, LOYAL AND UNCOMPLICATED RED WINES**
3. **BIG, MUSCULAR, ROBUST RED WINES**
4. **FINE, COMPLEX RED WINES**
5. **GREAT, COMPLEX RED WINES WITH DEPTH**

Country	Region	Wine	Light-bodied	Good, loyal	Big, robust	Fine, complex	Great, depth
FRANCE	Alsace	Pinot Noir					•
	Bordeaux	Graves, Médoc	•	•	•	•	
		St. Emilion, Pomerol	•	•	•	•	
		Bourgeais, Blayais		•		•	
		Canon Fronsac		•		•	
		Other Bordeaux appellations		•		•	•
	Burgundy	Côte de Nuits	•	•			
		Côte de Beaune	•	•			
		Côte Chalonnaise		•		•	
		Mâconnais				•	•
		Beaujolais				•	•
		Generic Burgundies				•	•
		Passetoutgrains				•	•
	Champagne	Still red wines (Coteaux Champenois)					•
	Côtes du Rhône	Côte Rôtie	•	•	•		
		Crozes Hermitage			•	•	
		Hermitage	•	•	•		
		St. Joseph		•		•	
		Cornas		•	•		
		Gigondas			•	•	
		Châteauneuf-du-Pape		•	•		
		Côtes du Ventoux				•	•
		Coteaux du Tricastin				•	•
		Côtes du Rhône				•	•
	Jura	Arbois				•	
	Loire Valley	Saumur Champigny					•
		St. Nicolas de Bourgueil		•		•	•
		Bourgueil, Chinon		•		•	•
		Gamay de Touraine					•
	Provence and the South West	Côtes de Provence				•	•
		Bandol		•		•	
		Palette		•		•	
		Cahors			•	•	
		Corbières				•	•
		Minervois				•	•
ITALY		Barolo		•	•	•	
		Barbaresco		•	•	•	
		Barbera			•	•	
		Dolcetto					•
		Grignolino					•
		Valpolicella					•
		Bardolino					•
		Pinot Nero, Merlot					•
		Chianti					•
		Chianti Classico		•		•	
SPAIN		Rioja		•		•	
GERMANY		Spätburgunder (Pinot Noir)					•
AUSTRIA							•
SWITZERLAND							•
OTHER COUNTRIES		Cabernet Sauvignon: *Argentina, Chile, South Africa,*		•	•	•	
		California, Australia		•	•	•	
		Pinot Noir: *Oregon, California*		•		•	
		Shiraz: *Australia, South Africa*		•	•	•	
		Pinotage: *South Africa*				•	
		Zinfandel: *California*			•	•	
		Zinfandel Primeur: *California*					•
		Pinot Noir Primeur: *California*					•

Matching names and character. Using the chart on the left for white wines and the chart on the right for red, identify a wine from the vertical list of regions and wine names. The dots will then signal the wine's likely character, described at the top of each of the bands of colour on the chart. Alternatively, if you want to find a wine of a particular type, begin with the general description, which will lead you to the name of an appropriate wine.

A Spectrum of Colours from the Grape

Of all a wine's attributes, its colour makes the most immediate impression. A wine's appearance may be determined by a particular grape variety or a specific method of vinification (*right*); or it can reflect the mellowing effects of ageing (*page 32*).

Besides its appeal to the eye, colour may serve as a guide to flavour. Sherry, for example—as a result of the selection and blending that goes into its making—displays a range of subtle gradations of colour and taste. The two basic styles are fino—pale, dry and delicate—and the mellower, more full-bodied oloroso, which is dark gold or amber (*right*). Both parent styles may be blended with sweetening and colouring wines; thus oloroso, for instance, is the basis of dark, sweet cream sherries.

The various styles of port may also be identified by colour (*right, below*), Young port displays a raw shade of reddish purple, which mellows with age. Tawny port derives its colour, and its soft nutty bouquet, from being kept in the barrel for as long as 15 years.

Each of the four types of Madeira is named after a grape variety, although nowadays the wines include grapes of more than one type. Malmsey is the darkest, sweetest and richest; Bual is slightly paler and less sweet; Verdelho is paler and drier still, and Sercial the palest and driest of all (*opposite page, above, left*).

Marsala (*opposite page, above, right*), the best-known dessert wine of Sicily, is made from Catarratto, Grillo and Inzolia grapes. Its colour is determined by age and blending, the deepest brown shades denoting the sweetest wines.

The colour of a rosé wine (*opposite page, below, left*) reflects the type of grapes used to make it, as well as the length of time the juice of the crushed grapes is left in contact with the skins before being pressed. The longer the skins remain in the wine, the deeper its colour.

Most classic Champagne (*opposite, below, right*) is a blend of red and white grapes, producing a white wine. Pink Champagne is coloured by contact with the skins of red grapes, or by the addition of red wine from the Champagne region.

Sherry: from Deepest Amber to Palest Straw

Variations from two main styles. Oloroso sherry (*far left*) ranges in colour from deep chestnut to warm amber; it usually has a soft, round taste due to blending with other wines. Palo cortado (*second from left*)—a rare style of oloroso—is slightly paler and drier. Amontillado (*second from right*) is a wine of fino parentage, which acquires an amber colour and a dry, nutty taste through years of ageing. Fino (*far right*) is the palest and driest of all sherries and has a fresh, delicate flavour.

Port: Red, Tawny and White

Colours that denote character. A young vintage port (*above, left*) has a distinctly reddish-purple colour. Tawny port (*above, centre*) has a red-brown hue; in the glass, it will often display a light lemon-yellow rim, which is indicative of good quality. White grapes yield the more unusual white port (*above, right*), which has a light golden colour and a relatively dry taste.

Madeiras: from Rich Brown to Mellow Gold

Basic styles named after grapes. The darkest and sweetest style Madeira is Malmsey (*above, left*), a luscious wine renowned for its intense richness, fragrance and body. The palest and driest is Sercial (*above, right*), which has a marked freshness and tangy bouquet. All types of Madeira are characterized by an underlying burnt flavour, the result of the wine being heated after fermentation.

Marsala: Dark Intensity

A warm shade of brown. Marsala is traditionally a rich sweet wine, brown in colour, with a tangy, burnt flavour and a faintly malty bouquet. It is now also vinified as a dry wine. The drier varieties are lighter in colour than deep-toned Marsalas of full-blown sweetness.

Rosé: Delicate Gradations of Colour

Subtle variations of rosé. Pinot Noir grapes from Sancerre in the Loire Valley yield a pink-tinted wine (*above, left*). A rosé wine from Tavel, in the Rhône Valley, is a deeper pink, and is made from Grenache grapes (*above, centre*). Bandol wines from the Côtes de Provence are made from a blend of grape varieties and are orange-pink in colour (*above, right*).

Champagne: White or Pink

Two styles from one region. Vintage Champagne (*above, left*) varies from palest straw to gold; the colour deepens as the young wine ages. In a good quality Champagne, the bubbles will be tiny and of uniform size, plentiful and persistent. Pink champagne is characterized by a rosy blush (*above, right*).

Hues that Mellow as Wines Mature

When a fine wine is laid down in a cellar to age, it slowly matures, evolving in taste and changing colour. The vast majority of wines have little potential for improving with age, and are best drunk young, but fine and complex wines need time to resolve their diverse elements into a harmonious whole. Some of the principal wines that fall into this category are listed on pages 28-29.

As they age, fine white wines darken, deepening to a golden hue. Complex red wines lose their tinge of blue, first becoming a warmer red, then eventually a lighter colour. Thus, an old white wine, such as a Sauternes, may actually be much darker in appearance than an old red wine, such as claret.

As an illustration of the ageing process in fine dry white wines, a complex, full-bodied Burgundy is the palest shade of yellow when young, and turns to burnished gold with age (*right*). Sweet white wines such as Sauternes and the late-harvest German wines, which are a pale lemon-yellow to begin with, change eventually to deep gold (*opposite page, below*).

In many fine young red wines, intensity of colour indicates an abundance of fruit and tannin. A young red Bordeaux (*opposite page, above*) is a raw purple-red; a Burgundy of the same age will have a ruby colour with violet overtones. Over the years, the wines lose their tannic harshness and bluish tones; they change first to a vivid red, then to a brick red, and in full maturity are a pale tawny colour with orange reflections.

Vintage port is produced in years when the wines are so promising that shippers declare the wine to be of vintage quality. In youth, vintage port is an intense, purple shade, so dense as to appear almost black. After many years in the bottle, it will fade to a tawny red (*right*), finally turning a pale rose-beige.

White Burgundy: Straw Turning to Gold

Deepening tones of a fine white wine. A cool, pale straw colour, with delicate greenish reflections, is typical of young white Burgundies—in this case, a 1979 Meursault (*above, left*). With age, the colour of the wine will gain in depth and warmth, acquiring progressively deeper tones of gold. The 1947 Meursault (*above, right*) has deepened to a clear amber.

The Softening Tones of Vintage Port

From purple-violet to mellow tawny. In its extreme youth, vintage port has a raw, purple-violet colour. The 1977 Taylor vintage port (*above, left*) has begun to lose its blue reflections and has softened slightly to a less harsh purple-red. With age, the port will turn to a warmer red, gradually gaining orange reflections until it eventually acquires a pale tawny hue. Here, a 1920 vintage port from an unknown shipper is a well-developed shade of tawny with a hint of orange, fading to yellow-gold at the rim (*above, right*).

A Century of Change in a Fine Bordeaux

Changes in fine claret. As the deeply coloured wines of the Médoc age, they change from a harsh purple-red to a soft brick colour. The deep garnet of a young Château Latour, drawn from the cask several months before bottling (*far left*) has a distinctly purple tone. Château Montrose 1937 (*centre*) is very deep in colour, but its tones are warm. Château Rausan-Ségla 1899 (*left*), still in perfect condition, has cleared to a terracotta colour without fading.

A Great Sauternes Darkening with Time

Ageing in a fine sweet wine. The path of a Sauternes to maturity is illustrated here by a Château Suduiraut. In the 1971, the cool lemon hue of the young wine has mellowed to a warm honey (*far left*). In the 1962 Sauternes (*centre*), the colour has deepened to gold. The 1924 has assumed a tone of limpid caramel (*left*).

Assessing a Wine Step-by-Step

Examining a wine to assess all its qualities involves the senses of sight and smell as well as that of taste. Following the sequence on the right and thinking about each impression in turn will heighten your awareness of a wine's attributes.

Choosing the right glass is important: the glass should narrow at the top so that the bouquet can concentrate in the space above the wine's surface (*page 46*). The glass must also be clean—free of the stale odours that can be picked up through storage in a cupboard or from careless washing and drying.

Make sure that the glass is no more than one-third full, to allow space for the bouquet to develop. However, the glass should not contain less wine than this, or its aromas will not be fully released.

The systematic analysis of wine begins with a good look at its colour (*Step 1*). Wines may contain all the colours of the spectrum, from the blue tinge that makes some young red wines purple, to the orange tones that in time can turn a white wine honey-gold. Thus a wine's colour may indicate its age (*page 32*).

The wine is then swirled, sniffed and tasted. Using the tongue to rotate the wine (*Step 6*) ensures that the liquid reaches all parts of the mouth that are sensitive to taste; these include the palate and the underside of the tongue.

The taste buds that are sensitive to the four basic tastes are located on different parts of the tongue: sweetness at the tip, acidity at the upper edges, saltiness at the sides, and bitterness at the back. These sensations, associated with the aromas and other stimuli such as the grating of tannin, the velvety smoothness of glycerine, the prickle of carbon dioxide and the burning sensation of alcohol, create the taste—or so-called mouth—of the wine.

1 **Examining the wine's colour.** Pour wine into a clean clear glass—here, a standard tasting glass—until it is one-third full. Hold the base so that your hand does not obscure the wine and tilt the glass so that you can see the wine's colour, preferably against daylight or against a white tablecloth. Examine the colour to assess its hue, clarity, depth and intensity.

4 **Sipping the wine.** Tilt the glass to your lips and take a mouthful of wine—about a tablespoonful—large enough to cover your tongue but leaving enough space in your mouth to draw in some air.

5 **Sucking in the wine.** Tilting your head forwards, purse your lips and draw air through the wine in your mouth, holding your tongue rigid. Exhale the air through your nose, thus ensuring that flavours and aromas are distributed throughout your entire palate.

2 **Swirling the wine.** Holding the base of the stem, rotate the glass gently to swirl the wine around. This action will expose more of the wine to the air, helping to release the fresh aromas of a young wine or the many volatile substances that form the bouquet of an older wine; these will concentrate in the top of the glass.

3 **Sniffing the wine.** Lift the glass to your nose and take sharp, shallow sniffs. This will reveal the fresh, fruity aromas of a young wine, as well as the more complex scents of an older one.

6 **Chewing the wine.** With your lips closed, relax your tongue and move your jaws with a chewing motion so that the wine flows all over your mouth and is in contact with the tongue and mucous membrane lining the palate. After savouring the wine, either swallow it or spit it out.

7 **Giving the wine a choppy shake.** If a young wine seems stubborn in releasing its bouquet, give it an abrupt, rough shake (*above*); this action may release further fruit in the wine's aroma. Sniff the wine again before tasting it. □

Wine-Tasting: a Basis for Comparison

During the first moments of tasting a wine, you will form distinct impressions about its aroma, taste and bouquet (*page 34*). However, these impressions are bound to be transitory and even a wine expert may find it difficult to remember them for long. A written record will help recall each wine you sample, and will act as a guide for buying—or not buying—the same or a similar wine in the future.

Your wine log may take any form you fancy—a notebook, like that shown on the right, a loose-leaf file or a card index. The essential consideration is that the record is clear and consistent, written in terms that will be easily comprehensible when you refer to it at a later date. The lexicon of terms generally used to describe wine on page 24 will help you to define a particular wine's qualities.

The basic information included in each entry should begin with the date of tasting, the name of the wine and its vintage; you might wish to remind yourself of the place and occasion too. This can be followed by a description of the wine's appearance, including information about age and origin that may be revealed by its colour (*pages 30-33*). The next points to note are your impressions of the wine's aroma and taste, and suggestions of foods that it would suit particularly well.

Any general remarks about the wine's state of maturity will help you decide whether a particular wine is best consumed immediately, or should be laid down to mature.

Simple Arrangements for Sampling Wines

A wine-tasting offers an opportunity for comparing a variety of wines, and can be organized as a small informal party or a more formal occasion with a larger number of guests. Any selection of wines may be sampled at a tasting, but it may be interesting to choose a theme to increase your knowledge of particular wines.

You might, for example, offer wines from the same vineyard but of different vintages, starting with the youngest wine and finishing with the oldest. Or the wines could be of the same vintage and approximately the same quality, but produced by different vineyards in any one region. Since German wines are graded according to quality (*page 28*), you could taste wines from one region and of approximately the same age, in ascending order of quality.

Other possibilities arise from comparing wines made from a particular grape variety of about the same age and quality. However, the wines should not originate from regions with very different climates, because the same grape variety may produce a more aggressive wine if it is grown in a hot climate, and might therefore overwhelm a finer wine from a temperate zone.

Whatever the theme of the tasting, there are a few general rules to follow. When tasting red or white wines, start with the least complex and progress to the most complex, and go from the youngest to the oldest. If both red and white wines are to be tasted, the white wines are usually presented first. However, the acidity of white wine can detract from the appreciation of the bouquet of a complex red wine, and if your red wines are particularly fine you may wish to taste them before the whites.

Make sure that you have enough wine glasses for the tasting—at least one glass for each guest. If both red and white wines are served, glasses should be changed or rinsed when you switch colours. Empty bottles with plastic funnels should be provided so that guests can empty their glasses of unwanted wine. Buckets or wooden wine cases containing sawdust are convenient for spitting after tasting.

Good lighting is essential so that the colour of the wine may be seen clearly. Natural daylight is best; if artificial lighting is necessary, white fluorescent light should be avoided, because it will distort your perception of the wine's colour. Tables should be covered with white cloths to provide a background for assessing the colour and clarity of the wine. A quiet atmosphere will help you to concentrate on analysing the wine, and guests should be discouraged from smoking or wearing perfume, which will interfere with the wine's aroma.

It is a good idea to serve a little simple food so that guests may cleanse their palates between wines. Bread or dry unsweetened biscuits, which are regarded as neutral in flavour, are the only food served at a professional wine-tasting. If you like, provide small cubes of mild cheese such as Gruyère or mild Cheddar, or other plain snacks, but avoid strong flavours since they would disguise the taste of the wine. Jugs of cold water should also be available.

All wines must be uncorked and, if necessary, decanted (*page 44*), in advance. Serve the wines at the correct temperature to bring out their flavour and bouquet (*page 45*), keeping them cool in buckets of water and ice.

Corks sometimes give the name of the vineyard and the vintage. If the wine has been decanted, the bottle can be placed beside the decanter, and the cork attached to the decanter's neck with an elastic band or a cork pin.

Guests at a wine-tasting will welcome copies of a short information sheet stating the theme of the tasting, the region from which the wines come, and specific details about the origins of the wines, their vintages and prices. Leave enough space on the sheet for guests to add their comments, which they can use as part of their personal wine log.

A Personal Record for Future Reference

15/8/81 Château Mouton Rothschild, 1962

Appearance. Still very young in colour. Fine ruby colour, with great depth and intensity.

Odour: Powerful aroma of blackcurrant and leaves, the latter providing a slight astringency to the bouquet.

Taste: A very big, muscular, direct wine, containing a considerable amount of tannin which, however, because the elements are perfectly balanced, is not bothersome. Tasted with grilled lamb chops – the robustness and strength of the wine can easily withstand the relatively rich flavour of the meat. Will go well with any grilled or roasted red meat. Long, deep persistence on the palate.

General: A powerful, elegant wine which, although perfect now, still has many years of life ahead of it.

16/8/81 Ridge California Zinfandel, Langry Road, 1973

Appearance: Deep red colour with purple edge, displaying youth.

Odour: Blackcurrant and wild berry odour.

Taste: Straightforward, open wine, rapidly showing all its qualities on tasting. Good acid and tannin balance.

Robust meat dishes, especially those in which fruit is used, would complement this very fruity wine – duck with cherries, rabbit with prunes, or pork with apricots. Medium persistence.

General: With age, this wine will soften. Will keep for another decade.

16/8/81 Dürkheimer Michelsberg, Bad Dürkheim Weingut Karl Schaefer, Rieslaner Auslese, 1973

Appearance: Colour of honey, bordering on caramel.

Odour: Distinct aroma of peaches and apricots.

Taste: Fruity taste, strongly reminiscent of the peaches and apricots detected in the bouquet. Vibrant, nicely balanced dessert wine with a slightly metallic edge. Lovely poured over peaches and served as dessert. Also good with other fruit – strawberries or other berries. Long persistence.

General: Drinkable now, but can easily be kept for several more years.

25/8/81 Vouvray Clos Naudin Sec, Foureau, 1959

Appearance: Delicate straw colour.

Odour: Sweetish fruit scent with a

Recording impressions on tasting. The entries in the wine log shown above provide a record for future reference. The basic information begins with the date of tasting and the name of the wine and its vintage. This is followed by a description of the wine's appearance, odour and taste, and some general comments indicating the wine's likely development in the future.

Sensible Approaches to Storage

If you buy only a few weeks' supply of wine at a time, you can store it in any convenient corner, away from heat and light. And wine to be stored no more than a year or so will keep well in any reasonably cool, dark place—an unheated spare room, perhaps, or a cupboard where the wine will be well clear of hot pipes or outside walls.

But for the long-term storage of fine wines—a period that can range from five to 20 years or even more—a good cellar, where wine can develop at its own pace, free from the damaging effects of heat, light and vibration, is indispensable. The ideal wine cellar should have a constant, cool temperature; it should be reasonably humid; and it should be well ventilated.

Such an environment occurs naturally in traditional underground cellars; or it can be artificially produced by air conditioning and humidifiers. In either case, the optimum temperature is between 10° and 14°C (50° and 57°F). Temperatures consistently lower than this range will slow a wine's maturation, but will do no other harm; higher temperatures cause the wine to age too rapidly to develop its finest qualities. The temperature should be as constant as possible: even in the best of cellars, it will inevitably vary with the seasons, but rapid fluctuations of temperature will damage the wine.

A degree of humidity prevents corks from drying out, and thus shrinking and letting in enough air to oxidize the wine. A cellar with a floor of beaten earth will be naturally humid; a stone or concrete floor may be covered with sand or gravel and sprinkled from time to time with water. Good ventilation and an odour-free atmosphere are also very important, because strong smells—or even stale air—can penetrate the corks and taint the wine.

Generally, bottles to be kept for any length of time should be stored lying down, so that the corks remain in contact with the wine, promoting breathing without shrinkage. In purpose-built cellars, wines are kept in bins, usually made of concrete (*right*). Single bottles of different wines are most conveniently stored in racks (*far right, above*). Labels are easily damaged by humidity; it is worth painting a permanent label on bottles that will be kept for a long period (*right, above*).

Indelible Identification

Painting a label. Long storage in a humid cellar will disintegrate labels. For permanent identification, paint a coded reference on each bottle, using oil paint thinned with turpentine (*above*). You can abbreviate the vintage and the grower's name—for example, Clos Duval Cabernet Sauvignon 1977 is coded DUV 77; Château Lanessan 1959 is LAN 59.

A Basic System for Easy Access

Storing bottles in racks. Single bottles of different wines may be stored in racks, so that one bottle can be removed without disturbing the rest. Metal racks are needed in a damp cellar; wooden racks, although suitable for the house, would soon deteriorate in a humid atmosphere. To ensure their stability, racks should be level and firmly fixed to the wall.

Serried Ranks of a Single Vintage

Stacking bottles in bins. In a large, purpose-built cellar, wine is usually stacked in concrete bins, one wine and one vintage to each bin. If there is more than one vintage or more than one wine in a bin, wooden slats may be laid between rows to facilitate removal from the bottom layers. Each bin is labelled to classify its contents.

The Miraculous Harvest

The quality of the wine produced by any vineyard in a particular year is determined not only by vinification methods, which can be controlled (*pages 8-17*), but by the weather, which cannot. Wine growers, especially in temperate regions, are at the mercy of natural phenomena. A severe winter can devastate whole vineyards; an untimely spring frost may kill tender young shoots. During the months when the grapes ripen, too much sun and not enough rain—or too much rain with little sun—will thwart the development of the grapes, and harm the wine.

Despite these hazards, there are certain years when harvesting conditions are so good that wines of these vintages attain a supreme quality. The greatest vintages prior to 1945 (*right*) have entered the mythology of wine lore; recent vintages are rated on the separate chart provided with this volume.

The wines listed here have all demonstrated great longevity. Besides these, the legendary Tokay Essence—a sweet Hungarian white wine no longer made—is reputed to have an almost limitless life; Madeira is also exceptionally long-lived.

The greatest vintage since wines were first bottled and corked for preservation is 1811, the year of the Great Comet, which was at its most spectacular in Europe at the time of the harvest. The great twin Bordeaux vintages—1864 and 65, 1874 and 75, and 1899 and 1900—belie the theory that a great vintage is always followed by a lesser year because it takes the vines' strength. The exceptionally prolific harvests of 1874 and 75 and 1899 and 1900 also prove that a large crop can produce a great wine.

1921 is the greatest white wine vintage of the 20th century; it yielded luscious wines of immense concentration which are still in perfect condition. Some vintages have only revealed their great quality with time. The red Bordeaux wines of 1870 and 1928 were, to begin with, harsh and unyielding. But with lengthy ageing, both vintages mellowed. By the early 1920s, the 1870 clarets were declared the greatest of all time; by the 1960s, the 1928s had achieved such perfect maturity that they have been acclaimed as the best of the present century.

Great Vintages of the Past

Golden vintages. The legendary vintages before 1945 are shown on the right. The wines listed are exceptionally long-lived, and were of superlative calibre in these vintage years.

★   Great vintages
★★   Very great vintages
★★★   The greatest vintages recorded

Year	PORT	GERMANY	RED BURGUNDY	SAUTERNES	RED BORDEAUX
1811	★★★	★★★	★★★	★★★	★★★
1815	★★				★★
1834	★★				
1844					★★
1847	★★★			★★★	
1851	★★				
1858				★★	★★★
1863	★★★				
1864			★	★★	★★★
1865		★★	★★	★★	★★★
1868	★★				
1869				★	★★
1870	★★★		★		★★★
1874				★★	★★★
1875			★	★★	★★★
1878	★★			★★	★★
1884	★★				
1893		★★			★
1896	★★				★
1899				★	★★
1900	★★	★★		★★★	★★★
1904	★		★	★★	
1906			★★	★	★
1908	★★				
1911	★	★★	★★		
1912	★★				
1915			★★		
1919			★★		
1920	★			★	★
1921		★★★		★★★	★
1923			★★		
1927	★★★				
1928			★★★	★★	★★★
1929		★★	★★	★★★	★★★
1931	★★★				
1933			★		
1934	★	★	★	★★	★
1937		★★	★★	★★★	

2
Serving Wine
Bringing Out the Best

There are times when the serving of wine invites an element of ceremony, with decanters, ice buckets and sparkling glasses heralding the moment when the wine is to be tasted. But correct procedure should be more than a series of gestures—a bottle chilled to the right temperature, a cleanly extracted cork, timely decanting for wines that need it and an appropriately shaped glass will all contribute to the realization of a wine's full potential.

If you have a reliable corkscrew, opening most wines will present no difficulty, but older red wines require special care because they contain sediment (*page 43*). Decanting the wine will ensure that the sediment stays behind. It also exposes the wine to the air (*page 44*), which releases its bouquet. The best time for decanting—immediately before serving or as much as 4 hours earlier—depends on the wine itself and your experience with it. Some fragile old wines may suffer from contact with the air, while others improve. Traditions can reflect these differences: old wines are rarely decanted in Burgundy, but in the Bordeaux region wines of the same age are almost always decanted. If in doubt, decant your wine nearer to serving time rather than hours in advance; then, with a foreknowledge of what the wine may offer, you can wait for it to reach its peak, rather than discovering that it has begun to fade.

Any wine will best reveal its qualities if served at the ideal temperature, which will vary according to the type of wine, its stage of development and the surrounding temperature (*page 45*). Champagne and dry white wines profit from thorough, rapid chilling, which tempers the wine's acidity and ensures a pleasant crispness. A red wine, however, may react markedly to variations in temperature. A degree or two below the ideal will deaden the bouquet and exaggerate the tannin's acerbity, but if the same wine is served too warm, its balance may shatter, so that the separate elements disperse and the alcohol becomes too dominant.

The ambient temperature is also important—a wine will require extra coolness to convey freshness on a hot day or in a warm room. The theory that red wines should be served at room temperature derives from the chilly dining rooms of the last century and is invalidated by modern heating; red wines usually need cooling to reveal their best qualities. Always remember that a wine served a little too cool will rapidly warm up in the glass, while a wine served too warm will never cool down in the glass.

A glass of freshly poured Champagne creates a mood of expectation. To present the wine at its best, the bottle has been chilled thoroughly in an ice bucket. The cork has been removed slowly, so that the wine has not foamed over. Poured into a chilled glass, the Champagne displays a continuous fountain of tiny bubbles.

Efficient Techniques for Opening Bottles

Any wine should be opened with care, using a reliable opener that extracts the cork cleanly and smoothly. Young wines may be opened without special precautions, but older red wines must be handled gently to avoid disturbing the tannic sediment in the bottle. Champagne and other sparkling wines must also be opened correctly to prevent the cork from emerging violently and the wine from foaming over.

All the openers shown below will remove a cork smoothly without disturbing the contents of the bottle. Whatever its design, a corkscrew should have an evenly coiled screw with smooth edges—this is especially important with older corks, which can crumble easily. An opener with sharp protrusions round a central shaft can tear corks apart. With the two-pronged extractor, you can remove a cork without piercing it—particularly helpful if you wish to re-use corks.

The procedures for opening old red wine are designed to prevent sediment

from clouding the wine when it is served. A day or two before the wine is to be opened, carefully ease the bottle from its horizontal storage position (*page 38*) and set it upright. The sediment, which has settled along the underside of the bottle, will slowly slip down to the base. Move the bottle carefully, and hold it immobile while you uncork it (*right*).

If an old red wine has not been set on end in advance for the sediment to settle, it may be served from a cradle (*box, opposite page*); make sure the position of the bottle never changes so that the sediment remains undisturbed on the lower side.

The wired-on corks of Champagne and other sparkling wines must always be removed slowly; otherwise the pressure in the bottle may propel the cork out violently the instant the wire is removed. A Champagne cork is less likely to pop if the wine has been well chilled (*page 45*), but even chilled Champagne must be opened with care (*box, right, below*).

1 **Removing the capsule.** Stand the bottle on a flat surface. With a sharp knife or the retractable blade on a wine-waiter's corkscrew (*above*), cut all round the capsule just below the projecting part of the bottle neck. Remove the top part of the capsule, so that it does not come into contact with the wine when it is poured.

Reliable Openers of Different Designs

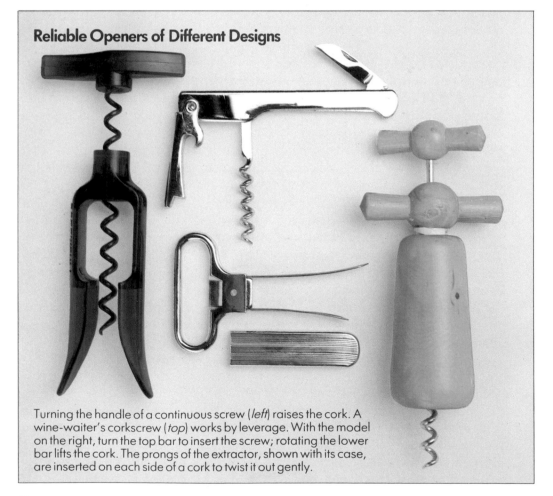

Turning the handle of a continuous screw (*left*) raises the cork. A wine-waiter's corkscrew (*top*) works by leverage. With the model on the right, turn the top bar to insert the screw; rotating the lower bar lifts the cork. The prongs of the extractor, shown with its case, are inserted on each side of a cork to twist it out gently.

Uncorking Champagne Safely

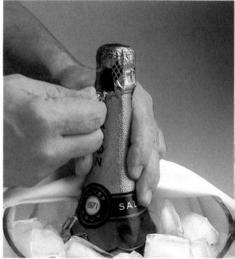

1 **Removing wire and foil.** Chill the bottle of Champagne to the right temperature (*page 45*). Lift the cork's wire toggle (*above*); untwist it anticlockwise, holding the cork with your other hand. To prevent accidents, keep your hand over the cork until the wire is completely untwisted. Remove the wire cap and foil together.

2 **Inserting the screw.** To remove any dust or mould accumulated during storage, wipe the bottle's neck and rim and the top of the cork with a clean cloth. Open out the corkscrew, folding the screw down at a right angle. Insert the screw into the centre of the cork (*above*), and twist slowly to embed the screw completely.

3 **Drawing the cork.** Flip down the short lever, hooking it on to the edge of the neck of the bottle; grip the lever and the neck together firmly. Hold the end of the long lever and pull it up (*above*). For a very long cork, unfold the corkscrew, enclose the cork and the neck in your hand, and gently pull out the cork.

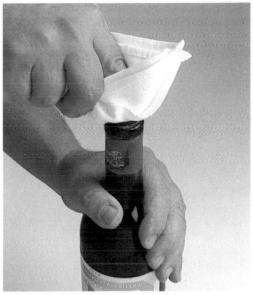

4 **Wiping the neck.** To remove any trace of mould from the bottle rim or fragments of crumbled cork from inside the neck, carefully wipe the rim and the inside of the neck with the cloth (*above*). The wine is now ready to be either decanted (*page 44*) or served directly from the bottle.□

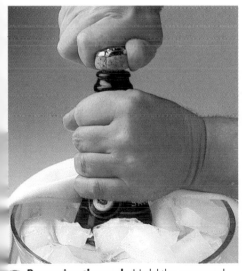

2 **Removing the cork.** Hold the exposed part of the cork firmly in place with one hand and turn the bottle slowly with the other hand (*above*). When you feel the cork beginning to rise, press firmly to prevent the cork from emerging violently. After removing the cork, blow into the bottle to discourage foaming. Wipe the bottle's neck and pour the Champagne.

Pouring Wine from a Cradle

1 **Uncorking the wine.** Keeping the bottle horizontal and its label uppermost, ease the wine—here, a Burgundy—from its storage rack to a napkin-lined cradle. To prevent any wine from spilling when the cork is drawn, place an upturned plate beneath the front of the cradle. Open the bottle (*Steps 1 to 3, above*) without changing its position in the cradle.

2 **Pouring the wine.** Wipe the bottle neck clean with a cloth. Slip one hand through the cradle's handle and grasp the bottle and cradle firmly together. Pour the wine steadily without changing the bottle's position. If the wine contains sediment, never twist the bottle, even if the wine drips as you move it from glass to glass.

How, Why and When to Decant

The practice of decanting wine is not merely a convention, but a procedure which positively benefits certain wines. If there is sediment in the bottle, pouring the wine into a decanter will ensure that this deposit remains behind. Decanting also exposes wine to the air, which will open up its bouquet. Indeed, this is the only effective means of aerating a wine; merely removing the cork exposes only a small area of the wine's surface, whereas decanting brings the entire contents of the bottle into contact with the air.

Whether a wine will profit from aeration, and choosing the best time for decanting, depends on the wine itself. In general, young red wines will open up and reveal their fruit if decanted shortly before serving (box, right). It is the older wines that will need time to open out, but these are also the wines that can suffer if they are exposed to the air for too long. Only your experience of a particular wine will indicate whether it profits from being decanted some hours before serving. Some older wines may be at their peak 2 to 3 hours after decanting, while others may have begun to fade. If you are in doubt, it is safer to decant the wine nearer the time of serving rather than too early.

Wines that are decanted to separate them from sediment include older red wines and aged port. However, fine old Burgundies are not usually decanted, because if exposed to air they may be susceptible to oxidation; instead, the wine may be served from a cradle (page 43).

If you plan to decant an older red wine, the bottle should be set upright a day or two in advance so that the sediment will settle at its base; if this is not possible, the wine should be poured from a cradle. When decanting these wines, position a candle flame or other point of light beneath the neck of the bottle, in your direct line of sight, to enable you to see sediment as it appears in the neck (box, right).

Old vintage port is always decanted; it throws a heavy sediment, and it may be impossible to remove the cork intact. Set the bottle upright several days before opening it, and decant the wine through muslin, which will trap heavy pieces of crusted sediment and fragments of crumbled cork (box, far right, above).

Exposing a Young Wine to Air

Decanting a young red wine. Open the wine (page 42)—here, a Beaujolais. Hold the decanter in one hand and pour the wine rapidly into the decanter, so that the wine splashes up and is well aerated.

Straining Port Through Muslin

Decanting old port. Place a funnel in the neck of a decanter; line it with several layers of clean muslin, well rinsed and wrung out. Pour the wine—here, a 1924 port—through the funnel to trap crusty sediment and crumbled cork. As soon as fine sediment appears in the wine, stop pouring at once—this powdery deposit would slip through the cloth.

Direct Light to Show Up Sediment

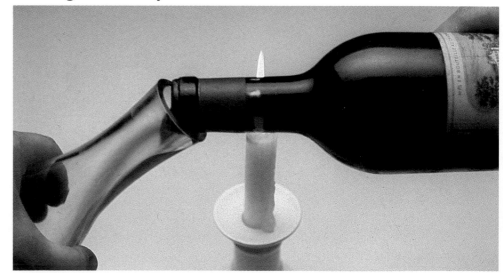

Decanting old red wine. With the lip of the bottle in the top of the decanter, slowly pour the wine—here, an old Bordeaux. Once the wine flows smoothly, move the bottle neck over a candle flame and pour more rapidly, tilting the bottle and the decanter without changing the angle at which they are held. When the first trace of sediment appears in the neck of the bottle, stop pouring at once.

Creating the Right Conditions

Every wine has an ideal serving temperature that best brings out its flavour and bouquet. To give an impression of coolness and freshness, wine should always be served at least a degree or two cooler than room temperature. The chart here indicates the range that generally suits different categories of wine (*page 28*).

Since cold tempers acidity, crisp, relatively acidic white wines should be served cooler than more complex white wines. Fresh, fruity red wines should be served cooler than more tannic and older red wines. A degree of coolness enhances the fruitiness of a fine young red wine; when fully mature it will need a slightly higher temperature to release its bouquet.

Red wines may be served directly from a cool cellar, or first cooled in an ice bucket (*below*). White wines and Champagne should be chilled in plenty of ice (*below, centre*). Champagne should also be served in chilled glasses to prevent it foaming up when poured (*below, right*). Alternatively, all wines may be cooled in the refrigerator for up to an hour, or in the freezer for no more than half an hour.

Finding the Ideal Temperature

15°-16°C (59°-61°F)	**Great, complex red wines:** first and second growth clarets **Fortified wines:** vintage port, old Madeira, old sherry
14°-16°C (57°-61°F)	**Great, complex red wines:** first growth Burgundies from the Côte de Nuits **Fine, complex red wines**
14°C (57°F)	**Big, muscular, robust red wines** **Fortified wines:** Marsala, young port, Madeira, sherry
10°-12°C (50°-53°F)	**Good, loyal and uncomplicated red wines** **Light-bodied, non-tannic red wines, drunk young and cool** **Complex, full-bodied white wines**
8°-10°C (46°-50°F)	**Crisp white wines** **Highly scented white wines with an edge of sweetness** **Soft white wines** **Muscular, vigorous white wines**
6°-8°C (43°-46°F)	**Rich, sweet white wines** **Champagne**

Bringing Out Freshness

Cooling red wine. Fill an ice bucket with cold water; add a handful or two of ice cubes. Position an opened bottle of red wine—here, a Beaujolais—in the bucket (*above*). To maintain the temperature, add more ice when the cubes begin to melt. If the wine is cool enough, and the surrounding temperature is not too high, remove the bottle from the bucket.

Packed Ice for Thorough Cooling

Chilling white wine. Put a few handfuls of ice cubes in the bottom of an ice bucket. Place a bottle of white wine—in this case, Champagne—in the ice bucket. Pack as many ice cubes as you can round the bottle, and then fill the bucket almost to the rim with cold water. Chill for about 20 minutes, twirling the bottle in the ice occasionally to help the wine chill evenly.

Cold Glasses for Sparkling Wine

Pouring Champagne. To prevent chilled Champagne foaming when it meets a relatively warm glass, put some ice cubes in each glass. Swirl them round until the glass becomes misty, then pour out the ice. Alternatively, chill the glasses in the freezer. Open the Champagne (*page 42*). Tilting a glass to prevent foaming, pour out the wine (*above*).

Glasses Designed to Enhance Wines

A few rules derived from simple logic govern the design of a good wine glass. All of the wine glasses shown below are made from uncoloured, uncut glass, so that the wine's colour and clarity are easily observed. Long stems permit a firm hold for swirling the wine to develop its bouquet (*page 35*), and ensures that its tempera-ture will not be affected nor its beauty obscured by holding the bowl in the hands.

The ideal wine glass has a rim narrow-er than the bowl at its widest point, so that the wine's bouquet concentrates in the space above the wine's surface. However, straight-sided glasses, such as glasses 3, 7 and 11, admired for the purity of their form, are also good for serving wine.

Here, glasses 1 to 7 are filled with red wine and glasses 8 to 13 with white. Most glasses may be used for either red or white wine, but certain forms are traditional for specific colours and regions. Glass 1, for-merly used for serving white Burgundies, is now mostly used for red wine; glasses 2 and 4 are traditional for red Burgundies, and glass 10 for German and Alsatian white wines. Glasses 6 and 8 are good for simple daily wines, but they are too small for the full appreciation of more complex

wines. For these wines, a large-bowled glass—1 or 4, for example—would be ideal. Glasses should be large enough to hold about 10 cl (3½ fl oz) of wine when no more than half full, so that the wine can be swirled without spilling. Very large glasses may be only about one-eighth full.

The best Champagne glasses (14 to 16) are long-stemmed, and they have fluted or tulip shapes in which the fine lines of tiny rising bubbles can be seen clearly. Since a Champagne's bouquet develops from the bursting bubbles at its surface, the wine is not swirled, and so the glasses can be filled almost to the top.

Fortified wines, being rich and concentrated, should be served in small glasses (17 to 19). You might choose a straight-sided glass, such as glass 18 or 19, for a lesser fortified wine with a relatively un-complicated bouquet. For a fine vintage port or Madeira with a more complex bouquet, glass 17, which narrows at the lip, is ideal. This well-proportioned glass may also be used at wine-tastings (*page 36*), where only a small quantity of any one wine will be served to each taster.

Wine in a Menu
Complements and Consonances

Meals are frequently planned with no wine consideration but a "white with fish, red with meat" afterthought. Except for being unnecessarily restrictive, this formula is quite suitable for planning everyday meals, for choosing pleasant, uncomplicated wines whose main virtue is their quaffability, and for deciding on accompaniments for high-spirited foods whose complicated flavours deaden the palate's sensitivity to finer wines.

This chapter presents a different approach to menu-planning. The meal is designed around a sequence of wines, instead of a series of dishes. The intention is to create a harmonious interrelationship between the wines themselves, as well as between the wine and the foods. The menus have been devised by Richard Olney, Chief Consultant to *The Good Cook* series, who has also provided the accompanying commentary. Each menu has a different theme—ranging from simple combinations of robust wine and rustic foods (*page 52*) to elaborate seven-course dinners built around a progression of seven different wines (*page 60*). The food for each menu, with suggested alternatives, is described in the texts; the wines and their possible alternatives are presented in the picture captions.

The wines must be chosen to complement each other; no wine should suffer by comparison to the one preceding it, and it must stand up to the wine that follows. If you change one wine, those that come before and after it must often change as well. There are many possible patterns, but one practice should be avoided: wines made from the same grape, but from different parts of the world, should not be placed next to each other in the sequence; otherwise you risk having the depth and subtlety of a fine wine overwhelmed by a brash emulator.

A few principles govern the choice of food. Complex flavours need simple wines; complex wines need simple flavours: the finer the wine, the simpler the food. In these menus, the climactic wine comes not with the main course but with the cheese. It is preceded by a salad, to refresh the palate, but because vinegar in a dressing is anathema to fine wine, water is this course's best companion. In general, sweetness in food will make a dry wine too acid and sour foods will turn it flat, but a young wine with rough fruit goes well with sweet and savoury dishes, and a somewhat acidic wine may show unexpected charm when drunk with sharp-flavoured dishes. Desserts should be less sweet than the accompanying wine.

young Graves is poured before the first
ourse is served for an all-red-wine menu.
efore each succeeding course of food, the
ccompanying wine will be poured so that it
ay first be tasted alone before being
voured with its chosen dish.

Marriages of Cheese and Wine

The particular affinities between cheese, wine and bread are said to reside in the fact that all three are fermented foods. The explanation may owe more to poetry than to commonsense, but it is certain that for many people a meal without a cheese course is incomplete. There are others, though, who categorically deny cheese a place on their menu, contending that its aggressive flavours damage their appreciation of the wine.

The wine merchant's motto, "Buy on bread, sell on cheese", would seem to support the second point of view. Its implication is that when a buyer is tasting a wine, only a nibble of bread will permit his palate to detect the wine's faults or its real qualities, whereas if he tastes a wine with cheese, its faults will be disguised and he will think it better than it is.

But "wine" and "cheese" are abstractions; there are many cheeses and there are many wines. Cheese is often spoken of in terms of its "bouquet" and shares many adjectives with wine—mature, full-bodied, heady, sharp, fruity, delicate, grassy or herbal, high or gamey, or floral. Its odours can range from the fragrant sweetness of fresh pasturage to the pungent ferments of decay and, surprisingly, the most terrifying of scents can announce the most refined, subtle and gentle of flavours with a gamut of voluptuous textures known to no other food.

Wines, for their part, can be powerful, huge, muscular, dense; they can be acerbic or supple, crisp or soft, fruity, thirst-quenching, simple and rustic. It is true that some delicate, frail old wines may be overwhelmed by a cheese, but most others will accompany a cheese platter admirably, the chosen cheeses corresponding to the nature of the particular wine.

Illustrated on the right are four traditional alliances, each between a specific wine and a specific cheese. Below, different cheeses accompany two fine red wines of divergent character.

Strength with Sweetness

Roquefort with Sauternes. Sauternes is traditionally served with Roquefort in the Bordeaux region. Whether they enhance each other, or are two mighty forces, each refusing to be vanquished, is a traditional point of contention. Whether you settle the question or not, tasting them together is a rewarding experience.

A Meeting of Powerful Personalities

Strong cheeses with robust wine. A powerful Barolo from Piedmont in Italy is served with Camembert (*centre*) and, clockwise from the lower left, Pont l'Évêque, Livarot, ripe goat cheese, fresh Parmesan, Gorgonzola, mature Cheddar and Maroilles.

Only a powerful wine can stand up to the rich, penetrating taste of most blue cheeses or the heady exhalations of a Maroilles or Livarot. Good companions for almost any wine are Camembert, Cheddar, Parmesan and Pont l'Évêque, though perhaps too aggressive for an old claret or a Burgundy. Châteauneuf-du-Pape or Gigondas from the southern Rhône Valley or Californian Zinfandel are among other red wines that can support strong cheeses.

A Neighbourly Match

Münster with Gewürztraminer. This is a marriage made in Alsace. The high, intimidating bouquet of Münster belies its creamy, melting texture and gentle flavour, which form a striking alliance with the spicy, floral Gewürztraminer.

Crisp Wine and Piquant Cheese

Goat cheeses with Sancerre. The crisp, flinty, thirst-quenching wine of Sancerre from the Loire Valley is drunk young while its fruit is still green and tender, often accompanied by the local goat cheeses, seen here in a semi-dry state. They are sometimes served so dry that they must be splintered with a hammer.

A Classic Combination

Stilton cheese with port. If it is drunk with Stilton, an immature vintage port—in this case, a five-year-old Taylor—still with the rawness and violence of youth, can be tamed remarkably. The unattractive habit of pouring port into a hollowed-out Stilton will destroy the wine and cheese.

A Delicate Encounter

Mild cheeses with delicate wine. Here, a mature red Graves from the Bordeaux region has been decanted in advance to be served with a selection of mild or delicately flavoured cheese—clockwise from the left, *reblochon,* Cheshire, St. Nectaire, Taleggio, Gruyère and fresh goat cheeses. Other mild cheeses that are suitable include Brie, Caerphilly, Edam, Wensleydale, *tomme de Savoie, fontina* and *stracchino.* The nature of these cheeses permits them to be served with any decent red wine or, somewhat less conventionally, with robust but fine white wines like the *vins jaunes* from the French Jura or dry Italian *vino santo.*

Fresh, Fruity Wines with Robust Foods

A substantial main course of braised meat and vegetables has a robust flavour that is best balanced by a vigorous young red wine. In this menu, for example, lamb stew is served with Zinfandel.

To provide an introduction to the exuberant fruit of the Zinfandel, a dry, fresh and uncomplicated white wine is the best choice with the first course. The food itself should have a clean sharpness to flatter the wine. Here, the effect is achieved with herring fillets that have been marinated briefly in lemon or lime juice, drained and dressed with olive oil, salt, pepper and fresh herbs. Split and marinated prawn tails or thin slices of filleted salmon could also pave the way for the meat course.

The wild-berry intensity of the Zinfandel is reflected in the more intricate bouquet of the Bandol—a wine with a similar character but greater complexity, which is served with the cheese. Because the menu is simple and includes no dessert wine, a rich dessert—in this case, poached pears, vanilla ice cream and hot chocolate sauce—is entirely appropriate.

WINES	MENU
Soave Classico 1979 (Pieropan)	Marinated Raw Herring Fillets
Ridge California Zinfandel 1978 (Paso Robles, Santa Clara)	Lamb Stew with Spring Vegetables
	Green Salad
Bandol 1975 (Domaine Tempier)	Cheeses
	Poached Pears, Vanilla Ice Cream, Hot Chocolate Sauce

1 Soave. This soft, refreshing, dry white wine from the Veneto region of Italy could be replaced by a crisper white wine such as a Swiss Dorin or Fendant, a Savoie Crépy from across the border in France or by a Sauvignon Blanc from California, South Africa or Australia. Any of these could serve also as an aperitif.

2 Zinfandel. The Californian Zinfandel grape produces a robust, fruity wine. Possible substitutes are a Cahors from the south-west of France, a Cornas from the Côtes du Rhône, a Dolcetto or a Nebbiolo, both from Piedmont in Italy, or a Shiraz, from South Africa or Australia.

3 Bandol. The solid structure and firm fruit of this red wine from the Mediterranean coast of France enable it to hold its own following the Zinfandel. A Châteauneuf-du-Pape from the southern Rhône Valley or a Barolo from Piedmont in Italy could also follow the Zinfandel or any of the suggested alternatives. □

A Sequence of Simple Harmonies

This menu is a further variation on the theme of simple wines with simple food. The meal begins with a salad of leftover meats or fish and vegetables. Its quality will depend on the excellence of the olive oil and vinegar, while garlic, fresh herbs and salad greens will enliven it. A vigorous white wine, whose qualities lie more in force of character than in finesse, will support the vinaigrette better than most reds. Asparagus vinaigrette or melon and prosciutto could replace the salad.

For the second course, fresh pasta is moistened with the braising juices of the veal that follows. In this instance, both pasta and veal are served with a Chianti, but a lighter Italian wine, such as a Dolcetto or Barbera, might advantageously accompany the pasta, the Chianti being reserved for the meat. Braised beef, lamb, pork or game could also be served this way, preceded, if preferred, by polenta or risotto instead of pasta.

A Barbaresco finishes the meal, served with cheese, fruits and nuts presented at the same time. Apples and pears, in particular, go well with both cheese and wine.

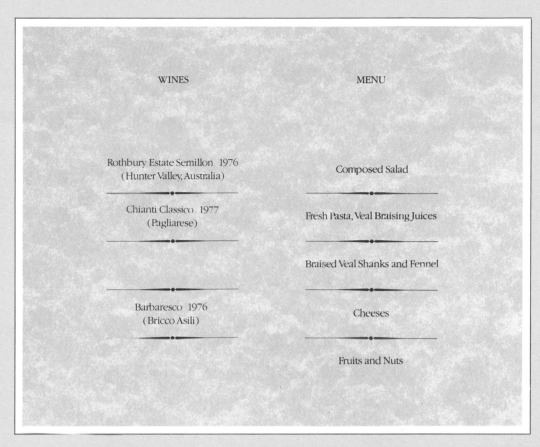

WINES	MENU
Rothbury Estate Semillon 1976 (Hunter Valley, Australia)	Composed Salad
Chianti Classico 1977 (Pagliarese)	Fresh Pasta, Veal Braising Juices
	Braised Veal Shanks and Fennel
Barbaresco 1976 (Bricco Asili)	Cheeses
	Fruits and Nuts

1 **Semillon.** The most important white grape variety from the Bordeaux region, Semillon produces a wine of a rougher and more earthy character when grown in Australia's Hunter Valley. The Tuscan Vernaccia di San Gimignano, Frascati from the Roman hills, Bellet from near Nice or a white Crozes Hermitage from the Rhône Valley are possible substitutes.

2 **Chianti.** From Tuscany, Chianti is one of the good-natured red wines of Italy that are happiest in the company of other traditional Italian red wines. Instead of the Chianti, a Nebbiolo or a Grignolino from Piedmont could precede the Barbaresco or, if both red wines are being replaced, a Coteaux d'Aix from the South of France would be a good choice.

3 **Barbaresco.** Barbaresco is one of the most distinguished wines of Piedmont. To follow the Chianti, the Nebbiolo or the Grignolino, a Barolo from Piedmont or a Brunello di Montalcino from Tuscany might replace the Barbaresco. Following a Coteaux d'Aix, a Palette, also from Provence, or a Châteauneuf-du-Pape from the Côtes du Rhône, is suitable.□

A Versatile Backdrop to a Wide Choice of Wines

A menu of simply cooked seafood followed by grilled meat, cheese and fruit would suit almost any balanced selection of white or red wines. Here, crayfish salad (*recipe, page 167*) precedes grilled guinea fowl and strawberries. Only dill imposes a restriction on the choice of wine: dill complements crayfish, but is often quarrelsome with wine. However, a solid, rustic wine—here, a white Crozes Hermitage—will support its presence. Shrimps, prawns or lobster might be substituted for the crayfish. If *fines herbes* replace the dill, the crustaceans could accompany a dry white wine of greater nuance.

The guinea fowl could be replaced by other grilled poultry, game birds, steaks or chops, all versatile companions to a red wine, be it a cool *primeur*, a venerable great growth or the young Médoc here.

A fine St. Emilion accompanies the cheese; strawberries, spooned into the last glasses, give a fresh reminder of the wine's complexity and vigour. The berries might be replaced by peaches; either will enhance the fruit of a young wine or give a last burst of life to an old one in decline.

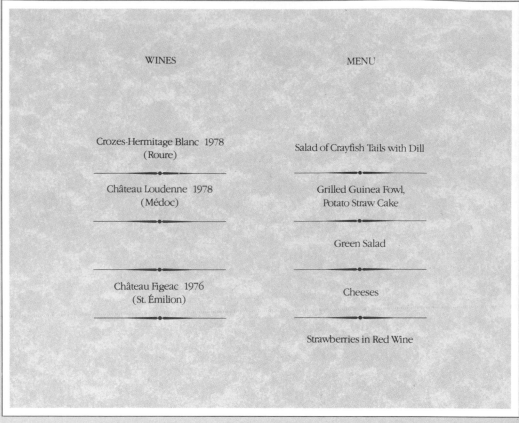

WINES	MENU
Crozes-Hermitage Blanc 1978 (Roure)	Salad of Crayfish Tails with Dill
Château Loudenne 1978 (Médoc)	Grilled Guinea Fowl, Potato Straw Cake
	Green Salad
Château Figeac 1976 (St. Émilion)	Cheeses
	Strawberries in Red Wine

1 Crozes Hermitage. The hills at Crozes Hermitage in the northern Côtes du Rhône produce sturdy, vigorous wines able to compete with many aggressive flavours. The dill-crustacean alliance goes well also with relatively dry German Rieslings or with the pronounced fruit of Californian Chenin Blanc.

2 Médoc. The light, cleanly defined style of this bourgeois growth—from Château Loudenne—is reflected with greater force and density in the Château Figeac that follows. A younger St. Emilion could be substituted for the Médoc. If both reds are changed, a light red wine, such as Gamay de Touraine, is possible or, for more substance, a Rhône Valley Cornas.

3 St. Emilion. From St. Emilion, Château Figeac is distinguished by the presence of a high proportion of the Cabernet Sauvignon grape. A classified Médoc could follow the Loudenne. Loudenne's replacements could be followed by a Bourgueil from the Loire Valley, a Corton from the Côte de Beaune or a Rhône Valley Hermitage, respectively. □

Rich Dishes with Powerful Wines

Composed around a hearty main course of braised game—here, braised, stuffed hare—this menu provides an opportunity for a harmonious succession of big, powerful wines. The richness of the hare would not be hospitable to a complicated dish preceding it. The cheese soufflés coated with cream, known as *petites suissesses* (*recipe, page 169*), not only leave the palate alert for the meat, but also throw into relief the cool, clear tonalities of the Chevalier-Montrachet. A ragout of morels or a fish terrine could play a similar role.

The heady amalgam of flavours from the hare's flesh, braising juices and its truffled, blood-bound forcemeat invites a match with an equally heady wine. Most appropriate is a red from the northern Côtes du Rhône—here, a Côte Rôtie, whose bouquet has a suggestion of game. A civet of wild rabbit or a roast woodcock with a sauce of innards and *foie gras* could replace the hare. A Hermitage from the same area accompanies the cheese.

After rich food, a sorbet is the lightest, most refreshing dessert. Fresh fruit or a Sauternes, or both, could be substituted.

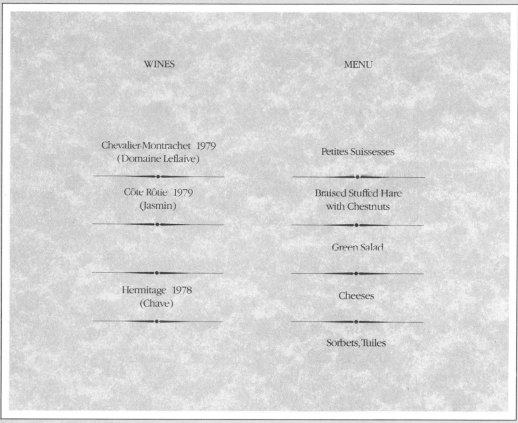

WINES	MENU
Chevalier-Montrachet 1979 (Domaine Leflaive)	Petites Suissesses
Côte Rôtie 1979 (Jasmin)	Braised Stuffed Hare with Chestnuts
	Green Salad
Hermitage 1978 (Chave)	Cheeses
	Sorbets, Tuiles

1 Chevalier-Montrachet. This is one of the cluster of appellations from the Côte de Beaune; for many, it represents the most perfect expression of white Burgundy. The Chevalier-Montrachet could be replaced by one of the unusual and lovely Pinot Blancs from Morey-St. Denis, a Nuits-St. Georges from the Côte de Nuits or by a Californian Chardonnay.

2 Côte Rôtie. Côte Rôtie and Hermitage, from the northern Côtes du Rhône, are difficult to place with other wines, their force obliterating the nuance of a fine claret or Burgundy, their finesse putting other big wines in an unflattering light. If the Hermitage is retained, a Cornas could precede it; or the Côte Rôtie could be replaced by Châteauneuf-du-Pape.

3 Hermitage. Like Côte Rôtie and other northern Rhône wines based on the Syrah grape, Hermitage will appreciate several years of bottle age and will, in a good year, support several decades. If a Châteauneuf-du-Pape from the southern Rhône replaces the Côte Rôtie, only an older bottle of the same appellation would be likely to stand up to it. □

Wines that Stand Up to Sweetness

The focal point of this menu is the fruit-garnished main course, whose sweetness can clash with many wines. One wine that thrives in such company, however, is the Chinon here, whose own fresh, fruit flavour—often likened to raspberries, and slightly astringent—complements the soft note of prunes in the rabbit's savoury, dark sauce. Quail with grapes, duck with cherries, pork with apricots or blood pudding with sautéed russet apples could be counterpointed in the same way.

The calm elegance of the Savennières that starts the meal provides a pleasant contrast to the vigorous, well-structured Chinon, while the bouquet of the following Pomerol recalls that of the Chinon with greater depth and maturity.

As a companion to the white wine, a vegetable gratin or soufflé would make an ideal first course. In this case, courgettes are shredded, combined with rice, chard, sautéed onion, eggs, Parmesan and garlic *persillade*, and baked. Any light dessert—here, fresh figs with a raspberry purée—will complete the menu.

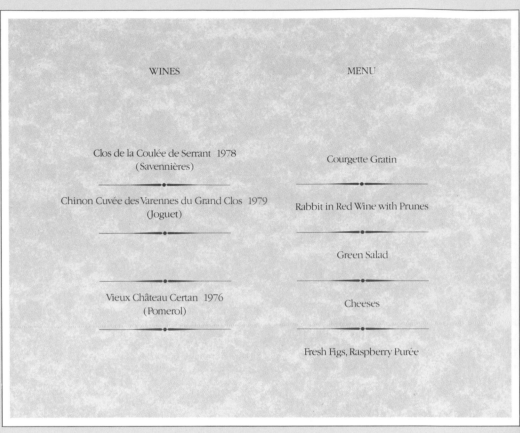

WINES	MENU
Clos de la Coulée de Serrant 1978 (Savennières)	Courgette Gratin
Chinon Cuvée des Varennes du Grand Clos 1979 (Joguet)	Rabbit in Red Wine with Prunes
	Green Salad
Vieux Château Certan 1976 (Pomerol)	Cheeses
	Fresh Figs, Raspberry Purée

1 **Savennières.** Made from the Chenin Blanc grape, often called Pineau de la Loire, the Coulée de Serrant is a dry wine from the Loire Valley. Possible replacements include a dry Vouvray from the same region, a white Graves from Bordeaux or, from outside Europe, a Chenin Blanc (or its equivalent from South Africa, known as Steen).

2 **Chinon.** This wine from Touraine in the Loire Valley is made from the Cabernet Franc grape, also known as Breton. From the same region and grape variety, a Bourgueil could serve instead—or the astonishing Château-Chalon from the Jura, a white wine that can fill the role of many a red and, like the Chinon, is at home with a sweet and savoury note.

3 **Pomerol.** Merlot and Cabernet grapes produce, in Pomerol, relatively supple wines with a more immediate flavour than those of the other great Bordeaux appellations. A St. Emilion might also follow a Chinon or a Bourgueil. The Château-Chalon could be continued with the cheese course or be replaced by a firm, barely mature growth from the Médoc or the Côte de Nuits.□

Red Wine with Fish: an Unconventional Theme

This unorthodox menu presents red wines with a succession of fish dishes. A first course of grilled scallops and monkfish, briefly marinated with lemon juice, olive oil, chopped green onion and *fines herbes*, is accompanied by a Saumur Champigny, whose light, fresh fruit will not overwhelm the fish. The meal could also be opened with grilled prawns or red mullets or deep-fried cuttlefish.

In the main course, the firm, rustic flavour of salt cod (*recipe, page 167*) is best served by a wine with the same description, and the garlicky *persillade* suggests a solid red—here, a Rioja. Other salt cod dishes, except those in tomato or cream sauce, or an eel stew might be substituted.

The menu breaks a further convention. Port is normally a post-prandial wine, only to be drunk with Stilton. Here, port is served with sharp, heady cheeses that would overwhelm most wines. Following the cheeses, the bitter fragrance of thyme, cooked with the dried figs and red wine, will flatter the port's sweet intensity. Pears or peaches in red wine syrup or almond pastries are alternatives.

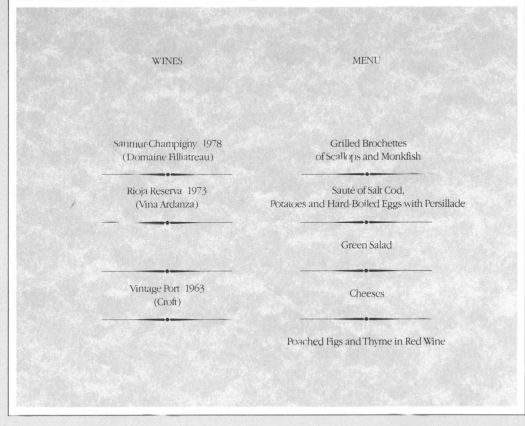

WINES	MENU
Saumur-Champigny 1978 (Domaine Filliatreau)	Grilled Brochettes of Scallops and Monkfish
Rioja Reserva 1973 (Vina Ardanza)	Sauté of Salt Cod, Potatoes and Hard-Boiled Eggs with Persillade
	Green Salad
Vintage Port 1963 (Croft)	Cheeses
	Poached Figs and Thyme in Red Wine

1 Saumur Champigny. This pretty wine from Anjou in the Loire Valley is made from the Cabernet Franc grape. Pinot Nero or Merlot from north-east Italy, Beaujolais, any of the red wines from France or California that are labelled *primeur*, or, more conventionally, a dry white wine, could stand in.

2 Rioja. A prolonged sojourn in wooden casks endows this Spanish wine with a smoothness many appreciate; others regret the inevitable loss of the wine's fresh fruit. Similar qualities may be found in Italian red wines labelled *riserva* from Piedmont or Tuscany—or a fresher note might be struck by a two-year-old Mercurey from the Côte Chalonnaise.

3 Port. Vintage port from the Portuguese Douro valley usually needs at least 15 years of bottle age for its violence to be tamed and its finesse to develop; it will continue to evolve for many decades. A Banyuls from the French Catalan coast, an old Madeira—either vintage or solera—a Sauternes or a rich, sweet Tokay Aszu could be substituted. □

A Succession of Contrasting Wines

A menu conceived around a selection of contrasting wines, each very different in character, is perhaps the most difficult to bring to a successful conclusion. Each wine must not only be enhanced by the food chosen to accompany it but must also be capable of expressing itself fully in the wake of the preceding wine. At the same time, it must be sufficiently discreet to pave the way for the wine to follow.

Old Madeira is an excellent choice as an aperitif. Although it more often shares with vintage port the role of an after dinner wine, Madeira's aptitude for exciting the palate makes it an admirable aperitif wine as well, on condition that its intense flavours are not permitted to alter one's appreciation of the wine to follow. A rich consommé, unaccompanied by wine, will provide the transition. Few other foods so sharpen the appetite while cleansing the palate. In this context, most other soups would be too heavy, too bland or too rich;

however, a concentrated, clear fish broth with a cautious hint of garlic would be an effective substitute.

The excellence of the grilled fish that follows in this menu depends on its absolute freshness, on its being only just cooked and on the quality of the olive oil that serves as its sauce. The fish will complement any fine, dry white wine and leave the palate unencumbered. Fritters of lamb's or calf's brains, grilled sweetbreads or scallops, sprinkled with breadcrumbs and olive oil and briefly baked, could be substituted.

A vigorous St. Emilion is very much in its element with the concentrated sauce of the meat course, an old-fashioned fricandeau (*recipe, page 168*); the wine supports the accompanying sorrel, whose light acidity counterpoints the sauce's richness. Fricandeau could be replaced by any stew or braise so long as the sauce is not dominated by tomatoes. Braised lamb's tongues, pig's ears or trotters; braised, stuffed lamb shoulder; beef *à la mode* and

coq au vin are a few of the possibilities.

A Chalone vineyard Pinot Noir from California accompanies the cheese. The two red wines have little in common besides colour, but neither the exuberance and fresh, chewy fruit of the St. Emilion, nor the massive dignity of the young Pinot Noir suffer from the proximity.

The peaches, peeled and sliced, are lightly sugared and macerated for a short time in a portion of the dessert wine. The wine should possess a certain vibrancy, here supplied by a German Auslese. The distinctive, bitter-sweet flavour that the noble rot bestows upon it seems to marry particularly well with peaches, both as a macerating agent and in a glass, separately. Mixed fresh fruits may be treated in the same way (*page 74*). A pistachio nut soufflé with an almond milk base would go well with the wine, as would any apple dessert that is slightly less sweet than the wine itself.

1 **Madeira.** Malmsey—one of four grape varieties associated with the island of Madeira—yields an intricate wine with an iron structure, sweet, pungent and vibrant. This Malmsey is a solera—a blend of old wines dated by the age of its most venerable component. It could be replaced most easily by either a fino or an amontillado sherry.

2 **Condrieu.** This dry white wine, with a cool fragrance of peaches, honey and almonds, is made from the Viognier grape, cultivated on the right bank of the northern Rhône Valley. It can be replaced by a white Burgundy or by a light-bodied young red wine—for example, a Merlot from the Veneto.

3 **St. Emilion.** Château Monbousquet is a solidly built wine yet well rounded and sufficiently supple to be enjoyed young, while it still retains its youthful fruit. If the following wine is replaced, a young, earthy Burgundy such as a Fixin or a Nuit St. Georges, from the Côte de Nuits, could be served in its stead.

WINES	MENU
Soleia Malmsey 1853 (Tarquino T. da Camara Lomelino)	
	Double Consommé
Condrieu Château du Rozay 1980	Grilled Sea Bass, Olive Oil
Château Monbousquet 1975 (St. Émilion)	Fricandeau of Veal with Sorrel
	Green Salad
Chalone Vineyard Pinot Noir 1978 (Monterey, California)	Cheeses
Wachenheimer Mandelgarten Scheurebe Auslese 1976 (Rheinpfalz, Dr. Bürklin-Wolf)	Peaches in Wine

4 **Pinot Noir.** From one of the rare parcels of calcareous earth in California, this big, intense sombre wine could hold its own in most company except, possibly, in that of a fine Burgundy. Following a Fixin or a Nuits, a noble growth from the Côte de Nuits—for instance, a Richebourg or Grands Échezeaux—will be safer.

5 **Rhine wine.** This sweet wine from the German Palatinate is vibrant, floral and lacy, with a delicately bitter background. It could be replaced by a late-picked Gewürztraminer or Riesling, from Alsace or California, a Barsac or a Loupiac from the Bordelais, or, from Touraine in the Loire Valley, a sweet, old Vouvray from a rich vintage such as 1959. □

A Stately Progression of Related Wines

The most classical of menu types, and ultimately, perhaps, the most satisfying, is that in which the wines for the body of the meal are chosen from a single region or neighbouring regions. Within that context, the wines progress from young to old and simple to complex. Here, the wines—mostly red—have been selected from Graves and Médoc in the Bordeaux region; alternatively, such a menu might well be built around the produce of a single vineyard, moving from lighter and more recent vintages to older and greater vintages of the same wine.

Champagne makes an exhilarating aperitif for both the food and the other wines; in this instance, it is followed by a white Graves, then a young red wine from Pauillac in the Médoc, then a succession of two older red Graves. The red wines culminate in a great Médoc from a great vintage, a 1961 Château Palmer from the commune of Margaux, and a fine,

old Sauternes rounds off the meal.

The food for this menu is chosen specifically to enhance the selection of wines. Smoked salmon is a particularly versatile starter: its delicately smoky flavour goes equally well with simple, refreshing, dry white wines, full-bodied Chardonnays or floral German Rieslings, as well as the Graves served with it here. The salmon could be replaced by another smoked fish, or even caviare.

As the next course, sweetbreads are a match for many wines, red or white. Here, cloaked in their braising essences and exhaling the bouquet of truffles, they marry perfectly with the Pauillac: few aromas or flavours form such a comfortable alliance with fine red wines as those of the truffle. Kidneys in wine sauce or fish in a red wine sauce are possible replacements.

The vegetable estouffade that follows (*recipe, page 169*) forms a bridge between the sweetbreads and the subsequent lamb, just as the red Graves that accompanies them links the young Pauillac

with the older Graves—Château La Mission Haut-Brion—served with the meat. The vegetables—a mixture of unpeeled garlic cloves, artichoke hearts, shredded lettuce, small onions and a bouquet garni, sweated until tender in butter—should be savoured alone first, then carried over to be eaten with the lamb. The estouffade might be replaced by a vegetable gratin or soufflé, and the lamb, for its part, by roast beef or game birds. The green salad forms an interlude before the cheese and its companion the Château Palmer.

For dessert, the vibrant Sauternes is presented with unsweetened apple slices, sautéed in butter until lightly coloured and wrapped in crêpes, then dabbed with butter, sprinkled lightly with sugar and quickly glazed in a hot oven. The apples could be replaced by a pear or almond-based dessert; or, if the vegetable course was not transformed into a soufflé, by a sweet soufflé.

4 **Graves.** This is a classified growth from a recent fine vintage; if preceded by a Mercurey, it could be replaced by a Santenay or a Monthélie from the Côte de Beaune. If a Côtes du Rhône came first, a Gigondas from the Rhône would be a suitable successor. A Cabernet Sauvignon could be followed by an older Californian Cabernet Sauvignon.

5 **Graves.** The second Graves here is a classified growth from a mature vintage. A Beaune, also from the Côte de Beaune, could follow the Santenay or Monthélie; a Châteauneuf-du-Pape from the southern Côtes du Rhône could follow its near neighbour, Gigondas, or another Cabernet Sauvignon its namesake.

6 **Margaux.** This Médoc third growth is from a great vintage—1961. In the pattern of the preceding substitutions, a Corton, also from the Côte de Beaune, or a Nuits-St. Georges from the Côte de Nuits could follow the Beaune. An older Châteauneuf-du-Pape could follow the preceding one and an older Cabernet Sauvignon follow the younger Cabernet.

1 Champagne. This most celebrated of sparkling wines is usually made from a mixture of white and red grapes—Pinot Noir and Chardonnay. It could be replaced with another sparkling wine or with a Graves that is lighter-bodied than the one that follows.

2 White Graves. The great white wines from Graves will develop for many years in bottle. In order to present the subsequent young red wine in the best light, the Graves chosen here is also young. It could be replaced by a first growth Chablis from northern Burgundy, a white Hermitage from the Rhône Valley or a Corton-Charlemagne.

3 Pauillac. This Grand Puy-Lacoste, a vigorous, young fifth growth claret from the Médoc, could be replaced by any of a number of young red wines, provided these are followed by older wines from the same general region—such as a Mercurey from the Côte Chalonnaise, a generic Côtes du Rhône or a Cabernet Sauvignon from California.

7 Sauternes. Sauternes and Barsac form an enclave in the south of Graves; the 1955 vintage shown here yielded great wines. A Loupiac or a Ste. Croix du Mont, from just across the Garonne river, a German Beerenauslese Riesling or a late-picked Gewürztraminer from either Alsace or California are alternatives. □

WINES	MENU
Champagne Laurent-Perrier (Cuvée Grand Siècle)	
Domaine de Chevalier Blanc 1976 (Graves)	Smoked Salmon
Château Grand-Puy-Lacoste 1978 (Pauillac)	Braised Veal Sweetbreads with Truffles
Château Malartic-Lagravière 1975 (Graves)	Mixed Vegetable Estouffade
Château La Mission Haut Brion 1966 (Graves)	Roast Saddle of Lamb, Gratin Dauphinois
	Green Salad
Château Palmer 1961 (Margaux)	Cheeses
Château Filhot 1955 (Sauternes)	Gratin of Crêpes with Apples

A Wine-Tasting Banquet

A menu in which two or more closely related wines are tasted—alternately, sip by sip—with each of several courses is a particularly instructive way to compare subtle distinctions. One approach is to choose wines of the same vintage from neighbouring vineyards—here, Californian Chardonnays and red Burgundies. Or you could select wines from the same vineyard but of different vintages.

So that you may approach the wines with a fresh palate, the aperitif should have a markedly different character from that of the wines opening the meal. These wines, as here, may originate in a climate very different from the one that produces the reds, but harmony among the reds depends on an overall similarity of characteristics, as in the menu on page 60.

Like that menu, the food should be chosen to exalt the wine. Here, seafood sausages (*recipe, page 168*) followed by sautéed ceps and roast partridges with braised cabbage support two Californian Chardonnays and a succession of great Burgundies. A Hungarian Tokay with a blanc-manger rounds off the meal.

The seafood sausages—casings stuffed with fish mousseline, diced crustaceans and pistachios—are poached and served with a butter sauce (*recipe, page 167*). Fish preparations in creamy sauces are particularly suited to rich, complex, dry white wines; turbot, John Dory or sole in a creamed velouté would do as well.

The following course should excite the senses without sating the palate. The firm, meaty flavour of the ceps, often reflected in the wine, goes well with red wine. Grilled, duxelles-stuffed cultivated mushrooms, a truffle baked in puff pastry or a truffle ragout are alternatives.

For their sake and that of the wine, the partridges should be roasted only until pink. Both birds and wines will ally themselves more intimately with the cabbage if it has been braised slowly with an old partridge. The flavour of any game bird mingles well with the delicately earthy bouquets of the Burgundies; roasted or grilled red meats might be substituted.

The blanc-manger, a Bavarian cream made of almond milk, could be replaced by most almond or apple-based desserts.

1 Moselle Kabinett. This light-bodied, not-quite-dry but steely young Riesling from the Saar valley, floral and laced with delicate fruit, could be replaced by any refreshing, young, dry white wine: a Swiss Fendant, or, from France, Crépy from Savoie, Quincy or Reuilly from the Cher valley or by a Champagne.

4 Gevrey-Chambertin; Bonnes Mares. The Clos St. Jacques is a *premier cru* from Gevrey-Chambertin in the Côte de Nuits; the Bonnes Mares is a *grand cru* straddling the two neighbouring village appellations of Morey-St. Denis and Chambolle-Musigny. If Pomerol or a St. Emilion were chosen for the previous course, their successors could be two older wines from different growths of the same appellation. If wines from outside France were used, two older wines from the same grape variety and region could follow.

5 Clos de la Roche. Alternatives to this Morey-St. Denis *grand cru* from the Côte de Nuits could be chosen from solid and mature vintages of the more distinguished *châteaux*—for instance, La Conseillante or Pétrus to follow the other Pomerols, or Château Cheval Blanc to follow the St. Emilions. The other suggestions could be followed by a still older Shiraz, Cabernet Sauvignon or Pinot Noir, coming from the same region as its predecessors.

2 **Sonoma Chardonnay; Napa Chardonnay.** The same vintage of complex white wines, made in northern California from Burgundy's noble Chardonnay grape, could be replaced by two different vintages of a single, complex dry white wine—such as Graves from Bordeaux, Chablis from northern Burgundy, a Clos des Mouches from the Côte de Beaune, or a Condrieu or Hermitage, both of which are from the northern Rhône Valley.

3 **Volnay; Pommard.** The Volnay and the Pommard, neighbouring *climats* in the Côte de Beaune, are known more for delicacy than for power. They could be replaced by two recent vintages of any red wine that will age well, making it possible to follow this course with older vintages of the same wine. Pomerol, St. Emilion from Bordeaux, Australian or South African Shiraz, Californian Cabernet Sauvignon, or Pinot Noir from Oregon in the north-western United States all fit this description.

6 **Tokay Aszu.** The sweet, richly flavoured Tokay from Hungary could be replaced by a Muscat from Corsica or Beaumes-de-Venise in the southern Côtes du Rhône, by a sweet Jurançon from south-west France, by a Sauternes or by one of the "Passito" wines made in Italy from semi-dried grapes, usually Muscat (Moscato). □

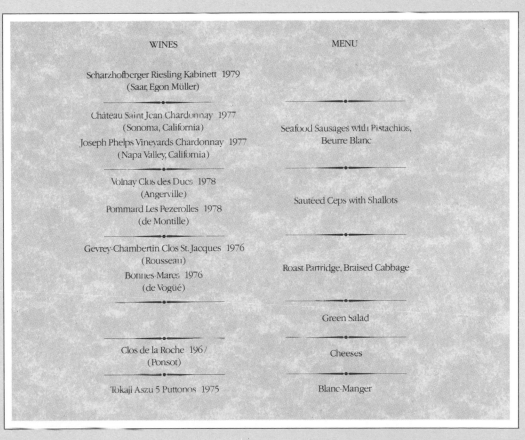

WINES	MENU
Scharzhofberger Riesling Kabinett 1979 (Saar, Egon Müller)	
Château Saint Jean Chardonnay 1977 (Sonoma, California) Joseph Phelps Vineyards Chardonnay 1977 (Napa Valley, California)	Seafood Sausages with Pistachios, Beurre Blanc
Volnay Clos des Ducs 1978 (Angerville) Pommard Les Pezerolles 1978 (de Montille)	Sautéed Ceps with Shallots
Gevrey-Chambertin Clos St. Jacques 1976 (Rousseau) Bonnes-Mares 1976 (de Vogüé)	Roast Partridge, Braised Cabbage
	Green Salad
Clos de la Roche 1967 (Ponsot)	Cheeses
Tokaji Aszu 5 Puttonos 1975	Blanc-Manger

4
Cooking with Wine
Alchemy in the Kitchen

A generous splash of young red wine completes the assembly of a pungent marinade in which beef will steep for several hours. Combined with the marinade's other ingredients—oil, aromatic vegetables and herbs—the wine will flavour the meat. The wine marinade will later serve as a braising medium and, finally, will become a rich sauce that moistens a hearty beef stew.

Food and wine form as natural a partnership in the kitchen as they do at the table, and wine has a role to play in every branch of cookery. Even before any ingredients are cooked, wine may be set to work as a flavouring agent in a marinade (*opposite and page 66*). Wine makes a fragrant poaching or braising medium for fish, shellfish, meat, poultry and game, and a sauce for sautés or roasts can be swiftly created by using a splash of wine to dissolve the rich residues in the pan (*page 69*). In desserts, combinations of wine and fruit provide many permutations of flavour (*pages 74-76*); wine can also enhance shimmering jellies, refreshing ices (*page 77*) and creamy egg custards (*page 78*).

The taste and texture of the wine you choose—whether it is tannic or acid, light or full-bodied—will influence the character of the completed dish. It is neither necessary nor desirable to sacrifice a great vintage wine to the cooking pot, but it is always essential to use a decent, drinkable wine. One that is not good enough for drinking at the table will never be good enough for use in the kitchen.

Some classic recipes and regional specialities call for quite specific wines—occasionally even by name—but a similar wine of the same type and quality may often be substituted with excellent effect. In many other cases, wines may be freely interchanged. The dictum that red meats and game must always be treated with red wine, and white meat and fish with white, should never be slavishly followed. The colour will determine the appearance of the sauce, but it is the wine's taste, texture and general character that attest its validity in a dish. Unconventional combinations can produce attractive results when, for example, a sweet white wine replaces the more usual dry white wines in preparing fish and pork, or when a fruity red wine is used to produce a red-brown sauce that is an enticing contrast to delicate sole fillets (*page 70*).

The fundamental principles of wine cookery are illustrated on the following pages. An Anthology of more than 60 recipes, gathered from 11 countries, begins on page 143; it further indicates the wide range of possibilities for using wine in cooking.

Infusing Meat with Robust Flavour

Wine combined with aromatic vegetables and herbs produces a fragrant marinade in which meat can be steeped before it is cooked. Olive oil, added together with the wine, helps to moisten the meat and distribute flavours. As well as flavouring the raw meat, the marinade serves as a cooking medium that can be made into a rich sauce and served with the finished dish (*right; recipe, page 156*).

Robust, simple red wines are a good choice for marinades, and those that are young and tannic (*page 28*) will give both colour and a strong flavour to the finished sauce. Some of the many suitable wines include a Côtes du Rhône, an Italian Barbera, or the Californian Zinfandel used here, a robust wine with an open, slightly herby taste. White wines may be used, but they will not impart colour to the sauce.

Lamb, pork, beef and game all benefit from a wine marinade. Here, chunks of beef are first larded with strips of pork fat coated with a *persillade*—a mixture of garlic and herbs; the fat will nourish the meat as it cooks and keep it succulent. The meat is left to marinate for several hours before the liquid is drained off.

Moistened with the marinade, which is supplemented by stock and more wine, the beef is then braised with aromatic vegetables in a closed vessel. Gentle cooking in a relatively small amount of liquid—just enough to keep the meat moist—ensures that the intermingled flavours of the braise are richly concentrated.

In this instance, the beef is garnished with sautéed strips of green bacon—first parboiled to remove excess salt—small onions and button mushrooms. These ingredients are cooked separately in order to preserve their texture and flavour. The cooking liquid, cleansed of impurities and reduced (*Step 7*), makes the dark savoury sauce that completes the dish.

1 **Larding meat.** With a pestle, pound garlic with coarse salt in a mortar; add chopped parsley and dried herbs—here, thyme, savory, marjoram and oregano. Slice pork back fat into 5 mm ($\frac{1}{4}$ inch) lardons about 5 cm (2 inches) long; roll them in the *persillade*. Put sliced onions and carrots in a bowl with a stick of celery, crushed garlic, sprigs of parsley and thyme, and bay leaves. Cut meat—here, boned leg of beef—into chunks weighing about 100 g ($3\frac{1}{2}$ oz) each. Cut slits in the meat; insert a lardon in each slit (*above*). Add the meat to the bowl; pour on olive oil and wine.

5 **Adding the marinade.** Pour a splash of cognac into the pan. Add the reserved marinade liquid (*above*) and enough beef or veal stock to cover the meat. With a wooden spoon, scrape the deposits from the bottom of the pan to dissolve them in the liquid. Add a bouquet garni—leek, celery, bay leaf, thyme and parsley sprigs, tied together with string.

6 **Straining the braise.** Cover and simmer over a very low heat or in a preheated 150°C (300°F or Mark 2) oven for about $2\frac{1}{2}$ hours. Put the meat in another pan, add the garnish and keep warm. Pour the contents of the braising pan into a fine-meshed sieve set over a pan (*above*). Discard the carrots and bouquet garni. Press the onions through the sieve.

2 **Draining the meat.** Cover the bowl and marinate the meat for 5 to 6 hours or leave overnight. To ensure that the meat marinates evenly, turn it occasionally. Pour the marinade into a colander set over a bowl. Put the drained meat on a towel and dry it with another towel. Discard the aromatic vegetables and herbs; reserve the marinade liquid.

3 **Preparing a garnish.** Cover strips of lean green bacon with water, bring to the boil and simmer for 3 minutes. Rinse in cold water and drain. Sauté the bacon in oil until golden; drain into a sieve set over a bowl. Return the fat to the pan; sauté small onions until golden and add to the sieve. Increase the heat, briefly sauté mushrooms and add them to the sieve.

4 **Browning the meat.** In the same fat, sauté chopped onions and carrots over a medium heat until lightly coloured, about 30 minutes; remove and set aside. Sear the meat for about 30 minutes until evenly browned on all sides. Return the sautéed onions and carrots to the pan. Sprinkle the meat with flour and turn it (*above*) until the flour browns.

7 **Finishing the braise.** Set the pan half on the heat and simmer the cooking liquid until it reduces and thickens slightly. At the same time, cleanse it by removing the skin of impurities that forms repeatedly on the cooler side of the pan (*above*). Pour the sauce over the braise (*right*). Simmer it gently for 15 to 30 minutes so that the flavours intermingle, and serve.□

Sauces and Glazes from Rich Residues

A little wine added to the caramelized deposits left behind in the pan by sautéed or roasted meat produces a richly flavoured sauce in a matter of moments. After the cooked meat and any fat have been removed, the wine is simply poured into the hot pan, which is stirred and scraped over a high heat until the residues dissolve in the wine—a process called deglazing.

Wines of all types may be used for deglazing. Red wines will produce a deeply coloured sauce and are often used with beef, lamb and game. Full-bodied, deep-coloured young wines are particularly suitable—for example, an Italian Barolo or Barbaresco, a Californian Zinfandel, or an Australian Shiraz.

White wines make a pale, caramel-coloured sauce that goes well with veal and pork. Any good quality, young dry white wine is suitable—a young Bourgogne, a Burgundian Aligoté, a Muscadet from the Loire Valley, or a Californian Chenin Blanc. One of the dry white Sauvignon Blanc wines would also be a good choice—a Graves, a Sancerre or Pouilly-Fumé from the Loire Valley, or a Californian Sauvignon Blanc. If you prefer to match the slightly sweet flavour of pork with a sweet wine, choose a Loupiac or a Ste. Croix du Mont from Bordeaux.

Here, slices of pork tenderloin—a delicate meat that cooks through quickly—are sautéed in just enough fat to coat the pan (*right, above*). The meat is removed from the pan and wine added. Vigorous scraping with a wooden spoon or spatula over a high heat dislodges the caramelized meat juices from the pan. The wine is reduced over high heat to make the sauce.

The same technique is used to create a sauce for the veal roast shown on the right. To give it extra flavour, the veal is rubbed with a marinade of wine, herbs and olive oil, and marinated for several hours. The meat is then wrapped in pig's caul—the fatty, lace-like stomach membrane, sold fresh or dry-salted—which nourishes the meat as it roasts. Towards the end of cooking, the veal is basted frequently with the marinade, which imparts a rich glaze to the surface of the meat. The pan is deglazed with the roasting juices, supplemented with wine, and the sauce is spooned over the carved meat.

A Swiftly Created Sauce for a Sauté

1 **Slicing meat.** Trim excess fat from pork tenderloin. Cut the meat into slices about 1 cm (½ inch) thick; here, the meat is cut on the bias (*above*) to give each slice a larger surface area. Coat the slices of meat on both sides with flour.

2 **Sautéing the meat.** In a large enough pan to hold the slices easily, melt butter until it foams. Add the slices of pork in one layer (*above*); if the slices overlap, they will stew instead of browning. Sprinkle them with salt and pepper, and cook over a high heat for about 3 minutes on each side, until lightly browned all over.

Marinating and Basting a Succulent Roast

1 **Pouring on wine.** To soften dry-salted caul and remove excess salt, soak it in tepid water for 5 to 10 minutes. Rinse fresh caul. Put it in a dish and cover with wine—here, a young Bourgogne. Place the meat—here, veal cushion weighing about 2 kg (4 lb)—in a shallow dish. Sprinkle with dried mixed herbs and olive oil. Add wine to a depth of 1 cm (½ inch).

2 **Drying the caul.** Rub the marinade into the meat; cover the dish and leave at room temperature for 3 to 4 hours, or overnight in a refrigerator; turn the meat occasionally. Spread the caul on a towel and dry it (*above*). Remove the meat from the marinade; pat it dry. Wrap the meat in the caul and put it in an ovenproof dish. Reserve both marinades.

3 **Deglazing the pan.** Transfer the slices of meat to a warmed serving plate. Pour a generous splash of wine—here, Muscadet—into the pan (*above, left*). Bring the wine to the boil, scraping the sides and bottom of the pan vigorously with a wooden spatula or spoon to loosen the caramelized deposits, and stirring them so that they will dissolve and blend into the wine (*above, right*).

4 **Spooning sauce over the meat.** Leave the pan over the heat for 1 to 2 minutes, until the wine reduces to a light syrupy consistency. If you like, add a garnish to the meat—here, apple rings, brushed with butter and grilled. Spoon the sauce over the meat (*above*) and serve. □

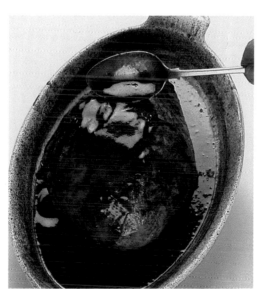

3 **Roasting the meat.** Put the meat in a preheated 230°C (450°F or Mark 8) oven. After 10 minutes, reduce the oven heat to 180°C (350°F or Mark 4). After a further 45 minutes, spoon off any fat in the dish and baste the meat with the remaining juices. Cook the meat for another 10 minutes, then pour on a little of the reserved marinade liquid (*above*).

4 **Basting the meat.** Scrape up the deposits from the bottom of the dish. Return the meat to the oven and increase the heat to 230°C (450°F or Mark 8). Roast it for another 20 minutes, basting the meat frequently with the marinade. When the marinade is used up, supplement it with wine. Put the meat on a heated serving plate in a warm place.

5 **Serving the meat.** Add wine to the juices in the dish and boil the liquid over a high heat until it thickens slightly, stirring to dislodge caramelized deposits from the dish. Pour the sauce into a sauceboat. Carve the meat and spoon the sauce over each serving (*above*). Here, the veal is served with parboiled spinach, drained and sautéed briefly in butter. □

Poaching Fillets in a Fragrant Fumet

Wine is a great asset in fish cookery, since it can provide both a cooking medium and a sauce for the finished dish. Although red wine is not normally associated with fish, it is used in this demonstration to create a deeply coloured sauce that makes an arresting contrast to poached fillets of sole (*right; recipe, page 146*). The wine here is a young Côtes du Ventoux from the Rhône Valley, a fairly tannic wine with plenty of body and colour. Other red wines that go well with fish include other wines from the Côtes du Rhône, and young Bordeaux and other wines vinified from the Cabernet Sauvignon grape.

If you prefer a white wine, any crisp, dry variety will serve admirably—a Loire Valley wine such as a Pouilly-Fumé, a Sancerre or a Muscadet, or a Graves. You could also try a lesser white Burgundy or a Californian Chardonnay. For fish dishes that call for a sweet white wine, a lesser Sauternes or a semi-sweet Chenin Blanc from the Loire Valley would be suitable.

In this demonstration, wine is first used in the creation of a fumet, a fish stock made from fish trimmings, herbs, aromatic vegetables, water and wine. The concentrated flavours of the fumet—with more wine added to cover the fish with liquid during cooking—infuse the delicate fillets of sole. The pan is tightly covered and the liquid brought to boiling point over a medium heat. The heat is then turned off and the fish cooks through. This gentle poaching will ensure that the fish remains intact and moist while absorbing the flavours of the fumet.

The cooking liquid is reduced by boiling, then thickened with cubes of butter. This procedure must be carried out over very gentle heat, so that the butter does not turn oily as it melts into the liquid. The result is the fine, velvety sauce in which the fillets are served.

1 Preparing the ingredients. Put fish heads and chopped carcasses in a large pan. Add sliced onions and carrots, unpeeled garlic cloves and herbs—here, fennel, parsley, bay leaves and thyme. Trim the edges and any dark flesh from sole fillets (*above*). To keep the fillets white, put them in iced water. Add the trimmings to the pan; pour over a bottle of red wine.

2 Skimming the liquid. Add salt to the pan. Pour in enough cold water to just cover the ingredients. Set the pan, uncovered, over a fairly low heat. As soon as the liquid approaches the boil, after about 15 minutes, use a ladle to remove the scum that rises to the surface (*above*).

6 Pouring in wine. Add enough wine to barely cover the fillets. To stop the fillets from drying out, cover with buttered greaseproof paper and place a lid on the pan. Cook over a medium heat, lifting the lid and paper occasionally to check the liquid's progress. When the liquid boils, turn off the heat at once; leave the pan, covered, to stand for 8 to 10 minutes.

7 Draining the fillets. Set a wire rack over a tray. Remove the lid and the paper from the fillets and, with a slotted spoon, carefully transfer them to the wire rack (*above*). Cover the fillets again with the paper to keep them moist, and leave them to drain while you make the sauce.

3 **Straining the fumet.** Half cover the pan, reduce the heat and simmer the fumet for 30 minutes. Set a colander lined with several layers of damp muslin over a bowl. Strain the fumet into the bowl (*above*); discard the trimmings, herbs and vegetables. To reduce the fumet slightly, return it to the pan and boil for a few minutes. Skim it and leave to cool.

4 **Scoring and folding.** Pat the fillets dry between two towels. To prevent them from distorting during cooking, slit the outer membrane six times diagonally. Season the fillets with salt and pepper, then smear them with softened butter. Fold them in half, covering the scored membrane (*above*), and arrange them in a well-buttered, heavy sauté pan.

5 **Adding the fumet.** Check that the fumet is cool; if necessary, you can accelerate the cooling by stirring the fumet over a bowl of iced water. Pour the cold fumet over the fillets in the pan (*above*).

8 **Making a butter sauce.** Pour the cooking liquid through a sieve into a heavy pan; add any liquid that has drained from the fish. Bring the liquid to the boil over a high heat to reduce it to a syrupy consistency. Turn the heat down to very low and put a fireproof mat underneath the pan. Whisk cubes of butter into the liquid, a small batch at a time (*above*).

9 **Finishing the dish.** When all the cubes of butter have been whisked into the liquid, the sauce is complete. Transfer the fillets from the rack to a warmed serving platter. Spoon some of the sauce over the fish and present the rest separately, in a warmed sauceboat (*above*). Serve the fish and its sauce immediately. □

Mussels Swathed in a Creamy Coating

A dry white wine blends especially well with shellfish, complementing its salty freshness. Such wines, exemplified here by a Muscadet, are therefore an excellent medium for steaming mussels and other bivalves (*right*). As an alternative to Muscadet, you could use any of the Sauvignon Blanc wines mentioned on page 68, or an Italian Verdicchio or Soave.

Start by cleaning the mussels (*Step 1*). Discard all mussels with broken shells, and those with shells that remain open when tapped smartly; such specimens are probably dead. Soak the live mussels in clean, salted water; they will expel any sand or grit they contain.

Only a relatively small amount of wine is required for steaming mussels, because they release liquid of their own while they cook. Herbs and aromatic vegetables, added to the pan, will bring extra flavour to the mussels—and fragrance to the liquid. A few minutes of steaming will open the bivalves and cook them.

The cooking liquid can be served with the mussels just as it is, or it may be reduced by boiling to concentrate its flavours. Should the liquid taste very salty, however, do not reduce it, because the salt taste would increase; use any excess liquid, with water, in a stock or a soup.

If you like, you can enrich the liquid by adding cubes of butter (*page 71*) or—as here—a blend of egg yolks and cream (*recipe, page 148*). The addition of yolks and cream will also make the liquid less salty. Gentle heat will thicken the yolks slightly, giving extra body to the sauce.

1 **Cleaning the mussels.** Immerse fresh mussels in a bowl of cold salted water. Clean each mussel thoroughly; first pull off its hair-like beard, then scrape away any growth or debris from its shell, using a small sharp knife (*above*). Transfer the mussels to a fresh bowl of salted water. After soaking for about 30 minutes, the mussels will expel any sand or grit.

2 **Adding wine.** Strain the cleaned mussels and tip them all into a large pan. Add flavourings—here, celery sticks, garlic cloves, bay leaves, chopped parsley and thyme—and then pour in a generous splash of white wine (*above*). Cover the pan and set it over a high heat. Shaking the pan frequently, cook the mussels until their shells open—3 to 5 minutes.

5 **Creating a sauce.** Place egg yolks and double cream into a mixing bowl and whisk the ingredients to blend them. Pour in 2 to 3 ladlefuls of the cooking liquid (*above*), continuing to whisk until all the ingredients are smoothly amalgamated.

6 **Adding the sauce.** Pour the egg yolk and cream mixture over the mussels in the pan (*above*). As you are pouring, distribute the mixture so that each mussel is coated as evenly as possible with the liquid.

3 **Straining the mussels.** Pour the mussels into a colander lined with several layers of damp muslin, set over a deep bowl to catch the cooking liquid (*above*). Taste the liquid; if it is not salty, reduce it by boiling. If the liquid is too salty, use only part of it for the sauce; do not reduce it.

4 **Opening the shells.** When the mussels are cool enough to handle, prise the shells apart with your fingers and thumbs, separating the two halves completely (*above*). Discard the empty half shells. Arrange the mussels—still attached to the remaining half shells—in layers in a wide-surfaced shallow pan. Set the mussels aside.

7 **Finishing the dish.** Tilt the pan gently from side to side over a medium-low heat (*above*), until the sauce has thickened to a custard-like consistency—about 10 minutes; during this time, the sauce must never approach the boil, or it will curdle. Ladle the mussels into individual soup plates and serve immediately (*right*). □

Perfect Partnerships of Wine and Fresh Fruit

The natural flavours of wine and fruit complement each other extremely well. The simplest way to enjoy their harmony is to pour wine over fresh fruit, sweeten the mixture if you like, and serve it as a dessert. Certain fruit and wine combinations are so perfect that they have become classics in their own right, but the ingredients may be varied in any way desired.

You can, for instance, moisten an assortment of fruits with a white wine. Here, a dry white German wine from the Franconian region is poured over strawberries, plums and melon (*right*). Other suitable wines include those made from Sauvignon Blanc and Riesling grapes, and Muscat wines from Alsace. If you prefer a sweeter wine, you could try a Bordeaux from Loupiac, Cérons or Ste. Croix du Mont, a Gewürztraminer, or a late-picked Riesling from California.

All red wines blend well with fruit, including fresh, fruity wines that are drunk young—a Beaujolais *primeur*, for example, a Californian Pinot Noir or Zinfandel *primeur*, or an Italian Bardolino.

The strawberry season provides an occasion for a particularly felicitous combination of fruit and wine. Strawberries, added to the last glass of red wine, are a perfect conclusion to a meal. Following a Bordeaux tradition, a fine old claret that has begun to decline may be poured over strawberries (*box, right*). When the fruit is lightly crushed, its fresh juices give the wine a momentary sparkle of life.

The hint of peaches in the flavour of sweet Botrytis wines (*page 16*) gives them a natural affinity with that fruit. Here, sliced peaches are macerated in a Sauternes (*box, opposite page*); you could substitute a naturally sweet German wine of good quality. For a further range of intermingled flavours, peaches may be steeped in different types of red wine.

Whichever wine you choose, the freshness and colour of the fruit are best preserved by preparing the fruit just before pouring on the wine. However, some desserts, such as sliced peaches or an assortment of fruits, will improve if allowed to macerate in the wine for an hour or two before serving. The quantity of sugar added depends on taste, but too much will obscure the flavour of the wine.

1 **Preparing fruit.** Plunge strawberries into cold water; with splayed fingers, transfer them at once to a colander to drain. Remove the stalks, cut the strawberries in half into a large serving bowl. With a small knife, peel ripe plums; cut each fruit along its natural indentation and extract the stone (*above*); add the halved plums to the strawberries in the bowl.

2 **Scooping out melon balls.** Cut a ripe melon in half. With your fingers, or a spoon, scoop out the seeds and the seed pulp from each half; discard the seeds and pulp. Using a melon ball cutter or a teaspoon, scoop out the flesh and add it to the bowl of fruit (*above*).

Revitalizing a Fading Bordeaux

Combining strawberries and wine. Wash strawberries (*Step 1, above*); drain them and remove their stalks. Put the fruit in wine glasses and pour on red wine—in this instance, a claret. If you are using an old wine, as here, decant the wine (*page 44*) or take care not to pour out any sediment. Serve the strawberries accompanied by a bowl of sugar so that sugar may be added to taste.

3 **Adding sugar to the fruit.** Sprinkle sugar over the fruit (*above*). To ensure that the sugar is evenly distributed, gently turn over the fruit with your fingertips, taking care not to crush the strawberries.

4 **Pouring on wine.** Pour a chilled white wine—here, a German Steinwein—into the bowl (*above*), so that the fruit is almost covered with wine. The dessert may be served at once, or you can leave it to stand in a cool place for an hour or two before serving, so that the flavours of the fruit and wine merge together.

5 **Serving the fruit.** Spoon the dessert into individual bowls, making sure that each bowl contains an assortment of fruits (*above*). If you like, sweet biscuits may be served as an accompaniment.☐

Echoing Flavours: Peaches and Sauternes

Slicing peaches. Plunge ripe peaches briefly into boiling water, then transfer them to a bowl of cold water to arrest cooking. Nick the skin with a knife and peel the peaches. Cut into segments (*above*). Sprinkle with sugar and pour on wine—here, a Sauternes. Let the fruit macerate for up to 2 hours, then serve.

A Crystalline Syrup for Tender Fruit

When fruits are poached with sugar in wine, the sugar dissolves in the wine, and the liquid can be transformed into a gleaming syrup (*right; recipe, page 162*). You can use a red or a white wine. A red wine will infuse the fruit with its colour, and the best choice is a fresh, fruity young wine with a deep colour—young Côtes du Rhône, for example, a Graves, a Cahors, or a Californian Zinfandel.

If you prefer a white wine, a Sauternes or a good quality German wine from the Rhineland is ideal. These wines have a warm and golden colour, with a hint of peaches in their flavour.

Both fresh and dried fruits can be poached in wine, and the wine's acidity helps to prevent the fruit from falling apart during cooking. Pears and apricots, in particular, benefit from the technique shown here for peaches. For poaching, fresh fruits should be slightly firm rather than completely ripe. Dried fruits should be soaked to soften them before cooking; red wine is best for poaching dried figs, and white is excellent for dried apricots.

1 Peeling peaches. To loosen their skins, plunge peaches into boiling water. After a few seconds, transfer them to a bowl of cold water to arrest cooking. Drain the peaches. With the aid of a small knife, peel the peaches (*above*). Dip each peeled fruit in lemon juice to keep it from discolouring, then put it in a large bowl.

2 Sweetening the fruit. Sprinkle sugar over the peaches and leave them for 1 hour to absorb the sugar. Transfer the peaches, and any juice that has run from them, to a pan. An untinned copper pan will help to keep the fruit's bright colour, but you can use a stainless steel or enamel pan instead. Do not use aluminium; it would react with the wine and spoil its taste.

3 Pouring on wine. Add more sugar to the peaches. If you like, add a blade of mace or a few cloves for extra flavour—here, a piece of cinnamon stick is added to the pan. Pour wine—in this instance, a red Graves—over the peaches. Cover the pan, set it over a low heat and gently simmer until tender, about 30 minutes.

4 Reducing the cooking liquid. Remove the cinnamon stick from the pan. Using a slotted spoon, transfer all the peaches to a large serving bowl. To reduce the cooking liquid, maintain it at a regular light boil, stirring occasionally (*above*). When the liquid is thick and syrupy, remove the pan from the heat.

5 Serving the fruit. Spoon the thick wine syrup over the peaches. Leave the fruit to cool in the syrup before serving. If you like, accompany the peaches with sweet biscuits or slices of sugared brioche.□

Locking in Sparkle: a Lemon Sorbet

Ices or sorbets, frozen mixtures of sugar syrup and puréed fruit or fruit juice, gain particular distinction from wine. Still or sparkling wines, both sweet and dry, may be used. White wines will blend particularly well with a purée of peaches, melon or apricots, and red wines with puréed strawberries or raspberries. Champagne or any sparkling wine will lend an exhilarating liveliness, and in this demonstration a sorbet is flavoured with lemon and sparkling Vouvray: a dry white wine from the Loire Valley (*recipe, page 162*).

Always begin an ice or sorbet by first preparing the sugar syrup. The syrup must be completely cold before it is added to the other ingredients, or the mixture will take a long time to freeze.

While the syrup cools, prepare the fruit or fruit juice. To retain a sparkling wine's liveliness, make sure that the wine is well chilled (*page 45*), and open the bottle just before mixing and freezing the sorbet. When the ice has frozen, the sorbet is thoroughly whisked to break up any large ice crystals and to ensure a relatively smooth consistency.

1 Extracting citrus zest. Prepare sugar syrup and leave it to cool. Rinse lemons in cold water and dry them. To obtain the aromatic oil and flavour from the lemon rind, rub sugar lumps over the surface of the lemons (*above*). Put the lumps into a large bowl. Squeeze the lemons and strain their juice into the bowl.

2 Adding wine. Open a bottle of well-chilled sparkling wine (*page 42*) and pour the wine into the bowl of lemon juice and sugar (*above*). Immediately add the cooled sugar syrup. Stir the mixture to blend the ingredients together.

3 Freezing the sorbet. Transfer the mixture to shallow metal trays. Put the trays in the freezer or in the freezing compartment of the refrigerator. After about 30 minutes, remove the trays and stir the mixture with a fork, moving the frozen section round the edges into the centre (*above*).

4 Whisking the sorbet. Return the trays to the freezer for a further 3 to 4 hours, stirring the mixture every hour. When the sorbet is firm enough to hold its shape and is evenly frozen, transfer it to a large bowl. Using a whisk, beat the sorbet until it is rather mushy in texture (*above*).

5 Serving the sorbet. If you like, you can keep the sorbet in the freezer for up to 2 hours; if it is kept much longer, the wine may lose its sparkle. When you remove the ice from the freezer, scrape or stir it to loosen the mixture and restore its mushy texture. Spoon the sorbet into individual glasses; serve with sponge fingers or sweet almond biscuits.□

Marsala Custard Enriched with Cream

Wine whisked over heat with egg yolks and sugar will produce a thick, foaming custard, permeated by the wine's flavour. Marsala, a fortified wine from Sicily, is used for the Italian version of this dessert, zabaglione (*right; recipe, page 164*). You can use another fortified wine, such as sherry or Madeira, or a white wine, sweet or dry. Cinnamon and lemon will complement a fortified wine, but a fine white wine requires no additional spices.

The custard must be cooked in a bain-marie filled with hot, not boiling, water. This ensures a gentle, even heat so that the mixture thickens without curdling. Whisking will trap air bubbles in the yolks for a light and fluffy mixture.

Once the consistency of the mixture has slightly thickened, you can serve it as a sauce, hot or cold. A white wine custard, used in this way, is a good accompaniment to soufflé puddings, chocolate gateaux and poached peaches or pears. Longer cooking will make the mixture thicker and more mousse-like. You can then serve it warm, or—as here—the cooled custard may be blended with whipped cream.

1 Pouring in wine. Put sugar—here, sugar flavoured with vanilla—and egg yolks in a large pan or heatproof bowl. Add grated lemon rind and a little ground cinnamon. Pour wine into the pan—in this instance, Marsala (*above*).

2 Whisking over heat. Place a trivet in the bottom of a large pan. Half fill the pan with water and heat the water to a simmer. Set the pan with the mixture on the trivet. Over a low heat, whisk the mixture (*above*), making sure that the water does not come to the boil.

3 Thickening the custard. Continue to whisk the mixture for about 10 minutes until the custard increases in volume and becomes pale and thick. When it has reached the desired consistency, take the pan off the heat; continue whisking the custard for a minute or so.

4 Whisking in cream. Set the thickened zabaglione aside to cool. Whisk double cream until it forms soft peaks. Add the whipped cream to the zabaglione, then whisk it gently into the cooled custard.

5 Serving the dessert. When the cream has been incorporated, and the mixture is smoothly blended, ladle the custard into individual glasses (*above*). If you like, accompany it with sweet biscuits.□

A Guide
to the World's Wines

A galaxy of great wines. The wines shown here are some of the aristocrats of the wine world, reflecting the highest achievements of the wine-maker's art. They include a selection of first-growth Bordeaux wines and *grands crus* Burgundies, a noble German Trockenbeerenauslese, and a rare Tokay Aszu Eszencia from Hungary.

t would take far more than a single lifetime to taste all the wines hat the world has to offer. From the cool, well-watered slopes of he Rhineland to the hot, sunny vineyards of South Africa's Cape f Good Hope, thousands of varieties of vine produce the grapes hat make wine. Many of these wines never leave their native istricts—they are consumed only by the people who produce hem, and by a few passing travellers, who bring home tales of onderful, unheard-of local wines. But as more and more people iscover the pleasures of wine, more and more wine of increasngly varied origins finds its way to wine merchants throughout he world. The legendary and well-travelled wines of France and ermany are now joined by such relative newcomers to the xport trade as the produce of Australia, California, Chile and ugoslavia. The choice is bewildering—and exciting.

The best way to learn about wine is to drink it; the pages that llow will help you understand what you are drinking. The ection begins with 10 pages of maps. The world wine map on age 80 is followed by maps of the major sources of wine outside urope: the southern section of Australia, California on the west ast of the United States, and the Cape of Good Hope in South frica. Maps of the major European wine countries begin on page , with Italy, Spain, Portugal and Germany. France, because of

the number of its wine regions and the variety of distinguished wines within them, is illustrated by six pages of maps: a map of the entire country, locating its important wine-producing regions, and more detailed maps of the regions themselves.

Following the maps, an alphabetical reference section defines terms that arise frequently in the discussion of wine, and introduces the countries whose wines are worth exploring. Most wines are covered by a single national entry—Rioja, for example, is discussed in the entry for Spain. The major exceptions, by virtue of the size and complexity of their wine production, are France and Germany. In addition to general information on wine-making in these countries, there are separate and more detailed entries on their major wine regions, such as Bordeaux and Mosel.

Just as the provenance of any wine provides a key to its character, so too do the grapes it comes from. The grape varieties illustrated on pages 18-21 are the most important sources of quality wine, while the catalogue on page 140 identifies well over 100 other important varieties.

This guide will be most helpful if used in conjunction with the general index to the volume, since a term, a wine or a region that does not have its own alphabetical entry may be discussed or defined elsewhere.

The Vineyards of the World

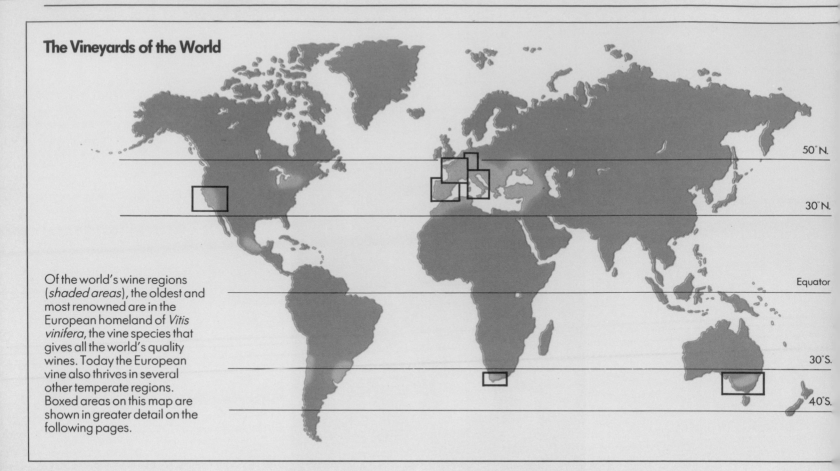

Of the world's wine regions (*shaded areas*), the oldest and most renowned are in the European homeland of *Vitis vinifera*, the vine species that gives all the world's quality wines. Today the European vine also thrives in several other temperate regions. Boxed areas on this map are shown in greater detail on the following pages.

50°N.

30°N.

Equator

30°S.

40°S.

California's Winelands

Even in California's generally over-hot weather, local conditions in a number of areas (*right*) make it possible to produce good wine. Foremost is Napa Valley (*far right*), the home of many of the most famous vineyards.

PACIFIC OCEAN

MENDOCINO

NAPA VALLEY

SONOMA

SOLANO

San Francisco Bay

SAN FRANCISCO

SANTA CLARA

SANTA CRUZ

SAN BENITO

MONTEREY

MONTEREY

SAN LUIS OBISPO

SANTA BARBARA

SANTA BARBARA

LOS ANGELES

SAN DIEGO

SAN DIEGO

SIERRA FOOTHILLS

EL DORADO

AMADOR

ALAMEDA

CENTRAL VALLEY

LOS ANGELES

RIVERSIDE

Sacramento

Russian

San Joaquin

San Benito

Salinas

Owens

NAPA VALLEY

CALISTOGA

CHATEAU MONTELENA

STERLING VINEYARDS

DIAMOND CREEK VINEYARDS

BURGESS CELLARS

SCHRAMSBERG VINEYARDS

CHARLES KRUG WINERY

STONY HILL VINEYARD

FREEMARK ABBEY

JOSEPH PHELPS VINEYARDS

HEITZ CELLARS

BERINGER VINEYARDS

ST. HELENA

LOUIS MARTINI WINERY

RUTHERFORD HILL WINERY

CHAPPELLET VINEYARDS

BEAULIEU VINEYARD

INGLENOOK VINEYARDS

CAYMUS VINEYARDS

ROBERT MONDAVI WINERY

STAG'S LEAP WINERY

YOUNTVILLE

CLOS DU VAL VINEYARDS

MAYACAMAS VINEYARDS

HIGHWAY 29

Napa River

CHRISTIAN BROTHERS WINERY

NAPA

CARNEROS CREEK WINERY

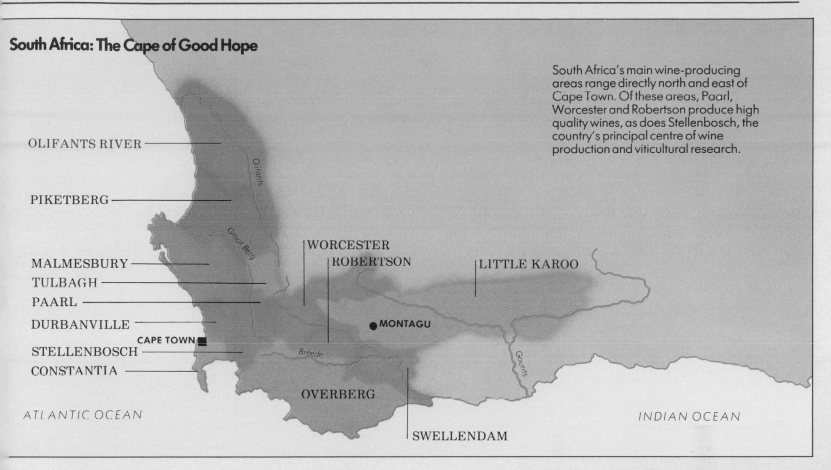

South Africa: The Cape of Good Hope

South Africa's main wine-producing areas range directly north and east of Cape Town. Of these areas, Paarl, Worcester and Robertson produce high quality wines, as does Stellenbosch, the country's principal centre of wine production and viticultural research.

OLIFANTS RIVER

PIKETBERG

WORCESTER
ROBERTSON

LITTLE KAROO

MALMESBURY
TULBAGH
PAARL
DURBANVILLE
CAPE TOWN
STELLENBOSCH
CONSTANTIA

● MONTAGU

Olifants

Groot Berg

Breede

Gourits

OVERBERG

ATLANTIC OCEAN

INDIAN OCEAN

SWELLENDAM

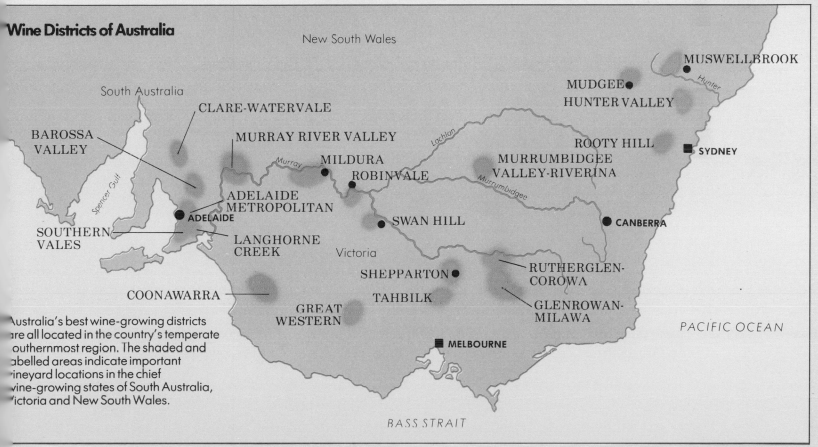

Wine Districts of Australia

New South Wales

South Australia

MUSWELLBROOK

Hunter

MUDGEE
HUNTER VALLEY

CLARE-WATERVALE

BAROSSA
VALLEY

MURRAY RIVER VALLEY

Lachlan

ROOTY HILL

■ SYDNEY

Murray

MILDURA
ROBINVALE

MURRUMBIDGEE
VALLEY-RIVERINA

Murrumbidgee

ADELAIDE
METROPOLITAN

● ADELAIDE

Spencer Gulf

SOUTHERN
VALES

LANGHORNE
CREEK

SWAN HILL

● CANBERRA

Victoria

RUTHERGLEN-
COROWA

COONAWARRA

SHEPPARTON

TAHBILK

GLENROWAN-
MILAWA

Australia's best wine-growing districts are all located in the country's temperate southernmost region. The shaded and labelled areas indicate important vineyard locations in the chief wine-growing states of South Australia, Victoria and New South Wales.

GREAT
WESTERN

PACIFIC OCEAN

■ MELBOURNE

BASS STRAIT

Italy and Its Regional Wines

Every one of Italy's 20 regions, from Piedmont to Calabria and including the islands of Sardinia and Sicily, produces wine; most can lay claim to wines of quality. Some of the best known of these wines are marked on the map in italics.

AUSTRIA

SWITZERLAND

TRENTINO ALTO ADIGE

FRUILI VENEZIA-GIULIA

YUGOSLAVIA

VALLE D'AOSTA

LOMBARDY

■ MILAN

VALPOLICELLA

VENETO

PIEDMONT

TURIN ●

BARBERA

BARDOLINO

● VENICE

NEBBIOLO
BARBARESCO
ASTI SPUMANTE
DOLCETTO
GRIGNOLINO
BAROLO

SOAVE

FRANCE

● GENOA

EMILIA-ROMAGNA

BOLOGNA ●

LAMBRUSCO

LIGURIA ——

VERNACCIA DI SAN GIMIGNANO

LIGURIAN SEA

● FLORENCE

CHIANTI

TUSCANY

VERDICCHIO

THE MARCHES

BRUNELLO DI MONTALCINO

ORVIETO

ELBA

UMBRIA

LATIUM

ABRUZZO

■ ROME

MONTEPULCIANO

FRASCATI

MOLISE

CAMPANIA

SARDINIA

■ NAPLES

PUGLIA

ISCHIA

BASILICATA

VERNACCIA DI ORISTANO

TYRRHENIAN SEA

MOSCATO

CALABRIA

● PALERMO

IONIAN SEA

MARSALA

MALVASIA

ETNA

SICILY

MOSCATO

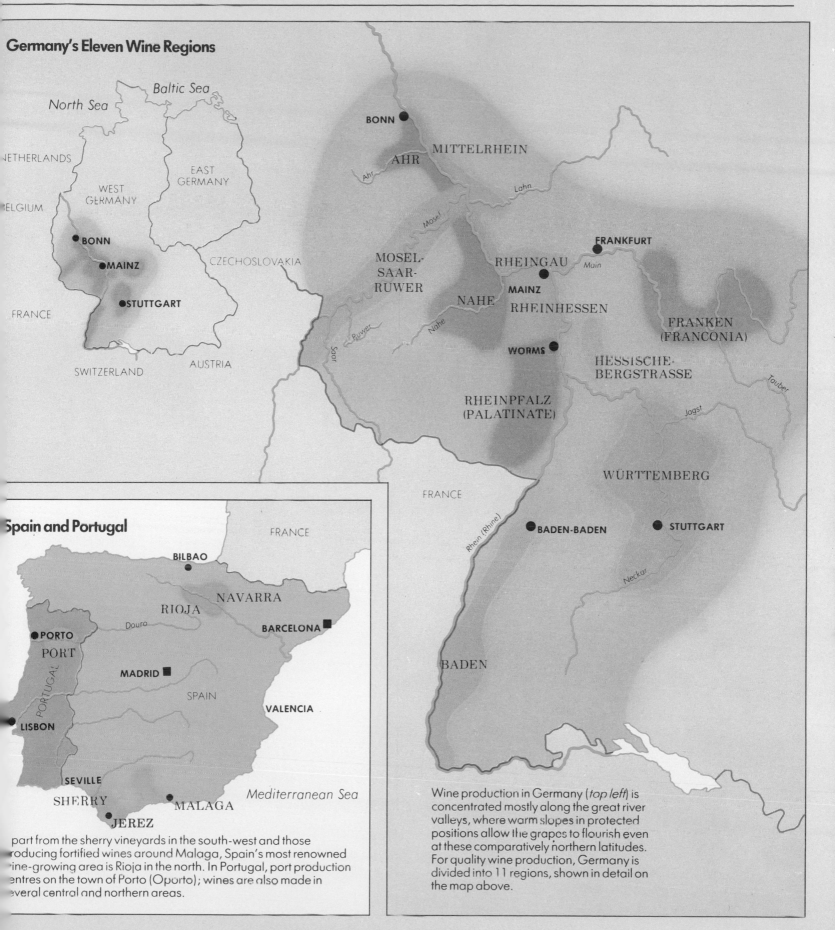

Germany's Eleven Wine Regions

North Sea

Baltic Sea

NETHERLANDS

BELGIUM

WEST GERMANY

EAST GERMANY

CZECHOSLOVAKIA

FRANCE

● BONN

● MAINZ

● STUTTGART

SWITZERLAND

AUSTRIA

BONN ●

AHR

MITTELRHEIN

Ahr

Lahn

Mosel

MOSEL-
SAAR-
RUWER

RHEINGAU

FRANKFURT ■

Main

MAINZ ●

NAHE

RHEINHESSEN

FRANKEN
(FRANCONIA)

Ruwer

Nahe

WORMS ●

HESSISCHE-
BERGSTRASSE

Saar

Tauber

RHEINPFALZ
(PALATINATE)

Jagst

FRANCE

WÜRTTEMBERG

Rhein (Rhine)

● BADEN-BADEN

● STUTTGART

Neckar

BADEN

Wine production in Germany (*top left*) is
concentrated mostly along the great river
valleys, where warm slopes in protected
positions allow the grapes to flourish even
at these comparatively northern latitudes.
For quality wine production, Germany is
divided into 11 regions, shown in detail on
the map above.

Spain and Portugal

FRANCE

BILBAO ●

NAVARRA

RIOJA

Douro

BARCELONA ■

PORTO ●

PORT

MADRID ■

PORTUGAL

SPAIN

VALENCIA

LISBON ●

SHERRY

SEVILLE ●

MALAGA

JEREZ ●

Mediterranean Sea

part from the sherry vineyards in the south-west and those
roducing fortified wines around Malaga, Spain's most renowned
ine-growing area is Rioja in the north. In Portugal, port production
entres on the town of Porto (Oporto); wines are also made in
everal central and northern areas.

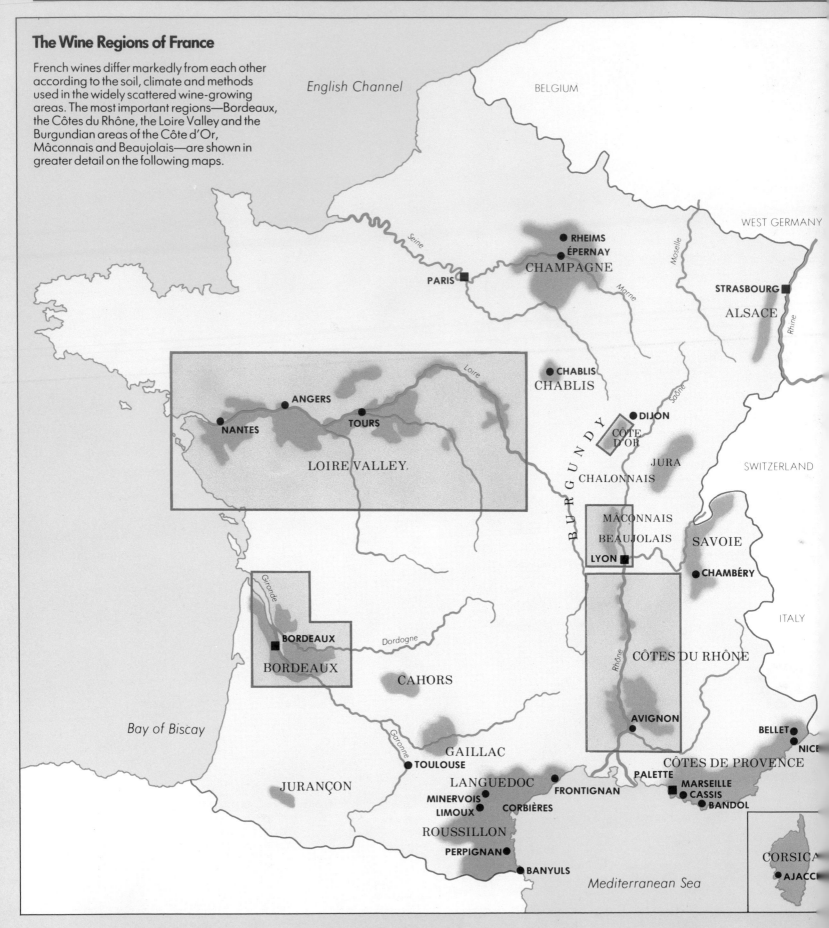

The Wine Regions of France

French wines differ markedly from each other according to the soil, climate and methods used in the widely scattered wine-growing areas. The most important regions—Bordeaux, the Côtes du Rhône, the Loire Valley and the Burgundian areas of the Côte d'Or, Mâconnais and Beaujolais—are shown in greater detail on the following maps.

English Channel

BELGIUM

WEST GERMANY

Seine

● RHEIMS
● ÉPERNAY
CHAMPAGNE

Morne

Moselle

STRASBOURG ■

PARIS ■

ALSACE

Rhine

Loire

● CHABLIS
CHABLIS

● DIJON
CÔTE D'OR

Saône

ANGERS ●

JURA

● TOURS

NANTES ●

B U R G U N D Y

CHALONNAIS

LOIRE VALLEY.

SWITZERLAND

MÂCONNAIS

BEAUJOLAIS

SAVOIE

LYON ■

● CHAMBÉRY

Gironde

ITALY

Dordogne

Rhône

CÔTES DU RHÔNE

■ BORDEAUX

BORDEAUX

CAHORS

Bay of Biscay

Garonne

● AVIGNON

BELLET ●

NICE

CÔTES DE PROVENCE

GAILLAC

PALETTE

● TOULOUSE

LANGUEDOC

● FRONTIGNAN

MARSEILLE ■ ● CASSIS

JURANÇON

MINERVOIS ●

CORBIÈRES

● BANDOL

LIMOUX ●

ROUSSILLON

CORSICA

● PERPIGNAN ●

● BANYULS

Mediterranean Sea

● AJACC

Bordeaux: Districts and Communities

Many of France's finest vineyards cluster near the Atlantic coast, on both sides of the rivers Gironde, Garonne and Dordogne. Names in large type on the map below are those of "limited areas" with their own official appellations. Also shown are smaller wine-producing localities—"communities".

MÉDOC

ST. ESTÈPHE

PAUILLAC
ST. JULIEN
ST. LAURENT

HAUT-MÉDOC

LISTRAC
MOULIS
MARGAUX
CANTENAC
LABARDE

LUDON

BLANQUEFORT

BORDEAUX
TALENCE
PESSAC
VILLENAVE-D'ORNON
CADAUJAC
LÉOGNAN
MARTILLAC

Gironde

CÔTES DE BLAYE

BLAYE

CÔTES DE BOURG

BOURG

CÔTES DE CANON FRONSAC

FRONSAC

GRAVES DE VAYRES

PREMIÈRES CÔTES DE BORDEAUX

GRAVES

CÉRONS

BARSAC
PREIGNAC

BOMMES
SAUTERNES
FARGUES

LALANDE DE POMEROL
POMEROL
NÉAC

LUSSAC
MONTAGNE
PUISSEGUIN
PARSAC

ST. GEORGES

ST. EMILION

CÔTES DE FRANCS

CÔTES DE CASTILLON

Dordogne

ENTRE-DEUX-MERS

STE. FOY BORDEAUX

CÔTES DE BORDEAUX

CADILLAC
LOUPIAC

STE. CROIX DU MONT
ST. MACAIRE

LANGON

Garonne

Mâconnais and Beaujolais

POUILLY-LOCHÉ
POUILLY-FUISSE
ST. VÉRAN
JULIÉNAS
FLEURIE
CHIROUBLES
MORGON

CÔTE DE BROUILLY

MÂCON

POUILLY VINZELLES

ST. AMOUR

CHÉNAS

MOULIN-À-VENT

BROUILLY

Saône

The southern part of Burgundy's wine-growing region is made up of the Mâconnais district in the north and, to the south, the Beaujolais district, with nine community appellations.

LYON

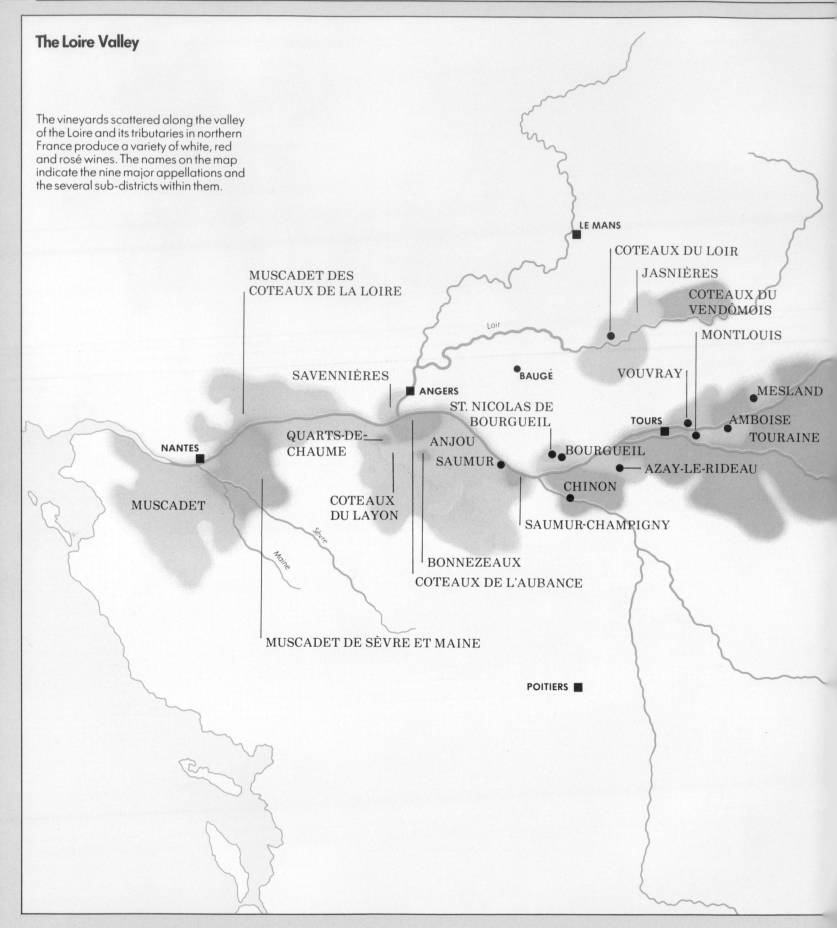

The Loire Valley

The vineyards scattered along the valley of the Loire and its tributaries in northern France produce a variety of white, red and rosé wines. The names on the map indicate the nine major appellations and the several sub-districts within them.

LE MANS

COTEAUX DU LOIR

JASNIÈRES

COTEAUX DU VENDÔMOIS

MUSCADET DES COTEAUX DE LA LOIRE

Loir

MONTLOUIS

SAVENNIÈRES

BAUGÉ

VOUVRAY

MESLAND

ANGERS

ST. NICOLAS DE BOURGUEIL

TOURS

AMBOISE

QUARTS-DE-CHAUME

ANJOU

SAUMUR

BOURGUEIL

TOURAINE

NANTES

AZAY-LE-RIDEAU

COTEAUX DU LAYON

CHINON

MUSCADET

SAUMUR-CHAMPIGNY

Sèvre

BONNEZEAUX

COTEAUX DE L'AUBANCE

Maine

MUSCADET DE SÈVRE ET MAINE

POITIERS

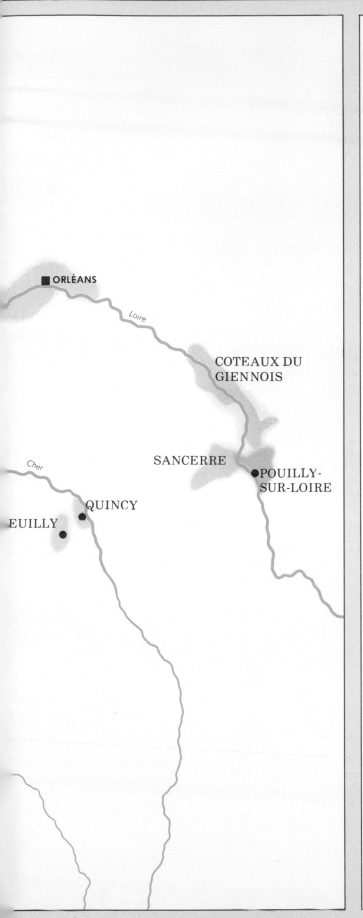

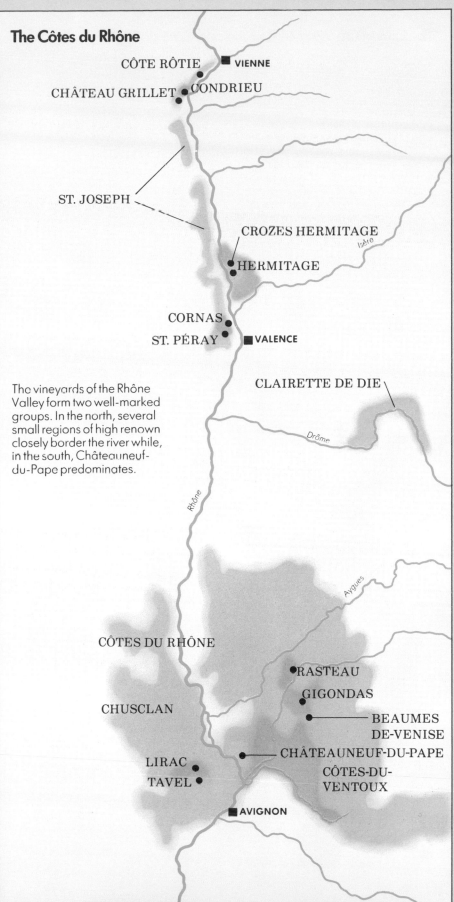

The Côtes du Rhône

CÔTE RÔTIE

■ VIENNE

CHÂTEAU GRILLET ● CONDRIEU

ST. JOSEPH

CROZES HERMITAGE

● HERMITAGE

Isère

CORNAS

ST. PÉRAY ● ■ VALENCE

CLAIRETTE DE DIE

Drôme

The vineyards of the Rhône
Valley form two well-marked
groups. In the north, several
small regions of high renown
closely border the river while,
in the south, Châteauneuf-
du-Pape predominates.

Rhône

Aygues

CÔTES DU RHÔNE

● RASTEAU

GIGONDAS

● ——— BEAUMES
DE-VENISE

CHUSCLAN

● ——— CHÂTEAUNEUF-DU-PAPE

LIRAC
TAVEL

CÔTES-DU-
VENTOUX

■ AVIGNON

■ ORLÉANS

Loire

COTEAUX DU
GIENNOIS

Cher

SANCERRE

POUILLY-
SUR-LOIRE

QUINCY

EUILLY

The Côte d'Or: Côte de Beaune and Côte de Nuits

Within Burgundy lies the Côte d'Or—a strip of vineyards running from south-west to north-east. The southern half is known as Côte de Beaune and the northern half as Côte de Nuits (*small map, below*). Here, the strip is divided into three, working from south (*near right*) to north. Names in large type show wine-growing communities; smaller type labels best vineyards (*shaded areas*).

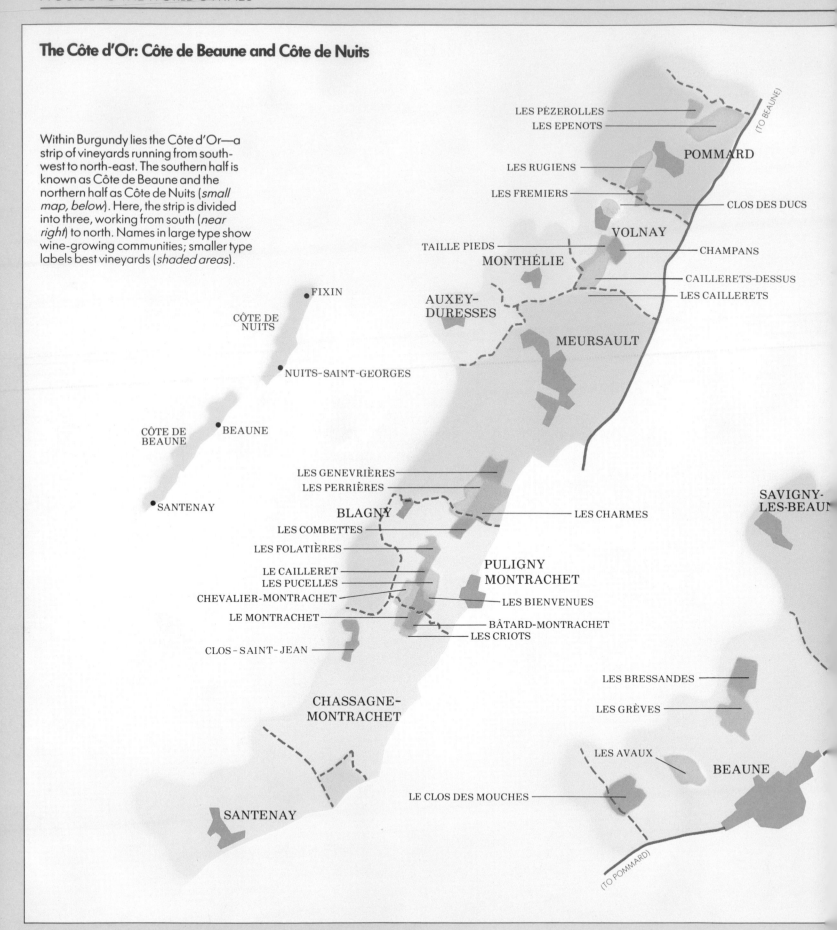

LES PÉZEROLLES
LES EPENOTS
POMMARD
LES RUGIENS
LES FREMIERS
CLOS DES DUCS
VOLNAY
TAILLE PIEDS
CHAMPANS
MONTHÉLIE
CAILLERETS-DESSUS
LES CAILLERETS
AUXEY-DURESSES
MEURSAULT

FIXIN
CÔTE DE NUITS

NUITS-SAINT-GEORGES

CÔTE DE BEAUNE
BEAUNE

SANTENAY

LES GENEVRIÈRES
LES PERRIÈRES
LES CHARMES
SAVIGNY-LES-BEAUN
BLAGNY
LES COMBETTES
LES FOLATIÈRES
LE CAILLERET
LES PUCELLES
PULIGNY MONTRACHET
CHEVALIER-MONTRACHET
LES BIENVENUES
LE MONTRACHET
BÂTARD-MONTRACHET
LES CRIOTS
CLOS-SAINT-JEAN

LES BRESSANDES

LES GRÈVES

CHASSAGNE-MONTRACHET

LES AVAUX
BEAUNE

LE CLOS DES MOUCHES

SANTENAY

(TO POMMARD)

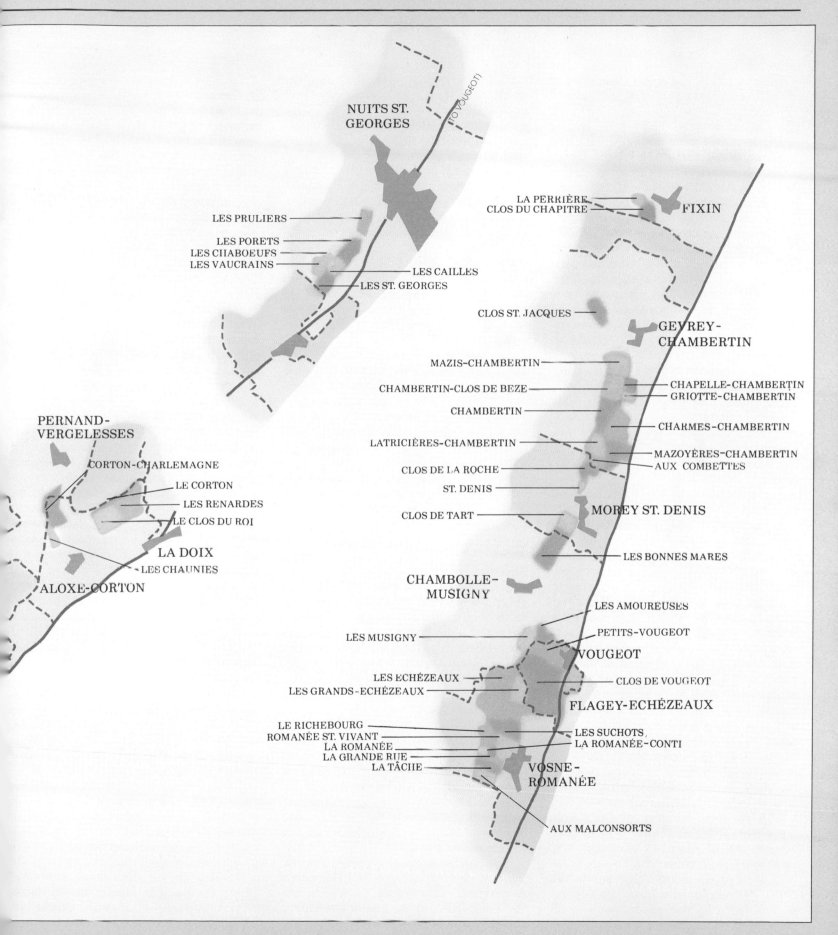

NUITS ST.
GEORGES

LES PRULIERS

LES PORETS
LES CHABOEUFS
LES VAUCRAINS
LES CAILLES
LES ST. GEORGES

PERNAND-
VERGELESSES

CORTON-CHARLEMAGNE

LE CORTON

LES RENARDES

LE CLOS DU ROI

LA DOIX

LES CHAUNIES

ALOXE-CORTON

LA PERRIÈRE
CLOS DU CHAPITRE
FIXIN

CLOS ST. JACQUES

GEVREY-
CHAMBERTIN

MAZIS-CHAMBERTIN

CHAMBERTIN-CLOS DE BEZE
CHAPELLE-CHAMBERTIN
GRIOTTE-CHAMBERTIN

CHAMBERTIN

CHARMES-CHAMBERTIN

LATRICIÈRES-CHAMBERTIN

MAZOYÈRES-CHAMBERTIN
AUX COMBETTES

CLOS DE LA ROCHE

ST. DENIS

CLOS DE TART

MOREY ST. DENIS

LES BONNES MARES

CHAMBOLLE-
MUSIGNY

LES AMOUREUSES

PETITS-VOUGEOT

LES MUSIGNY

VOUGEOT

LES ECHÉZEAUX

CLOS DE VOUGEOT

LES GRANDS-ECHÉZEAUX

FLAGEY-ECHÉZEAUX

LE RICHEBOURG
ROMANÉE ST. VIVANT
LES SUCHOTS
LA ROMANÉE-CONTI
LA ROMANÉE
LA GRANDE RUE
LA TÂCHE
VOSNE-
ROMANÉE

AUX MALCONSORTS

A.C. *Appellation Contrôlée.* See *French Wine Appellations; Wine Laws*

Ahr

A minor Rhine wine region, the second smallest in Germany (Hessische Bergstrasse is smaller). It is situated on the Ahr river, a tributary of the Rhine (*map, page 83*). The area under vine is less than 500 hectares (1,240 acres), the output only about 5 per cent of Germany's total.

The Ahr is the most northern of the German wine regions; the climate is very cold for vines, and to make any wine here is an achievement. Yet, uniquely for a German wine region, more red wine than white is made. Some is of good repute in Germany, but it is rarely sent outside.

Spätburgunder (Pinot Noir) and Portugieser grapes go into the red, Riesling and Müller Thurgau into the white wines. There is only one district (*Bereich*), Walporzheim Ahrtal, composed of over 40 single vineyards (*Einzellagen*), grouped into a single greater vineyard (*Grosslage*).

Algeria

Algeria is one of the world's major wine producers, but, because of Islamic injunctions against drinking alcoholic beverages, only about 2 per cent of the 5,000,000 or so hectolitres (about 110,000,000 gallons) produced each year is consumed within the country; the rest is exported, mainly to Russia, Germany and West Africa. The modern Algerian wine industry was established by French settlers in the 1870s, who brought with them their expertise and long tradition of making quality wines. The departure of many experienced wine growers when Algeria became independent in 1962 caused an initial fall in standards, but the government is now concentrating on improving the quality of the wines. Most of the wine is produced in bulk and exported for blending; some Algerian wines, however, achieve a really high standard.

The western province of Oran is a major vine-growing region; it holds over 70 per cent of Algeria's vineyards and nine zones that, under the French, were ranked as producers of VDQS wines (see *French Wine Appellations*). The Algiers region, east of Oran, produces about 25 per cent of the country's wine, while the

Constantine region, farther east, has the smallest output. The country's best wines, always red, come from the vineyards of Oran and Algiers, in the hills and north slopes of the Atlas mountain range, where the soil is calcareous and gravelly. The vineyards of the flat, alluvial plains near the coast produce most of the ordinary bulk drinking and blending wines, both red and white.

The most common red grape varieties are Carignan, Cinsault and Morrastel; in the hilly areas, Grenache, Pinot Noir and Syrah are grown. Some good dry rosés are made largely from Grenache and Cinsault grapes. White wines, mostly made from Clairette and Muscat grape varieties, are of generally poor quality.

Because of the hot climate, Algerian wines tend to be big and powerful. Red wines from Oran are dark-coloured, highly alcoholic and have very little acidity. The vineyards of Mascara, Tlemcen and Haut Dahra produce the richest and most robust of the Oran wines. The finest Algiers wines are generally lighter-bodied. Algiers red wines from the mountain vineyards are strong and fruity with a brilliant colour; those from the lower hills are more delicate and perfumed.

Alsace

The wines of Alsace have a character entirely their own. They are not like any other French white wines; indeed they have been called the German wines of France, but they are also quite unlike their German cousins farther along the Rhine. Nor do they have much in common with the many other wines made the world over from the same grape varieties, be they Riesling, Gewürztraminer, Muscat or Tokay.

Nonetheless, Alsace wines are good. The standard of the appellation wines, the only ones likely to be exported, is nearly always high. The vintners of Alsace are noted for their integrity and their painstaking determination to make the best possible and most natural wine from the resources given.

The north-eastern province of France, bordered by Switzerland and Germany, Alsace came into French possession under Louis XIV, at the end of the Thirty Years War in 1648. However, after being

French for 220 years, Alsace was annexed by Germany in consequence of the Franco-Prussian War in 1871. What followed were 50 years of vinicultural annihilation. To prevent competition with their own Rhine wines, the German administration proscribed the cultivation of noble grape varieties in the province. Alsace was left to produce small cheap wines that served only for blending with lesser German wines to make Sekt (q.v.).

At the end of World War I, Alsace was restored to France and an uphill struggle began, to replant vineyards and to establish a reputation and a market. This process was interrupted again during World War II, which brought German military occupation from 1940 to 1944, and much fighting and destruction over local ground. Afterwards the Alsatian grower-shippers—the *producteurs-négociants*—started up again, with great courage, working towards the splendid results of the last 30 years.

Alsace is one of France's two northern wine regions (*map, page 84*); the other is Champagne. Both make almost exclusively white wine; red grape vines do not give their best in such latitudes. The climate of Alsace is continental—hot summers, little rainfall, hard winters. To save them from ground frost the vines are trained to grow high off the ground.

About a quarter of the cultivated land in Alsace is devoted to vines. The vineyards are on a winding strip that extends for 110 km (70 miles) along the foothills of the Vosges mountains at altitudes between 180 and 365 metres (600 and 1200 feet), facing east towards the distant Rhine. The best wines come from a middle part of this strip. Administratively the province is divided into two departments, Bas-Rhin and Haut-Rhin. However, A.C. Alsace is the only appellation of origin for the entire region.

Label designations are different from those of the rest of France. They are not primarily geographical. Instead of being named after a district, commune or *château*, Alsace wines bear the name of the grape they are made of.

These grapes are divided into noble and lesser breeds. The lesser, known as *cépages courants*—Knipperle, Chasselas, Müller Thurgau—make crisp, refreshing little carafe wines to be drunk young in local cafés and restaurants. They are not exported, and they have no appellation.

There are six noble varieties, the *cépages nobles*. Foremost among these are Riesling and Gewürztraminer, the first certainly one of the five or six most distinguished wine grapes in the world, the second perhaps the most individual.

Riesling, which the people of Alsace regard as their greatest wine, is both firm and delicate, complex and fine. It is a steely wine, very very dry, with the balance between fruit, acidity and freshness entirely achieved. It goes well with all the foods that call for a fine dry white wine—oysters, fish, and other seafood. It turns a dish of *choucroute garnie*—sauerkraut garnished with sausages and smoked meats—into a feast. There will never be an abundance of true Riesling because the vine, here as elsewhere, is late ripening, delicate and yields very little fruit.

A true Gewürztraminer is a highly scented aromatic wine. *Gewürz* means both spice and seasoning and the wine literally tastes of flowers and spices. At the same time it has strength and weight—it is a solid wine for all its fragrance. Like all the bigger Alsace wines, it can be heady, as well as dry. (Only in years of exceptionally long warm autumns do the vintners decide to make a *Vendange Tardive*, a late-picking of the grapes equivalent to the German Spätlese, to produce a rich wine with some lingering sweetness.) Once tasted, a Gewürztraminer will always be easy to recognize by its smell and taste. It is a white wine that wonderfully enhances a wide range of foods normally associated with red wine; it brings out many rich and savoury dishes—cheese fondue, pork, goose or *charcuterie*, hot or cold. The wine is also a perfect, perhaps *the* perfect, companion to that other great Alsace speciality, *foie gras*.

Tokay d'Alsace or Pinot Gris (no connection with the Hungarian Tokay grape) makes a more full-bodied and deeper-coloured wine, soft without flabbiness, and with enough substance to complement *foie gras*, roast turkey and chicken, veal dishes and hot ham.

Muscat from Alsace, unlike all other wines made from that grape elsewhere in the world, is not sweet but bone-dry, yet still musk-scented and very grapey. It can be light with a discreet aroma, when it makes an easy aperitif, and does nicely with asparagus or scrambled eggs; it can also be full-bodied, luscious, even heady, and accompany creamy dishes of crab, prawn or lobster. Traditionally, Muscat is often served with cheese (Parmesan and Gruyère can be recommended), with desserts and with fruit.

Pinot Blanc makes a relatively uncomplex dry wine with a touch of sharpness. Sylvaner, the most widely planted of these grapes, with vines that yield a large amount of fruit, sometimes makes a thin, even acid, wine with a tendency to flatness. However, when good Sylvaner wine is drunk young, its dryness is clean and fruity. Both Pinot Blanc and Sylvaner are good summer aperitifs, and go well with quiches, eggs and shellfish.

Another agreeable, dry, refreshing wine is Edelzwicker, which means noble mixture, designating a wine blended from two or more noble grapes. The label does not say which grapes are used; more often than not though, Sylvaner is included in the blend.

By law, wines bearing the name of any one of the noble grape varieties must have been made solely from that grape. A similar 100 per cent rule applies to the labelling of vintage wines. If a wine is labelled 1978, for example, it has not been blended with a single drop from another year. Beyond these two restrictions, Alsace wines from different sources may be, and are, freely blended, provided they come from the same grape variety and have been grown within Alsace. Here, blending is not a short cut but a conscious art.

Sometimes the producer's home township appears on the label. This is an indication of origin, but does not mean that all the wine inside the bottle comes from the surrounding vineyards. Some of the most important or bustling wine townships are Barr, Bergheim, Ribeauvillé, Riquewihr, Ammerschwihr, Kienzheim, Kaysersberg, Eguisheim and Guebwiller.

Occasionally the name of a single vineyard is mentioned on an Alsace label—Kaeferkopf, Sporen, Schoenenberg, Le Rangen, Pfirsiberg, etc—there are some 30 of these favoured sites. When one of these vineyards is named, all the wine in the bottle must originate from this single source. Alsace also produces a large quantity of reliable minor wines, without appellation, marketed and exported under brand names.

Qualifications such as *Grand Vin, Grand Cru, Grande Réserve, Réserve Exceptionnelle* may also be found on labels—all four signify that the wine contains more than 11 per cent alcohol. *Cuvée Spéciale* or *Réserve* means a blend. All Alsace wine appears in the slim green bottles known as *flutes d'Alsace*, and must be bottled in the region.

Ampelography
The study and classification of grape vines.

A.O.C. *Appellation d'Origine Contrôlée.*
See *French Wine Appellations; Wine Laws*

Appellation Contrôlée see *French Wine Appellations; Wine Laws*

Argentina
Argentina is one of the largest wine-producing countries in the world. There is a huge demand for wine in the country and until recently very little has been exported. Red wines predominate, but whites, sparkling wines and rosés are also made. The industry is organized on a mass-production basis and 70 per cent of Argentine wine is simple table wine—quite sound and drinkable, but lacking any subtlety or individual distinction.

The principal wine-producing area is Mendoza, a semi-desert region bounded in the west by the Andean mountains. The first vineyards were established in the 16th century by Spanish Jesuit missionaries who planted the Criolla grape (the same variety became known as the Mission grape when the Spanish introduced it to California 200 years later). However, it was not until the end of the 19th century that the wine industry expanded. Improved communications opened up the interior, and many immigrants from Italy, France and Germany arrived in Mendoza, bringing with them European vines from their own lands and also modern wine-growing expertise. Today, there are more than 200,000 hectares (495,000 acres) of vineyards in Mendoza and a superb irrigation system waters the vines.

The arid climate helps to prevent the spread of disease and allows the grapes to ripen well in the summer heat; winters are cool enough to allow the vines to rest. Depending on the variety of grape, harvesting takes place between February and April. In some vineyards, however, the grapes are picked underripe in January in order to preserve more of their natural acidity.

Mendoza produces 70 per cent of all Argentinian wine, mostly red wines from the Malbec grape and the traditional Criolla. Recently, more Cabernet Sauvignon and Pinot Noir grapes have been planted and some of the Cabernets are very good indeed. The best white wines are made with Semillon, Tempranillo and Chenin grapes.

North of Mendoza, the region of San Juan has the second largest acreage of vines in Argentina. The climate is very hot and the wines are therefore heavier than those of Mendoza. Regions north of San Juan, such as La Rioja, produce white and rosé wines with a high alcohol content and low acidity. These are very popular in Argentina but seem flabby and flat to a European palate.

The southern wine-growing regions of Rio Negro and Neuquen make only 5 per cent of the country's wine, mostly still or sparkling white wines. The cooler climate produces wines with a lower alcohol content and more acidity, and many people consider them to be the best wines produced in Argentina.

The quality of wine exported from Argentina is uneven, but the National Institute of Vitiviniculture set up in 1959 is tightening controls and encouraging more growers to produce higher quality wines. One problem is the Argentinian preference for wines aged for a long period in wood, which destroys the fresh fruit of the wine, giving it a flat, rather stale taste. However, many more wines are being vinified today by modern methods to make fresher tasting wines.

Australia

Botany Bay, where the first shiploads of British settlers reached the Australian shore in 1788, lies at about the same distance from the equator as the vineyards of Jerez or Sicily. Vine cuttings and seeds picked up *en route* in South Africa on that first voyage were planted by the emigrants in the fertile soil of their new home, with some idea of creating vineyards that would free England from dependence on French and German wine. Although the earliest planting failed because an unpropitious site was chosen at first, others later succeeded elsewhere in the colony. By the 1850s, a modest Australian wine industry was established. Expansion, gradual for decades, speeded up dramatically in the early 1960s with increasing public interest in wine. By 1981, 30,000 hectares (175,000 acres) of vines were under cultivation and 4,000,000 hectolitres (90,000,000 gallons) of wine were being produced each year. Australian wine is freely available in Great Britain, Canada and Germany, and various South-East Asian countries are also importers.

For anyone trying to make top-quality wine, Australia's splendid climate is a mixed blessing. Reliably hot, dry summers and moderately wet, frost-free winters mean that little of the grape crop is lost and consistency is relatively easy to attain. But the heat can quickly produce overripe grapes that yield excessively alcoholic wines. It is, therefore, not surprising that for most of its wine-making history Australia was known chiefly as a source of undistinguished fortified wines and immensely heavy reds, high in alcohol and short on balance.

With the expansion of the 1960s, however, came a marked improvement in quality. A new generation of knowledgeable and innovative wine makers experimented with grape strains more suited to the scorching sun, and started to use modern methods of controlled-temperature fermentation, producing more consistently successful results. As a result, wines from Australia are now usually well balanced and some have distinction.

Many different grape varieties are grown, including virtually all the best grapes of France and Germany. The staple red grape variety is Shiraz, the Syrah of the Rhône Valley; its alternative Australian name is Hermitage, after the upper Rhône community that produces some of the best French Syrah wines. The Shiraz is popular in Australia because it is hardy, productive and resistant to the heat. The best wines made from it are firm and tannic and age extremely well.

Although it is not planted so often, Cabernet Sauvignon produces some fine Australian wines, and frequently Cabernet Sauvignon and Shiraz are blended together. Pinot Noir grapes have been less successful, clearly preferring the soil and colder climate of their origins.

The Riesling grape is grown widely in Australia, with some success especially in the cooler areas. Semillon, the principal white wine grape in Sauternes and Graves, is also grown in many Australian vineyards. In most places it produces rather bland dry wines but a mature Semillon from the Hunter Valley, north of Sydney, can be a very fine wine. When young, it is very acid and hard, but with at least five years' bottle age it develops a light golden colour and a rich and subtle flavour. Chardonnay, the white Burgundy grape, is being planted in increasing quantities and is considered very much the grape of the future. Other white grape varieties include Chenin Blanc, Marsanne, Muscat, Traminer and Sauvignon Blanc.

Australian wine makers cultivate such vast areas that growers with less than 40 hectares (100 acres)—immense by European standards—are regarded as small operators. Nearly all the vineyard areas are situated in the southern, cooler part of the country, between the 32nd and 35th degrees (*map, page 81*). The three most important wine-producing states are South Australia, New South Wales and Victoria.

South Australia accounts for 60 per cent of the wine produced in the country. Its pre-eminence is largely explained by a cool ocean current from the Antarctic, which moderates the climate. Its most important wine-producing areas are the Barossa Valley north of Adelaide; the Clare-Watervale Valley a little farther to the north and west; a zone south of Adelaide known as the Southern Vales with its neighbour Langhorne Creek and Coonawarra, a small strip of land some 300 km (200 miles) south-east of Adelaide. Coonawarra is thought by many experts to be Australia's finest red-wine producing area; it is best known for its Cabernet Sauvignon.

The Barossa Valley produces red, white and fortified wines. With its relatively cool climate, the valley is well suited to the Riesling grape, and with the help of modern technology, its wine makers are now producing a light, delicate white wine. The Barossa red wines are medium to full in body, and usually benefit from a few years' bottle age.

The Clare-Watervale Valley is South Australia's most northerly wine region. It has much the same rainfall as the Barossa but its higher temperature and heavier soil give fuller wines. The red wines are high in alcohol, and noted for their longevity. The white wines, made largely from the Riesling grape, also tend to be fuller than those of Barossa Valley.

The region known as the Southern Vales includes Reynella and McLaren Vale. Both have an ideal climate for the cultivation of vines. The weather conditions and rainfall are reliable, and the area is remarkably free of pests. A little farther east, Langhorne Creek has a rainfall too low to support vines, but the Brenner river floods every year, enabling the vines to survive. One or two of the wines are good, but most are ordinary.

Coonawarra, being far to the south and close to the sea, is one of Australia's coolest regions. Its soil, known as *terra rossa*, or red earth, is a strip of rich red loam, underlaid by limestone and clay. This strip is only 14.5 km (9 miles) long and less than 2 km (1 mile) wide; in places, it is only about 180 metres (200 yards) across. Beneath the limestone, an unusually high water-table helps the vines to thrive. The cool climate and red soil combine to produce red wines of great finesse, the best being made from Cabernet Sauvignon grapes. Shiraz grapes grown here produce a lighter wine for early drinking.

New South Wales, the birthplace of the Australian wine industry, produces about a quarter of Australia's wine. The Hunter Valley is by far the most famous vine-growing region in the state. The high quality of its wines is largely due to the comparatively cool climate, but the weather is rather more unpredictable than in many parts of the country, bringing problems to the wine makers and making the quality of the vintages correspondingly variable.

The long-established vineyards of the lower Hunter Valley are best known for red wine from the Shiraz grape, and white wine from the Semillon. With both these grape varieties, Hunter Valley wines are unsurpassed in Australia. The Shiraz may develop a characteristic and complex nose that is sometimes described—aptly if inelegantly—as "sweaty saddle". The upper Hunter Valley vineyards are newer and more modern, and most of them have irrigation to cope with years of drought. Quite different styles of wine are produced: the Upper Hunter is at its best with Riesling, Traminer, Sauvignon Blanc and, to a lesser extent, Chardonnay. Shiraz tends to produce light, almost thin wines, but some good wines are made from Cabernet Sauvignon.

Mudgee is a region some 260 km (160 miles) north-west of Sydney, at the same latitude as the Lower Hunter. Lying on the western slopes of the Great Dividing Range, it has less summer rain than the Hunter Valley and hence much less vintage variation. At some 460 metres (1,500 ft) above sea level, it is one of Australia's highest vineyard areas. The grapes—Cabernet Sauvignon, Shiraz, Riesling and Chardonnay—therefore ripen much more slowly and the vintage is usually five to six weeks later than in the Hunter Valley. The wines are good and fuller than in the Hunter Valley.

The third major wine-growing area in New South Wales, Riverina, is entirely under irrigation and planted with high-yielding vines. The accent has been on quantity rather than quality.

A glance at a map would suggest that the state of Victoria, being to the south of the country and relatively cool, would yield a higher proportion of the country's production than the 13 per cent it can claim. The explanation of its low yield goes back to the 19th century, when the vine pest, *Phylloxera vastatrix (page 7)*, struck Victoria but left the rest of the country almost unaffected. Most of the vineyards in Victoria were abandoned. At the beginning of the 1980s, however, the area under vine began increasing faster in Victoria than anywhere else.

Although the vines are grown all over the state, in terms of quality the most important region is the north-east, around the towns of Rutherglen, Corowa, Glenrowan and Milawa. This is the home of liqueur Muscat, a rich, luscious fortified wine. It is made from the Frontignan Muscat grape; after fermentation, the wine is fortified up to 19 or 20 per cent and matured with wines from older vintages in a modified solera system (see *Sherry*). Traditionally, the red wines of north-eastern Victoria have been high in alcohol, but lighter, more delicate styles are now being produced.

Some 160 km (100 miles) south-west of Rutherglen lies the fertile Goulburn Valley, renowned for its red and white wines. Château Tahbilk, the principal vineyard here, produces full-bodied reds from Shiraz and Cabernet Sauvignon grapes, and from the Marsanne grape, a light dry white that improves with bottle age. The other notable vineyard in the area is Mitchelton, which produces some excellent varietal white wines.

Farther south still, the Yarra Valley on the outskirts of Melbourne is being re-established as a wine-growing area after some 60 years of decline following the Phylloxera epidemic. To the west, the village of Great Western is of importance for the production of sparkling wines. The climate here is rather cooler than elsewhere in Victoria, but the rainfall is not sufficient for the vines and must be supplemented in summer by irrigation.

In the north-west of Victoria, the area around the city of Mildura is most important for fortified wines, produced chiefly by the same methods as those used for sherry. Here, summers are long and hot, and the rainfall is low. With the entire region under irrigation, a large volume of red and white wine of moderate quality is also produced. West of Mildura, the wine-making region stretches over the border with South Australia into an area known as Riverland.

Wine is also made in the states of Western Australia and Queensland, though on a very much smaller scale than the three main wine-growing states. Both have very hot climates that present problems for wine makers.

In Tasmania, however, 240 km (150

miles) off Australia's southern shore, conditions are cooler, and although the industry is very much in its infancy, Tasmania is well placed to produce good white wines in the future.

Unlike most other wine-producing nations, Australia does not have a law that specifically addresses wine-making and wine appellations. However, the Goods Description Act and general practice ensure certain standards of nomenclature. If a wine is a blend of two or more grape varieties, then the predominant grape must be the first named. Consequently, if a wine is made from 60 per cent Shiraz and 40 per cent Cabernet Sauvignon, it must be labelled as Shiraz Cabernet rather than Cabernet Shiraz. (The natural inclination would be to do the opposite, since Cabernet wines are, as a general rule, more expensive.)

Although very little information is required on the label by law, Australian wine makers often provide it in abundance for a public without the long-established wine-drinking traditions of Europe, specifying when the grapes were picked, and how the wine was made, and suggesting how to serve it.

Austria

Austria produces light white wines with a small proportion—about 11 per cent—of red wines. Some are of high quality and most are of a consistently good standard and make excellent everyday table wines. All the best wines are white.

Until recently, almost all Austrian wine was consumed inside the country. Demand exceeds supply and the traditional wine-making pattern is one of small vineyards and individual growers producing wine for local consumption. In the 1970s, mainly because of new technology and new wine laws that were passed in 1973, exports increased considerably and Austrian wines are becoming more widely appreciated.

The amount of wine produced in the mountainous western part of Austria is negligible; almost all the country's vineyards lie in the eastern part where the Alpine ranges give way to slopes that grade eventually into the vast Hungarian plains. The wine-growing country is divided by Austrian wine law into four regions: Lower Austria, Vienna, Burgenland and Styria.

Lower Austria, in the northern part of the country, includes the whole of northeastern Austria and has around 30,000 hectares (74,000 acres) of vineyards. In the fertile, wooded country watered by the Danube, there are cornfields, market gardens and farms as well as vines, and most of the wine is produced from small vineyards. The Retz and Falkenstein Matzen districts, north of the Danube, form the largest wine area in Lower Austria; they are mainly planted with Grüner Veltliner, Austria's most popular grape. The ubiquitous Grüner Veltliner makes a typical, light dry Austrian wine—at its best it is fresh and fruity with a good acid balance and a lovely green-gold colour; it is sometimes spicy, almost peppery, in flavour, and should always be drunk young. A small amount of good ordinary red wines are also made here.

The vineyards of Wachau, spectacularly situated on the banks of the Danube, produce some of Austria's best wines. The small vineyards have a mixed character; some vines are planted in deep soil, others cling tenaciously to rocky outcrops covered with a shallow layer of soil; some sites are well exposed, others are shady. The principal grapes are the Grüner Veltliner, Neuburger and Rheinriesling, and Silvaner. The best of the Wachau wines are characterized by an exceptionally flowery bouquet and more finesse than most Austrian wines; a good Rheinriesling—rarely found outside the area—is a complex wine of high quality. Spitz, Weissenkirchen, Durnstein and Loiben are all village names with good reputations.

The vineyards east of the Wachau in the Krems and Langenlois districts lie on lower hills and are planted in broad terraces intersected by winding lanes called *Kellergassen* that lead to cellars cut into the hills. The soil is mainly sandy and the wines are similar to those of the Wachau, though perhaps lacking in the extra finish that distinguishes the best Wachau wines. In the village of Rohendorf, in the Krems district, are the cellars of Lenz Moser, Austria's most renowned wine grower, whose innovative methods of cultivation have been adopted in many other Austrian and German vineyards. (The vines are planted in widely spaced rows to reduce the spread of disease and facilitate mechanical cultivation, and trained to twice the usual height to counteract the loss in yield.)

The monastery and wine school at Klosterneuburg, near Vienna, continues a long Austrian tradition of monastic wine-making and has a rapidly expanding export trade. South of Vienna some pleasant, dry red wines are made in Bad Voslau, but the district is most famous for its Gumpoldskirchens — late-gathered, medium-dry white wines made from a blend of the lively Zierfandler grape with the Rotgipfler and heavier Neuburger.

The Vienna wine area has only about 600 hectares (1,500 acres) of vines but it is rightly designated as a separate area, for its character is unique. The vineyards extend from the slopes of the Vienna woods right into the residential suburbs, and the wine villages of Grinzing, Sievring and Nussdorf are encompassed by the city. Most Viennese wine is drunk as *Heurige*—new wine—in the wine cellars and gardens of Vienna. The Heurigen wine laws, established in the 18th century by the Empress Maria Theresa, allow wine growers to sell their own wine on their own premises free of tax. The advent of the new wine is signalled by hanging a green bough outside the grower's premises; when the wine is finished, the bough is then taken down. This very heady new wine is light and sprightly, still prickling as it ferments; it is mostly produced from the Grüner Veltliner and Müller Thurgau grape varieties with some Riesling and Traminer.

Burgenland, another wine area, on the eastern border of Austria, was part of Hungary until the 1920s and the Hungarian influence remains. The area specializes in sweet wines. Its most famous wine Ruster Ausbruch, used to be compared to Tokay, the great Hungarian dessert wine and is made by a similar method. There are about 15,000 hectares (37,000 acres) of vines. The most important vineyards of Burgenland lie in the flat, sandy area around Lake Neusiedlersee where the microclimate is warm and dry, and the surface of the lake retains the sun's heat to the benefit of the surrounding vines. The principal grapes include the Furmint (which is used to make Hungarian Tokay) and the Traminer, Muskat Ottonel and Riesling grapes.

On the eastern side of the lake is an area called Seewinkel which, because of its sandy soil, is one of the very few places in Europe to escape Phylloxera (*page 7*). Around the villages of Podersdorf, Illmitz and Apetlon, ungrafted vines can be grown on their natural roots, and fine Ausleses, Beerenausleses and Trockenbeerenausleses are produced by the Esterhazy estate at Eisenstadt and by Lenz Moser at Apetlon. The best wines are of a high quality but they do not age well and have a tendency to oxidize.

The local Eiswein can be excellent (q.v.) but is rarely made because winters in the area are usually mild. Some distinctive rather fiery red wines are produced from the higher slopes at the western end of the lake, where the soil changes from sand to limestone. Red grapes include the Kadarka grape from the Balkans, Pinot Noir, Portugieser and Blaufrankisch (Gamay) grapes. Some pleasant red wines are made in south Burgenland but none of the reds matches the white wines.

Styria, on Austria's Yugoslavian border, has about 2,000 hectares (5,000 acres) of vines. There are few co-operatives or big producers and nearly all the wine is consumed locally. The principal white grapes include Pinot Blanc, Traminer, Riesling and Ruländer. A small amount of red wine is made, including Schilcherwein, a dark rather spicy wine made from the native Blauer Wildbacher grape.

Most Austrian wines are labelled with the year of the vintage and the name of the village or district of origin; the individual vineyard is rarely specified. The wines may also bear the name of the grape from which they are made, either on its own or with a place name.

Since 1973, wines bearing the Austrian Wine Seal label have been graded by a system similar to that used for German wines. The classifications include ordinary table wine (*Tischwein* or *Tafelwein*); quality wine (*Qualitätswein*), which may have some added sweetening; superior quality (*Qualitätswein Kabinette*), which must be completely natural, with no extra sweetening allowed; and quality wines of special ripening and harvesting methods (*Qualitätswein besonderer Reife und Leseart*). This last category includes those grades equivalent to high quality German wines—Spätlese, Auslese, Beerenauslese, Trockenbeerenauslese and Eiswein—as well as two that are specifically Austrian: Ausbruchwein and Strohwein, or straw wine, so named because the grapes are dried out on wooden frames, often covered with straw, to produce a result similar in quality to Trockenbeerenauslese.

Baden

A former province of Germany, now part of the Federal State of Baden Württemberg, making a diversity of wines under varying topographical and climatic conditions, in vineyards scattered among the agricultural lands. Baden is the southernmost corner of Germany, bordered by France in the west and Switzerland in the south (*map, page 83*). The climate is sunny and mild, sheltered by the Odenwald and Schwarzwald mountains.

About one-third of Baden wine is red, the rest white. Until recently, Baden wines—bottled like the Rhine wines in tapering amber-coloured bottles—have been little known in the outside world. The red is enjoyed locally and in Germany at large, as are the minor whites. There is a small but much appreciated export trade in the best whites; these wines are excellent, similar in some ways to fine Hock and Mosel, only a good deal drier.

Until 1870, when *Phylloxera vastatrix* (*page 7*) devastated the vines, Baden produced more wine than any other German area; now it yields about 14 per cent of the German total.

There is a profusion of grapes: a majority of Müller Thurgau; Spätburgunder (Pinot Noir); a little Riesling (here called Klingelberger); various amounts of Ruländer (Pinot Gris), Gutedel, Silvaner, Weissburgunder, Gewürztraminer.

Vineyard soil varies from area to area—volcanic and crumbled granite soils respectively in the two best regions, Kaiserstuhl and Ortenau; marl, gravel, clay and limestone elsewhere.

Baden wine growers have organized themselves into co-operatives—120 of them are linked to one enormous central co-operative situated at Breisach, which deals with 80 per cent of the vintage.

There are seven districts (*Bereiche*): Badisches Frankenland, Badische Bergstrasse, Breisgau, Bodensee (Lake Constance), Kaiserstuhl Tuniberg, Margräflerland and Ortenau. Sixteen greater vineyard groups (*Grosslagen*) exist and more than 300 individual vineyards (*Einzellagen*).

On the north shore of Lake Constance are produced white and pink wines called Seeweine (lake wines)—simple wines consumed agreeably enough on the lakeside's terraces and garden restaurants.

Beaujolais

Beaujolais is an easy red wine that goes with good-fellowship and simple hearty food. Indeed, it is so delicious and yet uncomplicated—a refreshing wine suitable for drinking casually at any time of day—that it has become one of the most popular wines in France and one that remains in huge demand internationally.

The Beaujolais region in the southernmost part of Burgundy begins at the border of the Mâconnais and ends not far above the gates of Lyon (*map, page 85*). This is wine-rich country—approximately 20,000 hectares (50,000 acres) under vines, worked by literally thousands of owners and growers, with a vintage averaging 1,000,000 hectolitres (22,000,000 gallons), much of it vinified in co-operatives and sold to local shippers. Yet the region can never produce enough Beaujolais, so huge is the demand. Most of its wine used to be drunk locally, and at Lyon, with a fair amount going to Paris; now, over half the vintage goes out into the world that is clamouring for it.

All the best wines are produced in the Haut-Beaujolais, the northern half of a jumble of granite hills. The grape is Gamay—specifically, the variety known as Gamay *à jus blanc*—and the Gamay, which can be so mediocre elsewhere, does wonders on granite soil. In the Bas-Beaujolais, the southern half of the district, the granite gives way to chalk, and here wines made from the same grape tend to be on the light side.

There are four grades in the Beaujolais classification. The lowest two are Beaujolais and Beaujolais Supérieur (none of the Bas-Beaujolais wines rise above these). Then comes Beaujolais-Villages, for which some 30 Haut-Beaujolais villages qualify; and at the top there are nine individual appellations which form Beaujolais' highest rank—St. Amour, Juliénas, Chénas, Fleurie, Moulin-à-Vent, Chiroubles, Morgon, Brouilly, Côtes de Brouilly.

Beaujolais is usually a wine whose best attributes are those of youth—vivid colour, exuberance of fruit, sprightliness, and a hint of effervescence. It should be drunk before these charms have faded, and it must be drunk cool, even chilled.

Wines bearing the plain Beaujolais appellation can be extremely agreeable when six months to a year old, and are usually reliable when marketed under the label of a trusted shipper. Beaujolais Supérieur and Beaujolais-Villages have the characteristic Beaujolais fruitiness, vigour and exuberance, but in an enhanced form; and the nine individual appellations should be Beaujolais at its most distinctive and delicious.

St. Amour from the most northerly Beaujolais vineyards is the lightest, and delicate in fruit; Juliénas is sturdy, a little hard at first, but always vigorous; Brouilly, fresh and grapey; Côtes de Brouilly, grown higher up, has a better-defined character; Fleurie is light as silk, brilliantly translucent, unmistakable in fruit; Chiroubles approaches Fleurie in lightness. Chénas, firmer than most, is sometimes said to have most distinction; while Morgon, full-bodied and fruity, is recognized as being one of the longer-living Beaujolais.

Of all Beaujolais, Moulin-à-Vent is the least typical, big and full and improving with—indeed needing—age. No sprightliness here, but it is a wine that should be kept, and when at last opened, not to be drunk chilled. Some regard Moulin-à-Vent as Beaujolais' best wine; it is certainly its most venerable, complex and uncharacteristic.

Beaujolais Nouveau or Primeur is at the other end of the time scale: a wine that is often drunk within weeks of its birth. New wine can be a delightful drink and, not so many years ago, Beaujolais Nouveau was drunk mainly in local cafés and bistros. It was hardly ever bottled, and it was not meant to travel except, perhaps, to Paris or nearby Geneva. It was a cheap drink, as well it might be, with no storage, no prolonged handling, no capital tied up in it. Now Beaujolais Nouveau has become the fashion—a profitable one for the wine trade—and is hurried to more distant places by November 15th, the earliest permissible date after the vintage.

There are several snags in marketing such young wine. To get the wine clear and quiet after fermentation, bottled and pronounced fit to drink by the French authorities in such a short time, it has to be raced through all its vinification processes—racking, filtering, fining etc.; and if the wine, which may be any basic Beaujolais, has little strength or character from the beginning, it will not stand up well to such treatment. As a result, the wine hailed on arrival in Brussels or London will be a thin and acid little affair—unless, for worse, it has been boosted with more than a pinch of sugar.

If, on the other hand, a first-rate wine has been brought forward by quick vinification, that infant prodigy is delectable but short-lasting. Treated in this way Beaujolais will have lost all its charm by the first spring after harvesting; raised more slowly the same wine will just begin to come into its own by the spring.

Bergerac

A small French wine region lying immediately to the east of Bordeaux and sharing, on a diminished scale, its neighbour's blessings of soil and climate (*map, page 84*). Bergerac has a cluster of *appellations contrôlées*. North of the Dordogne, which divides the region from east to west, Pécharmant produces fresh, fruity red wines that are perfect for everyday drinking. Other good reds bear the general Bergerac and Côtes de Bergerac appellations. Monbazillac, south of the Dordogne, produces sweet white wines; at their best, these resemble the wines of Sauternes. Lighter sweet white wines come from Rosette, while the Montravel and Haut-Montravel appellations produce a range of white wines from sweet to dry and crisp. As in Bordeaux, Cabernet Sauvignon, Cabernet Franc, Merlot and Malbec grapes are used for the red wines. For the whites, Semillon, Sauvignon Blanc and Muscadelle are the principal varieties.

Blanc de Blancs

White wine made from white grapes. Because most Champagnes are made from a blend of wines from white and red grapes, this term distinguishes the lighter-bodied Champagnes made only from white grapes. Except with reference to Champagne, the term has no real meaning.

Blanc de Noirs

When applied to Champagne, this term means white wine made only from red—or "black"—grapes. Because, with few exceptions, all Champagnes contain some white grapes, it is rarely used. It is commonly—and incorrectly—used in California for rosé wines to avoid saying "rosé" or "pink" on a label: American rosé wines have often been of poor quality, and consumers often shun wine so described.

Blaye

A large wine district of Bordeaux on the right bank of the Gironde, adjoining and often mentioned collectively with Bourg (*map, page 85*). Red and white wines are produced under three appellations: in ascending order of quality they are Blaye, Côtes de Blaye (white wines only), and Premières Côtes de Blaye. The reds are light and best drunk young and cool. The whites are dry or semi-sweet.

Bordeaux

City and trading port of 2,000 years' standing; the most important wine-producing area in France and one of the most illustrious in the world. Bordeaux is the capital of the department of the Gironde, and the boundaries of the Bordeaux appellation area are virtually co-extensive with those of the department.

Wine was already being made in the Bordeaux region in the first century A.D. and has been produced uninterruptedly since the end of the Dark Ages, with the resultant accumulation of immense knowledge and experience. The English have long had a special affection for the red wine they call "claret", and they have been linked with the area ever since the 12th century, when Eleanor of Aquitaine brought Bordeaux as part of her dowry to Henry II. The forerunner of claret was *clairet*, a very light, clear-coloured red wine. Methods of wine-making have changed over the centuries and the Bordeaux red wines no longer have their original pale colour; nevertheless they remain claret to the English.

This is a region of broad rivers, the Garonne and the Dordogne joining in the wide estuary of the Gironde. The vines are planted in the shallow valleys of these rivers and on the gravelly slopes and flat land between. The climate is humid, mild, with summers warm enough to ripen the grapes and winters cold enough to rest the vines, while not so harsh as to freeze them to death—except in a few disastrous unforgotten years, such as 1709 and 1956.

The soils of the region are as varied as its wines. The most desirable are poor soils in the ordinary agricultural sense: pebbly, even stony, lacking in organic matter (vines need a struggle to give their utmost), but rich in minerals, from which the complex, subtle flavours of a truly great wine are drawn.

Total output is enormous, with 113,000 hectares (280,000 acres) under vine—a tenth of the surface of the entire Gironde, which is the largest of the 90 departments in France. In an abundant year the area can produce about 5,000,000 hectolitres (110,000,000 gallons) of wine (rather more white than red) of which 3,000,000 hectolitres (66,000,000 gallons) rate an *appellation contrôlée*.

All red Bordeaux is dry wine, wine for the table—in the best, not in the official classifying sense of "table wine"—an admirable companion to almost any food except the very spicy, gamey or heavy. The gamut of red Bordeaux runs through all the categories: light-bodied and tannic; good, sound and uncomplicated; big, muscular and robust; fine and complex; of great depth and intricacy.

The dominant red wine grape varieties are the Cabernet Sauvignon, Cabernet Franc and Merlot. It is the tremendous Cabernet Sauvignon grape that gives claret some of its characteristics: a depth of flavour more easily experienced than described, sturdiness in youth, subtlety and softness in age and an astonishing longevity. A distinguished Bordeaux of a great year may still live—and show vigour, freshness even—after 40, 60, 80, sometimes more than 100 years.

White Bordeaux may be dry (whether crisp and refreshing; or soft; or muscular and vigorous) or outright sweet—the luscious rich sweetness of Sauternes and Barsac. The most distinguished white Bordeaux grapes are the Semillon, an indispensable ingredient of a true Sauternes, and the Sauvignon Blanc.

The whole Bordeaux region is divided into districts of varying size, which differ from each other in the character of the wines they produce. The very finest reds come from four renowned districts: the Médoc, Graves, St. Emilion and Pomerol. In the romantically named district of Entre-Deux-Mers, a large quantity of soft, light, dry white wine is made. Some very distinguished dry white wine is produced in Graves, and great sweet white wine in Sauternes, Ste. Croix du Mont and Loupiac.

Within some of the districts there are further subdivisions into villages or communities. Altogether, there are 40 different legally defined appellations of origin within the Bordeaux region (see *box*). The humblest appellations are those which have the broadest geographical reference—Bordeaux or Bordeaux Supérieur, for example; better wines from within a subdivision of the Bordeaux area, such as St. Emilion or the Médoc, may qualify for the more restricted appellation belonging to that area; the best may be labelled with the name of a single community, such as Pauillac or Margaux (both of which are in the Médoc).

Within the areas of appellation, large or small, the individual wine estates are situated—the *châteaux* as they are called in Bordeaux. These *châteaux* are not "castles"; they are country houses, often small and modest, a few large and ornate. Many date from the 18th century and are well proportioned and pretty; a few are beautiful. The fact that there are more than 2,000 of them, each with its own vineyard and outbuildings of cellars and wine sheds, gives one an idea of the profusion and diversity of *château*-bottled wines.

About 200 of the best *châteaux* are "classified"—that is, given official rank for the excellence of their wine. Such classification—a judgment of quality on individual vineyards and independent of the generally applied appellation laws—is a highly developed and established feature

Official Bordeaux Appellations

(in alphabetical order)

Barsac	Lalande-de-Pomerol
Blaye	Listrac
Bordeaux	Loupiac
Bordeaux Clairet (or Rosé)	Lussac-St.-Emilion
Bordeaux Côtes de Castillon	Margaux
Bordeaux Côtes de Francs	Médoc
Bordeaux Mousseux	Montagne-St.-Emilion
Bordeaux Supérieur	Moulis
Cadillac	Pauillac
Cérons	Pomerol
Côtes de Blaye	Premières Côtes de Blaye
Côtes de Bordeaux St. Macaire	Premières Côtes de Bordeaux
Côtes de Bourg	Puisseguin-St.-Emilion
Côtes Canon-Fronsac	St. Emilion
Entre-Deux-Mers	St. Estèphe
Fronsac	St.-Georges-St.-Emilion
Graves	St. Julien
Graves Supérieures	Ste. Croix du Mont
Graves de Vayres	Ste. Foy Bordeaux
Haut-Médoc	Sauternes

of the Bordeaux wine trade.

The best known classification is that made in 1855 for the Médoc and Sauternes regions (qq. v.). The wines of Graves were classified in 1953 with a revision in 1959, while those of St. Emilion were classified in 1954. Pomerol has as yet had no systematic classification.

Unclassified *châteaux* (the large majority) also label their wine with the appellation and with the *château* name, if it is bottled on the estate. Wine that they sell through brokers to one of the *négociants* in Bordeaux for maturing and bottling may be assembled in the same region with the products of other vineyards and sold under one of the more general Bordeaux appellations.

The question of the age at which different wines should best be drunk is an especially important one for Bordeaux. A wine with a high content of Cabernet Sauvignon cannot be hurried into quick maturity. It may taste rather hard and tannic in its youth (an austerity that is by no means unpleasant). Later it may also go through "mute", ungiving periods when it is what is called closed or tight. Ten years is not an unreasonable time to wait before drinking a classified *château* wine of a fairly good year.

At the lower end of the scale, a non-classified, run-of-the-mill wine with the most general Bordeaux appellation is usually at its best—light and easy to drink—when it is about one year old. As a rule of thumb, you can expect to wait another year or so before drinking a wine from one of the district appellations—for example, a St. Emilion or Blayais—and perhaps five years longer for a wine made and bottled at one of those innumerable small *châteaux*, many of which produce very good wine.

The light white wines of Entre-Deux-Mers are made to be drunk young. Some of those from the Graves district are very fine and complex, and should be drunk as long as 10 years after bottling. They may last for 40 to 50 years, while the greatest Sauternes can live as long as any wine produced in the world.

Bordelais

French adjectival form of the place name Bordeaux.

Bottles and bottle sizes

Standard bottle sizes vary from 70 cl (Mosel and Rhine) to 80 cl (Champagne), with the norm for most wines being about 75 cl. Tokay bottles contain 50 cl, and Beaujolais has its *pot* of 50 cl, considered the ideal size for a single person.

Most wines can be found in half bottles, and magnums are not unusual. Red Bordeaux wines are also bottled in a three-bottle size known as a Marie-Jeanne, in Double Magnums (four bottles), Jéroboams (six bottles) and Impériales (eight bottles). Champagne is not often seen in anything larger than a magnum but, for special occasions, it may be transferred under pressure from bottles or magnums to any of the following traditional sizes: Jéroboam (four bottles instead of six as in Bordeaux), Réhoboam (six bottles), Methuselah (eight bottles), Salmanazar (12 bottles), Balthazar (16 bottles) or Nebuchadnezzar (20 bottles). Outsize bottles of Champagne are useful only for the spectacle. Burgundy is also occasionally available in four-bottle Jéroboams, in Réhoboams and in Methuselahs. Port exists in magnums, rarely in the four-bottle Jéroboams, and in the specifically British Tappit Hen (three bottles), that is also known as a three-bottle magnum.

Wines for laying down will age better and more slowly in relatively large bottles, since the size of the cork and the air space in the bottle both remain approximately the same for a larger quantity of wine, and a smaller proportion of the wine is therefore in contact with the air in the bottle. A half bottle will age more rapidly than a bottle and a bottle more rapidly than a magnum.

Although many white wines are traditionally bottled in colourless glass, all wines keep better in dark-coloured glass.

Bourg

A district of Bordeaux with its own appellation, on the right bank of the Gironde, adjoining and often lumped together with Blaye (*map, page 85*). The wines are also spoken of as Bourgeais and Côtes de Bourg. The white wines are not outstanding. The reds are sound, soft, quite full-bodied wines, to be drunk fairly young.

Bourgeais see *Bourg*

Bourgogne see *Burgundy*

Brazil

Viticulture was initiated in Brazil by Jesuit missionaries, who transplanted the European *Vitis vinifera* vines from Argentina in the 17th century. Despite the efforts of Spanish and Portuguese colonists over the next 200 years, the sweltering, humid climate took its toll—many vines became diseased and vintages were poor. During the 19th century, Italian settlers expanded and developed vineyards in the more temperate southern regions of Brazil and the *vinifera* vines were almost completely replaced by an American hybrid grape—the Isabel—that proved better able to adapt itself to the conditions. After World War I, the Italians, using new techniques of cultivation and wine-making, reintroduced *vinifera* vines and the quality wines produced today come from the European stock.

Most Brazilian wines are consumed inside the country, but the export trade is growing. All types of wine are made—red, white, rosé and sparkling; none of them is distinguished but their quality is improving. The better red wines are made from the Italian Barbera and Bonarda grapes, and from Cabernet Franc, Merlot, Syrah and other fine grapes. *Vinifera* grapes used for good white wines include Trebbiano, Malmsey and Riesling.

Bulgaria

Bulgaria has a modern wine industry that is run extremely successfully by the state. The country produces no really fine wines but the output is high, the quality is improving, and the range is diverse.

Wine was made in what is now Bulgaria in ancient times, but for 500 years Bulgaria was dominated by the Turks, who imposed the Islamic faith, which forbids the drinking of alcoholic beverages. By the time the country became independent at the end of the 19th century, the tradition of wine-making was all but lost. In 1948, the state wine industry was set up with the help of German experts.

Bulgaria's temperate climate—with hot summers, long, warm autumns and no heavy rainfall—is well suited to viticulture. The majority of vines planted are the native Balkan varieties, but the introduction of European vines is increasing, notably Cabernet Franc, Cabernet Sauvignon and Pinot Chardonnay. Most vineyards are harvested mechanically and the huge state wineries serve large areas of the country.

Some brand names have been introduced for the export market, but most Bulgarian wines are named after the grapes used to make them. The Mavrud grape produces dark red, vigorous tannic wine that improves with age. Mavrud wines, from the Maritsa basin south of the Balkan mountains, are particularly well regarded. A fruity red wine of lighter character is made from Gamza grapes in the Danube valley in the north. The same area also produces an aromatic dry red wine of distinctive character from the Kadarka grape. The district of Melnik, in the south-west, is known for its powerfully concentrated, deep red wines. The best red wines are made from Cabernet Sauvignon; new plantings of Cabernet Franc are producing wine of great promise.

Eastern Bulgaria produces most of the country's white wines. The local taste is for heavy, sweet white wines, but demand from the German export market is encouraging the production of the fresher, lighter and more acidic whites that are popular in the West.

The local Dimiat grape is the most commonly planted white variety, producing a rather undistinguished dry white wine, lacking in character. Rcatzitelli, a grape of Russian origin, is used for pleasant dry or sweet white wines. Misket is a medium-sweet wine made from a variety of the red Muscat grape; its fragrance reflects the characteristic flavour and intense aroma of the Muscat vine. Sparkling white wines are also made, about 15 per cent being produced by the Champagne method (q.v.).

Burgundy

Burgundy, ancient province of France, rural, plenteous, vigorous-living, the very name evoking a roll-call of immortal wines—Chambertin, Corton, Clos Vougeot, Romanée-Conti, Montrachet—is one of the world's greatest wine regions, equal, not second or superior, to Bordeaux. Burgundian wines range from the flinty, dry white wines of Chablis to the incomparable red and white Burgundies of the Côte d'Or, from the honest, reliable wines of the Chalonnais and Mâconnais districts, to the youthful charm of the Beaujolais wines. The Burgundians take great pride and joy in their wine as an integral part of their daily life.

Situated in the centre of eastern France, Burgundy is far from the sea, and its heart, the Côte d'Or, is not even within sight of a river (*map, page 84*). The climate is hard, with severe winters and hot but unpredictable summers. Winemaking in northern latitudes is a perilous business, and Burgundy is in fact the world's northernmost region capable of producing great red wine. The quality of the vintages, however, is extremely susceptible to the weather. It is only in the finest vintage years that there is enough sun to bring the grapes to full ripeness and the Burgundian practice of adding sugar—chaptalization (*page 13*)—is a dire necessity at times. There is also the annual threat of too much or too little rain, and of hailstorms: one whipping of hail can strip off a year's harvest in a quarter of an hour. The Burgundian word for vineyard—*climat*, literally, a climate—reflects the local micro-variations of exposure to sun, rain, hail and winds.

The classic Burgundian vineyards are small and most are divided amongst many individual growers—a chaotic situation that originated when the large holdings of the Church and the nobles were broken up after the French Revolution and distributed among local citizens. The French custom of inheritance—division of property among all offspring—split the vineyards into smaller and smaller fragments with each successive generation.

Today, vineyards of, say, 12 hectares (30 acres)—a respectable size in Burgundy, there are many much smaller—are subdivided into six or more patches belonging to as many different owners.

The disadvantage of fragmented vineyards is confusion and uncertainty about exactly what wine you are buying, since the various owners of bits of the same vineyard may produce wines that differ from each other. The label may name the vineyard, but not whose vineyard, nor which corner of that vineyard. These factors matter because, unless the land is completely flat, no patch of earth is ever quite the same—in exposure to the sun, in the ways that the rain drains off it or soaks into it. One grower may own a well-sited part of the vineyard; another may own a less-favoured part. One grower's vines may be young and immature; the next grower's at their peak, or in decline.

Another factor to be considered is the way in which the wine is made. No two wine growers ever make wine in quite the same way: they will differ in experience, in enterprise, methods, skill and sheer luck—as well as in the results they set out to achieve.

Good Burgundy, then, is a rare wine. Great Burgundy is rare to the vanishing point. The entire output of Burgundy appellation wines is about a third of that of Bordeaux, and nearly half of it consists of Beaujolais. All the finest wines—the famous *grands crus* and *premiers crus* from Chablis to Pommard—make up less than a fifth of the whole output: a sobering fact, considering the huge world demand.

Burgundy has five wine districts. Chablis (q.v.) is an isolated enclave northwest of Dijon in the department of the Yonne. The other four districts are part of a continuous wine landscape, about 160 km (100 miles) long, stretching south from Dijon almost to Lyons—the glorious Côte d'Or (q.v.), a narrow strip of vineyards, barely 48 km (30 miles) long, which is divided into the Côte de Nuits and the Côte de Beaune; and the Chalonnais, Mâconnais and Beaujolais districts (qq.v.).

The red wine grapes are Pinot Noir, almost exclusively in the Côte d'Or and the Chalonnais (with a few lesser varieties, such as Pinot Beurot and Pinot Gris in small proportions); and Gamay in the Mâconnais and Beaujolais. The predominant white wine grape is Chardonnay, with some Pinot Blanc and Aligoté, the latter chiefly in the wine of that name.

As in Bordeaux, methods vary: some Burgundy is vinified to mature relatively soon; other wine growers vinify for long-lived wines. On the whole the reds are in cask for from 16 to 18 months, or sometimes two years, before bottling; the whites are bottled after six to nine months, with the exception of the great white wines which remain in cask for up to 18 months. (The optimum time to drink the various wines is discussed in the individual district entries.)

For the purposes of understanding Burgundy labels the system of *appellations contrôlées* may be described as having five levels, from the most general to the most specific. First, there are four basic appellations which may apply to wines made anywhere in Burgundy. Bourgogne, the most distinguished of the four and often of splendid quality, may be white, made exclusively from the Chardonnay grape, or red, made exclusively from Pinot Noir; if it is rosé or clairet, it must be made from Pinot Noir. A second appellation, Bourgogne Aligoté, is white wine made from the secondary Burgundy white grape variety, Aligoté—sometimes with an addition of Chardonnay. It is good, refreshing wine, perfect as an aperitif wine but never with the class of the Burgundy Chardonnays. Thirdly, Bourgogne Passetoutgrains may be red or rosé and is made from a mixture of various Pinots and the Gamay grape; it must contain a minimum of one-third Pinot grape. Finally, Bourgogne Grand Ordinaire and Bourgogne Ordinaire are rarely seen. They may be red, white or rosé and any grape varieties permitted in Burgundy may be used. Bourgogne Mousseux is usually made from wine of this category, treated by the Champagne method (q.v.); it may be white or rosé but, in fact, is nearly always white, although in the past, sparkling red Burgundies had a certain vogue on the export market.

At the next rank, there are the regional appellations which denote a better wine. Beaujolais and Beaujolais Supérieur may come from anywhere in the Beaujolais region, the latter having a higher minimum alcohol content. Beaujolais-Villages must come from a limited number of communities in the northern part of Beaujolais. Mâcon—red, white or rosé— may come from anywhere within the Mâconnais. Côte de Beaune-Villages and Côte de Nuits-Villages are both red wine appellations, restricted to wines from certain specified communities in the Côte de Beaune and the Côte de Nuits.

The community appellations—Fleurie, Gevrey-Chambertin, Chassagne-Montrachet, for example—indicate a further rise in quality. It is the practice of some, not all, Burgundian communities to tack the name of their most famous vineyard on to their own. Thus the village of Gevrey, for example, becomes, quite legitimately, Gevrey-Chambertin.

For their finest wines the Burgundians have two further ranks of classification: *premiers crus* and *grands crus*—first growths and great growths.

There are more than 200 *premier cru* Burgundies. A *premier cru* bears the name of the village it comes from, followed either by the words *Premier Cru* or by the name of the vineyard; sometimes the words *Premier Cru* are also added after the vineyard name. If the vineyard name is used on a *premier cru* label its lettering must be smaller than the village name. Thus, a wine may be labelled simply, Volnay, *Premier Cru;* or Volnay, Les Caillerets, indicating the village and the vineyard from which the wine comes, or even Volnay, Les Caillerets, *Premier Cru.*

A *grand cru* wine—of which there are about 30—belongs to the highest rank of all. Except in Chablis, where the district name of Chablis is also noted on the label, it bears the vineyard name alone without any further geographical indication. For example, a *grand cru* from Morey-St. Denis is labelled simply Clos de la Roche with no indication that the Clos de la Roche vineyard is near the village of Morey-St. Denis. (The term *tête de cuvée*, sometimes seen on a label, is not an official classification but has, traditionally, been used to distinguish certain of the *grands crus* that are considered to be in a class apart from the others—as, for instance, Chambertin and Chambertin-Clos de Bèze, as distinct from the other *grands crus* in Gevrey-Chambertin.)

A thorough knowledge of village and vineyard names is the only sure way to distinguish with confidence a *grand cru* wine label from that of a *premier cru*—as far as Burgundy is concerned one's homework is never done. Community appellations and *grands crus* vineyards are listed and discussed in separate district entries.

There is a self-perpetuating misconception that red Burgundies must be strong, dark, heavy, heady wines. The demand for such wines in the cold countries—Germany, Holland, Britain, for example—has ensured that they exist. It is certainly often less onerous to produce a dark, heavy, heady wine than to ensure its lucidity, elegance and finesse.

The finest Burgundies, however, have what one might call limpidity; there is an elusive depth. There can also be power, structure, strength, authority. If the balance is right, as in the great vintage years, this depth and power are not aggressive but reveal themselves gracefully.

A great Burgundy can be rich, magnificent, sensual, ripe, while still retaining an element of simple clarity. This may sound contradictory but the character of Burgundy is complex and hard to grasp.

Cadillac

A small area and appellation of the Bordeaux region, across the river Garonne from Graves and Sauternes. The area produces wines—sweet, white—that resemble those of the adjacent area of Ste. Croix du Mont (*map, page 85*)

Cahors

A town and wine district on the Lot river, south-west France (*map, page 84*). Given *appellation contrôlée* status in 1971, Cahors is noted for its dark red, so-called "black" wines, the classic accompaniment to *cassoulet*. The main grape is Cot or Malbec, with smaller proportions of Merlot, Syrah and Tannat—the traditional grape for the wines of Madiran (q.v.).

Cérons

A small sweet wine district of Bordeaux, within the Graves region and bordering on the community of Barsac in Sauternes (*map, page 85*). The wines with this appellation resemble in character those of the neighbouring community, Barsac, but they are less luscious and altogether not of the same class. Cérons also makes acceptable dry white wines under the Graves appellation.

Chablis

Chablis lies to the north of the Burgundian wine region, midway between Dijon and Paris, an outpost geographically isolated from the main wine land of Burgundy (*map, page 84*). The winter climate can be harsh and bitter. In Chablis, the vintage years are of enormous importance; if a summer has been poor in sunshine the wine will be thin and sharp. The soil—chalk with Kimmeridgian clay—is hard; the topsoil is thin, easily worn out and sometimes lying fallow for as long as 15 years. Under these Spartan conditions, the Chardonnay grape—known locally as the Beaunois—brings forth a steely, clean, elegant wine, bred to the utmost distinction: Chablis.

In the centre of the district, on the river Serein, lies the little wine town of Chablis, and just across the river on a hill are the vineyards of its finest *crus*, or growths. There are four appellations. The top one is *grand cru* Chablis—literally great growth Chablis—always designated by vineyard; the next in quality is *premier cru* or first growth Chablis, sometimes also designated by vineyard. The two lower appellations are Chablis and Petit Chablis. Wines classified only as Chablis come from the less exceptionally favoured vineyards (although they can still be excellent dry white wine) and they should be drunk young. Petit Chablis is what it says: a little wine. It is nicest drunk by the glass in a French café, and indeed it is seldom exported.

Great Chablis has breeding and distinction. Its attributes are a beautiful pale straw colour with a clear green tinge; a good hardness and a delicate, at times elusive, scent. It is as dry as a bone and it tastes of flint. It makes an incomparable partner to oysters.

The vineyards of the *grands crus* Chablis are tiny, with only 36 hectares (89 acres) between them. There are seven: Vaudésir, Valmur, Grenouilles, Les Clos, Les Preuses, Blanchots and Bourgros. An eighth—Chablis Moutonne—exists in name only. La Moutonne is not a vineyard but a former brand name, now recognized as a *grand cru*. The wine comes from parts of the Vaudésir and Les Preuses vineyards. There are about a dozen *premiers crus*; the best known are Monts de Milieu, Montée de Tonnerre and Fourchaume.

Chalonnais

Chalonnais, the area south of the Côte d'Or (*map, page 84*), is the least-known district of Burgundy, although the wines are very good. Much of the land is wooded or used for grazing (the Chalonnais is famed for its goat cheese) and the vineyards are not large. However, demand has been increasing over the last decade. As in the Côte d'Or, the grapes are Pinot Noir for red wines and Chardonnay for whites. There are four main appellations: Rully, Mercurey, Givry and Montagny.

Rully makes some red wine, the best of of it up to Côte de Beaune standards; a good deal of dry white wine, fairly full-bodied but without heaviness, and some sparkling wines, Bourgogne Mousseux and Crémant de Bourgogne. The latter has softer bubbles than the Mousseux and murmurs rather than fizzes in the glass. For sparkling wines, the grapes are Aligoté, sometimes with an admixture of Chardonnay, Pinot Noir and Gamay.

Mercurey has the largest production of the Chalonnais. Most of the wine is red and can be very good; its style is at times reminiscent of the lighter Pommard. Mercurey also produces some exquisite white wine. Givry makes some sound and pleasant red wines, and a little white. Montagny makes a good, distinguished dry white wine.

Chalonnais as a whole produces a large amount of Bourgogne Rouge and Blanc, and Bourgogne Passetoutgrains. All wines of the area should be drunk while young—the whites within two or three years. Although the reds would not deteriorate with slightly more bottle age, they would generally not gain in quality.

Champagne

The vineyards of Champagne make up the most northerly of the major French wine regions—a land of wooded limestone plains and gently sloping plateaux around the river Marne, about 145 km (90 miles) east of Paris (*map, page 84*).

The province of Champagne was once known mainly for its still wines, probably pink; but towards the end of the 17th century, the development of tightly corked glass bottles—first used in Champagne by Benedictine monks—made it technically possible to trap effervescence (*page 6*); and now French law restricts the name of Champagne to sparkling wine from a designated zone covering about 36,450 hectares (90,000 acres) between the city of Reims to the north and the river Seine to the south. Still red and white wines may not be called Champagne; they take the appellation Coteaux Champenois, sometimes with a community appellation—for example, Bouzy (a red wine).

Since mean annual temperatures in the region are just above the level at which grapes can ripen, the grape variety, location of vineyard and type of soil are of critical importance. The only red grapes used for Champagne are the Pinot Noir and Meunier, and the white grape is Chardonnay—all early ripening varieties. Most of the vineyards are planted on south-facing slopes out of the reach of cold river mists. The chalky soil, which gives the wine its character and finesse, also retains heat and reflects the warmth of the sun on to the growing vines.

The same Benedictine monks who pioneered the use of glass bottles and corks also developed and refined the art of combining grapes from different vineyards into a balanced whole—an art on which the differing characters of various Champagnes depend today. Champagne is sold under the names of about 150 Champagne houses in the region, some of them large enterprises, others small growers who make Champagne from a single vineyard. The best growths, which are used in the finest Champagnes, are concentrated in three distinct sections—the Montagne de Reims, named after the nearby city; the Vallée de la Marne, centred on the riverside town of Épernay; and the Côte des Blancs to the south of the Marne—the only district planted principally with the white Chardonnay.

Today, the making of Champagne is a carefully controlled operation. The red grapes are slightly more precocious than the white and are picked earlier, when only just ripe. If left to ripen longer, colour from the skins might bleed into the juices. The grapes are pressed rapidly, without a preliminary crushing, in wide, shallow presses to ensure that the juice does not become tainted by the grape skins.

The first operation peculiar to Champagne is the preparation of the *cuvée,* as the assemblage is called. Soon after the New Year, tasters from each Champagne house sample the new young wines to find a combination of growths that will produce a wine similar in quality and style to its Champagnes of previous years. Most Champagnes are made with red and white grapes from different vineyards; some, sold as Blanc de Blancs, are made only with the white Chardonnay. A few use only grapes from a single vineyard.

In most years, a little wine from previous harvests is added to the *cuvée* to help achieve a continuity of style. When the harvest is exceptionally good, however, promising a wine of superior taste, bouquet and ageing potential, the *cuvée* is allowed to retain its own distinctive merits; the finished wine is classified as vintage. Every Champagne house decides for itself when it will declare a vintage year for its wine. But this declaration is never made lightly—perhaps only three times in a decade—and not every house announces a vintage in the same year.

After the blending, the second fermentation is initiated (see *Champagne Method*). Fermentation takes only about three months, but the Champagne is left in cellars, cut deep into the chalky hills, for at least a year—three years for vintage Champagne—to develop its full finesse.

The jealously preserved reputation of Champagne is the guarantee of its quality, but each house produces its own Champagne, to suit varying preferences of markets in different countries. On Champagne labels, only vintage years are honoured with a date, and these wines rarely display their full complexity before they are 10 years old.

The word *crémant* denotes a wine that has a lesser degree of effervescence—a result of adding a smaller amount of sugar solution before the second fermentation. Sweetness varies considerably. Champagne labelled *brut* is bone dry; *extra sec* is dry; *sec* is slightly sweet; *demi-sec* more so; and *doux*—now rare—is very sweet.

Rosé is a pink champagne, which is produced in very small quantities, usually by the addition of a little red wine to the basic *cuvée*.

All Champagne should be served well chilled in a bucket of ice and water. Served too cold, its delicate structure goes unappreciated; served too warm, it will seem flabby.

The Champagne Method

The *méthode champenoise*—the Champagne method of making sparkling wine—takes its name from the French region where it was developed (see *Champagne*). A solution of sugar and yeasts is added to wine before bottling to launch a second fermentation in the bottle. The resulting carbon dioxide, unable to escape, is forced to dissolve in the wine, by the enormous pressure that the gas creates inside the specially made, strong and heavy bottles. The added sugar—enough to increase the alcohol by about 1 per cent or slightly more—must be precisely measured to limit the development of the pressure, lest the bottle explode.

This process starts in the spring following the vintage, when the new wine is first pumped into vats to aerate it, thus providing the oxygen necessary to nourish the yeasts. Sugar is dissolved in a small quantity of the same wine to which a culture of yeasts has been added and the solution is added to the vats. The wine is then bottled and sealed, either with temporary corks held in place by strong wire clamps, or with crown caps, and the bottles are laid down in cellars cold enough to ensure a slow fermentation; rapid fermentation would result in bubbles that are coarse instead of tiny, and their persistance, or holding quality, would be impaired. The bottom of each bottle is dabbed with a bar of whitewash, which is used like the hand of a clock to mark the bottle's position during future manipulations in the cellar.

After the bottle fermentation, which takes three months, the sparkling wines are aged for from one to several years, during which time the bottles are periodically given a twirl to shake up and homogenize the sediments—some heavier than others—that are precipitated. The bottles are then laid down again.

The next stage is the *remuage* (riddling), a process designed to collect all of the sediment in the neck of the bottle and permit its removal or *dégorgement* (disgorgement). The bottles are again shaken up and placed horizontally, neck first, in inverted V-shaped slotted racks, designed to hold each bottle by the neck with the body projecting, at any point in a 90-degree angle varying from horizontal to nearly upside-down vertical.

Once the sediment has again settled to the bottom surface of the bottles, their position is readjusted every two or three days, so that they both rotate and move from horizontal to vertical. The painted white bar on the bottom of the bottle acts as a guide for the cellarmen who perform the operation; each time, the bottles are given a complicated, jerking twist to displace the sediment and then repositioned, with the white markers advanced the equivalent of 10 to 15 minutes on a clock face, and the bottles set in a slightly more vertical position. The bottles will be given several complete turns over a period of six weeks to several months, the time depending on the willingness of the sediment to slide to the necks.

When the operation is finished, the bottles will be nearly vertical, necks down, and the sediment will have gathered into a concentration lying against the corks. The bottles are stored upside-down until ready to be disgorged—maybe immediately or years later; the wine and its bubbles hold better on the sediment.

Disgorging, today, is usually accomplished by immersing the necks of the bottles in a freezing solution. When they are opened, the pressure in the bottles discharges the plug of frozen sediment. The plug is replaced by more wine, usually sweetened according to the desired taste of the finished wine.

The final corks are inserted under intense compression and wired in place to resist the pressure of the carbon dioxide. The bottles are shaken to make sure the wine that has replaced the sediment is evenly distributed and the bottles are laid to rest for a few months before being labelled and put on the market.

Château

Used in Bordeaux simply to mean vineyard or property. Outside the Bordeaux region, a vineyard with a *château* on its property often takes the name of *château*.

Chile

A number of factors combine to make Chilean wines the best in South America. The soil is light and fertile; the oceanic climate is temperate, and although irrigation is a necessity almost everywhere, it presents no problems—the streams and rivers flowing down to the Pacific from the Andes ensure a plentiful supply of water. Phylloxera has never invaded

Chile and new vines can therefore be grown on their own roots without being grafted. In addition to those natural advantages, some of the best vineyards were planted in the 19th century by French growers, who left behind them their methods of making quality wines. Exceptionally strict government controls on the Chilean wine industry also help to maintain high standards.

The best wines come from the Aconcagua, Maipo and Maule valleys in central Chile, where there is a strong Bordeaux tradition. Cabernet Franc, Merlot and Cabernet Sauvignon—all Bordeaux grapes—produce good red wines, many of which are reminiscent of lesser Bordeaux, and some of the Cabernets are very good. The Burgundian Pinot Noir grape is also used, but with rather less success. Dry white wines are made from Sauvignon Blanc and softer, more rounded whites from the Semillon grape. The Riesling grape is also used, tending to produce stronger, drier wines than those vinified from the Riesling grapes in Europe.

In the north, the most common grape is the Muscat, which yields good quality, strong white wines that are high in alcohol. Some of the wines are fortified.

Southern Chile produces most of the country's ordinary red wine. It is usually made from the País grape, which is Spanish in origin and accounts for a majority of all Chilean vines. Some French vines, however, are grown in the south; the Vina San Pedro and Lomas de Pulmodon vineyards enjoy a reputation for fine, delicate Cabernets, and good red and white wines are produced from grapes from the Vina Santa Teresa vineyards.

The high quality of many Chilean wines and their relative cheapness—due to the low wages paid to the work-force—make them well worth buying. White wines for export must have an alcohol content of at least 12 per cent and red wines at least 11.5 per cent; all exported wines must be at least one year old. Exported wines are classified according to their age and altogether there are four categories: Courant, for wines that are one year old; Special, for two and three-year-old wines; Reserve, for four and five-year-old wines, and Gran Vino for wines that are six or more years old.

Clos (enclosure)

Usually the name of a specific, delimited growth or vineyard which may or may not be (or have been at one time) enclosed by walls: Clos de la Roche and Clos de Tart, both *grands crus* within the community appellation of Morey-St. Denis in the Côte de Nuits, are examples. A number of proprietors may possess land within the same *clos*.

Community (commune)

A local administrative area in France. Where a community contains vineyards that produce very good wines it may be distinguished by having a specific *appellation contrôlée* of its own, for example, Pauillac in the Médoc.

Corbières see *Languedoc and Roussillon*

Corsica

The island of Corsica, in the Ligurian Sea, belongs to France (*map, page 84*). Corsican wines, like those of Provence (q.v.), often reflect in their bouquet the herbal scents of the Mediterranean scrub—the *maquis*. Many of the grape varieties, although named differently, correspond to traditional Italian varieties. Two of the seven official wine areas—Patrimonia and the Coteaux d'Ajaccio—have earned *appellation contrôlée* status.

Most of Corsica's wines are red or rosé, but two of its finest wines, both from the northernmost tip of the island at Rogliano (Cap Corse) are white: Clos Nicrosi, a solidly constructed, dry, vibrant, earthy wine that can often accompany the foods usually served with red wine, and Muscatellu, a sweet dessert or aperitif wine of great delicacy, laced with the scents of peaches, apricots and unripe almonds.

Côte

Hillside.

Côte d'Or

The Côte d'Or is the heartland of Burgundy: it is an extraordinary concentration of small patches of land uniquely favoured by nature to bring forth an ultimate in wine. The chalky soil is packed with minerals, and the gentle slopes of the hillsides are perfectly angled to receive the full benefit of the sun. A little farther

north, and the wines could not attain their full power; farther south, they would lose in elegance and finesse. The two rather rugged lines of hillsides, the Côte de Nuits and the Côte de Beaune, stretch from below Dijon down to the little town of Santenay—no more than 48 km (30 miles) in all (*map, page 88*). The community appellations and *grand cru* vineyards of the Côte d'Or are listed separately for easy reference (see *boxes*).

The Côte de Beaune is the southern half of the Côte d'Or. Although most of the wine is red, including the well-loved Beaune, Pommard and Volnay wines, the greatest glories of the Côte are its supreme white Burgundies—Corton-Charlemagne and those from the communities of Puligny-Montrachet, Chassagne-Montrachet and Meursault. The vines that produce the great white wines are grown in the most favourable type of soil for white grapes: a base of hard rock covered with a thin layer of earth and a whitish marl. This type of soil predominates in the southern part of the Côte de Beaune, which is unofficially named Côte de Blancs or Côte de Meursault. The white Chardonnay grape is used exclusively for the white wines. As in the Côte de Nuits, the Pinot Noir grape is grown for red wines.

The taste and character of great white Burgundies are hard to convey. They do not have more than a faint family resemblance to the lesser breeds of their own kind. The great wines are complex, full-bodied, rich but dry. Their other striking features include the colour—extremely pale when young, but ageing to deep honey gold; the powerful nose; the long finish that is not only in the drinking—its scent can linger in an empty glass. Perhaps one comes nearest to the Burgundy essence by speaking of texture—there is density in the wine, a succulence, an invitation to chew, a suggestion of almond, hazelnut, earth and truffle.

At the most northerly end of the Côte de Beaune, the two communities of Ladoix-Serrigny and Pernand-Vergelesses have some fine vineyards, producing both red and white wines. Some of the best wine from Ladoix-Serrigny is marketed under the grander label of its neighbour Aloxe-Corton; the name Ladoix-Serrigny rarely appears on a bottle, and the community's lesser wines are sold as Côte de Beaune-Villages. Pernand-Vergelesses produces red and white wines, and has five *premiers crus*—the most prized is Ile des Vergelesses. Again the lesser red wines of Pernand-Vergelesses are often labelled Côte de Beaune-Villages.

Aloxe-Corton (the x pronounced like a soft s) is a *grand cru* community. Apart from Corton-Charlemagne, most Corton wines are red. Corton is the sole red *grand cru* of the Côte de Beaune, an overwhelming wine with all the depth and splendour of the grandees of the Côte de Nuits.

Some Corton wine comes from the vineyard called Le Corton; some from a number of other vineyards, which add their respective names to that of Corton, as in Corton Clos du Roi, Corton Les Bressandes and Corton Les Chaumes, all *grands crus*. Some of these vineyards are classified as *grand cru* in part only, and *premier cru* in other parts. For example, Corton Clos du Roi is a *grand cru*, Aloxe-Corton Clos du Roi is a *premier cru*. When the name Corton precedes any other name on the label, the wine is of *grand cru* classification and should be outstanding.

The *grands crus* of Corton-Charlemagne and Charlemagne are two of the Côte de Beaune's great white wines. They can be huge wines when drunk in maturity, firm, even steely, with a depth of flavours. The community also has nearly 30 *premiers crus*—the most renowned are Les Marechaudes and Les Renardes.

Chorey-les-Beaune has no classified vineyards. Its wines, nearly all red, are sold under the community name or as Côtes de Beaune-Villages. They should be drunk young.

Savigny-les-Beaune produces five *premiers crus*. Predominantly red, the Savigny *premiers crus* can be lovely wines—elegant, fragrant and on the light side.

Beaune makes more wine than any other community of the Côte d'Or and the charming old town of Beaune, with its gabled houses and cobbled streets, is the wine capital of the Burgundy region. The traditional wine auction is held every November at the 15th-century charity hospital, the Hospice de Beaune. The wines under auction come from the Hospice's own vineyards, many of them *premiers*

crus of Beaune; the ancient institution has also been endowed with parcels of some *grands crus* Cortons; prices obtained are always very high.

Beaune has over 30 *premiers crus*. Most of the wine is red, and the general character of Beaune wine is fruity, full-bodied and uncomplicated. There are, however, marked differences in style among the finest *premiers crus*, which range from round and full-bodied to light, elegant and delicate. Some of the most outstanding *crus* wines are the full, suave Les Grèves; Grèves L'Enfant Jesus, which has an exceptional elegance and finesse; the robust Theurons; Les Fèves, which is a more delicate wine with an intense aroma; Les Bressandes; and the full-bodied red and white Clos des Mouches.

Pommard, located to the south of Beaune, also has a wealth of *premiers crus*. Sadly, the popularity of these wines outside France has been abominably abused—partly because of the easily remembered, easily pronounced names. Not so many years ago, a great deal more Pommard was marketed than was grown inside the community; the wines were often heavy, heady and murky, and they gave Burgundy a bad name. Nowadays, following a tightening of the appellation laws, things are much improved. True Pommard is firm and deeply coloured with a sturdy character. Among the best *crus* are Les Epenots and Les Rugiens.

Volnay is the last major red wine community in the Côte de Beaune. Volnay is the most elegant and lacy of the red wines of the Côte de Beaune; the wine is suave, scented, round, and it matures more quickly than most red Burgundies. Of the 20-odd *premiers crus*, Les Caillerets, Les Champans and Les Chevrets are considered to be the best.

Monthélie is not a well-known community; however, it makes excellent wines, mainly red and with a very little white. It has about 10 *premiers crus*, relatively modestly priced and of a high quality.

Auxey-Duresses is another little-known community and its wines are therefore relatively cheap. It has several recently classified *premiers crus*. The white wines have a touch of the character of Meursault; at their best, they are charming drunk young and also age well.

Côte d'Or Community Appellations

Côte de Beaune
Ladoix
Aloxe-Corton
Chorey-les-Beaune
Pernand-Vergelesses
Savigny-les-Beaune
Beaune
Pommard
Volnay
Monthélie
Auxey-Duresses
St. Romain
St. Aubin
Meursault
Blagny
Puligny-Montrachet
Chassagne-Montrachet
Santenay
Cheilly-les-Maranges
Sampigny-les-Maranges
Dezize-les-Maranges

Côte de Nuits
Fixin
Gevrey-Chambertin
Morey-St. Denis
Chambolle-Musigny
Vougeot
Vosne-Romanée
Nuits-St. Georges

Meursault is one of the greatest white Burgundies. Compared with the wines of Puligny-Montrachet, Chassagne-Montrachet and Corton-Charlemagne, Meursault is the softest and roundest of the four, often referred to as a feminine wine. It is dry, but not bone-dry—a chewy wine, nutty and mealy like some celestial porridge. Rather oddly perhaps, none of the Meursault vineyards are classified as *grands crus*, and yet their dozen or so *premiers crus* are outstanding, and consistent in quality. The most regarded names are Les Perrières, Les Charmes, Les Genevrières, La Goutte d'Or and Le Poruzot.

Blagny is a small community adjacent to the south-east corner of Meursault. It makes a white wine of similar character, sold as Meursault Blagny or Blagny. The commune has three *premiers crus*.

The vineyards of Montrachet, the great white Burgundy, straddle the two communities of Puligny-Montrachet and Chassagne-Montrachet. Here, everything has come together to create that mysterious substance, an overwhelmingly great wine. The words, the eulogies, the analogies that have been heaped upon Montrachet for the last two centuries are fully merited. The wine has everything one looks for in a great white Burgundy, only more so. It is bigger, it has a deeper intensity of flavours and a longer finish, and it is longer-lived.

Altogether there are five *grands crus*: Le Montrachet, Chevalier-Montrachet, Bâtard-Montrachet, Bienvenues-Bâtard-Montrachet and Criots-Bâtard-Montrachet—and they have only 30 hectares (75 acres) of precious land between them. Chevalier-Montrachet is at least as fine as Le Montrachet and the other four Montrachet *grands crus* can be immense wines too, particularly Bâtard-Montrachet. The vineyard of Bâtard is also shared by the two communities. Chevalier-Montrachet and Bienvenues-Bâtard-Montrachet belong wholly to Puligny, and Criots-Bâtard-Montrachet belongs wholly to Chassagne.

The communities also produce more than 20 *premiers crus*. Les Combettes, Les Pucelles, Les Caillerets and Les Folatières are generally regarded as the leading *premiers crus*. Light-bodied red wine of great elegance is made in Chassagne.

The greatness of the Côte d'Or ends with Chassagne-Montrachet, although much sound-to-excellent wine is made in the four southern communities, Santenay, Cheilly-les-Maranges, Dezize-les-Maranges and Sampigny-les-Maranges.

Côte de Nuits wines are red, with rare exceptions; the soil is clay with chalk, rich in minerals; the vineyards face south-east, catching the early sun; the grape is the noble Pinot Noir. About a third of the entire output, which greatly varies with the weather and the years, is sold locally; around a tenth is kept as owners' reserves,

leaving just over half for French consumption and exports.

The wines have a family resemblance with considerable difference in colour, bouquet, taste, stature, staying power. More than 20 Côte de Nuits wines are classified as *grand cru*, the top Burgundy appellation; and more than 100 as *premier cru*—officially just below *grand cru* in quality. There are eight main wine villages, or communities, in the Côte de Nuits. The most illustrious wines come from Gevrey-Chambertin, Chambolle-Musigny, Vougeot, Vosne-Romanée. The lesser-known communities, however, are often the near equals of their more renowned neighbours.

The first community, on entering the Nuits from the north, is Fixin. It has six *premiers crus* wines. Fixin Clos de la Perrière and Fixin Clos du Chapitre are considered the best.

Gevrey-Chambertin has nine *grands crus*, Chambertin and Chambertin-Clos de Bèze indubitably heading the list. Their sizes are only 13 and 15 hectares (33 and 37 acres) respectively, while between them the two vineyards have nearly 30 owners. The other seven *grands crus* wines are Latricières-Chambertin, Charmes-Chambertin, Mazoyères-Chambertin (often labelled under the Charmes-Chambertin appellation), Mazis-Chambertin, Ruchottes-Chambertin, Chapelle-Chambertin and Griotte-Chambertin. There are about 25 *premiers crus*, of which Gevrey-Chambertin Clos St. Jacques and Clos des Varoilles are outstanding, and are said to merit *grand cru* rank.

Morey-St. Denis is a less well-known community, but it has five excellent *grands crus* to its credit: Clos de la Roche, Clos St. Denis, Clos de Tart, Clos des Lambrays and a part of the Bonnes Mares vineyard, which straddles the communities of Morey-St. Denis and Chambolle-Musigny. There are about 25 *premiers crus*, many of high quality, available at relatively low prices and well worth seeking out. A fine white wine, Monts Luisants, is also made in Morey-St. Denis.

Chambolle-Musigny has two *grands crus;* one is the community's share of Bonnes Mares, the other is the incomparable Musigny, a vineyard of only 10 hect-

Côte d'Or Grand Cru Vineyards

Côte de Beaune
Montrachet
Bâtard-Montrachet
Criots-Bâtard-Montrachet
Chevalier-Montrachet
Bienvenues-Bâtard-Montrachet
Corton
Corton-Charlemagne
Charlemagne

Côte de Nuits
Romanée-Conti
La Tache
Romanée St. Vivant
Grands Échezeaux
Échezeaux
Richebourg
La Romanée
Clos de Vougeot
Bonnes Mares
Musigny
Clos de la Roche
Clos St. Denis
Clos des Lambrays
Clos de Tart
Chambertin-Clos de Bèze
Chambertin
Charmes-Chambertin
Mazoyères-Chambertin
Chapelle-Chambertin
Griotte-Chambertin
Latricières-Chambertin
Mazis-Chambertin
Ruchottes-Chambertin

ares (25 acres). If Chambertin is the last word in grandeur, Musigny is the last word in elegance and lucidity. Some of the 20-odd *premiers crus* are also marvellous wines—above all, the delightfully named Musigny Les Amoureuses and Musigny Les Charmes. The community makes a small quantity of white wine called Musigny Blanc—a wine of great finesse.

Vougeot has one *grand cru*—from the famous Clos de Vougeot walled vineyard that encloses the historic castle, Château de Vougeot. It is a large vineyard of 50 hectares (123 acres), the largest *grand cru* vineyard in the whole of Burgundy;

but it is divided among about 80 growers and shippers, who sell under their various labels, with the consequent fluctuations in style and quality. Clos de Vougeot can be a very great wine. Outside the walls of the Clos de Vougeot vineyard there are a mere 5 hectares (13 acres) of land under vines. There are three Vougeot *premiers crus*—including Clos Blanc de Vougeot, a very fine white wine.

Flagey-Échezeaux is one of the Burgundian anomalies. Although this community produces two full-ranking *grands crus,* Grands Échezeaux and Échezeaux, its wines are included in the Vosne-Romanée appellation. The word Flagey is not used on wine labels because the village of Flagey-Échezeaux is situated at a distance from its quality vineyards, in flat country where not much wine of real distinction is produced.

Vosne-Romanée is often regarded as the very summit of Burgundy. Romanée-Conti, the top *grand cru*, is a wine of immense character and stature, nor do La Tache and Richebourg lag far behind in splendour. The Vosne wines—including the other two *grands crus* of the community, La Romanée and Romanée St. Vivant—sometimes have everything in perfect balance: backbone and velvet softness, vigour and finesse, opulence and delicacy in an extraordinary profusion of spice, scent and flavours.

The vineyards are tiny; the consequent rarity of these wines is extreme, and so, unfortunately, are their prices. Both Romanée-Conti and La Tache have a single owner—the Domaine de la Romanée-Conti, which also has holdings in the Richebourg and Échezeaux vineyards. Vosne-Romanée has about 10 *premiers crus* which share some of the resplendent characteristics of the commune.

Nuits-St. Georges, the last and southernmost of the Côte community appellations, has some extremely fine vineyards, producing an abundance of *premiers crus*—almost 40 in all. Nuits wines are usually big and high-flavoured and age well. Les St. Georges, Les Vaucrains, Les Cailles, Les Porets and Les Pruliers are among the most highly regarded Nuits wines. The community also produces a fine white *premier cru*—La Perrière, made from Pinot Blanc grapes. The back

country—where the hills have a less favourable exposure to the sun—produces very decent red and white wine, from Pinot Noir, Gamay, Chardonnay and Aligoté grapes, under the lesser appellation of Bourgogne Hautes-Côtes de Nuits.

Coteaux
Small hills.

Côtes de Bordeaux St. Macaire
A Bordeaux area and appellation on the right bank of the Garonne, bordering on the eastern end of the Premières Côtes de Bordeaux (*map, page 85*), and producing sweet white wine. The red wines are sold as Bordeaux or Bordeaux Supérieur.

Côtes de Bourg see *Bourg*

Côtes Canon-Fronsac see *Fronsac*

Côtes du Rhône
The vineyards of the Côtes du Rhône are probably the oldest in France. They produce red, white and rosé wines of considerable variety, including some—Châteauneuf-du-Pape, Hermitage, Côte Rôtie—that rank with those of Bordeaux and Burgundy among the very finest wines of France.

The river Rhône, which has its source in the same Swiss glacier as the Rhine, runs westwards through the Alps to Lyons, where it is joined by the Saône for its 300 km (190 mile) journey south to the Mediterranean. The Côtes du Rhône vineyards lie in the long narrow valley formed by the river between the mountains of the Massif Central to the west and the Alps to the east. They stretch from Vienne to Avignon, a distance of 225 km (140 miles), and fall into two areas (*map, page 87*).

In the northern area, from Vienne to Valence, the vines follow the river closely, clinging to steep granite terraces that catch the sun. In the southern vineyards, which begin just above Orange, the vines grow on broad, sun-baked terraces surrounded by the olive groves and herb-scented hillsides of Provence. Although granite remains the dominant element, the soil in the south is more varied and can be sandy, chalky or alluvial. Many of the southern vineyards—especially those of Châteauneuf-du-Pape—are full of large,

smooth stones that store the daytime heat of the sun and feed it back to the vines at night from below, protecting them from the danger of spring frosts and contributing to perfect ripening.

Rhône summers are long and consistently warm but, even so, the quality of the vintages varies because rain is variable and because the notorious Mistral wind that blows down the valley from the north can parch the grapes. To protect them from the wind, the vines are pruned low or protected by trees.

In any description of Rhône wines, the same adjectives are reiterated; full-bodied, vigorous, robust, assertive—qualities that are owed partly to the stony, granite soil and hot, arid summers, and partly to the type of grapes and the various methods of viniculture.

In the northern region of the Rhône, the principal red grape variety is the Syrah, which produces full-bodied, long-lasting, robust wines with an intense bouquet, including the best reds of the northern Rhône—Côte Rôtie, St. Joseph, Hermitage and Cornas. The most widely planted red grape in the southern Côtes du Rhône is the Grenache, which is used for the ordinary wines with general Côtes du Rhône appellations, and—in various combinations with other varieties—for the wines of Châteauneuf-du-Pape.

Among the most important white grapes is Viognier, grown only in the Condrieu region south of Vienne, where it makes the much-prized Condrieu and Château Grillet white wines, and contributes to the red Côte Rôtie wines of the same area. The Viognier grape is small and delicate and its yield is modest. The most distinctive characteristic of a Viognier wine is its strongly scented bouquet. The Marsanne and Roussane are used in the more robust white wines of Hermitage, Crozes Hermitage and St. Joseph. The Muscat grape is grown in Beaumes de Venise to make a sweet dessert wine—sometimes fortified—with an outstanding bouquet and a strong fruit flavour.

More than 1.5 million hectolitres (33,000,000 gallons) of wine are produced in the Rhône. All but 50,000 hectolitres (1,100,000 gallons) or so bear a general Côtes du Rhône appellation, with or without an additional regional or community name, depending on slight variations in the alcoholic strength of the wine. The appellation Côtes du Rhône-Villages is an accolade reserved for about 14 specific communities. For the best Rhône wines, there are separate appellations. The most esteemed of these are Côte Rôtie, Condrieu, St. Joseph and Hermitage in the northern Côtes du Rhône, and Châteauneuf-du-Pape in the south.

Just south of Vienne, the vineyards of the Côte Rôtie—literally, roasted hillside—are the most northerly of the Côtes du Rhône. The wines have great distinction, an intense flowery bouquet and a deep colour. The Viognier grape is used in small amounts (usually less than 10 per cent) with the Syrah here, to lend finesse.

At Condrieu, the wines typically have a deep, cool scent of fresh almonds and peaches. Within Condrieu, the tiny vineyard of Château Grillet has its own appellation for a white wine that is made in small quantities from the Viognier grape. The neighbouring St. Joseph wines may be red or white, light-bodied yet luscious and of great purity.

The widely known Hermitage wines are noble and vigorous. They age well, becoming softer and more delicate in maturity. Red Hermitage needs ample time to develop; wines from a good vintage may take 40 years to realize their full potential. The golden-coloured white Hermitage wines are dry and fruity, with a solid structure and a distinctive perfume. Wines from the neighbouring Crozes Hermitage vineyards can be full-bodied but they are less distinguished and more rustic than Hermitage.

Cornas wines come from a steep hillside sheltered from the Mistral, where the sun bakes the soil (cornas is a Celtic word meaning scorched earth) and the grapes ripen early. The wine is very dark in colour—almost black when young—and repays long keeping. Like many other fine red wines, it is hard in youth, but softens in maturity.

The sparkling white Clairette de Die comes from an isolated strip of vineyards to the east along the river Drôme, one of the Rhône's tributaries, and a sparkling white is also made at St. Peray, immediately south of the Cornas vineyards.

The reputation of southern Rhône wines is dominated by Châteauneuf-du-Pape. The extensive vineyards, established in the 14th century by the popes of Avignon, are situated below the papal summer palace. They cover about 3,000 hectares (7,400 acres) and usually produce some 1,500 hectolitres (33,000 gallons) of wine a year.

The wines from this large area vary in quality according to the different vinification methods and the grape varieties chosen by various growers, but the main characteristics of Châteauneuf-du-Pape are its deep colour, full body and typically "gamey" bouquet. Most producers use six or seven of the 13 different grape varieties permitted by the *appellation contrôlée* rules. Most Châteauneufs can be drunk at four or five years old, but if from a good year they may need as many as 15 years before they are at their best.

Among the other appellations in the southern Côtes du Rhône, Gigondas is a more rustic and aggressive wine than Châteauneuf, with less finesse; Tavel produces clean, fruity rosés from the Grenache grape; Tavel's near neighbour, Lirac, makes another full-bodied rosé, as well as a light red; and other light, fruity reds, whites and rosés come under the appellation of the Côtes du Ventoux.

Cross
A term used in viniculture to denote the result of crossing one variety of the species *Vitis vinifera* (*page 5*) with another variety of the same species (see *Hybrid*).

Cru see *Growth*

Cyprus
Wine-making in Cyprus has a history 4,000 years long. The wines of Cyprus are mentioned in Homer's epics and the Bible, and the island is today the most successful wine producer in the eastern Mediterranean, with a large domestic market and a flourishing export trade. Cypriots refer to the port of Limassol, which is the centre of the wine trade, as the Bordeaux of Cyprus. Most of the wine is good, ordinary table wine—strong, dark reds; rosés with character, and still and semi-sparkling white wines. The island also produces sherry-type wines and the renowned, sweet dessert wine called Commandaria.

The climate is very hot and dry, but the Troodos mountains in the west of the island attract rain, and nearly all the Cypriot vineyards lie on the south-facing mountain slopes. The vines receive the benefit of full sun together with the cooler temperatures that prevail above the sun-baked plains. The patchwork of small, terraced vineyards are generally farmed by peasant growers, who sell most of their grapes to big wine firms.

Phylloxera has never occurred on Cyprus and, in order to avoid the risk of contamination from European vines, most growers have remained faithful to their native, ungrafted *vinifera* varieties. The three traditional vines are the black Mavron, the white Xynisteri and the intensely perfumed Muscat of Alexandria. In recent years, however, some European grafted vines have been introduced under rigorously supervised quarantine conditions in an attempt to improve the quality of the wines.

The red wines of the island are dark, robust and high in tannin. The rosé wine, known as *kokkineli*, is usually quite dry with a deep colour and is full-bodied and high in alcohol.

White wines account for only a quarter of the island's output, and tend to be less successful; the hot climate produces flat-tasting wines, low in acidity, that oxidise easily. Nevertheless, selections from the new plantings of European vines, as well as the introduction of modern techniques and equipment, have contributed to the production of better quality white wines. White wine production is centred around Paphos, and Pitsilia is the best-known district for white Xynisteri.

Commandaria dessert wine has been made on Cyprus for centuries. It is produced in a limited area on the southern slopes of the Troodos mountains from black Mavron and white Xynisteri grapes, which are spread out and dried in the sun to concentrate their sugar. The mass-produced wine of today is no more than a pleasant, not particularly interesting, dessert wine. However, a small quantity of superb wine is still vinified in the traditional manner—aged for at least 30 years (sometimes in earthenware amphorae) and often blended by a method similar to the solera system used to make sherry (q.v.). Although the wine may contain four times as much sugar as port (q.v.), it is not cloyingly sweet. A really fine old Commandaria is deep mahogany or amber-coloured with an alcohol content of up to 25 per cent and a powerfully concentrated flavour.

Denominação de Origem see *Portugal; Wine Laws*

Denominacion de Origen see *Spain; Wine Laws*

Denominazione d'Origine Controllata see *Italy; Wine Laws*

Domaine (property)

A *domaine* that belongs to a single proprietor may contain more than one appellation. For example, the owners of the Domaine de la Romanée-Conti are proprietors of the Côte de Nuits appellations, Romanée-Conti, La Tache and parts of Grands Échezeaux, Échezeaux, Richebourg, Romanée St. Vivant and Montrachet.

Eiswein (ice wine)

Wine made from grapes that have been picked while frozen on the vine, rushed to the winery and crushed before they thaw. A proportion of the water content of the grapes is discarded in the form of ice crystals, and the juice from which the wine is made is therefore more concentrated than usual. The resulting wine is sweet, rare, rich—and expensive.

Entre-Deux-Mers

The largest of the Bordeaux wine districts, situated between the rivers Dordogne and Garonne—the name literally means Between Two Seas (*map, page 85*). The district used to produce a vast amount of mediocre light white, somewhat sweet, wine. In the 1970s, the growers turned to making dry wine based on the Sauvignon Blanc grape variety, which resulted in a much improved—and still improving—product: a pleasant clean aperitif or shellfish wine.

Only white wines bear the appellation Entre-Deux-Mers; the red wines produced in the area are sold as Bordeaux or Bordeaux Supérieur.

Fortified Wines

Sweet or dry wines that are strengthened by the addition of distilled spirits. Fortified wines normally have an alcoholic content of 17 to 18.5 per cent. The spirits are sometimes added to the must during fermentation, thus arresting the natural fermentation process and leaving a residue of unfermented sugar in the wine. Most port wines (q.v.) are made in this way, with a single addition of spirits to the must. Banyuls (see *Languedoc and Roussillon*) is made similarly, except that the degree of fermentation is controlled by several progressive additions of spirits.

Madeira wines (q.v.) are usually fortified during fermentation, or sometimes after the fermentation has been completed—as are some sweet wines in many other countries.

Sherries (q.v.), on the other hand, are always fermented until all their sugar has been converted into alcohol before they are fortified to stabilize them.

France

Who says wine, thinks France. France is the heartland of wine. By quantity; by diversity; by quality.

In most years, France produces more wine than any other country in the world; only Italy sometimes equals or surpasses her output. Nearly 1,215,000 hectares (3,000,000 acres) of vine yield an average of 75,000,000 hectolitres (1,650,000,000 gallons) a year—10 billion bottles or about a quarter of the wine produced in the whole world. Annual domestic consumption is calculated at 140 bottles per head—quite an amount, considering every man, woman and child in the whole of France is accounted for.

Wine and vine have been part of the fabric of French life for century upon century. The European vine, *Vitis vinifera*, is indigenous and wine has been made in France since well before the arrival of the Romans. You cannot sit down at a family table without finding beside the soup and the bread a bottle of wine, nor drive along a French road for many minutes (except in Brittany and the extreme north) without seeing vineyards.

The scale of cultivation is never large. Two hundred hectares (500 acres) in one ownership is rare, and some of the most renowned vineyards are minute. The *grand cru* Romanée-Conti, for example—which is considered by many people to be the greatest of all Burgundy red wines—issues from just one tiny vineyard of 1.85 hectares (4½ acres) in extent. There is an army of peasant owners, smallholding growers, *châteaux, domaines*, co-operatives and consortia.

The number of grape varieties, too, is wonderful and bewildering. Centuries of accumulated experience have determined which types do best in each region, and (at least for the best wines) complex legislation specifies which grapes may be used and even how they should be pruned.

Methods of cultivation and vinification vary, and not only from region to region. If a few individual growers follow new short cuts or sloppy old habits, many combine the best and wisest of the local traditions with the most helpful of recent scientific innovations.

No other country produces as wide a variety of types of wine: they are as diverse as the landscapes of France that give them birth, from the damp Atlantic seaboard to the sweltering Mediterranean hillsides and the cool Alpine foothills. Extremely sophisticated wine laws control the profusion with a rigorous system of identification according to place of origin (see *French Wine Appellations*).

Most of the huge flood of French wine is ordinary by fact and by legal definition. More than 80 per cent of the output is not of sufficient distinction to qualify for a local appellation of origin and is sold as *vin de table*. (After all, perfectly matched site, soil and microclimate are rare in nature, and so are the human integrity and devotion required to do them justice.) But these unsung and anonymous wines have their uses: when they are sound and honestly made, *vins de consommation courrante* (wines for current consumption) make pleasant enough drinking, in an offhand, daily way.

The better, and smaller, part of French wine production ranges from good through distinguished to very, very good and on up to the *ne plus ultra* of the world renowned *grands crus classés*. The great wine-producing regions of France (dealt with in separate entries under their own names) are Bordeaux, Burgundy, Cham pagne, the Loire, the Rhône and Alsace (*map, page 84*). But many other parts of the country too produce wines of specific character that add to the immense diversity of wine in France. Some of the more important areas are the Jurançon, Roussillon and Languedoc regions of southwest France; Bergerac, lying south-east of Bordeaux, Provence, which produces some fine complex red wines as well as whites and rosés; and the cooler Savoie and Jura regions near the Swiss border.

Expectedly, France exports wine—four hundred million bottles a year. A large proportion of this consists of the country's best wines, for the ordinary ones are usually drunk locally or used for making spirits and fortified wines. During the 1970s, the chief markets for French wines were West Germany, the United Kingdom, Belgium, Holland, Luxembourg and the U.S.A.

More unexpectedly, France imports twice as much as she exports. Her own enormous production, when depleted by export, does not entirely cover home consumption. The imported wines used to come chiefly from her North African possessions; now, since Algerian independence in 1962, they come generally from other Mediterranean countries, especially Italy and Spain. Such imports are usually strong ordinary wines, that are blended before bottling to stretch or strengthen some of the rather insipid wines of France's mass-producing southern departments.

Franken (Franconia)

A small but qualitatively important wine region of Germany to the east of the Rhineland, producing about 3½ per cent of the German total. The vineyards lie along both sides of the river Main (*map, page 83*). The wines of Franconia are the only German white wines that do not come in tall narrow bottles; instead they are sold in flat squat flasks called *Bocksbeutel.*

The climate is continental, the soil sandstone, lime, loess, clay and chalk. Practically all the wine produced is white. Franconia is the one region of Germany where the best wines come from the Silvaner grape, which accounts for over 40 per cent of the vines. Other varieties are Müller Thurgau and Riesling.

The general style and taste of Franconian wines are more akin to French dry white wines than to most other German wines. They are dry and firm, and can be very big. These excellent wines age well; unlike so many German wines, they are best when drunk with food.

There are three districts (*Bereiche*), Mainviereck, Maindreieck and Steiger Wald; within them some 150 individual vineyards (*Einzellagen*) are grouped into 17 greater vineyards (*Grosslagen*). The holdings are mostly small and worked through co-operatives, although there are some large estates too.

Near to the city of Würzburg lie the vineyards of Stein, home of the famous Steinwein. Although Steinwein is sometimes mysteriously interpreted in English as "stone wine", in German the word simply indicates wine from Stein. The vineyards are very stony, however, and the limestone of the soil imparts to the greenish wines the special character that has made them so well known.

French Wine Appellations

France has the oldest-established and most sophisticated body of wine law in the world. The laws define four ranks of quality in wines: AOC wines, VDQS (*Vins Délimités de Qualité Supérieure*), *Vins de Pays* and *Vins de Table.* The top category, AOC, is short for *Appellation d'Origine Contrôlée* (also often abbreviated as AC or *Appellation Contrôlée*). The phrase might be freely translated as "controlled entitlement to a place name". It means that a given wine's entitlement or right to call itself a Beaujolais or an Anjou is under the control of the French government. To qualify for an appellation a wine has to conform to a precise set of rules worked out specifically for that area by the *Institut National des Appellations d'Origine des Vins et Eaux-de-Vie* (INAO)—the National Institute of Appellations of Origin of Wines and Spirits. The body was set up in 1935, and eventually completed the considerable task of making a complete wine map of France, creating order out of many varied and conflicting traditions.

The ground rule of the appellation laws is geographical—the wine must be grown and made (not necessarily bottled) in the region or community (or, in some cases,

the individual wine estate) that the label lays claim to. There are about 300 AOC wines in France (perhaps 15 per cent of the country's annual production is of appellation standard) but there are infinite graduations in the AOC hierarchy: the more specific and limited the area, the more prestigious the appellation, and the more rigorous the conditions for obtaining and retaining it. A simple, generic *Appellation Bordeaux Contrôlée* tells us that the wine has come from anywhere within that region of huge wine output. *AC Médoc* limits provenance to one highly regarded district of Bordeaux. *AC Haut-Médoc* narrows it further to a part—the best part—of the Médoc, and *AC Pauillac* limits it further still to one of the great individual wine communities of the Haut-Médoc. In principle, it is possible for the same wine to qualify for as many as four different appellations, from the most general to the most specific—but the grower would, of course, always choose the most specific and therefore the most prestigious of them for his label.

Next, AOC wine must be made from the right variety of grapes for the area. The choice of grape varieties that may be used in a given appellation has been determined by tradition—an evolution and adaptation over the centuries of given varieties to specific climates and soil structures. The purpose of legislation is to enforce these traditions which are known to produce the best wines. Certain wines may be made only from a single variety: the *grands crus*, *premiers crus* and community appellations for red wine from the Côte d'Or, for instance, are made only from Pinot Noir (of which there are a number of strains, some producing better results than others), but the simple appellation, Bourgogne passetoutgrains, is a mixture of Pinot and Gamay. White Côte de Beaune *grands crus*, *premiers crus* and community appellations must be made only from Chardonnay, but the simple appellation Bourgogne Aligoté may be made from the Aligoté grape either alone or in combination with Chardonnay. No grape other than the Sauvignon Blanc may enter into Pouilly-Fumé or Sancerre; Chinon, Bourgueil and St. Nicolas de Bourgueil are made from Cabernet Franc to the exclusion of all other grapes.

There is also a limit to the permissible amount of wine produced, on the established viticultural principle that the lower the yield, the higher the quality. Low yields are induced by close planting, pruning, scant manuring, no watering—irrigation is forbidden in all AOC areas. Allotted yields are often as low as 35 or even 25 hectolitres (770 or 550 gallons) per hectare ($2\frac{1}{2}$ acres).

Lastly, the laws lay down the processes and methods of cultivation and vinification, as well as the raising of the wine during its formative years according to best local usage. Curiously, an actual tasting test for AOC wines was not required until recently. Now they are also supposed to pass a tasting panel.

The next rank, VDQS, *Vins Délimités de Qualité Supérieure* (Superior Quality Wines from a Limited Area) are the products of good if less distinguished regions. The qualifying rules run on the same lines but allow more scope, for example in choice of grapes and size of maximum yields. The grapes can—but need not—be more ordinary, that is less delicate, easier to tend, or more prolific. On the other hand, VDQS wines have always had to pass an official tasting test. The category was inaugurated in 1949, and the number of VDQS wines is increasing as standards improve locally. Some of the wines are very good.

Vins de Pays (Country Wines) are allowed an even wider choice of grapes, and even higher yields. Some growers, human nature being what it is, exploit this latitude, but many succeed in making quite delicious local wines. These may not always be easy to find; they do exist.

Vins de Table (Table Wines), the bottom rank as far as classification goes, must conform to certain reasonable standards of drinkability. *Vins de table* may be very good indeed, especially if they happen to be made in an appellation area, but they are bottled as *vins de table* by the grower because they were produced from vines too young to be accepted by the appellation rules.

Outside the four-part classification are the *Vins Ordinaires,* or *Vins de Consommation Courrante,* which are merely labelled by their alcohol content. These would be legion were they not sold under brand names. They are cheap wines, cheaper sometimes than a bottle of mineral water. The quality of these wines has improved greatly over the past 20 years.

Fronsac

A small district of Bordeaux on the right bank of the Dordogne (*map, page 85*), producing good red wine. There are two appellations, Fronsac and (the better one) Côtes Canon-Fronsac.

Frontignan see *Languedoc and Roussillon*

Gaillac

An appellation region in the Tarn valley west of Albi, in south-west France (*map, page 84*). Gaillac is a source of pleasant, refreshing white wines. The principal grape variety is Mauzac, supplemented by small amounts of l'En de l'El and Ondenc, as well as traditional Bordelaise varieties such as Cabernet Franc, Cabernet Sauvignon and Merlot. In the main the appellation Gaillac signifies dry wines and Gaillac Premières Côtes denotes the sweet wines traditional to the region. Some sparkling wines are also made.

Germany

River valleys, vine-covered hills turning to gold under the autumn sun, cheerful vintners, tall-stemmed glasses, cool slender bottles, flowery, fragrant and graceful wines—such is the image of the German wine land. It is a true one. The vineyards of Germany are river vineyards lying along the valleys of the Rhine and its tributaries, the Mosel, Main and Neckar; the men who work the vines are busy and devoted; the countryside is agreeable to the eye; the wines are lovely.

Yet Germany is not a wine country in the spontaneous way of France and Italy and Spain, where wine gushes forth in floods and is drunk by everyone with their food every day. Wine in Germany is scarce and hard won—by the wit and work of man and the tenacity of the vine. Much of the country lies too far north for vines to flourish. German wine is made only in a few south-western regions; it comes not in floods but in a trickle—perhaps a tenth of the output of France or Italy. Much of the trickle is very good, a minute part of it is exquisite. German Spitzenweine (peak wines) are great, unmatched in their own style, equal in rank to the white Burgundies and *grands crus* Sauternes of France.

Almost 90 per cent of German wine is white. Red wines do not do very well in such northern latitudes. Those that are made are rarely seen on the international market, though some, like Assmanshausen from the Rheingau region and from Baden, have a reputation in Germany.

The German wine lands lie between two climates—a humid maritime climate in the west and a drier, colder-in-winter, hotter-in-summer continental climate to the east. The great rivers of Germany, especially the Rhine, influence the temperature and the conditions, so that the land on their banks has something approaching a maritime climate. Without the moderating effect of the rivers, much of the land would not be suitable at all for wine-growing. With the grapes growing so close to their northern limit, local variations—a sunny bend in the river, a slope safe from the wind—can make a tremendous difference. By the same token, every nuance of weather has a direct effect on the wine, and no year is like another. In fine ones the grapes ripen late and rich; in bad they do not and are carted off to be made into the German sparkling wine called Sekt. There are also some favourable trends in the overall weather pattern, such as the frequency of warm early Junes (when the vine should flower) and long fine autumns; snow in winter is welcome as it protects the roots; morning mists soften the cold; and the water of the rivers retains and reflects the weak autumn sun. But disaster is always lurking—spring frost or too much rain at vintage time can spell disaster.

Yet there are advantages as well as problems in growing wines in a cool climate, and German wine makers exploit these natural benefits by specializing in styles of wine that can be produced successfully only under their particular conditions. One result of the latitude, for example, is that the sun does not ripen the grapes as fully as in a southern climate. With less grape sugar to be converted to alcohol, German wines are naturally less potent. But instead of adding sugar to their wine as a matter of course, German wine makers have made a virtue of its lightness and forbid chaptalization (*page 13*)—called in German *Anreicherung*—for all the better categories of wine.

The gentleness of the sun in this part of the world also ensures that some acidity remains in the grape at harvest time. The acidity is intrinsic to a good German wine, and is responsible for its clean finish and bite. But, unless it is counterbalanced by sweetness, it tends to result in an unpleasantly sour wine. Some German wines have residual sugar at the end of fermentation, but most are sweetened before bottling by the addition of natural unfermented grape juice.

Calculating the degree of sweetness is one of the German wine maker's most critical tasks. Just as in a fine red wine one looks for a perfect balance of fruit, tannin and acidity, so in a Rhine wine or Mosel one looks for a harmony of fruit, acidity and sweetness. Nowadays, in response to demand for a drier style, a number of German wines are being made with very little added grape juice, but few of these wines are a complete success; without the sweetness to balance the equation, they can seem sour and thin.

Yet another result of the climate is that the grapes mature very slowly. Each extra day on the vines compounds the risk from rain and storms, but the long ripening gives the grapes time to develop complex and subtle flavours not produced in quickly ripened fruit. The Germans accentuate this characteristic by growing highly scented grapes, of which the Riesling is the supreme example.

Thus one can summarize by saying that German wines are relatively low in alcohol, high in scent and flavours (that characteristic floweriness); and there is nearly always an edge, at least, of sweetness. The faults of German wines are the obverse of their virtues—lightness can become wishy-washy, acidity may turn into sharpness, fruit can seem like a fruit salad, and the sweet edge may cloy.

The most pleasing German wines are nearly always made from the Riesling grape, a variety which under the right conditions produces wines of the utmost distinction. It is a tight, greenish little grape, not much to look at, and it needs an arid soil. Its flavour is flowery but never sickly, and balanced by good acidity.

About a quarter of all German vines are of the Riesling type. Why not more? Because it has serious disadvantages: low yield, late ripening, and a proneness to some diseases, which is exacerbated by the wet autumns so common in Germany. On the other hand, the Riesling grape puts up a good resistance to frost, which makes it a stayer that can be kept long enough on the vine to develop the *Botrytis cinerea* (*page 16*) that is essential in the making of a great sweet wine.

The other two major grape varieties are the Silvaner and Müller Thurgau. Respectively, 15 per cent and over 30 per cent of all vines planted belong to these varieties. The Silvaner (spelt Sylvaner in Alsace and elsewhere) is easier to grow, ripens earlier and yields twice as much as the Riesling, but the softer, blander wine is not in the same class.

The Müller Thurgau is a cross between the Riesling and the Silvaner, achieved in the 1890s by a Herr Hermann Müller, a Swiss from Thurgau, and much experimented on by wine scientists since. It is bred to combine some of the virtues of both parents; it yields well, ripens early and produces a mild, fast-maturing wine, less firm than a Riesling but with a good balance. There is a hint of Muscat in its taste. Its use in Germany is spreading.

Other grapes planted in much smaller quantities are the Ruländer (elsewhere known as Pinot Gris) which likes richer soil and makes fuller, deeper-coloured wines; Weisser Gutedel (alias Chasselas), producing light wines to be drunk young; the Kerner, another cross-breed from the Riesling and the (red) Trollinger grapes; the Scheurebe, a Silvaner Riesling cross (to be distinguished from the Müller Thurgau, which is a Riesling Silvaner cross) named after a Herr Scheu who produced it (*Rebe* is a vine); and the Morio Muscat, a cross between Silvaner and Pinot Blanc, which produces a wine with a curiously strong Muscat bouquet. Another white wine grape, the Elbling, of small distinction, is grown for making Sekt. The grapes grown for red wine are of far less importance: they are Blauer Portugieser, Blauer Trollinger and Blauer Spätburgunder (alias Pinot Noir).

To understand German wine, it helps to understand German drinking habits.

Except in the small wine-growing regions of the country, Germans are beer drinkers. Beer is the drink that goes with meals, so Germans do not think as the French do, in terms of what wine goes with what food. Most Mosel and Rhine wines are too light or too rich to partner a savoury dish, and not dry enough.

There are, of course, many exceptions. German wine goes well with, to think of but a few things, an omelette or a cheese soufflé, sausages, asparagus, ham. Few wines are nicer than a Mosel with a light luncheon, or a cool bottle of Hock with cold chicken. Germans drink the drier Franconian and Palatinate wines with pork, partridge and pheasant—and they can be splendidly successful.

Yet German wine is more often a wine for leisure, to be drunk with friends in an evening, round a table, in a garden; a summer wine to be enjoyed perhaps with a basket of strawberries or peaches. If it is one of the great Spitzenweine, it is to be savoured slowly on its own—lingered over, discussed as wine for wine's sake.

German wine makers are exceptionally unanimous in their approach; with few other countries is it possible to generalize to the same extent about the style of wine and how to enjoy it. But that is not to say variations do not exist. There are huge differences in quality, nuances in taste.

The taste of German wines varies from vineyard to vineyard, year to year, month to month of picking, indeed from barrel to barrel. Many vintners do not standardize the year's vintage, but treat individual barrels separately. The more fundamental differences in taste, however, are between the produce of different parts of the country, which are chiefly attributable to variations in climate and soil. Several of the wine-growing districts of Germany are little known beyond their own boundaries. Indeed, to the world at large, German wine is made up of Rhine wine (Hock to the English, after the wine-growing district of Hochheim) and Mosel. Some wine drinkers may distinguish the Palatinate wines and perhaps the Stein wines of Franconia, a few may know about the drier wines of Baden, but when it comes to the Ahr, the Hessische Bergstrasse or the Mittelrhein, the outside world's response is blank.

For the purposes of quality wine production, the German wine authorities have divided all wine-producing areas into 11 regions (*map, page 83*). Seven of the quality wine regions produce Rhine wine; one produces Mosel; the other three each produce wines of a rather different character. The four major Rhine wine regions are Rheingau—head and shoulders above the rest—Rheinhessen, Nahe and Rheinpfalz (the Palatinate); the three lesser Rhine regions are the Ahr, Mittelrhein and Hessische Bergstrasse. The Mosel region now also comprises the wines of the rivers Ruwer and Saar, and is officially called Mosel-Saar-Ruwer. The remaining three regions are Franconia, Württemberg and Baden (qq.v.).

The way the regions are subdivided is in part the heritage of hundreds of years of wine-making, in part the result of recent legislation. Vine-growing along the Rhine began with the Romans and went on continuously through the Christian era. The large medieval holdings of the monasteries and nobles were broken up under the Napoleonic occupation, divided among the peasantry and carved by every generation into smaller and smaller portions. It was the same process that caused the vineyards of Burgundy to become so tiny; here it was carried to an even greater degree of fragmentation. Owning one-eighth of a hectare (one-third of an acre) of vineyard is commonplace rather than the exception. If the holdings of the Côte d'Or are of pocket handkerchief size, those of the Rhine and Mosel are postage stamps, with each minuscule patch producing its annual barrel or half barrel of wine bearing its own name. There used to be about 50,000 named wines registered in Germany; now there are nearly 3,000, which is still a considerable number.

This drastic reduction was achieved by a decree of 1971 which fixed the minimum size of any named vineyard at five hectares (13 acres). This meant that henceforth neighbouring patches smaller than those dimensions must go under one name, even though the land is shared between a number of owners each producing their own individual wine. This tidying-up operation, though sensible on the whole, brought some heartbreak when a long-established vineyard name had to be dropped into oblivion. Only one or two vineyards of exceptional renown were allowed to retain their identity.

One result of the change is that it is important for the wine buyer to get to know the name of growers as well as those of vineyards. A site may have acquired an excellent reputation through the products of one or two owners, and neighbouring growers now using the same name for their wine may not match their skills.

Intermediate between the 11 regions and the thousands of individually owned vineyards are three other categories of place names, all of which may appear on wine labels according to the provisions of the 1971 wine law.

The largest unit is the *Bereich* (district) of which there are 31 altogether. Within these are the *Grosslagen* (*gross* means large, *Lage* a site). These are units consisting of a number of individual vineyards (*Einzellagen* or single sites). There are now approximately 130 of these greater vineyards, encompassing between them some 2,600 single ones—and every name is duly registered. The names of towns and villages around which the vineyards are sited are also used in labelling the wines from the area.

A label will mention a pair of names—either town plus *Einzellage* or town plus *Grosslage*. If, for instance, a wine was grown on the single vineyard called Jesuitengarten—which is a part of the Grosslage Honigberg, near the wine town of Winkel—the wine will be called a Jesuitengarten from Winkel (in German, *Winkeler Jesuitengarten*). If, on the other hand, only some of the grapes came from Jesuitengarten and the rest from other sites within Honigberg, the wine will be labelled *Winkeler Honigberg*. Thus one cannot tell at a glance from a label if a wine comes exclusively from one vineyard or is a blend from several, unless one knows already which are the names of *Einzellagen* and which of *Grosslagen*.

The German wine industry is modern and innovative, looking diligently for ways to maximize productivity and minimize risks. Few countries set more stringent limitations than Germany on what goes into a bottle, or require such a complete description of its contents on the label. The thoroughness in this respect is not new: Germany introduced wine laws as far back as 1879.

The present law divides all wines into three categories. They are, in rising order of quality: *Deutscher Tafelwein; Qualitätswein; Qualitätswein mit Prädikat*.

Deutscher Tafelwein means German table wine, but *Tafel* is not the usual word for table (which is *Tisch*). *Tafel* means a board, and is used, in the context of meals, as a kind of Sunday word for table—you eat your supper on a *Tisch*, a banquet is served on a *Tafel*.

Official *Deutscher Tafelwein* is not for banquets, however, although it can be pleasant enough. Its style is lively, not very alcoholic. When the wine is good, it has a light fresh scent and an edge of sweetness; when it is not so good, more than an edge of sweetness masks more than an edge of acidity.

By law *Deutscher Tafelwein* must have a minimum of 8½ per cent alcohol, and it must consist of wine grown in a given German wine-growing region. (If not, it can only be called plain *Tafelwein* and could be made from any wine from any E.E.C. country.) *Deutscher Tafelwein* may be chaptalized (*page 13*). It does not have to pass a tasting test, but it has to conform to pure food and trade description acts which are quite strict.

The label will say *Deutscher Tafelwein* plus the name of the zone of origin. These zones do not correspond with the 11 regions producing quality wines, presumably to prevent a customer ever mistaking one kind of wine for the other. The five zones are: Rhein, Mosel, Main, Neckar and Oberrhein.

Many table wines are exported under a brand name, such as Goldener Oktober, or Prinz Rupprecht. They are blended to maintain a consistent standard so that once you have picked out the kind you like, you can be sure it will not disappoint you. German table wine is not improved by ageing, and should be drunk within a year of purchase.

It is interesting to note that actually very little table wine is made in Germany. In good vintage years, when wines are able to reach the standards required for the higher grades, it may be as little as per cent of the total output. The vintner's aim being to achieve the best possible wine under given conditions and the laws being what they are, it is perfectly possible for a wine of the same origin to be classed as *Deutscher Tafelwein* in one year and *Qualitätswein mit Prädikat* the next. (By the same token, if the third year should be a disaster, the wine may be sunk anonymously in a tank of Sekt.)

The next step up the scale is *Qualitätswein* (quality wine) or, to give it its full name, *Qualitätswein eines bestimmtes Anbaugebiet* (quality wine from a stated region), an expression always abbreviated to QbA. The "stated region" must be one of the 11 officially defined *Weinanbaugebiet* (wine-producing regions). To be ranked as QbA, a wine must conform to the rules of the region with regard to its grape variety, planting, yield and alcoholic strength. Chaptalization is permitted only within the limits prescribed individually for each region.

Having met these basic requirements, each wine aspiring to QbA rank is tested—first by laboratory analysis of such factors as alcohol, sugar and acidity, and then by a professional tasting panel. Note that the tests have to be passed by every candidate wine anew every year.

The wines are given points for colour, limpidity, nose and taste out of a possible maximum of 20 points. To pass as QbA, the wine must score at least 11 points out of the 20; if it falls below even by a fraction it can only be sold as a German table wine. A wine that passes both the laboratory and the tasting tests is given an official control number. On its label must appear the word *Qualitätswein* or the abbreviation QbA, the region of origin and the control number.

Optionally there may be numerous further items of information: German labels are full of words, and they are not empty ones. The vintage year is often given. A grape variety may be mentioned, if a single type accounts for at least 85 per cent of the bottle's contents. If the wine comes exclusively from a particular area within the region or from a particular vineyard, the name may be given. In addition, one often finds the name of the producer, bottler or exporter, accompanied by the word *Erzeugerabfüllung*, meaning bottled by the producer. (The former *Originalabfüllung*—bottled at origin—is

no longer permitted, nor is the word *Naturwein* or *Naturrein*, though they may still be found on older labels.)

QbA wines are often very good wines indeed. They can be said to be one of the mainstays of German wine production. The bigger QbA wines are long-lived: they can be kept to advantage for several years, gaining in complexity. But all of them can be drunk with pleasure a year after bottling, and the younger they are, the more fresh and lively their taste.

Qualitätswein mit Prädikat or QmP is the highest rank of German wine. It may be translated as quality wine with distinction. QmP wines must come exclusively from one district within a region and usually come from a particular vineyard within the district. No QmP wine may be chaptalized; it must attain 10 per cent of alcohol without the help of sugar added during fermentation. The law assures that in poor years few if any wines can make a QmP grade, and in that case the vintner may prefer to play safe, chaptalize his wine and go in for the lower QbA rank which permits the mite of sugar.

While chaptalization (which increases alcohol but never sweetens) is forbidden in QmP wines, sweetening with a controlled amount of unfermented grape juice, called *Süssreserve*, is permitted. This grape juice must be from the same vineyard, grape and year as the wine. It is added to the wine before bottling and treated so that it cannot ferment.

A QmP wine must undergo the same tasting test as the QbA wine and score at least 13 points out of the possible 20. The *Prädikat* or distinction will be one of five grades, each requiring a different score. These are: Kabinett, a wine made from grapes picked at the normal vintage time; Spätlese, made from grapes picked late; Auslese, made from selected bunches of grapes; Beerenauslese, made from berries selected from late-picked bunches of grapes; and finally, Trockenbeerenauslese, made from almost dried-out berries selected from bunches of very late-picked grapes.

A Kabinett wine will be the lightest in alcohol and usually the driest of the five. If it is true to form, it will be a fine wine, well made, with the pronounced characteristics of its type, be it Mosel, Hock or

Franconian. The word *Kabinett* (cabinet) is a loose term implying some prestige and suggesting the grower's private reserve kept in a cubby-hole.

To attempt a Spätlese wine, a grower must harvest late, waiting for the grapes to attain the maximum ripeness. The delay is always risky for the weather may break but, if all goes well, there will be a richer, fuller wine, probably higher in alcohol and commanding a higher price.

For an Auslese, only the ripest and the soundest grapes are chosen, and the wine gains accordingly. The name Auslese does not guarantee that the grapes were late-picked, but it is often the case that they were. Auslese wines are usually both sweeter and stronger than Spätleses.

Selection berry by berry, to produce a Beerenauslese, is practised in exceptional years when with the help of a fine, long, late autumn the grapes have been attacked by *Botrytis cinerea*. Beerenauslese has no need of added Süssreserve to sweeten it. The natural sugar content of the grapes is so high that plenty remains in the wine at the end of fermentation. The resulting wine is intensely sweet and aromatic, and rather more alcoholic than most German wines.

Trockenbeerenauslese is wine made by carrying the process used for Beerenauslese to more extravagant lengths. The longer the grapes are allowed to remain on the vines, the more intense in quality—and diminishing in quantity—the essence inside them becomes. By December—or even January at times—the berries have become wrinkled and nearly dry like raisins. After picking, the grapes are spread on tables and the best that is, the overripe berries with unbroken skins, properly attacked and shrivelled—are snipped out one by one with little scissors. The process is exacting, labour-intensive, appallingly expensive (20 times more so than making a Kabinett wine) yet it is immensely rewarding, because of the wonder and intensity of the wine. These Beerenausleses and Trockenbeerenausleses are the great wines of Germany.

Some wines in Germany may also be designated Eiswein (q.v.). This is not a rank or distinction but a descriptive term for the way the wine was made. German Eiswein, to be allowed that name, must attain QmP rank. It can be any of the five grades; most commonly it is Auslese.

Labels of QmP wines carry—by law— the words *Qualitätswein mit Prädikat*, or just QmP; the distinction itself, for example Spätlese or Kabinett; the wine region and the control number. There may also be the vintage year, the specific district, the vineyard, the grape variety and all the rest, as for QbA.

The QmP category embraces every style of German wine in its best form. Young wines of Kabinett standing are usually refreshing, light, admirably drinkable. After some years in bottle they can show their breeding: elegance, delicacy, firmness. There may be a hint of steel in the Riesling; the balance of fruit, acidity and body will emerge. QbA wines, together with QmP of Kabinett rank, make up about 75 per cent of German production; they are the typical wines.

Spätlese and Auslese wines are more special. Those of a good year well repay five to 10 years in bottle. The Beerenauslese and Trockenbeerenauslese wines are the exquisite rarities, the connoisseur's wines for considered occasions, and among the most expensive wines in the world. They can, like every German wine, be drunk young, but their peak comes after perhaps 15 to 20 years, and some will keep almost indefinitely.

Graves

A major district and appellation of Bordeaux, Graves produces both red and white wines. Situated on the left bank of the Garonne and bordering on the Médoc in the north, the region encloses the city of Bordeaux; indeed, the vineyards begin at the very edge of the suburbs, menaced by main roads, housing estates and rising land values.

The country is flat, with a depth of sandy gravel in the soil (*graves* in local French means gravel). In the rural areas some of the vineyards are planted in clearings surrounded by pine woods.

Graves used to be associated in most people's minds with white wine, semisweet and mediocre in character. In fact, from a quarter to a third of the wines of Graves were and are red. Many of these are very fine, and among them are some of the greatest of the great: Châteaux Haut-

Brion and La Mission Haut-Brion, to give but two examples.

The great red Graves when mature have an overwhelming richness, ripeness and subtlety of flavours that have more in common with the Médoc reds than with those of Pomerol or St. Emilion. The chief red wine grape varieties are Cabernet Sauvignon with Cabernet Franc, Merlot, and a little Petit Verdot.

The poorish whites are a thing of the past. The white wines are now mainly dry and of good quality. A few of them are exquisite wines—complex, rich, made for long-keeping (the incomparable white of Haut-Brion, for example, the outstand-

ing Domaine de Chevalier and Château Laville Haut-Brion). The grapes that produce the white wines of Graves are Semillon and Sauvignon Blanc with a small amount of Muscadelle.

An official classification of the wines of Graves was made in 1953 and revised in 1959. Fifteen *châteaux* in all received the accolade (see *box*)—some for their red wine, some for their white, some for both. Unlike the *châteaux* of the Médoc (q.v.), the classified vineyards of Graves are not divided into several ranks: all are designated simply by the words *grand cru classé Graves* on the label (along with the *château* name and *appellation contrôlée*).

Classified Red Graves

Community names are given in parentheses.

Château Haut-Brion
(Pessac)

Château Bouscaut
(Cadaujac)

Château Carbonnieux
(Léognan)

Domaine de Chevalier
(Léognan)

Château Fieuzal
(Léognan)

Château Haut Bailly
(Léognan)

Château La Mission Haut-Brion
(Talence)

Château La Tour Haut-Brion
(Talence)

Château Latour-Martillac
(Martillac)

Château Malartic-Lagravière
(Léognan)

Château Olivier
(Léognan)

Château Pape Clément
(Pessac)

Château Smith-Haut-Lafitte
(Martillac)

Classified White Graves

Community names are given in parentheses.

Château Bouscaut
(Cadaujac)

Château Carbonnieux
(Léognan)

Domaine de Chevalier
(Léognan)

Château Couhins
(Villenave d' Ornon)

Château Latour-Martillac
(Martillac)

Château Laville Haut-Brion
(Talence)

Château Malartic-Lagravière
(Léognan)

Château Olivier
(Léognan)

Château Haut-Brion
(Pessac)

The order of listing is alphabetical, with the exception of Château Haut-Brion, whose claret was so distinguished that it had already been included a century before in the 1855 Médoc list of first growths; it is customarily placed at the head of the Graves list.

There are also more than 300 unclassified vineyards in Graves, both making and selling wine under the name of their *château, domaine* or *clos*; and a further large number of small wine makers (chiefly in the south of the district) who sell their wine directly to the Bordeaux merchants for blending and marketing with a general Graves appellation.

Graves de Vayres

A small Bordeaux area with its own appellation, surrounded by the larger area of Entre-Deux-Mers (*map, page 85*). The gravel soil (*graves*) of the region produces white wines and a small amount of red that can be extremely good.

Greece

Vines are grown on the Greek mainland and on the islands. Most vineyards are situated near the sea, which moderates the hot, dry climate; and the poor soil, which varies between chalky, volcanic and rocky, is well adapted to viniculture. The bulk of production is ordinary red and white wine, of a rather unpredictable standard, which is consumed locally. The big wine firms produce their own brand-name wines, which are sound wines of a generally consistent standard; and about 2 per cent of the total wine production consists of better quality wines, with controlled denominations subject to government guarantee. The boost given to the export trade when Greece joined the E.E.C. in 1981 has resulted in efforts to improve quality and a closer application of the controls introduced in 1963.

The most extensive and important wine area is the southerly land-mass of the Peloponnese. A good red wine of renown, Nemea, comes from the hilly slopes around Corinth; made from the Agiorgitiko grape, Nemea is a heady, robust dry wine that is almost black in colour. Muscat wine from Patras in the north-west Peloponnese is a good quality dessert wine with a golden colour and a heavy

scent. Patras also produces the best Mavrodaphne—a sweet red dessert wine with a high alcohol content that matures well. Lighter, dry wines, including rosés—known as *kokkineli* in Greece—are made in the same area from the Rhoditis grape. A light, fragrant white wine called Mantinia is made in Arcadia, in the central Peloponnese; Monemvasia in the south makes the sweet wine whose name occurs as Malvasia, Malvoisie or Malmsey.

Some of Greece's best retsina wine comes from the Peloponnese. Retsina derives its distinctive turpentine-like flavour from the pine resin that is added to the must during fermentation. Most retsina is white, but a small proportion of *kokkineli* is also treated by the same method. Legend has it that the traditional Greek taste developed in the days of ancient Greece when a mixture of pine resin and plaster was used to seal the wine amphorae. Retsina is an acquired taste, but it is one that generations of visitors, as well as the Greeks themselves, have proved equal to acquiring.

In the northern Greek provinces of Thessaly, Macedonia and Thrace, thanks to wetter conditions and lower temperatures, the red wines can reach a good standard. Naoussa is a wine of vigour and distinction with a very dark colour; Rapsani, made in the region of Mount Olympus from several grape varieties, is rather rough and hard at first, but softens and improves with time; and the Amynteon vineyards near the north-western frontier produce somewhat tannic wines of deep colour.

The islands of Greece, scattered across the Aegean sea, contribute about 20 per cent of Greek wine production. Crete, the largest and most southerly of the islands, produces mostly big, heady red wines. Some of the best, especially those from Archanai, are produced in the central-northern part of the island around the port of Heraklion.

Samos, just off the coast of Asia Minor, has been famous over the centuries for its luscious Muscat wine, traditionally made without the addition of fortifying spirits, from grapes that are partially dried to concentrate their sugars. Today, drier, fortified versions are also produced. The people of Samos protect all their own wine

with unusually stringent regulations.

Among the smaller islands, most of which produce wines of varying quality, the tiny isle of Thera is remarkable for its highly alcoholic yet acidic wines. These wines are the product of volcanic soil and a climate that combines powerful sunshine with the cooling effect of the prevailing Aegean winds.

Growth (cru)

The word is used in France to refer to the product—either grapes or wine—of a single vineyard or wine-growing estate. The term therefore has connotations of high quality, since lower quality output is usually blended with that of other vineyards and does not keep its separate identity.

Haut-Médoc see *Médoc*

Hessische Bergstrasse

This tiny Rhine wine region, the smallest in Germany, is situated between the east bank of the Rhine and the river Main (*map, page 83*). The area under vines is only 350 hectares (865 acres); the output is about 30,000 hectolitres (660,000 gallons), which is less than 1 per cent of the German total. The wines are of the Hock style, soft and well balanced, mostly bottled early—the spring after the grapes were picked—and drunk at once. They are seldom if ever seen abroad. The two districts (*Bereiche*), Starkenburg and Umstadt, contain some 22 individual vineyards (*Einzellagen*) which are grouped into three larger units (*Grosslagen*).

Hungary

Hungary's most famous wine is the sweet, white Tokay from the north-east of the country. Bounded by the rivers Bodrog and Szerencs, the hills of the Tokay region contain approximately 6,000 hectares (14,800 acres) of vineyards, the source of one of the world's great noble rot wines (*page 16*). A sandy, loamy topsoil overlies a volcanic subsoil. Summer temperatures are high and rainfall slight, while the autumn is mild and damp, fostering the Botrytis fungus.

The grapes used are the sweet Hárslevelü, the aromatic Yellow Muscat and, above all, the thick-skinned Altesse, known in Hungary as Furmint, which is especially susceptible to the noble rot.

Unlike other noble rot wine, Tokay is not made simply from pressed and fermented Botrytis grapes; instead, a paste of Botrytis grapes is added to the must of normal white grapes. At harvest time the affected grapes, termed *aszu*, are mashed either by machine or by the traditional method of treading into a paste, and separated into 35-litre (8-gallon) containers called *Puttonyos*. The number of containers added to a standard fermenting vat of ordinary grapes determines the sweetness of the finished wine, whose label will eventually indicate how many Puttonyos are used. Tokay Aszu 5-Puttonyos is the sweetest usually sold; 6-Puttonyos wine is occasionally available.

The enriched must is subsequently filtered into barrels to finish fermenting and to mature for five to six years. The barrels remain unplugged and a benign, velvety mould grows on the wine's surface, lending further distinctive qualities to its bouquet.

Szamorodni, meaning self-born, is a Tokay wine made from bunches of grapes whose rotted berries have not been removed and treated separately. The sweetness of a Szamorodni vintage wine is determined by the proportion of Botrytis grapes in the crop.

Eszencia, the rarest of Tokay wines, is made from the juice of Botrytis grapes that oozes out under the natural pressure of berries piled high in a tub. Rich in sugar, *eszencia,* or essence, was once allowed to ferment slowly over many years. This wine—coveted at one time as an elixir and reputed to live for two centuries or more—has long since become too rare and expensive to be sold outside the auction room. Today, any *eszencia* that is made is used to enrich Tokay Aszu, which is then sold as Tokay Aszu Eszencia.

Tokay is so highly valued that it tends to overshadow the rest of Hungary's wine. In fact, the country's varied soils and climatic conditions produce a broad range of white and red wine, both sweet and dry. Red wines are made in the southern district around Szekszarda; white Pecsi Olasz Riesling—unrelated to the classic German grape of the same name—is produced in the south-western region of Mecsek; a red from the Oporto grapes is made

in the Villany-Siklos region to the south of Mecsek; and aromatic, powerful white table wines are the speciality of the northern shore of Lake Balaton, one of the largest lakes in Europe.

Hungary's most important red wine, the much-exported Bikaver (Bulls Blood), is produced around the north-eastern town of Eger. Made from Kadarka, Pinot Noir and Merlot grapes, Bikaver is deeply coloured and somewhat rough, growing in character with age. From the same region come both dry and sweet white wines, notably the full-bodied Egri Leanyka.

Hybrid

A term used in viniculture to denote the result of crossing any variety of the species *Vitis vinifera* (*page 5*) with a variety of a different species, usually *Vitis labrusca* (*page 7*).

Israel

Built anew on an ancient biblical tradition of viniculture, the wine industry of modern Israel has utilized modern equipment to overcome the problems of a searingly hot climate and produce a broad range of wines. The traditional taste for sweet, often sickly, red dessert wines and golden Muscatels is changing in favour of light, dry red and white table wines based on the newly introduced Cabernet Sauvignon and Sauvignon Blanc vines. Sparkling wines, ranging from dry to very sweet, are also made. All exports, mainly to the U.S.A., are quality controlled by the Israeli Wine Institute and certified as kosher.

The most important wine-growing areas include the slopes of Mount Carmel; the vineyards on the northern shore of the Sea of Galilee in the north of the country; the vast vineyards planted across the flat inland plains east of Jaffa and Tel Aviv; and the outskirts of Beersheba on the edge of the Negev desert in the south.

Until recently, the Carignan and Grenache grapes were used for nearly all Israeli red wines, and the Semillon, Clairette and Muscat grapes for white wines. However, the recent plantings of Sauvignon Blanc vines are producing wines of better quality and greater potential. Almost 75 per cent of the country's wine is made at the big co-operative, Zichron Jacob,

which is at the base of Mount Carmel.

The best-known red wines include Adom Atic, Atzmon, Carmelith, Primor and Château Windsor. Château de la Montagne, Mont Blem, Massadah and Carmel Hock are some of the most popular white wines. The foremost brand names for sweet dessert wines include Château Rishon, Topaz, Almog and Toda. Israel's leading sparkling wine, made by the Champagne method (q.v.), is labelled The President's Sparkling Wine.

Italy

Blessed with a reliable Mediterranean climate and a vinicultural tradition that dates back at least 3,000 years to Etruscan times, Italy vies with France as the world's largest producer of wine and generally surpasses France as the world's largest exporter. The quantity involved is prodigious—about 70,000,000 hectolitres (1,540,000,000 gallons) in 1980—and there is variety to match. Red and white, dry and sweet, still and sparkling, and fortified wines are produced by more growers than anyone has ever definitively enumerated.

Italian wines and wine-making techniques in the middle of the 20th century were the same as those described in books of a hundred years earlier—nothing had changed. The archetypal Italian wine-maker was a peasant who cared for crops planted beneath fruit trees, his vines winding up and overhead to form arbours from which abundant grapes were picked to make the family's yearly supply of wine. Now, the old ways have largely disappeared, and a more accurate image is of an accomplished young oenologist with advanced degrees in biochemistry and an acute awareness of everything that is happening the world over in the realms of viticulture and oenology. Many of the developments, particularly in southern Italy, Sardinia and Sicily, have resulted in mass-produced wines that are clean, pleasant and easy to drink. But the changes affect all Italian wines, from the humblest to the most highly valued.

Surprisingly for so passionately anarchic a country, the improvements were largely initiated by governmental action. In 1963, the Italian government introduced laws controlling wine production

Wine produced according to these government standards—broadly similar to the French *appellation contrôlée* system—is entitled to be labelled as a *Denominazione d'Origine Controllata* (DOC). There are now more than 200 DOC wines, and the general effect of the laws has been a considerable and continuing improvement in all Italian wines, not only those that merit a DOC rating. An even more rarified category is projected: *Denominazione d'Origine Controllata e Garantita* (DOCG). The first four wines already nominated for inclusion—Barolo, Barbaresco, Vino Nobile di Montepulciano and Brunello di Montalcino—indicate that, in the official view at least, these are the greatest Italian wines.

Recently, some lesser wines have been granted the subsidiary designation *vini tipici*—meaning typical wines and roughly equivalent to the French *vin du pays*. Wines that do not meet the standards for either DOC or *vini tipici* are sold simply as *vini da tavola*—table wines.

Every Italian region, from Val d'Aosta and Trentino-Alto Adige at the edge of the Alps to Calabria and Sicily in the far south produces wine (*map, page 82*). Little of it is made with long ageing in mind. Most Italian wines are destined to be drunk young—fresh, thirst-quenching, supple and fruity, often with a rustic earthy edge to them.

Some wines from the northern part of Italy, and in particular from Piedmont, are in a class apart. Piedmont is the home of the red Nebbiolo grape, Italy's noblest variety; and the two famous wines made from it, Barolo and Barbaresco, well merit their DOCG nomination. Both are massive wines, Barolo perhaps more so than Barbaresco, which can be more delicate. The wines are very similar, however, and both are best appreciated after eight to 20 years of bottle ageing. Other good Piedmont wines, also made from the Nebbiolo, are Gattinara and Crema. Some lesser Nebbiolo wines do not meet DOC standards, but are nevertheless clean and adequate drinking; they are sold as Nebbiolo or Spanna, a local name for the same grape variety. A certain amount of *vino novello*—a *primeur* wine, supple and tender, to be drunk very young—is also made, by carbonic maceration (*page 11*),

from Nebbiolo grapes. Other, less celebrated Piedmontese wines, especially pleasant when drunk in the year following the vintage, are made from the Barbera, Dolcetto and Grignolino grapes.

Piedmont for the most part produces red wine, but a pleasant, clean white wine is made from the Cortese grape, and Asti Spumante—a sweet, sparkling wine made from the Muscat grape—is known the world over.

Lombardy produces a number of Nebbiolo wines also: sparkling wines by the Champagne method (q.v.) and still white wines, mostly from recently introduced French and German grape varieties. The adjacent region of Trentino-Alto Adige produces a number of white wines from Sylvaner, Riesling and Gewürztraminer varieties, and reds from Cabernet and Merlot grapes.

Throughout north-eastern Italy, light-bodied, supple, seductive wines—both red and white—are produced from French grape varieties: Merlot, Cabernet Franc, Pinot Nero (Pinot Noir), Pinot Grigio (Pinot Gris) and Sauvignon Blanc. From native grape varieties, the Veneto region produces three of Italy's most exported wines: two reds, Bardolino and Valpolicella, and the white Soave. All are produced, industrially and individually, by small growers, and can be of great charm.

All three wines come from the area around the old city of Verona. Bardolino is made predominantly from the Corvina grape with some Rondinella, Malinara and Negrara, grown in vineyards on the eastern shore of Lake Garda near the village of Bardolino itself. Bardolino is a light, fruity wine that is often *frizzante*—slightly sparkling—and is best drunk young and cool. Valpolicella is made from the same grape varieties; it has slightly more colour and body than Bardolino, while sharing the same general characteristics.

The Valpolicella district also produces wines called Recioto or Reciote Amarone. These are made from the same grape as Valpolicella, but only the outermost grapes from each cluster, those that have received the most sunshine, are used. The grapes are then partially dried to concentrate their sugars; the resulting wine, after lengthy cask and bottle ageing, is

a rich, strongly alcoholic wine.

The white wine produced in the Soave vineyards is one of Italy's most popular. It is very pale, often with a greenish tinge. By no means complex, it is best enjoyed young for its fruit and light fragrance.

From the heartland of the nearby Emilia-Romana region comes the much-exported Lambrusco, made from the red grape of that name; at its best it is a light and refreshing wine. The region's best wines, though, have the name Colli Bolognesi, from around Bologna where Barbera, Merlot, Sauvignon Blanc and Pinot Bianco grapes, among others, yield light dry red and white wines—often *frizzante* and almost always enjoyed young.

Tuscany is celebrated above all for its Chianti, the red wine of Florence and Siena, made largely from the Sangiovese grape. The name Chianti has been in continuous use since the Middle Ages, but the nature of the wine has undergone many changes in that time, and it is still changing. Until recently, most Chianti was vinified according to the *governo all'uso Toscano*: a process in which must made from partially dried grapes was added to the new wine after its fermentation was complete. The result was a secondary fermentation that yielded a vigorous, lively wine, full of fruit and often lightly sparkling, meant to be drunk young. The *governo* has largely fallen out of favour in recent years, however, and growers have concentrated on producing a more orthodox wine aged in wood for two or three years (earning the titles *vecchio* and *riserva* respectively) and usually drunk after a few years' bottle age. The straw-covered flasks—known as *fiaschi*—that once signified young *governo* wine have largely been supplanted by sterner, Bordeaux-type bottles. Whether the wine these contain is a real improvement on its less serious but more good-natured predecessor is still a matter of some argument, but there is no doubt that much of modern Chianti is excellent wine of character and delicacy.

The area of the Chianti appellation is a large one, and it is subdivided into seven main sections. Chianti Classico, the heart of the region, is reputedly the best, and is made to somewhat stricter DOC regulations. However, each district has many growers, and the expertise of the individual grower—or the co-operative he belongs to—is more likely to determine a Chianti's quality than its precise geographical origin. Whatever its precise appellation, DOC rules insist that Chianti be made largely from the Sangiovese grape.

Tuscany also produces two DOCG wines: Brunello di Montalcino, made near Siena on the edge of the Chianti zone, and the nearby Vino Nobile de Montepulciano. The full-flavoured, fragrant Brunello is made from the Brunello grape, also known as Sangiovese Grosso, a strain of the principal Chianti grape. Vino Nobile is a big, well-balanced wine made largely from Sangiovese grapes.

There are other good Tuscan wines. A small vineyard, Saccicaia, produces a red wine that is excellent by any standards. It may only be sold as *vino da tavola*, however, because its independently minded proprietor plants only Cabernet Sauvignon—a variety not recognized under DOC rules for Tuscan wines.

Before the DOC legislation was introduced, a number of white Chiantis were produced. Now, Chianti must be red, and the best known of today's Tuscan DOC whites is Vernaccia di San Gimignano, a pleasant, dry wine with soft edges and a certain elegance.

Tuscany's offshore island, Elba, produces both red and white wines from local variations of the Sangiovese and Trebbiano grapes. The island's ferruginous soil gives the wines—some of which rate DOC status—a distinctly different flavour from that of their mainland cousins.

From the central province of Umbria comes Orvieto, a pale golden wine made largely from the Trebbiano Toscano grape grown in the hilly vineyards around the old Etruscan town of Orvieto. Originally, Orvieto wine possessed the moderate sweetness that is described in Italian as *abboccato*. However, the modern taste for dry white wines has greatly reduced *abboccato* production. Most Orvieto today is vinified as a dry wine, and has a flowery bouquet and a slight suggestion of bitterness.

Orvieto also produces a fine *vin santo*—an example of a species of dessert wine common all over Italy. *Vin santo* is made from grapes left to dry on straw after the harvest, and vinified only the following Easter, traditionally in Holy Week (the name means holy wine). Orvieto's *vin santo* spends five years in wood, emerging sweet and honeyed and deep yellow in colour; other similar wines may be dry, but all boast richness and deep colour.

To the east of Umbria lies the region of the Marches, best known for its Verdicchio, a light, attractive white wine usually sold in distinctive, amphora-shaped bottles. South of the Marches, along the Adriatic coast, is the region of the Abruzzi. Its most important DOC wine is the red Montepulciano d'Abruzzo, a robust, generous red wine.

From the Alban Hills near Rome comes what is perhaps Italy's best-known white wine: Frascati. It may be sweet, semi-sweet or dry; most now is dry and should be drunk young and fresh.

Farther south, the vine's fertility quickens, its output becomes prodigal and wines of distinction are harder to find. Yet it is in the south that improvements in Italian viniculture are having their greatest effect.

Sicily now produces first-class table wines, especially from the vineyards on the volcanic slopes of Mount Etna which yield red, white and rosé wines that have been awarded DOC status. The southern tip of the island produces sweet white wines from the Muscat grape, and its western point is the source of Marsala, Italy's most important fortified wine.

Like most of Europe's fortified wines, Marsala's origins are connected with British merchants of the 18th century. Noticing the similarity between the local wines of Marsala and those of Madeira (q.v.), the British set about developing a fortified wine from them. To a mixture of local wines is added a proportion of brandy and a proportion of heated—and, as a result, caramelized—must. The blend develops in cask from as short a period as four months for Marsala Fino to five years for Marsala Vergina, which is often aged by the solera system (see *Sherry*). Marsala has a curiously penetrating, nutty caramel flavour. It is appreciated both as a dessert wine and also as a useful adjunct to dessert cookery, where it provides the essential flavouring for a range of dishes, including zabaglione.

Italy's largest island, Sardinia, is the home of a number of DOC wines. From around the town of Cagliari come dessert wines made from the Muscat grape as well as Nuragus di Cagliari, a dry, lightly acidic white wine from the Nuragus grape. Sardinian red wines tend to be heavy and dark, earning them the name *vini neri*—black wines. The island also produces a Vernaccia di Oristano, an unfortified but sherry-like wine whose vinification depends on the workings of a flor-type mould (*page 16*), and Malvasia di Bosa, a rich dessert wine that is sometimes fortified.

Jura

A small enclave of vineyards in France near the Swiss border (*page 84*), Jura produces pleasant reds, whites and rosés. The lightest of these rosés are characterized as *gris* (grey).

The great wines of the district are the *vins de paille* (straw wines) and the *vin jaunes* (yellow wines).

The *vins de paille*—very rare today—are made from partially dried grapes that are laid out on straw mats to wither; the grape juices become concentrated and the resulting wine is very sweet.

The *vins jaunes* are made from the Savignin grape (the local name for Traminer). They are raised in wood on ullage (*page 15*) and affected by flor like fino sherries (see *Sherry*). The best of these wines is Château-Chalon—deep, rich, nutty and extraordinarily dry—which must be kept in casks for a minimum of six years before being bottled and may be aged for many years.

Jurançon

The traditional sweet white wines of Jurançon—a small appellation in the foothills of the French Pyrenees, south of Pau (*map, page 84*)—have a taste and aroma that have been likened to carnations, acacia flowers or hazelnuts. They are unique wines—rare, but worth seeking out.

Lalande-de-Pomerol and Néac

Two small areas next to the district of Pomerol that share the appellation Lalande-de-Pomerol (*map, page 85*). The best wines they produce—all red—can rival those of the Pomerol appellation.

Languedoc and Roussillon

France's most productive wine-growing area—adjacent regions extending from Avignon in the east to Limoux in the west, and from Carcassonne in the north to the Spanish border south of Perpignan (*map, page 84*). Languedoc and Roussillon are the homes of many of the wines used for blending in ordinary table wines, but there are also a number of wines that have deservedly earned *appellation contrôlée* and VDQS status.

The eastern boundary is marked by the VDQS district of Costières du Gard, which makes strong red wines. Plain white wines come from the Clairette de Bellegarde appellation, immediately to the south, and the Clairette du Languedoc appellation, farther to the west. Between these two districts are three appellations for fortified wines made from the Muscat grape—Muscat de Lunel, Muscat de Mireval and Muscat de Frontignan. From the same area, Picpoul de Pinet is a light, dry white wine with the rating VDQS.

Pleasant, refreshing red wines, fruity and supple, come from St. Chinain and Minervois, two large VDQS districts farther west, and from the Corbières district to the south. Within the VDQS area of Corbières, the *appellation contrôlée* district of Fitou makes strong red wines with good colour and bouquet. The district of Blanquette de Limoux makes a dry white wine, much of which becomes sparkling wine by the Champagne method (q.v.).

South of Corbières spreads the large viticultural zone of Roussillon, which produces robust red wines, some lively whites, and several fortified wines of considerable renown within France, though little known elsewhere. The red wines have only VDQS status, but the fortified wines have their *appellations contrôlées*, of which the best known are Banyuls, Rivesaltes and Maury. They are vinified in a similar way to port (q.v.)—except that, like sherries, the wines are raised on ullage (*page 15*)—and can achieve a comparable quality, developing the *rancio* (maderized) taste of tawny port from long ageing in the cask. The main grapes are Grenache and Muscat. The appellation Banyuls *Grand Cru* must have 75 per cent of Grenache and Muscat de Rivesaltes contains only Muscat.

Lichtenstein

This tiny principality, tucked between Austria and Switzerland, produces only about 800 hectolitres (17,500 gallons) of wine a year: virtually all of it is consumed locally. Most of the wine comes from the vineyards near its capital, Vaduz. Vaduzer wine is very light red, almost a rosé, and made solely from the Pinot Noir grape. Similar wines are made in the towns of Schdan, Triese and Balzecs and are named after their place of origin.

Listrac

A Médoc community that has been given its own appellation within the Bordeaux area. See *Médoc*.

Loire

The Loire Valley, the fourth largest wine-producing area in France and one of the most northerly (*map, page 84*), offers an abundance of different wines—dry and sweet white wines, which can be still or sparkling; dry and semi-sweet rosés; and a lesser amount of light, fruity red wines. There is no general "Loire" appellation; the river's name is used geographically to group the diverse wines that are produced—under a number of appellations—along its valley.

The river Loire flows for more than 1,045 km (650 miles), from mountains of the Massif Central in south-east France to the Atlantic coast in the west. The vineyards lie on both sides of the river and its tributaries between Pouilly-sur-Loire, half way along the Loire, and Nantes, at the river's mouth (*map, page 86*).

At Pouilly-sur-Loire and Sancerre, on opposite banks of the Upper Loire, are the easternmost *appellations contrôlées* vineyards. Pouilly-Fumé and Sancerre are both white wines made from the Sauvignon Blanc grape. In Pouilly the grape is known as Blanc Fumé because, when it is cultivated in the local chalky, flinty soil, it is considered to impart a distinctive, smoky scent and taste to the wine.

Pouilly-Fumé and Sancerre are both very dry, pale in colour, fragrant and fruity. Both wines are good with food, especially shellfish, and should be drunk within two to three years of bottling.

A lesser local wine called Pouilly-sur-Loire is made with the white Chasselas grape; only wines made with Sauvignon Blanc are classified as Pouilly-Fumé.

On the sheltered slopes of Sancerre the soil is more varied than at Pouilly and the quality of the wine is less even; in years with little sun, it may be rather acid.

South-west of Sancerre, two adjacent enclaves of vineyards at Quincy and Reuilly are known for clean, dry, crisp white wine made from the Sauvignon grape. They have a strong resemblance to Pouilly-Fumé and Sancerre. Reuilly also makes some red and rosé wines.

In the mid-Loire region, around the city of Tours, lies the large Touraine appellation area, which produces good ordinary wines. White wines, rosés and red wines are made in the local co-operatives. Three villages are permitted to add their names to the Touraine appellation: Azay le Rideau, Mesland and Amboise.

The climate is gentle and the vineyards, which have been cultivated since the eighth century, are set in fertile, softly undulating country of great beauty. The classic Touraine grapes are the white Chenin Blanc and the red Cabernet Franc. The soil for the most part is chalky; huge caverns, cut out of the hillsides centuries ago, are now used to store the wine.

Within the Touraine area are several more restricted appellations belonging to some of the very best Loire wines. Vouvray is the most famous wine of them all. Always white, it is made from the Chenin Blanc grape, known here as Pineau de la Loire. Depending on the methods of harvesting and vinification, Vouvray can be dry or sweet, still or sparkling.

With plenty of sun, the slow maturing grape will ripen fully and produce a fine, fruity wine with a honey-like sweetness. The greatest Vouvrays are made from grapes that have been allowed to develop *Botrytis cinerea* (*page 16*), but the fungus occurs only in exceptional years, when there is enough sun and humidity to promote its growth. These wines have a voluptuous honey and fruit flavour, and are sweet without being cloying. They benefit immeasurably from ageing and should be laid down for at least 10 years. They can last 20 to 30 years, or much longer, if from a great vintage.

As a result of demand for wines that are less sweet, a large amount of Vouvray is now successfully vinified to be dry; the result is full and fruity, with a good acid balance. These wines should be drunk within four to five years. Thin, acid wines of poor years are made into sparkling or *pétillant* Vouvray by the Champagne method (q.v.). Sparkling Vouvray is popular commercially and enables growers to go on making the prestigious, naturally sweet Vouvrays that do not yield a quick financial return.

The neighbouring vineyards of Montlouis have the same soil and climate as Vouvray, but the sites are not so well exposed to the sun; the resulting wines are similar to Vouvray, but lighter-bodied, always to be drunk young.

In Chinon and Bourgueil the soil is gravelly and the Cabernet Franc grape produces well-defined red wines with a sappy, fruity taste recalling fresh, grassy scents. Within the Bourgueil district, the community of St. Nicolas de Bourgueil has its own appellation. Chinon wines tend to be softer than Bourgueils. The wines are strongly scented and many people can perceive raspberries and violets in the bouquet.

North of Touraine around the Loir (a small tributary of the great Loire) is the appellation of the Coteaux du Loir, producing semi-sweet white wines. The best come from the chalky soil of the Jasmières region, which, although tiny, has its own appellation.

West of Touraine is Anjou, a large appellation that is famous especially for its rosé wines. Although rosés make up the bulk of wine production, sweet and dry white wines and a small amount of red wines are also produced. Saumur, for example, a limited district within the general Anjou appellation, produces red Champigny. At its best, Champigny can equal Chinon and Bourgueil for loveliness of fruit, although it is lighter in body than either. Most Saumur wine, however, is white; much of it is made into Saumur *mousseux*, a sparkling wine that is fuller and heavier than sparkling Vouvray.

Chenin Blanc and Cabernet Franc are Anjou's favoured grapes. Some rosés are made with a blend of Groslot or Gamay and Cabernet Franc, but the best use only Cabernet Franc. A shallow layer of flinty clay soil covers a bed of hard rock in most of the region; consequently, the wines tend to be slightly heavier than those from the light, chalky soil of Touraine.

Some of the finest still white wines of Anjou come from the vineyards of the Coteaux de Layon, south of the Loire. Quarts de Chaume and Bonnezeaux are both designated as *grands crus*; they are sweet, mellow and rich, and their alcohol content can reach 14 or 15 per cent. To allow their scent and character to develop, they should be aged for at least 10 years.

Across the Loire, the south-facing vineyards of the Coteaux de la Loire appellation are ideal for the late-ripening Chenin Blanc grape. Wines from the vineyards of La Roche aux Moines and Coulée de Serrant, an enclave with its own separate appellation within the Savennières area, have great delicacy. These used to be made from Botrytis-affected grapes, but now the grapes are picked earlier and the wines are dry.

The most western vineyards of the Loire are those situated in the Loire Atlantique department, the only vineyards in Brittany that have *appellations contrôlées*. The wine of the region has the general appellation Muscadet, because of the Muscadet grape from which it is made—originally, the Melon grape of Burgundy, transplanted to the Loire. Muscadet is a light dry wine with a fresh, clean taste that makes an excellent accompaniment for seafood. Until 30 or 40 years ago, Muscadet was simply the *vin du pays* of Britanny; today it is sold throughout France and exported widely.

The proximity of the Atlantic keeps the climate temperate and many of the vineyards have a high proportion of sand in their soil. To preserve the acidity of the early-ripening Muscadet grape, the harvest takes place earlier than for most grapes. If the grapes were allowed to become too ripe, the wine would lose much of its characteristic freshness and finesse.

The best Muscadets are bottled *sur lie*: in this process, they are not racked to remove sediment (*page 15*) but kept on their lees in barrels until bottled, with the aim of retaining their freshness and fruit.

There are three Muscadet appellations—Muscadet, Muscadet Coteaux de la Loire (to be distinguished from plain Coteaux de la Loire appellation of Anjou) and Muscadet de Sèvres-et-Maine, which produces more than 80 per cent of the total wine output of the region. All Muscadets have an upper alcohol limit of 12 per cent and they should all be drunk young.

Gros Plant, made from the grape of the same name, is a VDQS of the region (see *French Wine Appellations*). It is a lighter-bodied, more acid wine than Muscadet and can also be bottled *sur lie*. Other interesting VDQS are the light, attractive red wines produced in Coteaux d'Ancenis from Gamay and Cabernet grapes.

Loupiac and Ste. Croix du Mont

Two small adjacent districts of Bordeaux with their own appellations, situated across the river Garonne opposite Sauternes (*map, page 85*). They produce sweet white wines that have the same character if not the same quality as the Sauternes. In mediocre years they are apt to cloy. In propitious years, though, when *Botrytis cinerea* (*page 16*) has spread over the vineyards, the wines that are produced can be very good.

Lussac-St.-Emilion see *St. Emilion*

Luxembourg

The wines of Luxembourg are all white. Often compared to Alsace wines, they are generally lighter-bodied. They are crisp, fruity, acidic, light in alcohol and should be drunk young. Among the best of the wines are the elegant Rieslings and the spicily perfumed Traminers.

The Luxembourg vineyards, interspersed with cherry and plum orchards, form a compact strip along the banks of the Moselle from Remich, on the southern border with France, to Wasserbillig, on the eastern border with Germany. The vines are sheltered from the winds by the forested tops of the hilly river banks. The soil varies from clay to a mixture of chalk with marl, the latter being particularly suitable for the Riesling grape. The most commonly planted grapes include Traminer, Pinot Gris, Pinot Blanc, Sylvaner and, of course, Riesling.

Wine production in Luxembourg is in the hands of approximately 1,600 growers, each working individual plots; some 1,000 hectares (2,500 acres) of the country are under vine. Despite the large number of growers, the quality of the wine is consistent because most of it is produced by large co-operatives. Government controls established at the end of World War I are strictly enforced. The finest wines are labelled *appellation complète*, sometimes *appellation contrôlée*, and always bear the vintage date. Only a very little wine is exported, mainly to Belgium.

Mâconnais

Mâconnais, the area that extends from above Tournus to south of the wine-trading town of Mâcon (*map, page 85*), is the one district of Burgundy where quantity presents no problem. It produces large amounts of red and white wine, and a small quantity of rosé. Above all, it is the home of Pouilly Fuissé, the most coveted and celebrated white Burgundy after Chablis and the unrivalled great wines of the Côte de Beaune.

Pouilly-Fuissé (not to be confused with Pouilly-Fumé, which is a Loire Valley wine) is made from Chardonnay grapes. It comes from four communities, Solutré-Pouilly, Fuissé, Chaintré and Vergisson, which, altogether, have 600 hectares (1,490 acres) under vines. The Pouillys are very, very dry and pale gold in colour; they have fullness and depth, yet are fairly light—lighter and less complex than Meursault or Corton, softer and less steely than Chablis. There is a hint of *gout de terroir*, a taste of earth, which in this area is limestone and slate. Most Pouillys should be drunk young. They reach their peak quickly after about six months in bottle and hold it for about four years.

There are three satellite appellations: Pouilly-Loché, Pouilly-Vinzelles and the recently classified St. Véran. Here the wines are still very good, if not quite as distinguished as Pouilly-Fuissé.

Red Mâcon, Mâcon Blanc and Mâcon Supérieur are good, honest table wines. The reds are made from the Gamay grape with or without some Pinot Noir and Pinot Gris; the whites are made from Chardonnay grapes with the occasional addition of a small amount of Aligoté, the latter tending to give the wine a little more definition.

The appellation Mâcon Villages or a specific village name, such as Mâcon Lugny, indicates better quality. Mâcon

Viré, for example, is an excellent white Burgundy. There is also a small amount of dry white wine with the appellation Pinot Chardonnay Mâcon; it is made of Chardonnay and Pinot Blanc and mainly intended for export to the United States.

Madeira

Wine has been made on the island of Madeira since the 15th century. Situated in the Atlantic Ocean 644 km (400 miles) off the coast of Morocco, the island has a warm temperate climate and the vines flourish in the fertile volcanic soil. Madeira is famous for the sweet fortified wines that take the island's name, but its natural wine has a high acidity and tastes somewhat harsh. Today, about a third of the island's wine is made into fortified Madeira and exported.

The present style of sweet Madeira wine has developed since the beginning of the 18th century when the wines were first fortified with brandy. The wine so produced was coarse, but it was discovered, in the course of exporting, that Madeira improved during long sea voyages: motion and tropical heat hastened its very slow natural maturation and contributed to its "burnt" taste.

The principal Madeira grapes are all white. The varieties used include Malvasia, Bual, Verdelho (the local name for the Italian Verdia grape) and Sercial (the same as the Riesling grape). A wine called Tinta is produced from the Negra Mole, probably a strain of the Pinot Noir grape.

The big shipping firms buy selected grapes, and all the wines for export are produced in modern wineries using up-to-date equipment and techniques. Fermentation is arrested by raising the level of alcohol sufficiently to kill the yeasts, and a residue of unfermented sugar is left in the wine; the state at which natural fermentation is stopped depends on the required sweetness of the finished wine.

The fermented wines are racked (*page 15*) and classified, and then put into the *estufa*, or hot house—a modern substitute for the tropical sea voyage originally supposed to be of such benefit to the wine. Good quality wines are fortified and then stored in casks for a maximum of six months in a room brought up to an air temperature of 70°C (158°F).

A second method of heating—used for less fine wine—is to put it into a vat whose base is fitted with hot water pipes. As the heated wine rises from the base, the contents of the vat circulate, and the wine is further agitated by compressed air or a propeller. The wine is brought to a temperature of 45° to 55°C (113° to 131°F) for a minimum period of 90 days. The wines are fortified, then rested in wood for 12 to 18 months, a period called *estagio*.

The finest wines are set aside in wood to be sold as vintage wine. They may be kept in wood for many years; as the wines mature they are carefully watched, and those that do not live up to their original promise are removed and used for blending. To achieve consistency of style and quality for their products, shippers now use the sherry solera system (see *Sherry*) for blending wines, first adopted under the stimulus of Phylloxera (*page 7*), whose depredations caused a severe reduction in the quantity of vintage wines.

The two lower categories of Madeira are Reserve and Current. Reserves are finer wines than Current Madeiras. Current Madeiras are bottled and shipped after their fifth year; the other categories of wine may be aged for 10, 15, 20 years or more before being bottled. Madeira has the reputation of being among the longest-lived of all wines, second only to the legendary Tokay Essence of Hungary (q.v.). There are many, both vintage and solera, that date from the 19th century and remain in sublime condition today.

Most Madeira is labelled with the shipper's name together with the name of the grape from which it was traditionally made. Today, the names tend to be indicators of degrees of the sweetness or style of the wine, rather than a sign that it is made purely of that grape variety. The driest variety, made from the Riesling grape (sometimes blended with a little Tinta wine to mellow it), is the pale Sercial Madeira; it has an almond flavour and is usually drunk chilled as an aperitif. Verdelho is medium dry with a very dry finish; it is full-bodied with a golden colour that darkens as it matures. Bual is fruity, scented and quite sweet. Malvasia, or Malmsey, is the most luscious of the Madeiras, dark and richly perfumed, acquiring finesse as it ages.

A blend of Madeira called Rainwater is very popular, and the brand name is now used to refer to the type of wine—light-coloured and dry. Madeira that is labelled with the name of the district of origin with no indication of the grape variety is an inferior wine made from the Tinta grape.

Maderized

A term usually applied to white wines that, as a result of too long a sojourn in casks or bottles, have become oxidized, turned a dull brown colour and become flat-tasting.

Madiran

A small appellation area adjoining the Armagnac region, near the Pyrenees in the south-west of France. The local Tannat grape gives Madiran wine its characteristic deep purple colour and its high tannin content. The wine is very long-lived, developing a rich and complex flavour as it ages.

Margaux

One of the four most famous Médoc communities, which has been given the distinction of its own appellation within the Bordeaux area. See *Médoc.*

Médoc

The most renowned of the four great red-wine districts of Bordeaux, producing many famous clarets that are agreed to be among the finest wines in the world.

Topographically the Médoc forms a rough triangle, the base north of the city of Bordeaux, the long sides flanked in the west by the Atlantic, in the east by the Gironde (*map, page 85*). Most of the vineyards are concentrated in one narrow strip of country about 70 km (44 miles) long, along the eastern leg of the triangle. It is basically flat country, with a few gravelly hills and gentle slopes, planted exclusively with vines—no precious space is wasted on other crops.

The soil, like the climate, is ideal for what it is expected to do. It is gravelly, sandy, full of pebbles that soak up the sunshine during the summer days and reflect warmth back at night to the benefit of the ripening grapes above. Drainage is excellent. The subsoil is made up of chalk, clay, ironstone and gravel in varying com-

binations. Médoc soil can change from one side of a road or a small stream to the other; hence the difference in the wines even from neighbouring properties. The predominant grape is the tannic Cabernet Sauvignon, blended with lesser quantities of Merlot and Cabernet Franc. Often a tiny amount of Petit Verdot is included to add an edge of hardness.

For appellation purposes, the Médoc wine strip is divided into two parts: Bas-Médoc (Lower Médoc) downriver to the north, and Haut-Médoc (Upper Médoc) to the south. Wines from many parts of the region may take the appellation Médoc, but the Haut-Médoc—the larger and more distinguished—has its own more restricted appellation: Haut-Médoc.

It is here that we enter, as it were, the Aladdin's cave of Bordeaux, with many treasures lying on every side. The pre-eminence of the Médoc clarets was recognized in the famous classification of Bordeaux growths, made in 1855 and confined (for red wines) to the Médoc—with the single exception of one Graves *château,* Haut-Brion. The classification was not the first attempt at an official grading of what is one of France's most prestigious products, and it will probably not be the last. The system, which was worked out by a committee of Bordeaux wine brokers (*courtiers*) and approved by the Chamber of Commerce of Bordeaux, bestowed the accolade of classification on the clarets of about 60 Médoc *châteaux,* including Château Haut-Brion, which was then considered part of Médoc. Today, although the *château* is officially part of the Graves region, it continues to be classed with the great Médocs.

The Médoc élite were allowed to call themselves *cru classé* on the label, and were graded into five classes, from first growth (*premier cru*) to fifth (see *box*). Let no one think that a fourth or fifth *cru* is a fourth or fifth-rate wine! It is a wine that proudly holds a rank in the highest order of the land. Below the *crus classés* came an unofficial category of more than 400 *crus bourgeois,* the great majority of them admirable wines.

The 1855 classification is still in use today. Is it still accurate? It would be more just to say that it is not strictly up to date, rather than that it is completely obsolete.

Vineyard sites, climate and soil do not change; owners and circumstances do. One or two *châteaux* no longer make any wine, others no longer make such good wine, some have succeeded in making better wine than their more highly ranked neighbours. Some *crus bourgeois* have reached *cru classé* standard and they should be promoted.

As well as demands for some demotions and promotions, there have been various schemes for reforming the framework of the classification itself. Nothing has come of it so far (wine politics being little different from politics elsewhere). The one and only formal change since 1855 is the belated admission to the first rank of Château Mouton-Rothschild (its initial place was at the head of the second *crus*). The elevation, which had long been regarded as overdue, came at last in 1973—by presidential decree, no less. They order these things seriously in France.

Almost all the classified *châteaux* are to be found in four great Médoc communities, each of which has an *appellation contrôlée* in its own right. From south to north these are Margaux, St. Julien, Pauillac and St. Estèphe. (There are two other communities—Listrac and Moulis—that also have the privilege of a separate appellation, but are less renowned since they possess none of the *crus classés.*)

Starting in Margaux, we have one first growth, Château Margaux, one of the best known and most loved wines; no fewer than five second and 10 third growths among them many internationally known wines, such as Château Brane-Cantenac and that English favourite Château Palmer; another handful of fourth and fifth growths, as well as some 20 *crus bourgeois* and *petits châteaux* (unclassified) which make delicious, and often by no means little, true Margaux.

A step north takes us to St. Julien, the smallest of the great communities, with five outstanding second growths: the Léovilles, the Châteaux Gruaud-Larose and Ducru-Beaucaillou; two third and four fourth growths (no fifths) and comparatively few *petits châteaux.*

Next comes Pauillac with its three tremendous firsts—Lafite-Rothschild, Latour, Mouton-Rothschild; two seconds, no thirds, one fourth and as many as 12 fifth

Médoc Classified Growths

Community names are given in parentheses.

Premiers crus

Château Lafite-Rothschild
(Pauillac)

Château Latour
(Pauillac)

Château Mouton-Rothschild
(Pauillac)

Château Margaux
(Margaux)

Château Haut-Brion
(Pessac, Graves)

Deuxièmes crus

Château Rausan-Ségla
(Margaux)

Château Rauzan-Gassies
(Margaux)

Château Léoville-Las-Cases
(St. Julien)

Château Léoville-Poyferré
(St. Julien)

Château Léoville-Barton
(St. Julien)

Château Dufort-Vivens
(Margaux)

Château Lascombes
(Margaux)

Château Gruaud-Larose
(St. Julien)

Château Brane-Cantenac
(Cantenac)

Château Pichon-Longueville Baron
(Pauillac)

Château Pichon-Longueville Comtesse
de Lalande (Pauillac)

Château Ducru-Beaucaillou
(St. Julien)

Château Cos d'Estournel
(St. Estèphe)

Château Montrose
(St. Estèphe)

Troisièmes crus

Château Giscours
(Labarde)

Château Kirwan
(Cantenac)

Château d'Issan
(Cantenac)

Château Lagrange
(St. Julien)

Château Langoa-Barton
(St. Julien)

Château Malescot-St.-Exupéry
(Margaux)

Château Cantenac-Brown
(Cantenac)

Château Palmer
(Cantenac)

Château La Lagune
(Ludon)

Château Desmirail
(Margaux)

Château Calon-Ségur
(St. Estèphe)

Château Ferrière
(Margaux)

Château Marquis-d'Alesme Becker
(Margaux)

Château Boyd-Cantenac
(Margaux)

Quatrièmes crus

Château St. Pierre-Sevaistre
(St. Julien)

Château Branaire-Ducru
(St. Julien)

Château Talbot
(St. Julien)

Château Duhart-Milon-Rothschild
(Pauillac)

Château Pouget
(Cantenac)

Château La Tour Carnet
(St. Laurent)

Château Beychevelle
(St. Julien)

Château Prieuré-Lichine
(Cantenac)

Château Marquis de Terme
(Margaux)

Château Lafon Rochet
(St. Estèphe)

Cinquièmes crus

Château Pontet Canet
(Pauillac)

Château Batailley
(Pauillac)

Château Haut-Batailley
(Pauillac)

Château Grand Puy-Lacoste
(Pauillac)

Château Grand Puy-Ducasse
(Pauillac)

Château Lynch-Bages
(Pauillac)

Château Lynch-Moussas
(Pauillac)

Château Dauzac
(Labarde)

Château Mouton Baronne Philippe
(Pauillac)

Château du Tertre
(Arsac)

Château Haut-Bages-Libéral
(Pauillac)

Château Pédesclaux
(Pauillac)

Château Belgrave
(St. Laurent)

Château Camensac
(St. Laurent)

Château Cos-Labory
(St. Estèphe)

Château Clerc Milon
(Pauillac)

Château Croizet-Bages
(Pauillac)

Château Cantemerle
(Macan)

growths, beautiful wines more than half of which could be promoted in rank; and a few excellent non-classed *châteaux*.

Then there is St. Estèphe with two second *crus*: Châteaux Cos d'Estournel and Montrose, plus three other classed *crus* and the largest number of *crus bourgeois,* many of them outstanding.

Very well—but what do these wines taste like? How much do they differ from community to community? Starting with the wines of Margaux, one might describe them as delicate. (The light soil, with fine white gravelly pebbles that cover many of its vineyards, contributes to this delicacy.) They are perfumed, flowery wines, silky of texture, showing great elegance and breeding. They are the least "big" wines of the four communities, the most velvety, with the most finesse.

The wines of St. Julien tend to be rather darker in colour, more full-bodied (the soil is often heavier: gravel mixed with clay). A typical St. Julien has been described as glossy, subtle, luscious; it will have more "vinosity" than a Margaux—a term not easy to define but suggesting a kind of inner strength. St. Juliens are wonderful wines; in character as well as geographically, they are the connecting link between Margaux and Pauillac, having something of the subtlety of the first and the vigour of the other.

Pauillac is the heart of the Médoc. Here the appropriate terms are depth, bigness, weight. The wines are deep-coloured, massive, vigorous, ripe and rich. The great Pauillacs are the slowest to mature and the longest lived.

The wines of St. Estèphe have the most sturdiness and the least subtlety of all the Médoc wines. The soil is heavier: clay, gravel, lime. These are firm, robust wines, with a hint of earthiness at times, yet easy to drink. In youth some can have much lightness, fruit and charm; the greatest St. Estèphes take their time, then wax full-bodied and deep; they age well and live long.

North of St. Estèphe is the Bas-Médoc, where the land is more flat and the soil less gravelly than in the Haut-Médoc. There are no classified *crus*. Nevertheless, much good—and some distinguished—claret is produced by the many *châteaux* and co-operatives.

Minervois see *Languedoc and Roussillon*

Mittelrhein

One of the minor Rhine wine regions of Germany, stretching from south of Bonn to north of Bingen (*map, page 83*). The wines are unremarkable and rarely if ever exported. The chief grape is the Riesling. Three districts (*Bereiche*), Rheinburgenau, Siebengebirge and Bacharach, encompass 11 vineyard groups (*Grosslagen*) made up of some 110 single sites (*Einzellagen*).

Montagne-St.-Emilion see *St. Emilion*

Morocco

The modern wine-making industry of Morocco dates from after World War II, when most of the vineyards now in existence were planted. Prior to that time, there were some vineyards established by French settlers in the 1920s, but most peasant farmers cultivated their vines for table grapes. Although a newcomer to the wine league, Morocco's production is closely controlled for quality by the government and there is substantial investment in modern mechanization and skills. Moroccan vineyards total some 55,000 hectares (136,000 acres) and produce approximately 1,000,000 hectolitres (22,000,000 gallons) of red, rosé and white wines each year—50 per cent of which is drunk, in spite of Islamic law prohibiting alcohol, by the home market and tourists.

The most commonly planted red grape varieties are Carignan, Cinsault and Grenache. Some of the best red wines come from the regions centring on the towns of Meknès and Fès, where the vineyards are sited on the northern slopes of the Middle Atlas mountain range. The vines benefit from the gravelly soil and the cooler temperatures that prevail in the mountains, producing full red wines with a deep tone and distinctive bouquet. Vineyards on the light, sandy soil of the coastal plain around Rabat provide very pleasant soft, heady red wines that should be drunk young—their lack of tannin and a low acidity tends to give them an oxidized, flabby taste with age. The young dry rosés of Morocco have a particularly good reputation, especially those from the north-eastern area around Oujda. Gris de

Boulaouane is a very good pale dry rosé produced south of Casablanca. Because of the very hot climate, the white wines—made from many varieties of grape, including the native Rafsai—lack freshness and acidity.

Mosel-Saar-Ruwer

One of the great wine regions of Germany, beloved throughout the world. Fed by its tributaries, the Saar and the Ruwer, the Mosel river (Moselle in France, where it rises in the Vosges) winds and loops its way through a deep-cut valley, with vineyards on both sides, to join the Rhine (*map, page 83*). The river's convolutions give the south-facing aspect sometimes to one bank and sometimes to the other.

The Mosel-Saar-Ruwer is not a large wine region: less than 12,000 hectares (30,000 acres) are under vine, producing some 15 per cent of the German total. There are five districts (*Bereiche*): Mosel Tor (Mosel Gate); Ober Mosel (Upper Mosel); Saar Ruwer; Bernkastel (Middle Mosel); and Zell (Lower Mosel).

The climate throughout the region is cold and northern. For the most part it is hard poor land—here both man and the vine must struggle. More than half of the Mosel region is planted with the Riesling grape, and there are substantial proportions of Müller Thurgau and Elbling. But nowadays increasing numbers of growers are tempted to experiment with the modern grape crosses that can tolerate the cold climate more easily.

The overall character of Mosel wine—always sold in slender green bottles, not the amber bottles used for Rhine wines—is one of floweriness and delicacy combined with the elegance and steeliness characteristic of the Riesling grape. The colour is limpid pale with a shimmer of green. The young wines are light and undemanding. Some of those from the Middle Mosel are genuinely great, of a grace and complexity that tempts writers to seek analogies to Schubert's music.

In the upper reaches of the Mosel valley there is lime, marl and sandstone in the soil, and the wines are light and soft. Lower down, where the river approaches the Rhine, the soil is less impoverished and the wines fuller. But the fame of Mosel wine is chiefly based on the prodigious vineyards of the Bernkastel or Middle Mosel district, a 65-km (40-mile) strip where the river cuts its way through a range of slate-stone hills. The Riesling grape responds particularly well to the slate-based soil.

In this stretch, the river's banks are very steep cliffs. To work them is inhumanly arduous. No plough, no engined device can go up such slopes, only men on long ladders. Helicopters are used for spraying. Yet such is the value of the soil, and of the protection from cold afforded by the deep-cut gorge, that every possible terrace is planted.

The valleys of the Saar and Ruwer benefit from the same slatey soil. Wines from the little Ruwer river are very very light—to the point of thin sharpness in bad years. But in good ones they are delightful: gossamer fine and delicate.

Saar wines, grown in the coldest part of the region, are successful only in about three or four years out of 10. In the bad years they are too acid for anything but drowning in a vat of sparkling wine. In fine years they are superlative and can even more outclass those from the Mosel.

There are many small growers in the region, though distribution is chiefly handled on a large scale by the big wine shippers. More than 500 single vineyards (Einzellagen) are grouped into 20 greater vineyards (Grosslagen). A certain quantity of wine is made by co-operatives, and a substantial amount is sold locally direct to the customer—chiefly tourists, both German and foreign.

Nahe

A small but important wine region of Germany, one of the seven Rhine wine districts. The total area under vines is less than 5,000 hectares (12,300 acres), yielding less than 5 per cent of Germany's output. Almost all the wine is white.

The vineyards lie along the Nahe, a tributary river of the Rhine, and its own two small tributaries to the right and left, as well as on the land between (map, page 33). A sheltering forest lies to the northwest of the vineyards, and the climate is relatively temperate.

The Müller Thurgau, Silvaner and Riesling grapes make up between them 50 per cent of the vines planted; the rest

are Morio Muscat and some of the new grape crosses. The soil is extremely varied—from slate to red sandstone, quartzite, loam, loess, clay and volcanic rock.

Nahe wines exhibit the best qualities of wines from both the Rhine and the Mosel regions. They are pale in colour, and often achieve the perfect balance between acidity and sweetness. They combine the clean, racy, crisp taste of some Mosels with the richness, flavour and complexity of the Rheingaus.

The region has two districts (Bereiche), Kreuznach and Schloss Böckelheim; seven greater vineyards (Grosslagen) and over 300 single vineyards (Einzellagen). There are some large estates but most of the holdings are small and owned by local farmers. About 20 per cent of the wine is made and marketed by co-operatives.

Néac see Lalande-de-Pomerol and Néac

New Zealand

Vines were planted in New Zealand as early as 1840, but it was only in the 1960s that any sort of wine industry developed, and much of the wine produced is consumed locally. The majority of vineyards are in North Island, where the most important regions are Poverty Bay, South Auckland and Hawke's Bay. Marlborough is the main vine-growing region of South Island.

Most wines for the middle and the lower end of the market are blends of grapes grown in different areas. The best quality wines are usually made from grapes grown in a single place, but as yet no regional styles have developed.

The climate is cool and summer rains are common—conditions well suited to the production of white wines, particularly the light, aromatic German style. The principal white grape varieties used are the Müller Thurgau, Gewürztraminer, Chasselas, Pinot Gris, Chenin Blanc and Chardonnay. Some very acceptable reds are also being produced, mainly from the Cabernet Sauvignon, Pinotage and Pinot Noir grapes. As might be expected in such a young industry, the wine makers of New Zealand are technologically advanced, making use of mechanical harvesting and controlled fermentation in stainless steel vats to ensure consistent quality.

Noble

"Noble" grape varieties are those renowned for making the world's greatest wines: Pinot Noir, Chardonnay, Cabernet Sauvignon, Riesling, Altesse (Furmint), etc. A "noble" wine is a great wine whose complexity and nuance place it in a class of its own.

Noble Rot see Botrytis cinerea (page 16)

Pauillac

One of the four most famous Médoc communities, which has been given the distinction of its own appellation within the Bordeaux area. See Médoc.

Pomerol

The smallest of the four great red-wine districts of Bordeaux. It adjoins St. Emilion; in fact, its most celebrated cru, Château Pétrus, is grown only some 640 metres (700 yards) from the famous Château Cheval Blanc across the border. The vines of Pomerol occupy a slightly hilly plateau; the soil is clay, gravel and sand on a subsoil rich in iron, the proportions varying from vineyard to vineyard.

The wines are of a very high standard. Unlike Médoc, Graves and St. Emilion, Pomerol has never been officially classified. Indeed, up to less than half a century ago its wines were not considered to be great. Now they are, with a vengeance. Château Pétrus—considered, rightly, one of the world's eight greatest clarets— fetches prices equal to and sometimes surpassing Lafite-Rothschild, Mouton or Latour. The next 10 outstanding châteaux, generally considered to be comparable with second growth Médocs, do not lag far behind—again rightly, for they are wonderful wines: Vieux Château Certan, Châteaux La Conseillante, La Fleur Pétrus, Trotanoy, L'Evangile, Gazin, Lafleur, Latour Pomerol, Petit Village.

Other excellent châteaux to look out for are Châteaux Beauregard, Certan de May, La Croix de Gay, La Pointe, Clos l'Église, Moulinet, Nenin, René de Sales, Tailhas. It is also worth remembering that anything sold under the plain appellation Pomerol is likely to be good value and good wine.

Pomerols are chiefly produced from Merlot, the grape that makes for roundness and smoothness in the wine, with a little—about 20 per cent—of Cabernet Franc, locally called Bouchet.

A fine Pomerol may be expected (by rule-of-thumb) to reach reasonable maturity at five years of age, and its best between 12 and 15. The *robe* or colour is a deep glistening ruby. The wines are highly, almost sweetly, scented: soft, round and deep-flavoured, with some of the astringency of the Médocs. In spite of their differences, they are clearly related to their distinguished cousins from the Médoc communes—in fact, even experienced tasters have taken a Pomerol for a Pauillac, or the other way round.

Port

Port, named after the city of Oporto (also known as Porto) from which it is shipped, is a fortified wine from the Upper Douro region in Portugal (*map, page 83*). Both red and white ports are made and, with the exception of some dry white port, the wines are powerful, heady and sweet. Port derives its particular character from the fact that the wine is fortified with brandy when it has only partially fermented. The natural grape sugars yield no more than 3 or 4 per cent alcohol before the yeasts are muted by the addition of brandy: the residue of unfermented sugar is left behind in the wine.

Until recently, when they were overtaken by the French, the British drank the most port; and British wine shippers have been closely associated with the port trade in Portugal since the 18th century (*page 6*). Port has been officially made in its present style only since the middle of the last century.

The port industry is subject to wine laws passed by the *Instituto do Vinho do Porto,* which delimits the area in which port can be made and lays down standards of classification. Only wines made from grapes grown in the demarcated area of the Douro region, and shipped from Oporto, may be sold as port.

The Douro port region extends from Mesâo Frio, about 136 km (85 miles) east of Oporto, to Barca d'Alva on the Spanish frontier in north-east Portugal. The terrain is mountainous and most of the vineyards are steeply terraced. Schist, which is excellent for both red and white grapes,

predominates in the soil, with some granite. The alluvial soil on the valley bottoms produces coarser wines of a lesser quality.

The middle of the region around Pinhâo, where the finest wines are produced, has the best climate—a mixture of Atlantic and Mediterranean. The rainfall is adequate and the winters not too severe, with plenty of sun in summer. Downriver near the Atlantic coast, the climate is cooler; farther upriver, the summers are very hot and the rainfall drops sharply.

Within the differing climates a remarkable number of microclimates also exist and over 80 varieties of grape are grown in the Douro, each one chosen for its suitability to a particular site and climate. Nowadays, there is much serious study and experimentation with native varieties and different soils to simplify the choice and improve the quality of the wine. Among the best red grapes are Bastardo, Tinto Cão, Mourisco and Donzelinho Tinto; principal white grapes include Esgana Cao, Donzelinho, Gouveio and Malvasia Fina.

Although many of the grapes are produced by small growers, almost all the wine is produced in modern wineries that are owned by the big shipping firms or farmers' co-operatives.

The length of fermentation—nowadays nearly always in temperature-controlled tanks—is usually 36 hours, depending on the degree of sweetness required in the finished wine. The fermented must is fortified with enough brandy to give it an alcohol content of about 18 per cent—at which point, the natural fermentation slows down and ceases within 48 hours.

The wines are stored in oak casks called pipes, each pipe containing 522 litres (115 gallons); half a pipe is a "hogshead". After about six months, the new wine is taken to the wine lodges at Vila Nova de Gaia near Oporto, where it is tasted and categorized. The finest wines become vintage ports, declared by each individual shipper. In years of exceptional quality, most shippers will declare a vintage but some may prefer to keep the vintage wine for adding to their quality blends. Shippers submit samples of their vintage wine, which may be the product of a single vineyard or a blend from several *quintas,* or estates, to

the *Instituto do Vinho do Porto,* between January and September of the wine's second year—that is, 16 to 24 months after harvest. The wine is bottled at about two to two and a half years.

Vintage port is sold under the *Selo de Garantia,* the seal of guarantee. Depending on a vintage year, it is not likely to reach full maturity until it is at least 20 years old. Indeed, a great vintage needs well over two decades to open out in elegance, its colour evolving as it does so (*page 30*) and it may be sublime when more than a hundred years old. As port matures, it throws a heavy sediment. Because it is matured in the bottle, vintage port still contains this sediment, which is known as the crust.

Wine from lesser years not declared as a vintage may also be aged in bottle like vintage port, precipitating the same sediment or crust. This type of wine is known as crusted port. It is an assemblage of young ports from different years, bottled early. The wine is made for drinking much earlier than vintage port—sometimes only three years after bottling.

Wood ports are the shippers' staple commercial wine, usually less big and full-bodied than vintage or crusted ports. They are blended wines, matured in wood casks until they are ready for drinking. Each shipper has his own mark, or brand, and the wines are blended to achieve consistency of style. The cheaper ports are a blend of young wines, while the more expensive varieties may contain some very fine old wine.

Wood ports are named according to their colour as ruby, tawny or white. Ruby port is deep red, full-bodied, rather sweet and is usually aged in wood comparatively briefly—sometimes for only two or three years. It should be drunk young, and will not mature in bottle.

Tawny port is generally aged for much longer and is a lighter, smoother, more mellow wine that usually tastes less sweet than ruby port. The best tawnies—some are very good indeed—are aged for 20 years or more before bottling, but once bottled they do not profit from keeping. Most white port is vinified to the same degree of sweetness as red port, but there is also a growing trend to make dry white ports that are drunk as aperitifs.

Portugal

Portugal's famous export wine is port (q.v.); but port accounts for a very small proportion of the wine made in the country. Far more red than white wine is produced, although the whites and rosés remain the most popular exports.

Most Portuguese wine comes from the temperate zones north of Lisbon (*map, page 83*). Apart from the Douro, where port is made, there are only six other demarcated wine regions, and approved wines that reach the required standard for each region are labelled *Denominação de Origem*.

Vinhos verdes or "green wines" make up about 25 per cent of Portugal's wine production. They are made in the Minho wine area which lies between the Minho and Douro rivers in north-west Portugal. The wines are called "green" because of their acidic youth, not because of their colour (most are red). They lose their freshness and sparkle if kept, and they are drunk during the year after harvesting. Although the red *vinhos verdes* make up about three-quarters of the wines, only the whites are exported—possibly because the astringency of the red is thought to be unappealing to foreigners.

A large range of grape varieties unknown in other countries is used for these wines. Land is scarce in this densely populated but still rural region, and here the wines are traditionally grown high above the ground, supported on fences and arbours in order to free enough land below for other crops.

The upland region of Dão, in the centre of northern Portugal, produces good red and white wines. Here, in general, the grapes are grown in small vineyards but industrially vinified by co-operatives. The red wines, deeply coloured and astringent as a result of prolonged maceration of the grapes, improve with age. The white wines are dry, with a refreshing, clean taste and should be drunk young.

The other four demarcated wine areas, Setubal, Bucelas, Carcauclos and Colares, are centred around Lisbon. All have greatly diminished in size and importance in modern times. The most notable is Setubal, where Moscatel do Setubal, a fortified dessert wine, is made from the white Moscatel grape.

In the Bucelas area, fresh dry white wines are made and exported. The red wines of the dwindling Colares vineyard are very tannic, acidic and astringent in youth; but they take age well.

Outside the six demarcated areas, the Ribatejo vineyards in central Portugal produce a large quantity of red and white carafe wines. Their higher quality wines include the popular Serradayres, a blend of the best Ribatejo wines.

Other wines deserving mention include the Periquita, Pasmodos and Camarate red wines from around Setubal, and some robust, substantial reds made at Borba, near Evora.

Premières Côtes de Bordeaux

Large district of Bordeaux with its own appellation, on the right bank of the Garonne, producing red and white wines (*map, page 85*). The reds are easy wines, best drunk young; the whites range from *moelleux* (slightly sweet) to sweet.

Provence

Provence, in the South of France, is an important source of good local wines—mainly rosés and reds, with a smaller proportion of whites. From the Rhône in the west to the Italian border in the east, there is a string of VDQS districts making wines to suit most tastes and pockets. Provence also has five *appellations contrôlées* for the distinguished wines from Palette, Cassis, Bandol, Bellet and Côtes de Provence (*map, page 84*).

Palette makes a full-bodied white wine and a firm, elegant red that ages well. Cassis produces reds, whites and rosés, but is best known for its distinctive white wine, rustic and vigorous, the traditional accompaniment to seafood in Marseilles.

Bandol produces pale elegant rosés and long-lived red wines with a deep colour and an intense fruit in youth that develops into a bouquet of great finesse. The Mourvèdre grape (a minimum of 50 per cent in the reds) imposes its intense fruitiness on the wines. A few Bandol vineyards also make some white wine.

Bellet makes reds, whites and rosés of consistent good quality. Côtes de Provence, promoted from VDQS status in 1977, produces red, rosé and white wines, the last often lacking in character.

Puisseguin-St.-Emilion see *St. Emilion*

Rheingau

The smallest and most renowned of the seven Rhine wine regions of Germany, regarded as one of the greatest wine areas in the world. The vines lie along the Rhine which makes a great bend on its way from Switzerland to the North Sea, so that for one brief stretch of 35 km (22 miles) the vineyards face the south and sun, protected from cold winds by the foothills of the Taunus mountains (*map, page 83*). The climate is about the mildest of the whole of Germany. The Rhine is at its widest and the reflections from its broad waters are another source of warmth, while the rising mists of autumn favour the development of *Botrytis cinerea* (*page 16*).

A large proportion of Rheingau wines are of the highest quality: superb Spätlese and Beerenauslese wines that are deep and complex in all their luscious ripeness and big, balanced beauty.

The soil varies: there is slate, loam, loess, quartzite, schist. The grapes are Riesling (a large majority), with some Müller Thurgau and Silvaner and a little Spätburgunder (Pinot Noir) for the small amount of red wine made (less than 2 per cent of the total) at Assmanshausen.

The output of this small region is between 2 and 3 per cent of Germany's total. There is only one district (*Bereich*), Johannisberg, comprising the 10 greater vineyards (*Einzellagen*) of the region.

Besides many smallholdings there are a number of more extensive vineyards, some of which have been owned by the same families for several hundred years.

Rheinhessen (Hesse)

A Rhine wine region that is one of the largest wine areas in Germany. Its output each year is a quarter of the whole German production, and its wines the most exported, chiefly to Britain and the U.S.A. The area under vines is more than 22,000 hectares (54,000 acres), with an average annual output well above 2,000,000 hectolitres (44,000,000 gallons)—more than 90 per cent of it white.

The vineyards are situated along the left bank of the Rhine (*map, page 83*), where the climate is mild for these latitudes, and relatively free from frost and snow. The type of soil varies—marl, loess, red sandstone, some slate and quartzite.

The grape of Rheinhessen used to be the Silvaner, but that has now been overtaken by the Müller Thurgau. There are much smaller quantities of Riesling, Scheurebe and Morio Muscat. A few Portugieser vines are grown for the minor amount of red wine that is made.

Rheinhessen wines are very popular, and they are pleasing enough, although it cannot be said that the majority of them have any great distinction. They are soft, mild, flowery wines, downright sweet or with a sweet edge. The best can be round, full and fruity; the lesser ones have a blandness one may tire of. Except for the very fine wines—of which there are a few—most of them should be drunk before attaining any great age in bottle.

One of the best known and most exported of Rheinhessen wines is Liebfraumilch. Fifty or more years ago it came only from the vineyards (not very outstanding ones) belonging to the Liebfrauenkirche (Our Lady's Church) at Worms. Since then, the law has given a good deal of leeway in the use of the name: it may appear on any wine or blend of wines that has passed the quality test for QbA wine (see *Germany*) and that has come from any of the four main Rhine wine regions, be it Rheinhessen, Rheingau, Nahe or Rheinpfalz. (The name may not be used on either table wine or a superior QmP wine.)

Liebfraumilch is usually a mild sweetish wine but there can be considerable differences in quality. As the grape variety is not allowed to appear on the label, the buyer had best rely on the name and reputation of the shipper.

The region is divided into three districts (*Bereiche*)—Bingen, Nierstein and Wonnegau—with between them 24 greater vineyards (*Grosslagen*) and more than 400 single ones (*Einzellagen*). There are some largish estates, often run by the wine trade or by co-operatives, but most of the vineyards belong to peasant growers who also farm other crops and do not depend on wine alone for their living.

Around the wine town of Bingen, which gives its name to the *Bereich*, there is some slate in the soil and some Riesling grown; some fine lively wines result.

Rheinpfalz (Pfalz, Palatinate)

This major Rhine wine region is one of Germany's largest and most productive wine areas. The Pfalz or Palatinate lies south of the Rheinhessen region. It is bordered by the Rhine in the east and French Alsace in the south and west (*map, page 83*).

The region is sheltered by the Haardt mountain range, a continuation of the French Vosges, and enjoys a temperate climate, milder even than the Rheingau. Summers are dry and sunny—peaches, almonds, figs, even lemons ripen. Most of the vineyards lie 15 km (9 miles) from the river along a road known as the Deutsche Weinstrasse.

There are more than 20,000 hectares (50,000 acres) under vines, with an output of some 2,500,000 hectolitres (55,000,000 gallons). The soil is various, with sandstone, granite, slate and in the best areas some chalk, lime and basalt. Two districts (*Bereiche*), Mittelhaardt-Deutsche Weinstrasse and Südliche Weinstrasse, contain 26 greater vineyards (*Grosslagen*) and some 300 single vineyards (*Einzellagen*).

The Müller Thurgau and Silvaner varieties account for about half of the grapes planted, with a lesser quantity of Riesling (chiefly in the Middle Haardt vineyards, which produce the most distinguished wine). Some red wine is produced in the Palatinate—about 15 per cent of the region's output—mostly in the south and not of very high quality; the grape used is the Portugieser.

Palatinate wines should be considered in two groups. First, there are the wines grown in abundance in the southern and northern extremes of the region. These are heady young wines with pronounced flavours, sometimes earthy, and with much sweetness. Often they are not bottled but drunk as carafe wines in local wine rooms. In their own style and place, they are seductive—even too seductive, since they are more alcoholic than most of Germany's wholesomely light wines.

The other kind of Palatinate wines come—not by any means in the same abundance—from the very best inner section of the region: the Middle Haardt, where the Riesling flourishes. Many of the wines are bred to become Beerenaus-leses and Trockenbeerenausleses—big, true, full-bodied wines with a depth of sweet flavours, weightier than their Rheingau peers. They go perfectly with heavy, savoury food—venison, perhaps, or wild boar. And yet they are too manifold in their layers of flavours not to be explored on their own too—the great vintage Palatinates are wonderful wines.

Rumania

Straddling the same latitudes as France, Rumania has a history of wine-making that dates back to the seventh century B.C. Now, with an annual output of more than 7,000,000 hectolitres (15,000,000 gallons), it is second only to the Soviet Union among the wine-producing countries of Eastern Europe. Moreover, its wine industry—unlike that of the Soviet Union and its neighbours, Hungary and Bulgaria—is largely independent of the state. There are about 300,000 hectares (750,000 acres) of vineyards altogether. Fifty per cent of the vineyards are owned by co-operatives, 34 per cent are private plots. Only 16 per cent of the vineyards are state-owned and are closely monitored by research stations to maintain and improve standards.

The chief wine-producing regions lie to the east and south of the country's central Carpathian mountain chain. In the east, the province of Moldavia has two main vineyard areas. One, in the foothills of the mountains, is noted chiefly for its Cotnari, a white dessert wine somewhat similar to Hungary's Tokay (see *Hungary*). The other, farther south, is centred on the town of Focşani in a territory of limestone, loess and sandy soils. This is Rumania's largest wine-growing region. It produces a diversity of red and white wines, and the towns of Odobeşti, Coeşti, Panciu and Nicoreşti give their names to the best known of them. The grape varieties grown in this region include the classic Cabernet Sauvignon and Pinot Noir, plus the indigenous white Feteasca, Grasa and Tamiioasa (Muscat) grapes.

The sun-drenched Dealul Mare vineyards on the south-east foothills of the Carpathians produce for export red wines of high alcohol content, especially those made from Cabernet (both Franc and Sauvignon) and Pinot Noir grapes. Some of Rumania's newest vineyards are situated on the flat southern plains of Wallachia. Here, pleasant, fragrant white wines come from the Dragaşani area, red and rosé wines from Segarcea and Sadova, and a wide range of reds and whites from the Argecs vineyards.

Two of Rumania's finest white wine regions lie at opposite ends of the country. In the north-west, on the lofty Transylvania plateau, 600 metres (2,000 ft) above sea level, the Tirnave zone grows a number of aromatic white varieties, such as Wälschriesling (Grey Riesling), Muskat Ottonel, Traminer and Feteasca. In the extreme south-east, close to the coast on the sunny, mild Dobruja plateau, a small wine region produces a dessert Muscat known as Murfatlar (the area's main town) as well as red and white wines produced from recently planted French grape varieties.

St. Emilion

One of the four major red-wine districts of Bordeaux. Situated on the right bank of the Dordogne, it contains the small old wine town of St. Emilion and the river port of Libourne (*map, page 85*). Though geographically small (about a quarter of the size of the Médoc), it has a large output—some 380,000 hectolitres (8,350,000 gallons) of appellation wine a year, including that from various outlying satellite communities.

The general character of the wines is soft, fruity, full; they are said to be more easily appreciated by the newcomer to claret than the relatively drier, more astringent wines of the Médoc and Graves.

On the whole, St. Emilions mature sooner than Médoc or Graves, although the greater wines among them can sometimes last to great age. An average fine St. Emilion will be good, if not yet at its best, at four to five years old, as against eight to 10 years for a comparable Médoc.

Prevalent grapes are Cabernet Franc and Merlot, with a smaller quantity of Cabernet Sauvignon. Malbec (here called Pessac) used to be included, but has largely been dropped because of its local susceptibility to disease. Cabernet Franc and Merlot are early ripeners and make for softer, less tannic wines than the Cabernet Sauvignon.

The region of St. Emilion proper con-

St. Emilion Classified Growths

Premiers grands crus classés

Château Ausone
Château Cheval Blanc
Château Beau-Séjour
  Duffau Lagarrosse
Château Beau-Séjour Bécot
Château Belair
Château Canon
Clos Fourtet
Château Figeac
Château La Gaffelière
Château Magdelaine
Château Pavie
Château Trottevieille

---

sists of two parts, a hilly area known as the Côtes and the stony, sloping Graves. The Côtes are an irregular collection of hills, with soil of silicon, clay and chalk. Their most outstanding wine is Château Ausone; other extremely distinguished vineyards are the Châteaux of Belair, Canon, La Gaffelière, Magdelaine, Pavie and the Clos Fourtet.

The Graves—a sloping plateau with low hills of gravel and sand—produces many fine wines, among them Château Cheval Blanc—undisputedly one of the all time greats—and Château Figeac, also a glorious wine.

St. Emilion also has an outer region that consists of four communities with the right to use their own compound appellations (these are Lussac-St.-Emilion, Montagne-St.-Emilion, Puisseguin-St.-Emilion and St.-Georges-St.-Emilion) together with seven satellite communities that lack separate appellations but are entitled to take the plain name of St. Emilion. The wines, though not as fine or lasting as those of inner St. Emilion, can be round, full of fruit and a pleasure to drink, especially when still fairly young.

The St. Emilions were officially classified in 1954. There are two classes only, *premiers grands crus classés* (classified first great growths) of which there are 12 (see *box*) and *grands crus classés* (clas-

---

sified great growths) of which there are now about 70. The order is alphabetical, except for Châteaux Ausone and Cheval Blanc, which head the first growth list.

In addition to the original classification there is also a huge listing made each year by analysis and official tastings, naming more than 500 *châteaux, clos* and *domaines* as *grands crus* (principal growths) and some 200 as minor *crus*.

St. Estèphe

One of the four most famous Médoc communities, which has been given the distinction of its own appellation within the Bordeaux area. See *Médoc*.

St.-Georges-St.-Emilion see *St. Emilion*

St. Julien

One of the four most famous Médoc communities, which has been given the distinction of its own appellation within the Bordeaux region. See *Médoc*.

Ste. Croix du Mont see *Loupiac and Ste. Croix du Mont*

Ste. Foy Bordeaux

A small area in the north-east corner of Entre-Deux-Mers, on the perimeter of the Bordeaux region (*map, page 85*), traditionally producing sweet, white wines, and a very small amount of red. Today, however, the white wines are often dry.

Sauternes

If Bordeaux is the home of claret, it is also that of some of the greatest of sweet white wines: those vinified in the five communities of Sauternes—Barsac, Bommes, Fargues, Preignac and Sauternes. The last is at once the name of the whole region, of a village and one of the communities therein—and of course the wine. Barsac is also a special case, since it has its own *appellation contrôlée* used by some growers.

Sauternes lies in an enclave of Graves, where there is much sand and gravel in the soil. The microclimate is warm and humid, with morning mists and mild heat in the autumn. These encourage the beneficent fungus, *Botrytis cinerea* (*page 16*), to spread through the vineyards in September. When it is established, the grape harvest begins.

Then we have a further complication and refinement: because the rot does not attack all the berries on the vine at the same time or rate, there has to be a picking of single berries, selected in their individual ripeness day after day, week after week, into October, into frost-threatened November. It is hard, slow, repetitive work and a perilous undertaking. Much can go wrong and when it succeeds there will be a little, a very little—the yields are infinitesimal—of richly sweet, flower-scented, golden wine. The "noble rot" does not attack every year, and when it is absent—say, because of a clear, cool autumn—no true Sauternes can be made.

True Sauternes is an entirely natural product. Its alcoholic strength is high—an average of 14 per cent—but no boost of sugar, no fortifying brandy ever goes near it. The master grape is Semillon, with about a third of Sauvignon Blanc. Usually a very little Muscadelle is added.

The Sauternes were the only wines classified along with the Médocs in the original 1855 classification of Bordeaux growths. Château d'Yquem was put in a top class of its own, as *premier grand cru* (first great growth). The other outstanding *châteaux* were ranked *premier* and *deuxième crus*. Since then some of the *châteaux* have split their properties into two; a few have ceased to exist. There have also been minor changes in naming and spelling. There are now 11 *premiers crus* and 13 *deuxièmes crus* (see *box*), as well as more than 300 minor growths.

Most of the classified *châteaux* make wonderful wines; in a right year, some of the first and a few of the second *crus* make a great wine. Château d'Yquem still is the summit. There the perfectionism of the perilous process is carried to its limits— the picking, if need be, goes on into December. The wine evolves in barrel for three and a half years. It requires constant topping up—with more of the precious wine—to make up for losses through evaporation; the yield in a good year is one glassful of Château d'Yquem from a vine; and in a wrong year, none.

Great Sauternes are immensely long-lived. Ideally one should not begin to drink them before they have been 20 or 30 years in bottle. They are always luscious, but in youth the honeyed sweetness still

Sauternes Classification

Community names are given in parentheses.

Premier grand cru

Château d'Yquem
(Sauternes)

Premiers crus

Château La Tour Blanche
(Bommes)

Château Lafaurie Peyraguey
(Bommes)

Clos Haut-Peyraguey
(Bommes)

Château Rayne-Vigneau
(Bommes)

Château Suduiraut
(Preignac)

Château Coutet
(Barsac)

Château Climens
(Barsac)

Château Guiraud
(Sauternes)

Château Rieussec
(Fargnes)

Château Sigalas-Rabaud
(Bommes)

Château Rabaud-Promis
(Bommes)

Deuxièmes crus

Château Doisy-Daëne
(Barsac)

Château Doisy-Védrines
(Barsac)

Château Doisy-Dubroca
(Barsac)

Château d'Arche
(Sauternes)

Château Filhot
(Sauternes)

Château Broustet
(Barsac)

Château Nairac
(Barsac)

Château Caillou
(Barsac)

Château Suau
(Barsac)

Château de Malle
(Preignac)

Château Romer du Hayot
(Fargues)

Château Lamothe Despujols
(Sauternes)

Château Lamothe Guignard
(Sauternes)

masks some of the subtleties—an underlying trace of flintiness perhaps, a hint of bitter almond to cut the cloying. In age the golden wine darkens, the flavours grow deeper. Michael Broadbent, the English wine authority and director of the wine department of Christie's Auction Rooms in London, notes having drunk an Yquem 1869 in 1969, a century after the wine was made, and finding it still "in perfect condition and balance", and an Yquem of 1875 in 1978 "still sweet, thick and rich".

Traditionally, Sauternes is drunk as a dessert wine at the end of a meal. This rather limits it. One may find that a glass of it taken by itself in mid-morning, cold but not iced, is restoring and refreshing in a most agreeable way. (Note that, unlike most other table wines, an opened bottle of Sauternes will keep reasonably well for a week or so, in a refrigerator with the cork stuck back in the bottle.)

Some people advocate drinking Sauternes during a meal proper with *foie gras* or fish, or serving it with Roquefort cheese at the end of the meal. Sauternes goes well with rather bland puddings, without excess of sweetness, creaminess or spice; better still with fruits—a ripe pear or some raspberries. Best of all perhaps, is Sauternes as the dessert itself.

Savoie

'Clean and fresh" are adjectives frequently applied to the wines of Savoie—a little enclave of vineyards in the mountains along the French-Swiss border near Geneva (*map, page 84*). Most of the wines are white, either still or sparkling. At their best, they have a flinty dryness and an exquisitely delicate flavour.

The appellation Vin de Savoie covers a large number of communities that produce red, white and rosé wines, and there are three more specific *appellations contrôlées* producing exclusively white wine: Seyssel and Roussette de Savoie, both made from the Altesse grape (locally called Roussette); and Crépy, made from the Chasselas grape.

Sekt

The usual German word for white sparkling wine, whether it is *Qualitätschaumwein* (quality sparkling wine) made by the Champagne method (q.v.) or ordinary sparkling wine made by fermenting in a pressurized vat. Large quantities of wine, both from within Germany and imported from outside, are devoted to the making of sparkling wines.

Sherry

Sherry is a complex blend of wines, fortified by the addition of distilled spirits. It is made principally from the white Palomino grape, and its style ranges from pale, straw-coloured wines of great delicacy and finesse to darker, fuller wines that have a mellow, nutty flavour. All the basic wines are dry by nature, and are often drunk this way in Spain itself, but before they are bottled for export they are usually combined with small amounts of wines specially made for blending with sherry, which add varying degrees of sweetness and colour.

Sherry derives its name from the Spanish town of Jerez; situated 30 km (20 miles) north of the port of Cadiz in Andalusia (*map, page 83*), Jerez is the capital of the sherry industry. The vineyards form a rough triangle between Jerez and the two coastal towns of Sanluca de Barrameda and Puerto de Santa Maria. The best vineyards are on the dazzling white chalky soil called *albariza*, which gives the Palomino grape finesse and a clean flavour.

The fine, even texture of the soil is of vital importance: the soil absorbs the heavy spring rains and then develops a hard crust on its surface when the rains stop. The crust prevents the moisture in the subsoil from evaporating and the vines can feed on the trapped water throughout the long, arid summer. To protect them from the *levante*, the east wind that blows in winter, the vines are grown low. In summer, the sun is reflected back from the white soil and the grapes ripen to a voluptuous sweetness.

Grapes that are grown in a hot climate tend to lack acidity when completely ripe. To increase the acidity of sherry, the harvested grapes are traditionally sprinkled with gypsum before they are pressed. The gypsum reacts with the cream of tartar that is naturally present in the grape, breaking it down into tartaric acid. Tartaric crystals precipitate out of the wine and settle as sediment during the first few months of storage in the cask.

Because of the hot climate, the very sweet pressed grape juice—the *mosto*, or must—starts fermenting almost immediately. Traditionally, the must was run directly into new oak barrels to ferment but nowadays technological advances make it more likely to be fermented in temperature-controlled vats.

After about six months in the wine barrel, the process of classifying the wine begins. Although an experienced grower will have some idea of what type of wine to expect from a certain slope of the vineyard or a particular crop of grapes, there are no guarantees as to how the wine will develop. The initial classification—made either by tasting or, with great experience, by nose—is often only a tentative assessment of the wine; the classification of individual barrels frequently alters as the wine evolves.

There are three main sherry classifications: fino wine, which evolves either into an old fino or into an amontillado; oloroso; and the hard-to-find palo cortado. Fino sherries are light, delicate wines, very pale when young, with a penetrating fresh scent. The characteristic that distinguishes fino wines is the vigorous growth of yeasty scum, known as flor (*page 16*), which forms on the surface and imparts a distinctive taste to the wine. Flor needs air to grow; and, unlike most wines, sherry is matured on ullage—that is, with a space for air at the top of the barrel (*page 15*).

Certain fino wines change their character as they mature and are then reclassified as amontillado. Amontillado sherries are softer, darker wines with a more mellow flavour than finos, and an almost nutty scent. Such naturally aged amontillados are of very high quality and the best of them are not fortified.

Manzanilla is a type of fino sherry made only in Sanluca de Barrameda. The grapes are harvested a little earlier than in other sherry vineyards and are therefore less ripe and more acid. Manzanillas are distinguished by their slightly salty flavour—said to result from the storage of the wines so near to the sea. They are light wines that do not travel well.

Olorosos are heavier, richer but less refined wines, often with a silky texture. They do not usually develop flor, and if flor does begin to develop on a wine initially classified as oloroso, the wine is fortified with distilled spirits to a strength sufficient to destroy the growth.

Palo cortado, which is raised without flor, is an extremely rare wine, somewhere between a fino and an oloroso in style. It is more delicate than an oloroso, but without the qualities bestowed by the flor on a fino. Mature palo cortado is dry but soft, with a rich, full flavour—a wine of great distinction. Inexplicably, the pre-Phylloxera grapes (*page 7*) produced far more palo cortados than are seen today.

Following the initial classification, the wines are racked and then fortified with distilled spirits. Fino-type wines, including amontillado, are brought up to an alcoholic strength of around 15 per cent—sufficient to stabilize the wine without killing off the flor. Oloroso-type wines are brought up to around 18 per cent alcoholic strength, which is sufficient to prevent accidental formation of flor.

The wines at this stage are vintage wines, called *añadas*, each barrel containing wine from one harvest and vineyard. After two to three years, the añada wines enter the solera system, the method used by sherry producers to achieve and maintain a standard of quality for their wines.

The solera system is based on the principle that a small amount of young wine, added to an older wine of the same kind, will take on the character of this older wine. Thus, when a barrel of mature wine is supplemented with a similar wine of a younger age, the wine in the barrel will gradually revert to its original style. After about six months it will regain its original taste.

The solera system consists of several different sets of barrels. All the barrels contain the same type of wine, but each set holds wine that has reached a different stage of maturity. Barrels containing the oldest wine are called soleras, like the system itself; the supporting barrels, of progressively younger wines, are known as criaderas, *criadera* being the Spanish word for nursery.

Only wine from the oldest barrel, the solera, is ever drawn off for bottling; no more than a third (sometimes only a fifth) of the barrel is drawn off. The solera is then refreshed with wine from the second oldest stage, which is in turn refreshed with wine from the third stage and so on. The criaderas containing the youngest wine are refreshed with a suitable añada wine being introduced into the system.

There are different soleras for each type of sherry, as well as soleras of varying ages. Some soleras date from the last century and are imbued with the memory of wines a hundred years old. The sherries produced from these venerable sources have a richer, deeper, more intense taste than younger wines.

Very few wines are bottled on their own straight from the solera; such wines are among the finest sherries, but their dryness gives them a limited appeal and they are very expensive. Normally, the solera wines form the base wines for blended sherries, and it is the skill and judgment exercised in this blending process that is the essence of the sherry-maker's art.

The sherry may be a blend of wine from different soleras, or a blend of solera wine with young sherries that have not passed through the solera system at all. There are therefore no vintage sherries and no date, place or vineyard on a sherry label.

Once blended, the sherry is then flavoured with a carefully regulated amount of sweet wine—finos are slightly sweetened, olorosos much more so. Traditionally, a black treacly wine made from Pedro Ximenez grapes was used to sweeten sherries, but it is being replaced by *dulce apagado*, a finer sweet wine made from the Palomino grape. A little colouring wine, made from reduced must, may be added, and the blended sherry is then fortified by about 1 to 2 per cent before being bottled.

Fino sherries should be drunk young. If they are kept, they lose their flavour and finesse. Indeed, in Jerez, young unfortified fino wines are appreciated as fine table wines. Amontillados and olorosos change very little in the bottle and can be kept longer.

South Africa

South Africa is one of the newcomers to the ranks of producers of fine wine. In the 18th century, it produced Constantia, a strong, sweet dessert wine from the Cape, that was celebrated in Europe and seen as a rival to port and Tokay. But in recent years, the country became known as a source of reliable if unexciting fortified wines, heavy red table wines and sweet whites. Now though, using modern vinification methods, it produces clean, easy-to-drink red wine—in particular, those made from Cabernet Sauvignon and Pinotage, a South African cross between Pinot Noir and Cinsault. A few of the white wines are also pleasant.

The country's wine industry has been steadily advancing since 1918, when the Co-operative Winegrowers' Association (*Kooperatieve Wijnbouwers Vereniging* or KWV) was established; this association was later given statutory powers to control production and quality. Controls became more and more stringent, most especially with the introduction of Wine of Origin (*Wyn van Oorsprong*) legislation in 1973 to enable Cape wine to be sold to member countries of the E.E.C. The Wine of Origin seal guarantees the truth of the label with regard to place of origin, wine variety, and vintage year.

South Africa's main wine-producing areas fall within an L-shaped region whose arms run approximately 300 km (185 miles) north and 400 km (250 miles) east from a point near Cape Town (*map, page 81*). The best wines come from the area immediately to the east of Cape Town, round the towns of Stellenbosch, Paarl, Worcester and Robertson, where the climate is a little cooler and the rainfall is higher than elsewhere. There is some granite in the soil, providing propitious conditions for the red wine grapes.

Traditional South African grapes for table wines were mostly rather coarse varieties, but in recent years these have been gradually giving way to nobler ones. The South African Riesling is being replaced by the true Rhine Riesling, which produces a greenish-tinged wine with clear, light fruitiness and a crisp finish. Steen is a traditional South African grape which yields wines that are light and fruity and usually semi-sweet. However, Steen is now recognized as a form of Chenin Blanc, and it is gradually being replaced by modern Chenin Blanc varieties.

The grape traditionally known in South Africa as Green Grape (*Groendruif*) has been identified as Semillon; it has been joined in recent years by such other European varieties as Sauvignon Blanc, Chardonnay, Gewürztraminer and Clairette. The Muscat d'Alexandrie, known to the Afrikaaners as Hanepoot, is one of several Muscat varieties that are used today for their characteristically scented wines.

Among the reds, there are two chief South African varieties: one is the prolific Cinsault, which produces a wine that can be rather thin and is often used for distilling and blending. The other, Pinotage, is capable of producing an excellent wine, robust and full-bodied. Both these strains, however, are increasingly being used with other grapes in blends such as the popular Roodeberg, which contains a high proportion of Cabernet Sauvignon. This grape is as reliable in South Africa as elsewhere in the world, producing its characteristically ruby-red wine with a strong bouquet.

Spain

Spain ranks as the third largest producer of wine in the world; it is surpassed only by France and Italy. The bulk of its production—34,000,000 hectolitres (748,000,000 gallons) in 1981—is ordinary wine from the vast central plateau, but there are also fine wines of several types produced in several regions—and, of course, sherry (q.v.) from the vineyards of Jerez in the south-west.

Wine laws passed in 1970 have raised standards in the wine industry throughout the country and modern methods of viniculture are becoming much more widespread. Wines labelled *Denominacion de Origen* are of a guaranteed standard, although the controls are not as stringent as for the French *appellation contrôlée* system. As well as demarcating special regions, the authorities are encouraging the modernization of the large co-operatives that produce the Spanish ordinary wines, *vinos corrientes*.

Undoubtedly, Spain's best wines come from the Rioja district, in the north of the country. Besides having the advantage of a climate more benign than that of the sweltering central tableland, the region has benefited from its position less than 160 km (100 miles) from the French border (*map, page 82*). In the 1880s, French

wine growers from Bordeaux crossed the border to escape *Phylloxera vastatrix* (*page 7*) and found the Riojan vineyards conveniently near home. Although the disease eventually reached Spain and the French recrossed the border, they left behind them their traditions of vinification and the care of wine.

White Riojas have in the past been kept too long in the wood, becoming flat and oxidized before bottling, but controlled-temperature fermentations and earlier bottling now allow fresh, crisp, lively wines to be made. The best red Riojas are soft and fruity, with a good body and acid balance. They are much lighter in colour than most Spanish wines, with a brownish tinge imparted by long ageing in wood. Light reds—*claretes*—are drier, lighter wines with a very slight acidity; good-quality rosés are also made.

The Rioja vineyards are situated on either side of the river Ebro, which flows east from the Sierra de Cantabria mountain range. There are some 45,000 hectares (111,200 acres) of vines, many of them planted in small vineyards that are interspersed among fields of vegetables and wheat. The terrain is hilly and the best vineyards are 450 metres (1,500 ft) above sea level. The commercial capital of the Rioja wine industry is Logroño.

The climate encourages wine-growing: a good rainfall, summers hot enough to ripen the grapes, but not long enough to parch them, and relatively mild winters.

Rioja vines are planted in three types of soil: calcareous clay, ferruginous clay and alluvial silt. The district is divided into three areas: Rioja Alta, in the south-west, has a mixture of clay and alluvial soils; in Rioja Alavesa, in the north-west, the vineyards are on calcareous clay soil and produce the best wines of the area. Rioja Baja, in the east, has a hotter, drier climate, less propitious for quality wines.

The primary red Riojan grape is the Tempranillo, which imparts a good acid balance. The Garnacho grape (Grenache) lifts the level of alcohol, while the Graciano lends freshness and aroma, and the Mazuelo gives tannin for longevity.

Many good vintners grow less than half their own grapes and purchase the rest of the grapes they need from growers whose standards they trust. Others buy grapes

on the open market and some buy ready-made wine from the co-operatives and then blend and mature it themselves.

Most Rioja wines are blended; the year on the wine label refers to the vintage of the predominant wine in the bottle. Some high-quality *reservas*, however, are single-vintage wines, made in an especially good year. To qualify as a *reserva*, a Rioja must be aged for six or more years in the wine cellar (*bodega*), and a *gran reserva* must be aged for at least eight years.

The Penedes district in Catalonia has a long tradition of wine-making and some Penedes wines are very fine indeed. A greater variety of wines is produced here than in other parts of Spain, including reds, whites and rosés, sparkling wines and dessert wines.

The climate is temperate with a good rainfall, and the chalky soil gives the wines finesse. The climate is hottest in the coastal region of Bajo Penedes, where good red wines are made from the Carinena (Carignan), Garnacho and Tempranillo grapes. The mountain vineyards of the Alto Penedes have a cooler climate and are mostly planted with the Parallada grape. The wines are light, delicate and aromatic—amongst the best white wines produced in Spain.

A number of grapes from outside Spain, including the Pinot Noir, the Cabernet Sauvignon, and white varieties such as Riesling, Chardonnay and Gewürztraminer are cultivated in the Penedes area. The wines of the Torres estates, vinified from these grapes, are among the highest quality still table wines in Spain and, unlike most Spanish wines, are always labelled with the vintage year.

From the vineyards of the Tarragon region, just south of the Penedes, comes Tarragona Classico, a wine matured by the solera system (see *Sherry*). Red wines of a distinctive character are made at Priorato from the Carignan and Grenache grapes; the wines are high in alcohol, very dark, dry and heavy-bodied. North of the Penedes, the Alella district is one of the smallest demarcated regions in Spain. The white wines are best, exported under the name Marfil, meaning ivory; the dry wines are crisp and light, and the medium-dry are smooth and fragrant.

The wines from most of Spain's other demarcated regions are not exported. In the Navarre region, which adjoins the Riojan vineyards, some good ordinary red and white wines are made, and in northwest Spain, where the climate is wet and the summers are unreliable, the slightly sparkling Basque Chacoli is produced—an astringent wine, very low in alcohol. Galicia, in the far north, produces a large amount of wine—the reds very astringent, the whites rather better.

On the Pyrenean border with France, Perelada, in the Ampurdan-Costa Brava region, produces the high quality Reserva Don Miguel wine and also some good sparkling wines.

La Mancha, the huge plain south-east of Madrid in the centre of the country, yields the largest amount of wine in Spain. It includes the demarcated regions of Mentrida, Mancha, Manchuela and Valdepenas, but much of the wine, from whatever region, is inaccurately labelled Valdepenas after the area's most distinguished wine. The subsoil is a mixture of gravel, chalk and clay; and the dry, hot climate produces strong wines with a high alcohol content. The principal red grapes are the Cencibel, Monstrel and Tintorea, and the most commonly planted white grape is the Lairen. Most of the wine is red; it is sound, everyday wine and is drunk young.

East of La Mancha lies the Levante, which encompasses the fertile land of the Mediterranean seaboard and the mountainous hinterland. One of the best wines is Fondillon from Valencia. Sweet, amber-coloured wines are also made from the Muscatel and Malvasia grapes.

To the west of La Mancha, the Extremadura region on the Portuguese border extends down into southern Spain. A great deal of wine, both red and white, is made but none of it is demarcated. Much of the best wine is produced by small local growers and drunk within the region.

Southern Spain is renowned for its sherry vineyards in the Jerez region but it also produces the excellent Montilla wines, which are very similar to sherry, and a dessert wine from Malaga, besides ordinary reds and whites from the Huelva district to the west.

The Montilla vineyards are about 160 km (100 miles) inland from Jerez and are centred around the towns of Montilla and Moriles. They lie on the same chalky soil that is found in Jerez, but the inland climate is even hotter, producing wines with a natural alcoholic strength of about 16 per cent. Montilla wines are not usually fortified for export.

Malaga, formerly known as Mountain Wine, is a dark sweet wine, made principally from the Moscatel and Pedro Ximenez grapes. The vineyards are situated in the hills behind the port of Malaga. The wine is either vinified where it is grown, or in one of the large *bodegas* in the town of Malaga itself.

Among the Spanish Islands, which all produce their own wine, Majorca makes very good red wines, and the Canaries, which used to be world famous for their sweet wine, make mostly plain white *vinos corrientes* for local consumption.

Sparkling Wines

The effervescence that characterizes sparkling wines is caused by the sudden escape of dissolved carbon dioxide, produced during fermentation, when the bottle is opened. The degree of effervescence may vary from a slight prickle resulting from a residue of sugar remaining unfermented in the wine when it is bottled—such wines are called *pétillant* in France—to a stronger sparkle achieved by adding sugar and yeasts to induce the wine to ferment a second time under pressure in a sealed vessel.

All the best sparkling wines are made by the Champagne method (q.v.), whereby the second fermentation takes place in bottles. Much sparkling wine is also made more cheaply by fermenting in bulk in pressurized vats, and bottling under pressure. Wine that is made fizzy by pumping carbon dioxide into still liquid does not merit serious consideration.

Switzerland

Switzerland has more than 12,000 hectares (nearly 30,000 acres) under vine—an impressively large number for such a small and mountainous country. Its vineyards are generally cultivated along efficient and scientific lines, and inevitably the majority of them are sited on steep valley slopes. The most important wine areas are in the south French-speaking cantons of the country. Roughly, these areas follow the course of the Rhône as it flows west through the Valais canton and then north into Lake Geneva. Thereafter, within Vaud canton, they follow the northern arc of the lake. The lake water reflects sunlight on to the vines, warming their environment and encouraging the growth of the grapes.

The vines of the Valais grow on some of the most dizzily steep terraces in the country. Situated on the sunny, south-facing slopes of the valley, the vineyards are watered by mountain streams and melted snow carried down by little wooden aqueducts, or *bisses*. The supreme white grape of this region is the Chasselas—here called the Fendant and known as the Dorin in Vaud canton. It makes a light, crisp, refreshing wine with a pleasant bouquet and a barely perceptible sparkle. The great majority of wines produced in this canton are white. Its chief red wine—rich, powerful and grapey with a clear ruby colour—is Dôle, based on Pinot Noir and Gamay grapes.

Some 40 per cent of Switzerland's wines come from vineyards planted in Vaud canton, along the north shore of Lake Geneva and most particularly along the Lavaux, the name given to the 16-km (10-mile) strip from Lausanne to Montreux. Chasselas is again the main grape, and it produces a light dry wine to be drunk young. Farther north, the region of Lake Neuchâtel in the canton of the same name produces good rosés and red wines made from the Pinot Noir grape, and some light, semi-sparkling white wines made from Chasselas.

The majority of Switzerland's 19 other cantons also make wines, but these are rarely exported. The German-speaking cantons to the north rely on the Müller Thurgau grape for some fragrant white wines. The red wines of the Italian-speaking Ticino canton in the south-east are made mostly from the Merlot grape, and rarely appear outside that region.

Turkey

Turkey has one of the world's most ancient wine-making traditions, dating back at least 6,000 years. Wine production virtually ceased in the eighth century, however, when Turkey adopted the Islamic faith, which forbids its followers any alcoholic beverages. Political reforms in the 1920s and 1930s—including the declaration that Islam was no longer Turkey's official faith—encouraged wine production; wine regions have since been demarcated, modern technical equipment provided and steady attempts made to enforce standards. Although progress has been slow and the export of Turkish wines is still minimal, the potential for growth is enormous.

Most of Turkey, with the exception of its western coastline and the area around the Sea of Marmara in the north, is rocky and mountainous. The climate is well suited for grape-growing, with hot sunny summers and plentiful rain in winter. The most commonly planted wine grapes are native, but the use of finer European varieties, such as the Pinot Noir, Chardonnay and Riesling grapes, is gradually becoming more widespread. All types of red and white wine are produced—dry, semi-dry, sweet, fortified and sparkling. None of the wine is of a very high quality but much of it is sound and reliable. Most wines are rather light with a low acidity; they are best drunk within a year.

Some of Turkey's best wines come from central Anatolia. Red wine is made in the area around Ankara from Kalecik, Çubuk and Dimrit grapes and white wines from the Hasandede, Narince and Emir varieties. New plantings include the Gamay, Carignan, Clairette and Riesling grapes. The region's best-known wine, Buzbağ, is a good quality red wine—full-bodied, heady, and intricate in structure.

In south-east Turkey, some medium quality red and white wines are produced. Gaziantep, a red wine made from Dergikarasi grapes, is well regarded, and wines that are similar in style to Buzbag are made from Horozkarasi and Bogazkarasi grapes.

The European influence is most prevalent in the green and fertile region of Thrace and Marmara, the largest wine-producing area in Turkey. Good and medium quality red and white wines—generally labelled Trakya, the Turkish name for Thrace—are made. The local Papazkaras grape yields reliable red wines; Gamay, Cinsault and Pinot Noir

and Cabernet Sauvignon grapes are also grown. White grapes include new plantings of Rieslings, Chardonnay and Sylvaner. Good, sweetish white wine, called Tekirdag, is made from the Yapincak grape, the local version of Semillon.

The Aegean region, which extends more than 240 km (150 miles) inland from the west coast, produces over a quarter of Turkey's grapes, including the seedless sultana. Although most of the grapes grown in the region are table grapes, the area does produce sound red and white wines, together with good, naturally sweet or fortified wines from the Bornova Muscat grape. The ancient city of Smyrna, known today as Izmir, is the centre of the region's wine production.

United Kingdom

England is too northerly a country to produce outstanding wine in other than exceptionally hot years. But a number of pleasant, light wines are made, mostly by small individually owned vineyards. The most favoured grapes are German varieties such as Müller Thurgau and the wines often have a flowery style reminiscent of Mosel. As in Germany, the wines are often sweetened with grape juice before bottling, but most are somewhat drier than their German counterparts. They are produced only in small quantities and are generally obtainable only through wine merchants in Great Britain itself.

U.S.A.

In terms of quantity, the U.S.A. is the second most important non-European wine producer, accounting for 13,000,000 hectolitres (286,000,000 gallons) in 1980. (Outside Europe, only Argentina produces more.) In quality terms, it ranks higher still. California, the major wine-growing state, produces some wines of very high quality and many of the cheaper table wines or "jug" wines from California and elsewhere are carefully made, reliable beverages.

Wine has been made in the U.S.A. since the arrival of European settlers in the 17th century, although not without difficulty. The American species of vines the Europeans found growing wild are unsuitable for wine-making, and early attempts to cultivate the European grape

encountered setbacks. Efforts by the colonists to grow *vinifera* along the east coast failed because the vines were attacked by the Phylloxera parasite (*page 7*), which was endemic to the wild *labrusca* vines but remained unidentified as the cause of the failure for another two centuries.

On the west coast, things at first went better. Spanish missionaries brought *Vitis vinifera* to Mexico, also in the 17th century, and later to California; the vines flourished because the climate was excellent and Phylloxera was then unknown on that side of the continent. The sweet Mission wine, originally produced for Communion use, remained popular for most of the 19th century.

From the mid-century on, many European grape varieties were brought into California; but in 1870 Phylloxera too made its entry and the vineyards were devastated. As in Europe, their recovery depended on grafted vines. Thereafter, wine productioin made marked advances both in quantity and in quality. But in 1918, an amendment to the Constitution forbade Americans to consume alcoholic drinks except as medicine or sacrament. Prohibition lasted until 1933 and denied a generation of Americans the chance to develop their taste for wine.

The most active phase in the improvement of North American wines came in the second half of the 20th century. Some good wines were made in California in the 1930s after the repeal of Prohibition, but a general demand for really fine wines did not spread until after World War II. Subsequently, progress has been rapid. In the 1960s countless new vineyards were planted in California and during the 1970s wine-making from *vinifera* varieties spread among the nearby northwesterly states—Washington, Oregon and Idaho—and, on a smaller scale, to other states throughout the country. In New York State, and especially around the Finger Lakes, large quantities of wine—much of it sparkling—are made chiefly from native American vines, and from hybrids created by crossing these vines with *vinifera* (*pages 7-8*).

California is currently the centre of good quality American wine production. It has an equable climate, fertile soil, an enthusiastic public and wine makers ambitious to produce the best possible wines.

Almost all the better wines and a large proportion of cheaper wines are sold under the name of a single grape variety as varietal wine. California law requires only that 51 per cent or more of the bottle's contents must be from the named grape variety, but most wine makers use 100 per cent or near it, in an attempt to capture the unique qualities of a grape strain. Very few producers concentrate on only a single wine; most make separate varietal wines from at least half a dozen different grape varieties.

California has gained much of its reputation with its Chardonnay whites and Cabernet Sauvignon reds. Other white wine grapes grown with success include the German Riesling, termed Johannisberg Riesling in California, and the Sauvignon Blanc, often called the Fumé Blanc. Recently, some late-harvested Botrytis-affected Rieslings (*page 16*) have been successful. The Sauvignons are dry wines with that grape's unmistakable metallic scent.

Red varieties other than Cabernet Sauvignon include the Syrah of the Rhône and another variety until recently confused with it—Petite Sirah. Both yield tannic, complex wines for long ageing. Pinot Noir, the grape of red Burgundy, is grown with only infrequent success.

Finally there is Zinfandel, a variety that is prominent only in California. Zinfandels are spicy, exuberant wines made in a bewildering variety of styles: there are light ones intended for drinking young—"California's Beaujolais"; there are thick, tannic ones intended to be aged for years; there are even sweet Zinfandels with 16 or 17 per cent alcohol made from late-picked, sun-withered grapes.

Vines are grown all over California but there are geographical variations in quality, based largely on climate and partly on chance, giving some vine-growing areas an advantage over others (*map, page 80*).

California lies at the same latitude as southern Italy and north Africa, areas considered rather too hot for the production of fine wines. But climate is not simply a matter of latitude—a series of mountain ranges running parallel to the coast divides California into a succession of microclimates, from the cool coastal

stretch to the hot interior. Predictably, the cooler microclimates—those in the northern part of the state—produce all the best wines.

The Napa valley, in Napa County north of San Francisco, has the densest concentration of California's great names. The 40 km (25 mile) long Napa valley has a climate moderated not only by the Pacific Ocean to the west but also by San Francisco bay, adjoining the southern end of Napa County. The nearby bay makes the weather generally cooler at the southern end of the county, providing optimal conditions for white wine grapes; many sites at the warmer northern end are ideal for red wine grapes. The distribution is not, however, smooth or continuous, and as yet little has been done to choose specific grapes particularly well adapted to certain soils and microclimates. The soils are varied, alluvial or volcanic; chalky soil is extremely rare.

A few of the wineries in the Napa valley are old-established firms from the 19th century, some of which kept going with Communion wine through the Prohibition period. Many more were established in the 1960s and 1970s and the pace of development has been very rapid.

Many wineries use grapes grown in several parts of California to make inexpensive but sound varietal wines. Others use only their own grapes or ones carefully chosen from other sites in Napa, and muster all their skill and equipment to produce the best wines in their power. Many wine makers—not only in Napa, but throughout California—who buy their grapes insist on a say in their nurture, and may well dictate the picking date and even the pruning methods. Virtually all the outstanding Napa wines are from single grape varieties.

Sonoma County, west of Napa, has a similar climatic range but rather more rain and fog from the adjacent Pacific Ocean. The main river valleys—Alexander, Sonoma, Russian and Dry Creek—encompass a variety of soils and microclimates. Wine was grown in the area even earlier than at Napa, but until the 1970s the emphasis was on ordinary wines. New efforts have been concentrated on quality wines, and the climate should allow results at least as good as Napa's.

Mendocino County, on the coast north of Sonoma, is the coolest of California's wine-growing regions. High-yielding grape varieties are being progressively replaced by finer varieties. The cool climate lends itself to delicate whites and some good light Zinfandels are produced.

South of San Francisco bay, vines are grown in the coastal counties of Alameda, Santa Clara, Santa Cruz, San Benito, Monterey, San Luis Obispo, Santa Barbara and—right at the southern end of the state—San Bernadino, Riverside and San Diego. The climate ranges from cool and windy on the central coast to near-desert in the far south. The coastal counties have the potential to produce fine wine, but have not yet acquired a reputation to rival those of the northern counties. The more interesting wines are made in Alameda's Livermore valley, on the slope of the Santa Cruz mountains spanning the Santa Clara-Santa Cruz border, along the Edna valley in San Luis Obispo and the Santa Ynez valley in Santa Barbara County.

California's fertile Central valley is too hot for the production of fine wines but modern technology, especially temperature-controlled fermentation, has made a tremendous difference to the quality and now huge quantities of pleasant, easy-drinking wine are produced. A few wines of more distinction are made at the cooler, northern end of the valley.

North of California, the states of Washington, Oregon and Idaho offer more difficult conditions for viniculture but wine makers are tempted by the hope of subtler, more delicate wines. The latitude is similar to that of France and Germany, but the cold ocean current makes the climate less agreeable, and rainfall is heavy near the coast. The climate is cool but with long hours of summer sunshine to ensure that grapes ripen slowly and have good acidity; it lends itself well to the cultivation of noble *vinifera* varieties. Oregon produces some very good Pinot Noir (a particularly difficult variety to adapt outside Burgundy) and Idaho Chardonnays can be remarkable.

In states outside California and the north-west, increasing amounts of *vinifera* vines have been planted recently, for example in the eastern states—even in cold New York. There are undoubtedly many areas in North America that would lend themselves perfectly to *vinifera*.

U.S.S.R.

The Soviet Union is one of the major wine-producing countries in the world; it has some 1,250,000 hectares (3,090,000 acres) under vines and produces more than 32,000,000 hectolitres (704,000,000 gallons) of wine a year. The most important vineyards extend round the north coast of the Black Sea, from Moldavia on the Rumanian border in the west through the Ukraine and Russia to Georgia, Armenia and Azerbaijan. The climate is severe: although summers are hot, there are the hazards of soil erosion caused by heavy downpours, late frost, hail and intense winters with temperatures plummeting to −40°C (−40°F). Much of the wine is sweet, but sparkling and fortified wines, dry reds and whites are also produced. The most commonly planted vines are native varieties, although the introduction of European stock is increasing all the time.

Very little wine is exported to the West. There are three wine classifications—ordinary, for unmatured wines that are not labelled with a place name; named wines, which are labelled with the place of origin; and *kollektsionye* wines, which have been bottle-aged for at least two years and are usually labelled with place of origin and grape variety.

The Soviet preference is for sweet and sparkling wines, especially those from the Crimean vineyards in the Ukraine. Sweet white wines made here include Ay-Danil and Livadia Muscats. The brand name Massandra is used by a combine of vine collectives for a range of dessert wines, notably rich, honeyed Muscatels. Good sparkling wines, including the well-regarded Kaffia, are made in Sevastopol and Balaclava in the Crimea. Kokur Nizhegorsky and Sylvaner Feodosiisky are two full-bodied, dry white wines.

Like the Crimea, the Republic of Georgia—lying between the Black and Caspian Seas in the shelter of the Caucasus—makes reputable wines. The Georgian dry whites, Tsinandali and Ghurdjurni, the red Mukuzani, which is heavy and dry, and the lighter Saperavi red wine are all good ordinary wines. Tbilisi is the centre of production for the Georgian sparkling wine Champanski.

The westerly province of Moldavia produces some good red wines, including Romanest and Negru de Purkar which are made with Cabernet Sauvignon, Merlot and Malbec grapes.

In the mountainous southern province of Armenia, nearly all the wines are heavy and sweet; although they are often labelled as port or Madeira, these names are no more than a nod in the direction of their European prototypes. Azerbaijan, on the western shore of the Caspian Sea, also produces dessert wines, of which Matras and Shemakh are the best known.

Vatting

A phase in traditional red wine vinification. The crushed grapes—skin, pulp and juice, with or without the stems—ferment in vats and, after fermentation, are left to macerate, the juices absorbing additional tannin from prolonged contact with the skins and (if they are present) the stems. The thickness of the skins and the amount of tannin they contain not only differs from one grape variety to another but from one year to another, depending on weather conditions such as the hours of sunshine or quantity of rain the vines have received. It is essential to wine-making that the length of maceration—which may be varied greatly from year to year—should be controlled by a sound intuition, drawn from long experience.

Vin Gris see *Vin Rosé*

Vin Rosé (pink wine)

In certain parts of France a distinction is made between *vin gris*—a very pale pink wine made by pressing the red grapes immediately after they are picked and fermenting the juice out of contact with the skins—and *vin rosé* or *vin clairet* (whence the English claret). For *vin rosé*, the juices are left in contact with the skins for a few hours after the grapes are crushed to draw more colour from the skins before being pressed and the juice fermented. Until the end of the 18th century, many of the Burgundies that are red today were vinified as *vins clairets*, and were said to have the colour of a partridge's eye—*l'oeil de perdrix*.

Vintage

A vintage wine is a wine from a single year (or vintage). Although the word is regularly misused in English, simply to mean good wine, its basic meaning has absolutely nothing to do with quality; it simply means the year a wine, good or bad, was made. The nearest approach to a legitimately qualitative use of the word is in connection with port and Champagne (qq.v.), whose producers do not label their wines with the vintage year unless they consider the harvest to be of sufficient distinction to warrant specific identification. Their best wines are therefore referred to as vintage Champagne and vintage port—that is, "Champagne with a date" and "port with a date".

Wine Laws

Wine laws are designed to ensure that what is inside the bottle is what the label claims. The words *St. Emilion, Chianti Classico* or *Riesling Kabinett* are not mere names but coded legal indicators of the authenticity—though not necessarily the quality—of the wine. Wine laws exist to protect both the consumer and the honest wine maker and trader from being cheated by fraudulent producers.

Wine laws control such matters as grape varieties, cultivation methods, pruning methods, alcoholic content, labelling, bottle sizes and many other aspects of wine production. But for the lay wine buyer and drinker, the most relevant provisions are those that govern the accurate and truthful attribution of the wines to their place of origin, and guarantee that it has been produced according to specified standards.

Wine laws vary widely in sophistication from country to country. In France, which leads the way in this as in so many aspects of viniculture, there is a complex and refined body of legislation that has evolved over generations (see *French Wine Appellations*). Germany (q.v.) has a history of scrupulous quality control but of a different structure from most European countries, which usually base their systems on the French tradition.

Spain and Italy have laws governing the rights of growers to label their wine with its place of origin. The European Economic Community has elaborated a set of general wine regulations that are binding on all its member countries, and most other wine-producing countries are attempting to develop wine laws to meet their own particular needs.

Württemberg

This former German province, now part of the Federal State of Baden Württemberg, is one of the two German wine regions producing rather more red wine than white (see also *Ahr*). The vineyards lie along the valley of the Neckar river (*map, page 83*). The region is a difficult one for wine-growing, since it is situated at the clash point of two climates, the continental and the maritime, with the consequent sudden and violent changes of weather: storms and spring frosts are always a danger.

Württemberg wines are seldom seen outside Germany. The best known among Germans is Schillerwein (*schillern*—to shimmer), a bright pink wine made, unlike other rosés, by crushing and fermenting red and white grapes together.

The three districts (*Bereiche*) are Kocher Jagst Taubertal, Württembergisch Unterland and Remstal Stuttgart. Fifteen greater vineyards (*Grosslagen*) comprise some 200 individual vineyards (*Einzellagen*). Most of the holdings are cultivated by small-scale growers working through co-operatives. The soil is varied, and so are the grapes: Trollinger, Spätburgunder (Pinot Noir) and Portugieser for the reds; Riesling, Silvaner and Müller Thurgau for the whites.

Yugoslavia

The rich variety of Yugoslavian wines reflects the number of different soils, microclimates and vinicultural traditions which influence wine production in the six provinces. The wines range from the fresh, acidic white wines of Slovenia in the north through a spectrum of aromatic,

heavy, golden wines, dry rosés—*ruzica*—to the dark, powerful reds of Macedonia on Yugoslavia's southern border. The wine industry is run by a number of large co-operatives that operate independently from the state. About 12 per cent of the country's large output is exported, and definitions of origin and quality are subject to legal controls. Wines are generally labelled with their predominant grape variety, or the region of production.

The province of Slovenia produces what are traditionally regarded as Yugoslavia's best white wines. Close to the borders of Austria and Hungary in the north, the vineyards of Slovenia's Drava region extend over the hilly slopes at the foothills of the Alps. The terraced vines grow on a subsoil of limestone, marl and clay, and the temperate, moist climate gives the grapes their freshness and acidity. Excellent white wines of varying character are made from the Sylvaner, Gewürztraminer, Ruländer, Wälschriesling, Sauvignon Blanc, Rhine Riesling and Sipon grapes. For export, most wines are vinified to retain some sugar to offset their natural acidity. Wines from Drava's Ljutomer district are highly regarded and widely exported—notably, the sweet, late-picked Tiger Milk.

Farther south in Slovenia, the Sava region makes reliable Sylvaners and Wälschrieslings and also some red and rosé wines, including a pleasant dry, light rosé called Cviček. The red wines, made from the Austrian St. Laurent grape, as well as Gamay and Portugieser varieties, are intensely coloured, with a hard edge.

More than three-quarters of Yugoslavia's wine comes from the provinces of Serbia and Croatia. The most prolific wine region in Serbia is Vojvodina. The hilly, sun-soaked vineyards of the Fruška Gora zone of Vojvodina produce white wines from Riesling, Sylvaner and Traminer grapes, as well as from

Pinot Blanc, Semillon, Sauvignon Blanc and the local Plemenka and Smederkevka vines. The Fruška Gora zone also produces a sparkling wine called Fruškagorski Biser.

The mountainous vineyards of Kosovo, in the southern Serbian province of Kosmet, make good red wines from classic French grapes, such as Cabernet Franc, Merlot and Pinot Noir. Amselfelder, made from Pinot Noir, is probably the best red wine of the area. Excellent, well-balanced reds come from the Venčac Oplenac region on the Morava river, south of Belgrade.

The Croatian Adriatic coast produces some of the country's most distinctive wines. The vineyards are sheltered from the north and east by mountain ranges; the proximity of the sea tempers the climate and the vines gain character from the rocky soil, which is rich in minerals. The best wines are the full-bodied reds; the area is also known for Malvasia, a rich dessert wine, and for sparkling wines.

The wines made farther down the Dalmatian coast include Plavac, a scented, dryish red wine with a smooth texture; Dingač, a round, rather heavy red with a high alcohol content; Prošek, a rich, sweet dessert wine high in alcohol.

Macedonian red wines are excellent value. Much of the wine is dark and vigorous with a high alcohol content and the new plantings of Cabernet, Merlot and Pinot Noir are producing wines of great potential. Zilavka, a white wine of great character, is produced in the Mostar region of Bosnia Herzegovina. The finest Zilavka is dry, fruity and strong with a good acid balance. A pleasant red wine, Blatina, is also made in Bosnia Herzegovina, but their Muslim tradition has not encouraged wine production. Very little wine comes from Montenegro; the best known is Vranac, an astringent red which ages well.

Bibliography

Aaron, Sam, and Clifton Fadiman, *The Joys of Wine.* Abrams, New York, 1975.

Allen, H. Warner, *A History of Wine.* Faber and Faber, London, 1961.

Allen, H. Warner, *Sherry and Port.* Constable, London, 1952.

Amerine, M. A., and E. B. Roessler, *Wines: Their Sensory Evaluation.* Freeman, San Francisco, 1976.

Amerine, M. A., and V. Singleton, *Wine. an Introduction.* University of California Press, Berkeley, 1978.

Anderson, Burton, *Vino: the Wines and Winemakers of Italy.* Little, Brown, Boston, 1980.

Andrieu, Pierre, *Notre Ami, le Vin.* Albin Michel, Paris, 1961.

Arlott, John, and Christopher Fielden, *Burgundy: Vines and Wines.* Davis-Poynter, London, 1976.

Arlott, John, *Krug: House of Champagne.* Davis-Poynter, London, 1976.

Athaneus, *The Deipnosophists,* Vol. 1 (trans. C. B. Gulick). Heinemann, London, 1969.

Bavard, Abbé E., *Histoire de Volnay.* 1870.

Bespaloff, Alexis, *The New Signet Book of Wine.* New American Library, New York, 1980.

Bourquin, Constant, *Connaissance du Vin.* Marabout-Gérard, Vervier, 1970.

Broadbent, Michael, *The Great Vintage Wine Book.* Mitchell Beazley, London, 1980.

Broadbent, Michael, *Wine Tasting.* Cassell, London, 1979.

Bréjoux, Pierre, *Les Vins de la Loire.* Paris, 1957.

Bréjoux, Pierre, *Les Vins de Bourgogne.* Revue du Vin de France, Paris.

Burroughs, David, and Norman Bezzant, *The New Wine Companion.* Wine and Spirit Education Trust, London, 1980.

Burroughs, David, and Norman Bezzant, *Wine Regions of the World.* Wine and Spirit Education Trust, London, 1979.

Chabot, Georges, *La Bourgogne,* Armand Colin, Paris, 1945.

Champagne: Wine of France. Comité Interprofessionel du Vin de Champagne, Lallemand, Paris, 1968.

Chancrin, E., *Le Vin.* Hachette, Paris, n.d.

Chaptal, Comte J.-A., *L'Art de Faire le Vin* (1819). Laffitte Reprints, Marseilles, 1981

Cocks and Féret, *Bordeaux et Ses Vins, Classés par Ordre de Mérite.* 12th edition, Féret, Bordeaux, 1969.

Columella, *De Re Rustica,* 3 vols. Heinemann, London, 1977.

Constantin-Wayer, M., *L'Âme du Vin.* Rieder, Paris, 1932.

Cooper, Derek, *Wine with Food.* Artus Books, London, 1980.

Croft-Cooke, Rupert, *Madeira.* Putnam, London, 1961.

Croft-Cooke, Rupert, *Sherry.* Putnam, London, 1955.

Danguy and Aubertin, *Les Grands Vins de Bourgogne* (1892). Laffitte Reprints, Marseilles, 1978.

Dion, Roger, *Histoire de la Vigne et du Vin en France des Origins au XIXème Siècle.* Flammarion, Paris, 1959.

Dormontal, Charles, *Florilège des Grands Vins de Bordeaux.* Éditions des Roses, Bordeaux, 1931.

Dormontal, Charles, *Sauternes, Pays d'Or et de Diamant.* Bière, Bordeaux, 1930.

Dovaz, Michel, *Encyclopédie des Crus Classés du Bordelais.* Julliard, Paris, 1981.

Dumay, Raymond, *Guide du Vin.* Stock, Paris, 1967.

Duyker, Hubert, *Grands Bordeaux Rouges.* Fernand Nathan, Paris, 1979.

Duyker, Hubert, *Grands Vins de Bourgogne.* Fernand Nathan, Paris, 1980.

Escritt, L. B., *The Small Cellar.* Herbert Jenkins, London, 1960.

Evans, Len, *Australia and New Zealand: the Complete Book of Wine.* Paul Hamlyn, Sydney, 1974.

Faith, Nicholas, *The Winemasters.* Hamish Hamilton, London, 1978.

Féret, editor, *Dictionnaire du Vin.* Bordeaux, 1962.

Féret, Édouard, *Dictionnaire-Manuel du Négociant en Vins et Spiritueux et du Maître de Chai* (1896). Laffitte Reprints, Marseilles, 1981.

Ferré, Louis, *Traité d'Oenologie Bourguignonne.* Institut National des Appellations d'Origine, Paris, 1958.

Fletcher, Wyndham, *Port.* Sotheby, London, 1978.

Forbes, Patrick, *Champagne: the Wine, the Land and the People.* Gollancz, London, 1967.

Forgeot, Pierre, *Guide de l'Amateur de Bourgogne.* Presses Universitaires de France, Paris, 1967.

Galet, P., *Cépages et Vignobles de France,* 4 vols. Déhan and Imprimerie de Paysan du Midi, Montpellier, 1958-64.

Galet, P., *Précis de Viticulture.* Déhan, Montpellier, 1970.

Gaudilhon, René, *Naissance du Champagne.* Hachette, Paris, 1968.

Goffard, Robert, *Le Service des Vins.* Cahiers de l'Académie Internationale du Vin, No.1, Geneva, 1980.

Got, Norbert, *Le Livre de l'Amateur de Vins.* Causse, Montpellier, 1967.

Grands Vins de Bordeaux. Société d'Action et de Gestion Publicitaire, Bordeaux, 1973.

Guide de Vins Européens Appellation d'Origine Contrôlée. Éditions Vilo, Lausanne, 1980.

Halasz, Zoltan, *The Book of Hungarian Wines.* Corvino Kiado, Budapest, 1981.

Hallgarten, F., *Alsace and Its Wine Gardens.* Wine and Spirits Publications, London, 1974.

Hallgarten, Peter, *Guide to the Wines of the Rhône.* Pitman, London, 1979.

Hallgarten, S. F., *German Wines.* Faber and Faber, London, 1976.

Hallgarten, S. F., *Rhineland, Wineland.* Arlington Books, 1965.

Hallgarten, S. F., and F. L., *The Wines and Wine Gardens of Austria.* Argus Books, Watford, 1979.

Harveys Pocket Guide to Wine. Octopus Books, London, 1981.

Hesiod, *Homeric Hymns and Homerica,* trans. H. G. Evelyn-White. Heinemann, London, 1950.

Jacquelin, Louis, and René Poulain, *The Wines and Vineyards of France.* Paul Hamlyn, London, 1962.

Jeffs, Julian, *Sherry.* Faber and Faber, London, 1970.

Johnson, Hugh, *Wine.* Mitchell Beazley, London, 1974.

Johnson, Hugh, *The World Atlas of Wine.* Mitchell Beazley, London, 1971.

Jullien, A., *Topographie de Tous les Vignobles Connus.* Paris, 1832.

Laborde, J., *Cours d'Oenologie.* Féret, Bordeaux, 1970.

Lacoste, P.-Joseph, *La Route du Vin en Gironde.* Delmas, Bordeaux, 1948.

Lacoste, P.-Joseph, *Le Vin de Bordeaux.* Delmas, Bordeaux, 1947.

Lafforgue, Germain, *Le Vignoble Girondin.* Larmat, Paris, 1947.

Lamalle, Jacques, *Les Côtes-du-Rhône.* Balland, 1981.

Langenbach, Alfred, *German Wines and Vines.* Vista Books, London, 1962.

Léglise, N., *Une Initiation à la Dégustation des Grands Vins.* Défense et Illustration des Vins d'Origine. Lausanne, 1976.

Lichine, Alexis, *Guide to the Wines and Vineyards of France.* Weidenfeld and Nicolson, London, 1979.

Lichine, Alexis, *Encyclopaedia of Wines and Spirits.* Cassell, London, 1967.

Livingstone-Learmouth, John, and Melvyn C. H. Master, *Wines of the Rhône.* Faber and Faber, London, 1978.

Mathieu, L., *Vinification.* La Maison Rustique, Paris, 1925.

Meinhard, Heinrich, *The Wines of Germany.* Oriel Press, London, 1971.

Meredith, Ted, *Northwest Wine.* Nexus Press, Kirkland, Washington, 1980.

Morrison, L. W., *Wines and Spirits.* Penguin Books, London, 1957.

Nègre, E., and P. Françot, *Manuel Pratique de Vinification et de Conservation des Vins.* Flammarion, Paris, 1941.

Olken, Charles E., Earl G. Singer and Norman S. Roby, *The Connoisseurs' Handbook of California Wines.* Alfred A. Knopf, New York, 1980.

Ordish, George, *Vineyards of Britain and Wales.* Faber and Faber, London, 1977.

Pama, C., *The Wine Estates of South Africa.* Purnell, Cape Town, 1979.

Penning-Rowsell, Edmund, editor, *German Wine Atlas.* Mitchell Beazley, London, 1977.

Penning-Rowsell, Edmund, *The Wines of Bordeaux,* Michael Joseph, London, 1969.

Peynaud, Émile, *Connaissance et Travail du Vin.* Dunod, Paris, 1971.

Peynaud, Émile, *Le Goût du Vin.* Dunod, Paris, 1980.

Pfitzinger, Paul, *Précis de Vinification Pratique.* Baillière, Paris, 1960.

Pijassou, R., *Un Grand Vignoble de Qualité: le Médoc.* Tallendier, Paris, 1980.

Pijassou, R., *Le Seignerie et le Vignoble de Château Latour.* Fédération Historique de Sud-Ouest, Bordeaux, 1974.

Poupon, P., *Nouvelles Pensées d'un Dégustateur.* Confrérie des Chevaliers du Tastevin, Nuits-Saint-Georges, 1975.

Poupon, P., *Pensées d'un Dégustateur.* Confrérie des Chevaliers du Tastevin, Nuits-Saint-Georges, 1957.

Poupon, P., and P. Forgeot, *Les Vins de Bourgogne.* Presses Universitaires de France, 1952.

Puisais, Jacques, *Le Vin Se Met à Table.* Valtat, Paris, 1981.

Puisais, Jacques, R.-L. Chabanon, A. Guiller and J. Lacoste, *Précis d'Initiation à la Dégustation.* Institut Technique du Vin, Paris, 1969.

Rainbird, George, *Sherry and the Wines of Spain.* Michael Joseph, London, 1966.

Ramain, Paul, *Les Grands Vins de France* (1931). Laffitte Reprints, Marseilles, 1981.

Ray, Cyril, *Bollinger.* Peter Davies, London, 1971.

Ray, Cyril, *The Wines of Germany.* Penguin Books, London, 1971.

Ray, Cyril, *The Wines of Italy.* Penguin Books, 1979.

Read, Jan, *Guide to the Wines of Spain and Portugal.* Pitman, London, 1973.

Redding, Cyrus, *A History and Description of Modern Wines.* London, 1833.

Renaud, Jean, *Biologie du Vin.* Presses Universitaires de France, Paris, 1950.

Revue du Vin de France. Paris, 1964-79.

Ribéreau-Gayon, J., *Traité d'Oenologie,* 2 vols. Béranger-Dunot, Paris, 1961.

Ribéreau-Gayon, J., and E. Peynaud, *Conseils Pratiques pour la Préparation et la Conservation de Vins.* Conseil Interprofessionnel du Vin de Bordeaux, 1952.

Ribéreau-Gayon, J. and P., E. Peynaud and P. Sudraud, *Science et Techniques du Vin.* Dunod, Paris, 1975.

Roberge, Earl, *Napa Wine Country.* Balding, Portland, 1975.

Rodier, Camille, *Le Clos de Vougeot* (1949). Laffitte Reprints, Marseilles, 1980.

Rodier, Camille, *Le Vin de Bourgogne* (1948). Laffitte Reprints, Marseilles, 1981.

Roger, J.-R., *Les Vins de Bordeaux.* Compagnie Parisienne d'Éditions Techniques et Commerciales, Paris, n.d.

Roncarati, Bruno, *Viva Vino DOC: Wines of Italy.* Wine and Spirits Publications, London, 1976.

Rouget, Charles, *Les Vignobles du Jura et de la Franche-Comté* (1897). Laffitte Reprints, Marseilles, 1981.

Saintsbury, George, *Notes on a Cellar-Book.* Macmillan, London, 1963.

Schoonmaker, Frank, *Encyclopaedia of Wine.* Adam and Charles Black, London, 1979.

Shand, P. Morton, *A Book of French Wines.* London, 1928. Revised and edited by Cyril Ray, Penguin Books, London, 1964.

Sichel, Allan, *The Penguin Book of Wine.* Penguin, London, 1971.

Siegel, Hans, *Guide to the Wines of Germany.* Pitman, London, 1978.

Simon, André L., *Know Your Wines,* Coram, London, n.d.

Simon, André L., *The Noble Grapes and the Great Wines of France.* London, 1957.

Simon, André L., *Port.* Constable, London, 1934.

Simon, André L., *The Wines, Vineyards and Vignerons of Australia.* Paul Hamlyn, London, 1967.

Stephens, Patrick, *The Great Book of Wine.* Cambridge, 1970.

Sutcliffe, Serena, editor, *André Simon's Wines of the World.* Macdonald Futura, London, 1981.

Thompson, Bob, *Pocket Encyclopaedia of California Wines.* Mitchell Beazley, London, 1980.

Todd, William, *A Handbook of Wine.* Jonathan Cape, London, 1922.

Turpin, Émile, *Les Vignes et les Vins du Berry* (1907). Laffitte Reprints, Marseilles, 1981.

Vandyke Price, Pamela, *The Taste of Wine.* Macdonald, London, 1976.

Les Vins du Rhône et de la Méditerranée. Éditions Montalba, Paris, 1978.

Wasserman, Sheldon, *The Wines of Italy.* Stein and Day, New York, 1976.

Yoxall, H. W., *The Wines of Burgundy.* Pitman, London, 1968.

A Glossary of Grape Varieties

Aleatico
Red grape of the Muscat family. Grown in Italy for sweet red wine.

Alicante Bouschet
Very productive red wine grape yielding ordinary wines that are high in alcohol. A 19th-century cross between Grenache and Petit Bouschet, the most widely grown of the *teinturier* grapes today, especially in southern France, Algeria and California.

Aligoté
White wine grape of Burgundy, producing pleasant dry wines that are best drunk young.

Altesse
White wine grape called Roussette in Savoie and Furmint in Hungary, where it is the chief grape grown for Tokay.

Aramon
Red wine grape that is hugely productive but poor in colour, producing wine of a greyish tinge. Still grown for ordinary wines in southern France, but largely superseded by improved crosses.

Barbarossa
Italian red wine grape grown especially in Liguria.

Barbera
Italian red wine grape, originally from Piedmont but now grown throughout Italy and in California.

Biancone
Corsican white wine grape.

Blauer Portugieser
German and Austrian red wine grape.

Bourboulenc
White wine grape of Provence.

Bouschet
Petit and Gros Bouschet are both crosses between the prolific but feebly coloured Aramon and a *teinturier* variety.

Braquet
French red wine grape, a component of Bellet, one of the best Provençal wines produced near Nice.

Brunello di Montalcino see *Sangiovese*

Bual
A Madeira grape that produces fine sweet Madeira of that name (though not all Bual Madeira is necessarily made from the Bual grape).

Cabernet Franc see *page 21*

Cabernet Sauvignon see *page 20*

Calabrese
Sicilian red wine grape.

Canaiolo
Italian red wine grape, a component of Chianti.

Cannonau
Sardinian red wine grape.

Carignan (Mazuelo)
Red wine grape originally from Spain, producing good robust wines. Grown in southern France, Spain and California (where it is spelt Carignane). It is a component of Rioja.

Carricante
Sicilian white wine grape.

Chardonnay see *page 18*

Chasselas
European white wine and table grape, known as Gutedel in Germany and Fendant in Switzerland. Produces light, agreeable wines usually best drunk young, including Pouilly-sur-Loire, and Crépy in Savoie.

Chenin Blanc see *page 19*

Cinsaut (Cinsault)
Red wine grape grown in the Rhône Valley (where it contributes to Châteauneuf-du-Pape), in Provence (used in red Bandol) and in Spain.

Clairette
White wine grape, grown in Provence.

Colombard (Blanquette, Pied-Tendre, Bon Blanc)
Very productive white wine grape, grown in the Dauphiné and Charente regions of France (where it is also used for making into Cognac) and in California.

Concord
Native North American blue-black grape of the species *Vitis labrusca*. Concord is very widely grown in the United States. It does not make good wine.

Cortese
Italian white wine grape, grown chiefly in Piedmont.

Corvina
Italian red wine grape, used in Valpolicella and Bardolino wines.

Cot
One of the red wine grapes of Bordeaux, where it is known as Malbec (and in St. Emilion as Pressac). It is progressively disappearing from Bordeaux where it has proved vulnerable to disease, but remains the principal variety in Cahors.

Dolcetto
Italian red wine grape of Piedmont. Produces a soft red wine of the same name.

Douce Noire (Dolcett Nero)
Red wine grape, grown in Savoie and Switzerland.

Elbling (Kleinberger)
White wine grape grown in Alsace, Luxembourg and Germany, where some of it goes into Sekt, the German sparkling wine. The grape is traditionally supposed to have been brought in by the Romans—and this may be true, because it is unlike any other indigenous German grape varieties.

Erbaluce
Italian white wine grape, grown in Piedmont.

Folle Blanche
French white wine grape grown in the Loire—where in the Nantes region it is known as Gros Plant, and produces a light, crisp, slightly acid wine of the same name. It also flourishes in the south of France and in California, where it makes light still and sparkling wine.

Freisa
Italian red wine grape, grown in Piedmont and Corsica.

Fuella
French red wine grape, used as a component in the red and rosé wines of Bellet, near Nice.

Furmint see *Altesse*

Gamay As well as the Beaujolais grape known as Gamay Noir *à jus blanc*, there are several *teinturier* or red-fleshed varieties of Gamay. See *page 20*.

Garganega
Italian white wine grape grown round Verona and used—generally with Trebbiano—in Soave wines.

Genove (Genovese)
Italian white wine grape; also grown in Corsica.

Gewürztraminer see *page 19*

Grenache see *page 21*

Grey Riesling
Not a true Riesling but a minor white wine grape grown in California, Austria, Italy, the central European countries, South Africa and Australia. Also known as Welsh Riesling and Italian Riesling.

Grignolino
Italian red wine grape, grown in Piedmont and California.

Grillo
Sicilian white wine grape, component of Marsala.

Gropello
Red wine grape of Lombardy.

Groslot (also spelt Grolleau)
Red wine grape of the Loire Valley.

Gros Plant see *Folle Blanche*

Grüner Veltliner
White wine grape grown in Austria and the Italian Alto Adige. There is also a little in California.

Gutedel see *Chasselas*

Hárslevelü
Hungarian white wine grape. Used, with Furmint and some Yellow Muscat, in Tokay.

Inzolia
Sicilian white wine grape.

Klevner see *Pinot Blanc*

Lagrein
Red grape used in red and rosé wines. Grown in Trentino and the Italian Tyrol.

Lemberger
German red wine grape grown in Württemberg.

Malbec see *Cot*

Malvasia (Malmsey)
White grape of ancient Greece and the Aegean, now grown in Madeira, South Africa and California. It produces the rich, sweet, long-lived Madeira called Malvasia.

Marsanne
French white wine grape, a component—with Roussane—in Hermitage and St. Joseph, some of the best white wines of the northern Rhône Valley.

Marzemino
Italian red wine grape of Lombardy.

Mazuelo see *Carignan*

Melon see *Muscadet*

Merlot see *page 20*

Mourvèdre see *page 20*

Morio Muscat
German white wine grape, a cross between Silvaner and Pinot Blanc. Often used in fragrant Rhine wines.

Müller Thurgau
German white wine grape, a cross between Riesling and Silvaner. Increasingly widely planted throughout Germany's wine region.

Muscadelle
White grape used in very small quantities the wines of Graves and Sauternes.

Muscadet
White grape transplanted from Burgundy to the Loire Valley around Nantes, where it produces wine of the same name.

Muscat
General name for many related varieties of sweet white grape, usually with a pronounced fragrance and used for making sweet wines.

Nebbiolo
Italian red wine grape—the noble grape of Piedmont. It is used to make Bardolo, Gattinara and Barbaresco wines. The grape is also called Spanna and its wine is labelled as such in parts of Piedmont.

Negrara Trentina
Italian red wine grape, grown in the Veneto and used in Valpolicella and Bardolino wines.

Nerello Mascalese
Red wine grape from southern Italy and Sicily.

Nielluccio
Corsican red wine grape.

Nocera
Red wine grape grown in Sicily.

Nosiola
Italian white wine grape grown in Trentino.

Nuragus
Sardinian white wine grape that makes the straw-coloured Nuragus di Cagliari.

Pagadebit
White wine grape grown in Italy and Corsica. It is extremely prolific, hence its name "debt-payer".

Palomino
White grape grown in Spain as the basic sherry grape.

Pamid
Bulgarian grape that produces ordinary red wine.

Pascal Blanc
White Provençal grape used in the fine wines of Cassis.

Pedro Ximenez
Spanish white wine grape used in sweet wines and as a sweetener for sherries.

Perle
German grape used in the dry white wines of Franconia.

Petit Verdot
Tannic and acidic red wine grape used in Bordeaux, in very small quantities to add an edge of hardness.

Picpoule
White wine grape from southern France.

Pineau d'Aunis
French grape, used with other varieties in rosé wines from Anjou and, decreasingly, in the red wines of the Loire Valley.

Pineau de la Loire see *Chenin Blanc*

Pinot Blanc
A natural mutation of Pinot Noir, called Klevner or Weissburgunder in Germany. There are plantings in Burgundy but, it is not common there. It gives good results in Italy and California.

Pinot Gris (Tokay d'Alsace)
A light-coloured mutation of Pinot Noir producing good white wine in Alsace and Italy. In Germany, it is known as Ruländer.

Pinot Noir see *page 21*

Pinotage
South African red wine grape, a cross between Pinot Noir and Cinsault.

Plant Droit
French red wine grape similar to Cinsault, used in Châteauneuf-du-Pape.

Poulsard
Red wine grape from the Jura region of France, also used in rosé wine.

Primitivo
Italian red wine grape, probably the origin of the Californian Zinfandel.

Prosecco
Italian white wine grape from the Veneto, often used for sparkling wine.

Raboso
Red wine grape from the Veneto.

Riesling see *page 19*

Riminese
White wine grape from Corsica.

Rolle
White wine grape grown in Provence, specifically in the Alpes Maritimes around Grasse.

Rondinella
Italian red wine grape grown in the Veneto, and used in Valpolicella and Bardolino wines.

Rosanella
Italian red wine grape from Lombardy.

Rossese
Italian red wine grape from Liguria.

Roussanne
One of France's finest white varieties, used in the white wines of Hermitage on the Côtes du Rhône, and in Savoie.

Ruby Cabernet
A cross from Cabernet Sauvignon and Carignan grown in California and used in red wines.

Ruländer see *Pinot Gris*

St. Emilionnais see *Ugni Blanc*

Sangiovese

Italian red wine grape used in Chianti and other wines. The variety Sangiovese grosso is used in Brunello di Montalcino wines of Tuscany.

Sauvignon Blanc see *page 19*

Savignin

The only grape used in the *vins jaunes* and *vins de paille* of the Jura region in France. See *Traminer*.

Scheurebe

White wine grape grown in Germany; a Silvaner and Riesling cross.

Schiava

Red wine grape grown in northern Italy.

Sciaccarello

Corsican red wine grape.

Semillon see *page 18*

Sercial

White grape producing the fine Madeira of the same name. This grape is the same as the Riesling.

Shiraz

Australian name for Syrah (q.v.).

Spanna see *Nebbiolo*

Sylvaner (Silvaner)

White wine grape grown in Alsace and Germany.

Syrah see *page 21*

Teinturier

Unlike most red grapes, whose colour resides only in the skins, *teinturier* grapes have red-coloured flesh. Wines derived from them therefore have a deep, rich hue, and may be used to boost the colour of paler ordinary wines.

Tempranillo

Red wine grape used in the Rioja wines of northern Spain.

Teoulier

Red wine grape of Provence.

Teroldego

Red wine grape of Trentino, in northern Italy.

Tibouren

Red wine grape of Provence.

Tinto Cão, Tinta Francesca

Black grapes grown in Portugal for port.

Tocai

White wine grape grown in north-eastern Italy.

Tokay d'Alsace see *Pinot Gris*

Touriga

Red wine grape from the Dão region of Portugal. Also used in port.

Traminer

White wine grape grown in Germany and Alsace. In the Jura region of France it is known as Savignin.

Trebbiano see *Ugni Blanc*

Ugni Blanc

White wine grape grown in France (in Cognac its name is St. Emilionnais) and in Italy, where it is known as Trebbiano.

Vaccarèse

Red wine grape grown in the Rhône Valley and used in Châteauneuf-du-Pape.

Verdelho

Portuguese grape used in white port. It also produces Verdelho Madeira.

Verdesse

White wine grape grown in the Dauphiné region of western France.

Verdiso

White wine grape from north-eastern Italy.

Verdot

Red wine grape used mainly in the ordinary wines of Bordeaux, where it is usually known as Gros Verdot.

Verduzzo

White grape from north-eastern Italy.

Vernaccia

Italian white wine grape used especially for Vernaccia di San Gimignano.

Viognier

White wine grape grown only in the northern Rhône Valley. It is the only grape used for Condrieu and Château Grillet white wines, and is associated, in small amounts, with the Syrah grape in Côte Rotie wine from the same region.

Viura

White wine grape grown in Rioja, northern Spain.

Weissburgunder see *Pinot Blanc*

Zinfandel

Red grape probably of Italian origin, now planted widely in California, where it produces a variety of fruity red wines. Also grown in Hungary and Yugoslavia.

Anthology of Recipes

In selecting recipes for the Anthology that follows, the Editors and consultants for this volume have drawn upon the cooking traditions of many different countries, spanning four centuries of culinary literature. The recipes for using wine in cooking range from simple preparations, such as peaches lightly poached in red wine, to elaborate Meursault soup, a delightful combination of shellfish, fish and wine. The 38 authors whose work is represented range from the 17th-century English cookery writer, Will Rabisha, to such modern food authorities as Jean and Pierre Troisgros. A number of the recipes—some of them from rare and out-of-print books in private collections—have never been published in English. Whatever the sources, the emphasis of the recipes is on authentic dishes prepared with fresh, high-quality ingredients.

Since many early recipe writers did not specify quantities or cooking times and temperatures, these have been judiciously provided. Where appropriate, introductory notes in italics have been added by the Editors. Modern terms have been substituted for archaic language, but to preserve the character of the original recipes and to create a true anthology, the authors' texts have

been changed as little as possible. Cooking terms and ingredients that may be unfamiliar are explained in the combined General Index and Glossary at the end of the book.

In some cases, where the author of a recipe specifies a wine which may not be easily available, alternatives are suggested in the editorial note.

For ease of use, the Anthology is organized into categories representing different courses in a meal. Recipes for standard preparations—stock, fish fumet and sugar syrup, and some of the more elaborate dishes recommended in Chapter 3, *Wine in a Menu,* such as vegetable estouffade, crayfish salad with dill and seafood sausages—appear at the end.

All recipe ingredients are listed in order of use, with the main or title ingredients placed first. Metric and imperial measurements for each ingredient are listed in separate columns. The two sets of figures are not always exact equivalents, but are consistent for each recipe. Working from either metric or imperial weights and measures will produce equally good results, but the two systems should not be mixed for the same recipe. All spoon measures are level.

Soups

Meursault Soup

Soupe au Meursault

Any white Burgundy or other full-bodied, complex, white wine could be substituted for the Meursault.

To serve 6 to 8

2 bottles	Meursault	2 bottles
¾ litre	water	1¼ pints
1	celeriac, sliced	1
10	carrots, sliced	10
7 or 8	shallots, peeled	7 or 8
6	leeks, sliced	6
2	onions, quartered	2
	salt and pepper	
1 bottle	dry white wine	1 bottle
15 cl	white wine vinegar	5 fl oz
24 to 40	live crayfish, washed	24 to 40
1 slice	smoked bacon, 4 to 5 cm (1½ to 2 inches) thick	1 slice
1	eel, skinned, cut into 5 cm (2 inch) pieces, bones removed	1
1	salmon trout, cleaned, cut into 5 cm (2 inch) pieces, bones removed	1
1	carp, cleaned, cut into 5 cm (2 inch) pieces, bones removed	1
4 tbsp	roughly chopped parsley	4 tbsp

Pour the two bottles of Meursault and the water into a large stew-pot, add the celeriac, seven of the carrots, four of the shallots, all the leeks and both the onions. Season and simmer gently for 1½ to 2 hours. Purée the mixture in a blender, then pass the purée through a very fine sieve so that the soup will be creamy and smooth—this is an essential step.

Pour the wine and the wine vinegar into a large pan, add the rest of the shallots and carrots, and season with salt and pepper. Bring the court-bouillon to the boil, then lower the heat, cover the pan and simmer for 30 minutes. Put the crayfish into the court-bouillon, cover the pan and cook over a high heat until they just turn red all over. Turn off the heat and leave the crayfish in the court-bouillon to keep warm.

Put the smoked bacon into another pan, cover with water and bring to the boil. Remove the pan from the heat and pour off the water. Cover the bacon with fresh water, so that it will not be too salty, and simmer until tender, about 40 minutes. Cut the bacon into six to eight pieces, each 4 cm (1½ inches) thick. Keep the bacon pieces warm.

About 10 minutes before serving the dish, poach the fish in the soup over a moderate heat, taking care not to let the soup boil. Start with the eel, which will take 8 to 10 minutes to cook. After the eel has been cooking for 5 minutes, add the salmon trout and the carp—these will cook in about 5 minutes, so that all the fish will be cooked at the same time—then add the smoked bacon pieces and the crayfish to the soup. Taste and, if necessary, adjust the flavour by adding some of the court-bouillon in which the crayfish were cooked. Ladle the soup into soup plates, arranging the fish, smoked bacon and crayfish (four or five per person) in each plate as decoratively as possible. Sprinkle the soup with the chopped parsley and serve very hot.

LALOU BIZE-LEROY
LE NOUVEAU GUIDE GAULT MILLAU, CONNAISSANCE DES VOYAGES

Peach Soup

To serve 4

350 g	peaches, sliced	12 oz
½ litre	water	16 fl oz
2	cloves	2
	ground cinnamon	
½ litre	white wine	16 fl oz
	sugar	
	croûtons	

Put the peaches, water, cloves and a pinch of cinnamon into a pan and cook until the peaches are tender. Discard the cloves and strain the liquid through a sieve, mashing the peaches to a purée with a wooden spoon. Return the strained liquid and peach purée to the pan and boil for a few minutes. Stir in the wine and add sugar to taste. Heat to just below boiling point and serve in hot soup plates, garnished with croûtons.

CORA, ROSE AND BOB BROWN
THE WINE COOKBOOK

White Wine Bisque

Other dry white wines can be substituted for the Chablis. The author recommends serving the bisque with small finger sandwiches of rye bread and butter.

To serve 6

1 litre	Chablis	1¾ pints
1 kg	white grapes, stalks removed, 72 grapes skinned, seeded and reserved for the garnish	2 lb
75 to 125 g	sugar	2½ to 4 oz
2.5 cm	stick cinnamon	1 inch
2	cloves	2
2 tbsp	quick-cooking tapioca	2 tbsp
3	egg yolks	3
½ tsp	salt	½ tsp

Put the unseeded grapes in a saucepan, cover with cold water and stir in 75 to 125 g (2½ to 4 oz) of sugar, depending on the sweetness of the grapes. Add the cinnamon stick and cloves and gradually bring to the boil. Lower the heat, and simmer gently for 20 to 25 minutes. Pour the contents of the saucepan through a fine-meshed sieve set over a clean pan and rub the grapes through the sieve. Keep the strained mixture warm by placing the pan in a bowl of hot water.

Cook the tapioca in ¼ litre (8 fl oz) of water until it is clear and transparent—about 20 minutes; then beat in the egg yolks one at a time, beating briskly after each addition; add the salt with the last yolk. Combine the tapioca mixture and the grape mixture, beating thoroughly with a rotary beater, or purée the two mixtures together in a blender. Heat the wine to boiling point, that is until beads appear on the surface, but do not allow the wine to boil. Stir the wine into the grape and tapioca mixture, beating well. Serve in hot soup plates, garnishing each serving with a dozen skinned and seeded grapes.

LOUIS P. DE GOUY
THE SOUP BOOK

Sparkling White Wine Fruit Soup

A consommé is a concentrated broth made with lean beef. To ensure it is absolutely clear and free of fat it should be strained through muslin.

To serve 8

¾ litre	sparkling white wine	1¼ pints
125 g	redcurrants, stemmed	4 oz
185 g	raspberries, hulled	6¾ oz
2 tbsp	sugar	2 tbsp
1	lemon, rind grated, juice strained	1
¾ litre	consommé	1¼ pints
3	egg yolks, lightly beaten	3
	salt	
	nutmeg (optional)	
	whipped, salted cream (optional)	

Put the redcurrants, raspberries and sugar into a fine-meshed sieve set over a pan and rub them through. Place the pan over a low heat and bring to boiling point to extract the juice thoroughly. Strain the fruit and sugar again through a fine-meshed sieve into a clean pan. Add 2 tablespoons of lemon juice and the rind and stir in the consommé and wine. Bring the mixture to boiling point but do not let it boil. Remove from the heat and stir in the egg yolks with a generous pinch of salt to taste. Heat well, but without boiling, stirring the soup constantly from the bottom of the pan with a wooden spoon. Serve hot in heated soup plates, each sprinkled with a fresh grating of nutmeg. Alternatively, leave the soup to cool, then chill it and serve in chilled soup cups, topped with a spoonful of whipped and salted cream.

LOUIS P. DE GOUY
THE SOUP BOOK

Fish and Shellfish

Sole in Red Wine

The technique of poaching fish in wine is shown on page 70.

To serve 8

Four 500 g	sole, filleted and soaked in iced water, carcasses, heads and trimmings reserved	Four 1 lb
1 bottle	red wine	1 bottle
1 or 2	fennel stalks	1 or 2
1	carrot, sliced	1
1	onion, sliced	1
4	sprigs thyme	4
1	bay leaf	1
4	sprigs flat-leafed parsley	4
2 or 3	unpeeled garlic cloves, crushed	2 or 3
	salt and pepper	
300 g	butter, 250 g (8 oz) cut into small cubes	10 oz

Chop or break up the carcasses and trimmings into fairly even-sized pieces. Put them, with the heads, in a large pan and add the fennel stalks, carrot, onion, thyme, bay leaf, parsley and garlic cloves. Pour in the wine, season with salt and add enough cold water to cover the contents of the pan by about 2.5 cm (1 inch). Place the pan, uncovered, over a fairly low heat and bring the liquid gradually to the boil, skimming off the scum that rises as the liquid approaches the boil. This will take about 15 minutes. Lower the heat, place the lid slightly ajar on the pan and simmer the fumet for 30 minutes.

Strain the fumet into a bowl through a colander lined with several layers of dampened muslin. Discard the trimmings, carcasses, heads, vegetables and herbs. Return the strained fumet to the pan and bring it to the boil again, skimming off any scum that rises. Continue to boil until the fumet is reduced by about two-thirds, then remove the pan from the heat and leave the fumet to cool.

Butter the bottom and sides of a heavy sauté pan. Remove the fillets from the iced water, place them between two towels and pat them dry. Slit the surface membrane of each fillet six times·diagonally, then season with salt and pepper. Smear the fillets with softened butter and fold each one in half so that the scored membrane surface is folded in upon itself. Place the fillets in the buttered pan.

Ensure that the fumet is cold; if it is still warm, place it over a bowl of iced water and stir until it has cooled. Pour the cold fumet over the fish fillets, adding more red wine if necessary to barely cover them. Cover the fillets tightly with buttered greaseproof paper and place a lid on the pan. Bring the liquid to the boil over a medium heat, checking occasionally to see whether it is boiling. As soon as it comes to the boil, turn off the heat immediately and leave the pan to stand, still tightly covered, for 8 to 10 minutes. Set a wire rack over a tray. Remove the buttered greaseproof paper and lid from the fillets and carefully lift them on to the wire rack. Cover the fillets again with the buttered greaseproof paper and leave them to drain.

To make the sauce, strain the poaching liquid through a sieve set over a heavy pan and add any liquid that has drained from the fish. Reduce the liquid to a syrupy consistency over a high heat. Set the heat to very low and put a firepoof mat under the pan. Whisk the cubes of butter into the liquid, a few at a time. Arrange the fillets on a warmed serving dish and ladle a little of the sauce over them. Serve the rest of the sauce separately, in a warmed sauceboat.

PETITS PROPOS CULINAIRES 11

Fish Tumbet

Tumbet de Pescado

To serve 4

500 g	sea bass, monkfish or hake, cleaned, skinned and cut into small fillets	1 lb
	salt	
1	lemon, juice strained	1
$\frac{1}{4}$ litre	oil	8 fl oz
10 cl	dry white wine	$3\frac{1}{2}$ fl oz
4	medium-sized potatoes, cut into rounds	4
2	large aubergines, peeled and cut into rounds	2
30 g	flour	1 oz
2	large sweet green peppers	2
1	medium-sized onion, chopped	1
1	garlic clove, chopped	1
1	bay leaf	1
3	large tomatoes, roughly chopped	3
	ground cinnamon	
1 tsp	sugar	1 tsp

Put the fish fillets into a shallow ovenproof dish, season them with salt, pour in the lemon juice, 4 tablespoonfuls of the oil and all the white wine. Place in a preheated 180°C (350°F or

Mark 4) oven for 20 minutes or until cooked through. Remove the fish from the dish and reserve the cooking liquid.

Heat 4 tablespoonfuls of the oil in a frying pan, sprinkle the potato rounds with salt, add them to the pan and cook, covered, for 20 minutes. Remove the potatoes from the pan, add another 4 tablespoonfuls of oil to the pan, coat the aubergine rounds with the flour, shaking off any excess, and fry them for 5 minutes or until tender. Put the sweet peppers under a hot grill, turning occasionally until their skins have blistered. Peel off the skins, remove the seeds and cut the peppers into fairly large strips. Sprinkle the peppers with salt and fry them for 4 minutes.

Pour the remaining oil into a saucepan, or, if there is any oil left over from frying the vegetables, use that. Fry the onion, garlic and bay leaf until the onion is brown. Add the tomatoes, a pinch of cinnamon and the sugar. Cook the sauce over a low heat for 20 minutes, occasionally adding small amounts of the liquid in which the fish was cooked. Strain the sauce through a sieve—the sauce should be fairly thick at this stage.

Cover the base of an ovenproof serving dish with a layer of fried potatoes, put a layer of fish fillets on top of the potatoes, then a layer of sweet peppers and aubergines on top of the fish. Repeat this step until all the fish and vegetables have been used. Cover with the sauce and put in a preheated 190° to 200°C (375° to 400°F or Mark 5 to 6) oven for 20 minutes. Serve hot in the ovenproof dish.

NESTOR LUJAN AND JUAN PERUCHO
EL LIBRO COCINA DE LA ESPAÑOLA

Salmon in Red Wine

Saumon au Vin Rouge

The wine sauce can be cooked several hours in advance, but the salmon steaks must be baked just before serving as they would dry out if reheated.

To serve 6

6	salmon steaks, 2.5 cm (1 inch) thick	6
1 bottle	red wine	1 bottle
6	shallots, sliced	6
1	bay leaf	1
¼ tsp	dried thyme	¼ tsp
4	sprigs parsley	4
	salt and pepper	
90 g	butter, cut into cubes	3 oz

Put the wine, shallots, bay leaf, thyme, parsley, salt and pepper in a small, heavy saucepan. Bring the wine to the boil, reduce the heat, cover the saucepan and simmer for 20 minutes. Strain the sauce into a bowl.

Put the salmon steaks in a baking dish that will hold them snugly. Lightly salt and pepper the salmon and pour about 20 cl (7 fl oz) of the wine sauce over them. Cover the dish and place it in a preheated 190°C (375°F or Mark 5) oven for 10 to 15 minutes, or until the fish flakes easily. Do not overcook.

While the salmon is cooking, reduce the remaining wine sauce to a thick syrup by boiling it rapidly, uncovered, in the saucepan. Remove the saucepan from the heat and gradually whisk in the butter cubes. Keep the sauce warm on a very low heat and do not let it boil again. Lift the salmon out of the wine on to a warm serving dish. If the sauce seems a little thick, thin it with a tablespoonful of wine from the baking dish. Spoon the sauce over each salmon steak and serve at once.

CAROL CUTLER
THE SIX-MINUTE SOUFFLÉ AND OTHER CULINARY DELIGHTS

Fresh Herrings in Red Wine

Harengs Frais au Vin Rouge

To serve 4

4	fresh herrings, with soft roes	4
20 cl	red wine	7 fl oz
1 tsp	mustard	1 tsp
1 tbsp	chopped parsley	1 tbsp
1 tbsp	chopped tarragon	1 tbsp
2	spring onions, chopped	2
	salt and pepper	
45 g	butter, cut into small pieces	1½ oz
4 tbsp	breadcrumbs or crushed rusks	4 tbsp

Scale the herrings, remove the heads and fins. Wash the herrings and slit them along the stomachs. Remove the soft roes. Put the roes in a bowl, mash them and mix in the mustard. To make the stuffing, stir the chopped herbs and onions in to the roe and mustard mixture, and mix thoroughly. Season the herrings with salt and pepper and put some stuffing inside each one. Dot the herrings with the butter. Place the herrings in a buttered ovenproof dish and pour the wine over them. Put the dish in a preheated 200°C (400°F or Mark 6) oven and cook for 10 minutes. Remove the dish from the oven, sprinkle the breadcrumbs or crushed rusks over the herrings, then return the dish to the oven for 5 minutes to brown the breadcrumbs. Serve the herrings straight from the dish, accompanied by jacket potatoes.

GASTON CLÉMENT
GASTRONOMIE ET FOLKLORE

Red Snapper Louisiana

If red snapper is unavailable, sea bream can be substituted.

To serve 8 to 10

2 kg	red snapper, cleaned, head and backbone removed	4 lb
2 tbsp	olive oil	2 tbsp
2	onions, finely chopped	2
2	sweet green peppers, finely chopped	2
2	mushrooms, finely chopped	2
1	garlic clove, crushed	1
6	tomatoes, skinned	6
$\frac{1}{2}$ tsp	powdered saffron	$\frac{1}{2}$ tsp
$\frac{1}{4}$ litre	dry white wine	8 fl oz
	salt and pepper	
1 tbsp	chopped parsley	1 tbsp

Heat the olive oil over a moderate flame and cook the onions, peppers, mushrooms and garlic in it for a few minutes; add the tomatoes and cook for 30 minutes. Add the saffron. Place the red snapper in a buttered, ovenproof dish. Pour the wine over the fish and season very lightly with salt and pepper. Add the sauce and cook for 30 minutes in a preheated 180°C (350°F or Mark 4) oven. Garnish with the parsley before serving.

RUTH MOUTON HAMILTON
FRENCH ACADIAN COOK BOOK

Mussels "Poulette"

The techniques of cleaning and steaming mussels are demonstrated on page 72.

To serve 8 to 10

3 litres	live mussels, scrubbed clean and soaked in salted water for 30 minutes	5 pints
1	stick celery, chopped	1
1	bay leaf	1
2 tbsp	chopped flat-leafed parsley	2 tbsp
2	sprigs thyme	2
2	garlic cloves, crushed	2
	dry white wine	
6	egg yolks	6
20 cl	double cream	7 fl oz

Put the mussels in a large pan, add the celery, bay leaf, parsley, thyme and garlic and pour in a generous splash of white wine. Cover the pan and open the mussels over a high heat, shaking the pan often until all the mussels have opened

—3 to 5 minutes. Line a colander with several layers of dampened muslin, then tip the mussels into the colander. Taste the liquid for salt: if it is not salty, reduce it by boiling. If it is very salty do not reduce it, but use only part of it to make the sauce. The remainder can be used to make soup or stock.

Once the mussels are cool enough to touch, pull the shells apart, discarding each empty half shell. Arrange the mussels in their half shells in a large shallow pan. Whisk the egg yolks with the cream and gradually whisk in 10 to 15 cl ($3\frac{1}{2}$ to 5 fl oz) of the cooking liquid. Pour this mixture over the mussels. Place the pan over a gentle heat, shaking it gently from side to side until the sauce thickens—about 10 minutes. Make sure that the sauce does not boil whilst it is thickening. Ladle the mussels and sauce into soup plates and serve immediately.

PETITS PROPOS CULINAIRES 11

Sea Bream with Mussels

Pagre aux Moules

The technique of cleaning mussels is shown on page 72.

This recipe is suitable for various members of the bream family, and also for grey mullet.

To serve 4 to 6

800 g to 1.2 kg	sea bream, cleaned and scaled, head removed	$1\frac{3}{4}$ to $2\frac{1}{2}$ lb
1 kg	live small mussels, cleaned	$2\frac{1}{4}$ lb
15 cl	dry white wine	$\frac{1}{4}$ pint
3 tbsp	olive oil	3 tbsp
1	leek, white part finely sliced	1
3	tomatoes, skinned, seeded and roughly chopped	3
4 tbsp	chopped parsley	4 tbsp
1 or 2	garlic cloves, chopped	1 or 2
2	fennel leaves, chopped	2
	salt and pepper	
	lemon quarters	

Put the mussels in a wide pan with the wine and let them open over a fairly high heat. Remove them from the pan as soon as they open. Strain the stock left in the pan through a layer of muslin, and take the mussels from their shells. Heat the olive oil in a small frying pan and soften the leek in it. Then add the tomatoes, parsley, garlic, fennel leaves and salt and pepper. When the mixture begins to look like a purée, thin it with a little of the strained mussel stock. Then, off the heat, add the mussels to the pan.

Spread a large sheet of aluminium foil or greaseproof paper with a film of olive oil. Lay the bream on this. Surround it with the prepared sauce; wrap the foil or paper round, twisting the edges so that no juice can run out. Put on a baking dish and cook in a preheated 180°C (350°F or Mark 4) oven for about 40 minutes. To serve, turn the fish out on to a heated dish with the sauce and juices all round. Add lemon quarters.

ALAN DAVIDSON
MEDITERRANEAN SEAFOOD

Asparagus, Scallop and Oyster Fricassée

*Fricassée aux Asperges,
Coquilles Saint-Jacques et Huîtres*

The author recommends a Pouilly-Fuissé with this dish.

The asparagus can be replaced by *petits pois* or mange-tout. Once the dish is cooked, its flavour can be further enhanced by the addition of fresh, chopped herbs such as mint, basil, chervil or chives; or better still, by the addition of caviare or *julienne* of truffle.

To serve 4

12	large asparagus spears	12
8	scallops, flesh cut into 2 or 3 slices, corals kept whole	8
8	oysters, shelled and drained of their liquor	8
80 g	butter, 70 g (2¼ oz) cut into small pieces and reserved in a cold place	2½ oz
2	shallots, finely chopped	2
20 cl	dry white wine	7 fl oz
3 tbsp	white wine vinegar	3 tbsp
20 cl	*crème fraîche* or double cream	7 fl oz
	rock salt and freshly ground black pepper	
	cayenne pepper	
	fines herbes (optional)	

Cut about one-third off each asparagus stalk; each one should then be roughly 9 cm (3½ inches) long. Starting at the stem base, use a paring knife to pare off the tough skin of the stalks, peeling off less as the skin becomes tender towards the tips. Wash the asparagus and leave them in a colander to drain.

Melt 10 g (¼ oz) of the butter in a casserole over a moderate heat, add the shallots, stirring them well with a wooden spoon, and cook for about 2 minutes until the shallots are translucent. Pour in the wine and wine vinegar, stir, and cook for 10 minutes to reduce the liquid.

In the meantime, pour 3 litres (5¼ pints) of water into a deep pan, add 3 teaspoonfuls of rock salt and bring to the boil. Add the asparagus, bring the water back to the boil and cook for 13 minutes. Remove the asparagus from the pan and leave to drain on a kitchen towel. Season the scallop flesh and coral with salt and a little black pepper and set them aside.

Stir the *crème fraîche* or double cream into the reduced wine liquid and cook over a low heat for 5 minutes, whisking from time to time. The shallots will flavour the cream. Put four plates to warm. Season the sauce with salt, black pepper and a touch of cayenne pepper. Remove the pan from the heat and whisk in the cold butter, a piece at a time. Set a sieve in a small saucepan placed over a low heat and strain the sauce into it. Gently simmer the sauce again for 3 minutes.

Put the scallop flesh and coral and the oysters into the sauce and poach them gently, making sure that they are well covered by the sauce. The shellfish will be cooked by the time the sauce starts to simmer again. To serve, place three well-drained asparagus stalks and equal amounts of oysters, scallop flesh and coral on each warmed plate; pour a moderate amount of sauce over the asparagus and shellfish. If you wish, sprinkle *fines herbes* over the sauce; serve immediately.

ALAIN AND EVENTHIA SENDERENS
LA CUISINE RÉUSSIE

Cuttlefish in White Wine

Seppie al Vino Bianco

To serve 6

2 kg	cuttlefish, cleaned, sponged dry and cut into small pieces	4 lb
About ½ litre	dry white wine	About 16 fl oz
	salt and pepper	
10 cl	olive oil	3½ fl oz
3	garlic cloves, crushed	3
1 tsp	lemon juice	1 tsp
2 tbsp	chopped parsley	2 tbsp

Season the cuttlefish pieces with salt and pepper, put them in a bowl and pour the olive oil over them. Cover the bowl and leave for 1 hour. Strain the olive oil into a pan, add the garlic and heat until the garlic starts to colour. Remove the garlic and discard it. Put the cuttlefish into the pan and cook over a moderate heat, moistening them from time to time with tablespoonfuls of wine, since the liquid will reduce during cooking. When the cuttlefish are cooked, about 45 minutes, transfer them to a serving dish and add the lemon juice. Sprinkle all over with the chopped parsley.

VINCENZO BUONASSISI AND PINO CAPOGNA
IL VINO IN PENTOLA

Poultry and Game

Chicken in Wine and Lemon Sauce

Poulastron aux Citrons

Patrimonio, a dry white wine from Corsica, is used in this recipe. If unavailable, any dry white wine can be substituted.

To serve 4

1.75 kg	chicken, cut into serving pieces, giblets (except liver) cut into small pieces	3½ lb
1 bottle	Patrimonio	1 bottle
2	lemons	2
20 cl	olive oil	7 fl oz
	salt and pepper	
1	carrot	1
1	leek, white part only	1
4	shallots	4
1	bay leaf	1
1 sprig each	thyme, sage, marjoram, rosemary, mint, savory and basil	1 sprig each
4	egg yolks	4
30 cl	double cream	½ pint

Heat 10 cl (3½ fl oz) of the olive oil in a frying pan, season the giblets and chicken pieces and brown them in the oil. Pour the rest of the olive oil into a cast-iron casserole, add the giblets, the carrot, leek, shallots, all the herbs and the wine. Bring to the boil and season with salt and pepper. Put the chicken pieces into the casserole. Cover the casserole and cook over a low heat for about 1 hour.

Meanwhile, using a small, sharp knife, carefully pare the rinds off both lemons in very thin strips—it is essential that no white pith is removed with the rind. Cut the rinds into *julienne.* Squeeze the lemons and strain their juice.

Remove the chicken pieces and giblets, strain the cooking liquid, raise the heat and reduce the liquid by about half. Take off the heat and leave to cool a little. Mix the egg yolks with the cream and stir them into the casserole. Return the casserole to a low heat and cook without boiling, stirring constantly until the mixture barely coats the spoon. Add the lemon juice and the *julienne.* Put the chicken pieces and giblets back into the sauce and warm over low heat for about 5 minutes.

ROGER LALLEMAND
LE COQ AU VIN

Chicken in Two Sauternes Sauces

Les Poulets aux Deux Sauces Sauternes

Other sweet white Bordeaux wines such as Cérons and Ste. Croix du Mont may be used instead of Sauternes.

Use the other parts of the chickens to make chicken stock.

To serve 6

3	chickens, breasts and thighs only	3
40 cl	Sauternes	14 fl oz
3 or 4	leeks, cut into 12 sticks, 3 cm (1¼ inches) long	3 or 4
3 or 4	turnips, cut into 12 sticks, 3 cm (1¼ inches) long	3 or 4
3 or 4	young carrots, cut into 12 sticks, 3 cm (1¼ inches) long	3 or 4
12	sticks celery	12
4 tbsp	olive oil	4 tbsp
1	shallot, chopped	1
1 tsp	mustard	1 tsp
20 cl	reduced chicken stock (*page 166*)	7 fl oz
4 tbsp	Armagnac	4 tbsp
12	large white grapes, pips removed with a needle	12
	salt and pepper	

Cook the vegetables in a pan of salted boiling water or, better still, steam them in a *couscoussier* or a vegetable steamer, until they are just tender. Strain them and keep them warm.

Sauté the chicken thighs in the oil over a moderate heat for 15 minutes without letting them become too brown, and then remove them. Pour the fat out of the pan, put the pan back on the heat and add the chopped shallot and mustard; cook for a moment or two then deglaze the pan with the Sauternes. Moisten with the reduced chicken stock. Put the thighs in the sauce and simmer over a low heat for 10 minutes. Take the thighs out of the pan and keep them warm. Raise the heat and reduce the sauce until it is fairly thick. Strain the sauce through a fine-meshed sieve set over a pan.

Put the Armagnac and grapes into a small pan and warm them over a very low heat for a few minutes; the Armagnac will most probably ignite, but the flames will die down. Remove the grapes and keep them for the garnish. Add half the reserved sauce to the bit of liquid left in the small pan, and keep the separate pans of sauce warming.

Season the chicken breasts with salt and pepper and arrange them side by side on a baking sheet, making sure they do not overlap. Grill the breasts for 2 minutes on each side.

Have six warmed plates ready, and prepare the dish for serving, working quickly so that the food does not get cold. Place two celery sticks in the middle of each plate, and in the hollow of each stick, arrange alternately the sticks of carrot, turnip and leek. Put a chicken breast on one side of the plate and a chicken thigh on the other. Coat the thighs with the sauce in which they were cooked and the breasts with their sauce. Just before serving, arrange two grapes on each breast.

ANDRÉ DAGUIN
LE NOUVEAU CUISINIER GASCON

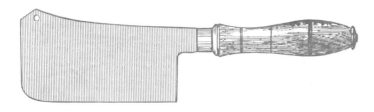

Chicken Sauté Basque-Style

Poulet Sauté Basquaise

The white wine recommended by the author comes from Irouléguy in the extreme south-west corner of France. It may be replaced by another dry white wine. Bayonne, famous for its ham, is also in this area of France.

Serve the dish with ceps and potatoes, sautéed together in olive oil or chicken fat. In the Basque region, some people add cooked, unpeeled garlic cloves to the sauce at the same time as the tomatoes, but the garlic must be peeled before serving.

	To serve 4	
1.75 kg	chicken, cut into serving pieces	3½ lb
	salt and pepper	
60 g	lard	2 oz
250 g	small white onions, peeled	8 oz
45 g	Bayonne ham or raw ham, cut into short strips	1½ oz
1	large sweet red pepper, cut into thick strips	1
30 cl	Irouléguy	½ pint
20 cl	veal stock (*page 166*)	7½ fl oz
1 or 2	tomatoes, skinned, seeded and coarsely chopped	1 or 2

Season the chicken pieces and fry them in the lard until they are golden. Add the onions, the ham and the peppers. Stir the mixture and cook over a low heat for 15 minutes. Drain off as much fat as possible and pour in the wine. Bring to the boil, cover the pan and cook for 30 minutes over a very low heat. Add the veal stock and the tomatoes to the chicken and simmer for several minutes. Correct the seasoning.

ROGER LALLEMAND
LE COQ AU VIN

Chicken in Yellow Wine

Le Coq au Vin Jaune

If vin jaune is unavailable, you can use a mixture of dry white wine and dry sherry instead.

	To serve 4	
2 kg	chicken, preferably a young cock, cut into serving pieces	4 lb
30 cl	*vin jaune du Jura*	½ pint
	salt and pepper	
	flour	
60 g	butter	2 oz
200 g	morels, blanched	7 oz
20 cl	double cream	7 fl oz

Season the chicken pieces with salt and pepper, and roll them in flour. Heat the butter in a heavy pan and fry the chicken pieces in it without allowing them to brown. Drain off the butter, pour in the wine and correct the seasoning. Cover the pan and cook over a gentle flame for 30 to 40 minutes. Add the morels and cook for another 15 minutes. Remove the chicken pieces, turn up the heat and reduce the sauce. Stir in the cream. Reduce the sauce again to ensure a thick, creamy consistency. Replace the chicken pieces in the sauce, bring to the boil once and serve.

ROGER LALLEMAND
LE COQ AU VIN

Poultry Livers with Onions and Madeira

Geflügelleber mit Zwiebeln und Madeira

Goose liver is particularly popular for this dish.

	To serve 4	
600 g	poultry livers, sliced	1¼ lb
2	medium-sized onions, finely chopped	2
12.5 cl	Madeira	4 fl oz
2 tbsp	flour	2 tbsp
80 g	goose fat or lard	2¾ oz
	salt and pepper	

Sprinkle the flour over the livers. Fry the onions in the fat over a moderate heat until golden. Raise the heat, add the livers and fry them quickly—they taste best when they are still pink inside. Remove the livers to a heated plate and keep them warm. Pour the Madeira into the pan, bring to the boil. Season the livers, then pour the Madeira sauce over them.

HANS GUSTL KERNMAYR
SO KOCHTE MEINE MUTTER

Drunken Quail

Codornices Emborrachadas

To serve 4

8	quail, cleaned	8
	salt	
30 g	lard	1 oz
100 g	streaky bacon, cut into 2 cm (¾ inch) squares	3½ oz
½ litre	dry white wine	16 fl oz
17 cl	brandy	6 fl oz
1	egg, beaten with 1 tsp sugar	1
10 cl	milk	3½ fl oz

Season the quail inside and out with salt. Heat the lard in a low, pot-bellied, fireproof stewpan over a medium heat and add the bacon squares and quail. Cook until the quail are browned all over. Skim off any excess fat in the pan. Add the wine and brandy. Place a sheet of brown paper over the top of the pan and put the lid on it. Cook over a medium heat until the liquid has reduced by half, about 15 minutes. Remove the quail and keep them warm. Mix the egg with the milk and add this mixture to the liquid in the pan. Swirl the pan round to mix the liquid with the egg and milk. The sauce will thicken slightly. Return the quail to the sauce and serve from the pan.

NESTOR LUJAN AND JUAN PERUCHO
EL LIBRO DE LA COCINA ESPAÑOLA

Partridges in Wine

Pernici al Vino

To serve 4

4	partridges, plucked and cleaned	4
35 cl	red wine	12 fl oz
60 g	butter	2 oz
	salt and pepper	
½ tsp each	chopped sage and rosemary	½ tsp each
250 g	leeks, thinly sliced	8 oz
4	shallots, peeled	4
1 tsp	sugar	1 tsp
125 g	ceps, heads separated from stalks, stalks thinly sliced	4 oz
2 tbsp	flour mixed to a paste with 30 g (1 oz) softened butter	2 tbsp

Heat 30 g (1 oz) of the butter in a large, heavy-bottomed pan, put the partridges into the pan and season them. Add the sage, rosemary and leeks and sauté for 20 minutes. Remove the partridges, put them in a fireproof serving dish and keep them warm. Heat the rest of the butter in a small pan, add the shallots, a pinch of salt and the sugar and cook over a low heat for 15 minutes. Add the cep heads and cook for a further 15 minutes. Arrange the shallots and cep heads round the partridges in the serving dish.

Place the pan in which the partridges were cooked over a high heat, pour in the wine and stir vigorously with a wooden spoon. Add the cep stalks and boil until the liquid is reduced by about a quarter. Whisk small pieces of the flour and butter paste into the boiling liquid, reduce the heat and cook for 5 minutes. Strain the sauce into another pan and leave it to cool for a few minutes, then skim off the fat from the surface. Pour the sauce over the partridges. Cover the serving dish and warm over a low heat for another 10 minutes.

GIORGIO GIOCO
LA CUCINA SCALIGERA

Mallard in Red Wine

Civet de Colvert

Serve with carrot or celeriac purée or fresh egg noodles, accompanied by a 1964 Volnay or a Côte de Nuits.

To serve 4

2	fresh mallards	2
1 bottle	fine red wine	1 bottle
15 cl	red wine vinegar	¼ pint
5 or 6	shallots, finely sliced	5 or 6
2	onions, finely sliced	2
1	bay leaf	1
1	bouquet garni	1
5 or 6	carrots, sliced	5 or 6
3	large leeks, sliced	3
1	stick celery, sliced	1
1	celeriac, sliced	1
50 g	butter or 4 tbsp olive oil	2 oz
	salt and pepper	

Remove the breasts and livers from the ducks and set them aside in a cool place or in the refrigerator. Chop the legs and wings and the rest of the carcasses into small pieces, put them in a bowl and cover them with the wine and wine vinegar. Add the shallots, onions, bay leaf and the bouquet garni and leave to marinate overnight. Next day, remove the duck pieces from the marinade, drain them in a colander set over a pan and then dry the pieces on a towel.

Pour the marinade into the pan, add the carrots, leeks, celery and celeriac. Place the pan over a low heat and cook gently so that the wine keeps its bouquet and taste—only the alcohol should evaporate during cooking. When the vegetables are tender, remove the bay leaf and strain the liquid into a blender. Add 1 tablespoon of the vegetables and blend; if the liquid is too thin, blend in some more of the vegetables. To ensure that the sauce is perfectly smooth, strain it through a fine sieve set over a pan. Correct the seasoning.

Heat the butter or olive oil in a heavy pan and fry the duck pieces over a high heat for 5 minutes on each side. Season. Remove the duck pieces and drain them thoroughly so that they do not make the sauce greasy. Put them in the sauce and cook gently for 5 minutes. Heat the grill until very hot, season the duck breasts and liver, place them on a metal tray and grill them for about 2 minutes on each side. The breasts and livers must be rare; add them to the sauce and duck pieces with their cooking juices. Serve very hot.

LALOU BIZE-LEROY
LE NOUVEAU GUIDE GAULT MILLAU, CONNAISSANCE DES VOYAGES

Marinated Duck Breasts

Le Magret de Canard Mariné

Côtes de Buzet is a red wine from south-west France made from the same grape varieties as red Bordeaux wines; a Bordeaux wine could be substituted.

Place the duck breasts in a glass dish with the onion, carrot, thyme, *quatre épices* and garlic cloves. Pour the wine into the dish and leave the duck breasts to marinate overnight.

For a really sumptuous vegetable to accompany this dish, cut a celeriac into rounds, 2 to 3 mm ($\frac{1}{8}$ inch) thick; blanch and drain them. Fry the rounds in butter for 10 minutes. Some of the sauce can be kept to pour over the celeriac.

	To serve 6	
6	duck breasts, boned, skinned and trimmed of fat and tendons	6
1	onion, sliced	1
1	carrot, sliced	1
1	sprig thyme	1
	quatre épices	
2	garlic cloves, crushed	2
1 bottle	Côtes de Buzet	1 bottle
30 g	goose fat	1 oz
90 g	butter	3 oz
4 tbsp	Armagnac	4 tbsp

Place the duck breasts in a glass dish with the onion, carrot, thyme, *quatre épices* and garlic cloves. Pour the wine into the dish and leave the duck breasts to marinate overnight.

Next day, remove the duck breasts from the marinade and drain them. Reserve the marinade. Melt the goose fat and 30 g (1 oz) of the butter in a sauté pan over a high heat, add the duck breasts and sauté them for 5 minutes on each side. Cover the duck breasts and keep them in a warm place or in an oven set

at its lowest temperature whilst finishing the sauce. Remove all fat from the pan and deglaze it with the Armagnac. Pour in the unstrained marinade and reduce over a high heat for at least 15 to 20 minutes, then strain the sauce and boil it again. Cut the remaining butter into five or six equal-sized pieces and add these to the sauce, whisking constantly. When all the butter is incorporated into the sauce, remove it from the heat immediately and pour over the duck breasts.

ANDRÉ DAGUIN
LE NOUVEAU CUISINIER GASCON

Rabbit Fricassée

Fricassée de Lapin

The author recommends accompanying this dish with pommes gaufrettes—potatoes sliced into wafer-thin waffles with the corrugated blade of a mandoline, then deep fried until they are golden.

	To serve 5	
One 1.5 kg	young, tender rabbit, cut into 8 serving pieces, liver reserved	One 3 lb
2 tbsp	groundnut oil	2 tbsp
30 g	butter	1 oz
	salt and pepper	
3	shallots, finely chopped	3
15 cl	crème fraîche or double cream	$\frac{1}{4}$ pint
2 tsp	strong French mustard	2 tsp
10 cl	dry white wine	$3\frac{1}{2}$ fl oz
1 tbsp	finely chopped chives	1 tbsp

Heat the groundnut oil and butter in a large, heavy pan over a moderate heat. Season the pieces of rabbit. When the butter is sizzling, brown the pieces of rabbit on each side—about 5 minutes. Stir in the shallots and cover the pan; reduce the heat to low and cook gently for 3 minutes.

In the meantime, pour the *crème fraîche* or double cream into a bowl, add the mustard and mix well together. Uncover the pan, add the wine, raise the heat high and bring the mixture to the boil. Add the cream and mustard mixture and mix well. Lower the heat, cover the pan and leave the fricassée to cook gently for 10 minutes.

Cut away and discard any fibrous connective tissue from the liver and purée the liver in a blender. Transfer the pieces of rabbit from the pan to a warmed serving dish. Remove the pan from the heat, pour in the puréed liver and whisk well—the sauce will thicken instantly. Pour the sauce through a fine-meshed sieve over the pieces of rabbit, sprinkle with the chopped chives and serve.

MICHEL OLIVER
MES RECETTES À LA TÉLÉ

Meat

Beef Stew in Barbera

Stufato di Manzo al Barbera

Any young red wine could be substituted for the Barbera. The cuts of beef best suited to braising are shin, chuck and leg.

To serve 4

1 kg	beef, cut into 100 g (3½ oz) pieces	2 to 2½ lb
1 bottle	Barbera	1 bottle
500 g	onions, sliced	1 lb
1	carrot, sliced	1
1	stick celery, chopped	1
2	bay leaves	2
3	garlic cloves, crushed	3
4	juniper berries	4
6	cloves	6
Two 2.5 cm	cinnamon sticks	Two 1 inch
50 g	butter	2 oz
4 tbsp	oil	4 tbsp
	salt and pepper	
500 g	potatoes, quartered	1 lb

Put the meat into an earthenware pot with the onions, carrot, celery, bay leaves, garlic, juniper berries, cloves and cinnamon sticks. Cover with the wine. Cover the pot and leave it in a cool place for two days, turning the meat occasionally.

Remove the meat from the marinade and drain it. Heat the butter and oil in a flameproof casserole over a moderate heat and, when the butter starts to foam, add the meat. Fry the meat for about 20 minutes, turning the pieces until they are lightly browned, then add the marinade and salt and pepper to taste. Cover the casserole and cook over a low heat at a bare simmer for 4 hours.

Add the potatoes to the casserole after the beef has been cooking for 3 hours. At the end of the cooking time, remove the meat and potatoes, arrange them in a heated, deep serving dish and keep them warm. Set a sieve over a clean pan and pour the sauce through the sieve. Degrease the sauce and, if necessary, reduce it over a high heat for a few moments. Pour it over the meat and potatoes.

LAURA GRAS PORTINARI
CUCINA E VINI DEL PIEMONTE E DELLA VALLE D'AOSTA

Minced Beef in Red Wine

Tapôlon

The wines recommended by the author for cooking this dish—Gattinara, Ghemme or Boca—are all red wines from Piedmont in Italy; any robust, young red wine can be used instead.

Tapôlon, from the word tapôlé, meaning "cut into tiny pieces with a knife", is usually eaten as a first course.

To serve 8

1 kg	lean beef, cut into small dice	2 to 2½ lb
½ litre	Gattinara, Ghemme or Boca	16 fl oz
2 tbsp	olive oil	2 tbsp
30 g	butter	1 oz
4	garlic cloves, crushed	4
1 tsp	rosemary, chopped	1 tsp
1	bay leaf	1

Heat the oil and butter in a large pan, add the garlic, rosemary and bay leaf and sauté until the garlic is softened but not coloured. Increase the heat, add the chopped beef and brown it. Season. Lower the heat, add a small amount of wine and cover the pan. Simmer for 2 to 2½ hours, adding small quantities of wine at regular intervals as the cooking liquid reduces.

FELICE CÙNSOLO
LA CUCINA DEL PIEMONTE

Beef in Gravy

Boeuf au Jus

The cuts of beef best suited to braising are shin, chuck and leg.

To serve 4

1 kg	braising beef	2 lb
15 g	butter	½ oz
3 or 4	slices pork back fat	3 or 4
20 cl	water	7 fl oz
20 cl	red wine	7 fl oz
100 g	shallots, sliced	3½ oz
1	strip lemon rind	1
1	sprig basil	1
2 tbsp	breadcrumbs	2 tbsp

Pound the beef on both sides with a mallet. Put the butter and the slices of pork fat in the bottom of a heavy saucepan, place the beef on top and cover the saucepan. Brown each side of the beef over low heat, turning occasionally. Pour in the water and the wine, add the shallots, lemon rind and basil; cover the pan and simmer over a very low heat until the beef is tender—about 2½ hours. Skim off fat from the surface of the liquid, add the breadcrumbs and simmer for another 15 minutes.

MARGUERITE SPOERLIN
LA CUISINIÈRE DU HAUT-RHIN

Tarhoniya Goulash

The cuts of beef best suited to braising are shin, chuck and leg. The author recommends serving potatoes baked in their jackets with the goulash.

To serve 4

1 kg	braising beef, cut into 5 cm (2 inch) cubes	2 lb
About ¾ litre	red wine	About 1¼ pints
60 g	flour	2 oz
¼ tsp	salt	¼ tsp
	black pepper	
2 tbsp	oil	2 tbsp
4	onions, chopped	4
4	tomatoes, quartered	4
2 tbsp	pearl barley	2 tbsp
2	bay leaves	2
4	large prunes	4
1	garlic clove, chopped	1
1 tsp	sweet paprika	1 tsp
2 tbsp	double cream (optional)	2 tbsp

Put the flour into a paper bag with the salt and plenty of pepper; put in the meat, shut the bag tightly, and shake it vigorously a few times, until the meat is evenly coated with flour. Heat the oil in a frying pan and brown the meat and onions quickly. Put the meat and onions in an ovenproof casserole that has a tight-fitting lid. Add the tomatoes, pearl barley, bay leaves, prunes, garlic and paprika. Pour ½ litre (16 fl oz) of the wine over the mixture, cover the casserole and put it in a preheated 180°C (350°F or Mark 4) oven for 20 minutes. Then turn the oven to its lowest setting—about 130° to 140°C (250° to 275°F or Mark ½ or 1) and leave the goulash to cook for at least 4 to 5 hours. After 2 to 2½ hours, stir the goulash gently and, if it looks dry, add 15 cl (¼ pint) more of the remaining wine. Continue adding small quantities of wine from time to time, but do not add too much or the gravy will not thicken.

If you wish, stir in the cream just before serving—do not let the cream cook in the oven or it will curdle.

LESLEY BLANCH
ROUND THE WORLD IN EIGHTY DISHES

Beef Stew, Burgundy-Style

Boeuf Bourguignon

The cuts of beef best suited to braising are shin, chuck and leg.

To serve 8

1.5 kg	braising beef, cut into 5 cm (2 inch) cubes	3 lb
1	large onion, sliced	1
4	sprigs parsley, finely chopped	4
1	sprig thyme	1
1 or 2	bay leaves, crumbled	1 or 2
	black peppercorns, coarsely crushed in a mortar	
2 tbsp	olive oil	2 tbsp
1 bottle	red wine	1 bottle
20 g	lard	⅔ oz
200 g	green bacon, cut into large dice and blanched	7 oz
3 tbsp	marc or brandy	3 tbsp
2 tbsp	flour	2 tbsp
½ litre	stock (*page 166*)	16 fl oz
1	garlic clove, crushed	1
24	small onions, peeled	24
20 g	butter	⅔ oz
	salt	

Put the cubes of meat in a large bowl; add the onion, chopped parsley, thyme, bay leaves and a good pinch of crushed peppercorns. Pour in the olive oil and the wine and leave to marinate for 3 hours, turning the meat four or five times.

Melt the lard in a skillet over a low heat, add the bacon strips and sauté them for about 10 minutes. Take the meat out of the marinade and drain it. Place the skillet over a medium heat, add the meat and brown well on all sides. Heat the marc or brandy in a small heavy pan, set the liquor alight and pour it over the meat when the flames have died. Reduce the heat to low and sprinkle the flour over the meat, stirring well until the meat is coated in flour. Add the stock, marinade and garlic; cover the pan and simmer for 2 hours.

Whilst the stew is cooking, sauté the small onions in the butter over a low heat. Add the sautéed onions to the stew after it has been cooking for 2 hours, season with salt to taste, replace the lid and cook for another hour. Remove the meat, bacon and the onions from the skillet, arrange them on a serving dish and keep them warm. Strain the sauce through a sieve into a pan and reheat it, half on, half off the heat, skimming until the sauce is free of grease and impurities. Pour the sauce over the meat and serve.

CÉLINE VENCE
ENCYCLOPÉDIE HACHETTE DE LA CUISINE D'HIER ET D'AUJOURD'HUI

Marinated Beef Braised in Red Wine

The technique of assembling a marinade with herbs and vegetables is demonstrated on page 66.

	To serve 4	
1 kg	leg of beef, cut into 90 g (3 oz) pieces	2 lb
60 g	pork back fat, cut into lardons 5 mm (¼ inch) thick and 5 cm (2 inches) long	2 oz
4 tbsp	olive oil	4 tbsp
250 g	onions, coarsely chopped	8 oz
250 g	carrots, coarsely chopped	8 oz
3 tbsp	flour	3 tbsp
3 tbsp	cognac	3 tbsp
About ¼ litre	beef or veal stock (*page 166*)	About 8 fl oz
1	bouquet garni, including celery and leek	1
	Persillade	
1	garlic clove	1
	coarse salt	
1 tbsp	finely chopped parsley	1 tbsp
½ tsp	dried mixed herbs	½ tsp
	Marinade	
1	large onion, sliced	1
1	carrot, sliced	1
1	stick celery	1
3 or 4	garlic cloves, crushed	3 or 4
3 or 4	sprigs parsley	3 or 4
1	sprig thyme	1
2	bay leaves	2
1 bottle	red wine	1 bottle
2 tbsp	olive oil	2 tbsp
	Garnish	
3 tbsp	olive oil	3 tbsp
150 g	green bacon, cut into strips, parboiled for 2 to 3 minutes, rinsed in cold water and drained	5 oz
20 to 25	small onions, peeled	20 to 25
250 g	small mushrooms	8 oz

To make the *persillade*, crush and pound the garlic clove in a mortar with some coarse salt. Mix in the chopped parsley and a pinch of dried herbs. Roll the lardons in the *persillade* and set them aside. Start assembling the marinade by putting the sliced onion and carrot in a large bowl, then adding the celery,

crushed garlic, parsley and thyme sprigs and the bay leaves.

Using a small knife and following the grain of the meat, cut deep, narrow incisions in the pieces of meat. Insert a lardon in each incision. Add the meat to the bowl containing the vegetables and herbs for the marinade, then pour the wine and olive oil into the bowl. Cover the bowl and leave the meat to marinate for 5 to 6 hours or overnight, turning occasionally.

Pour the meat pieces into a colander set over a bowl, drain them well, then lay them on a towel and use another towel to pat them dry. Discard the aromatic vegetables and herbs; reserve the strained marinade liquid.

To prepare the garnish, heat the oil in a heavy pan over a medium heat and sauté the bacon strips until they are golden. Remove the bacon and put it into a sieve set over a bowl. Pour any oil that has drained from the bacon back into the pan; add the small onions and sauté them over a low heat until they are golden, then drain them in the sieve. Increase the heat, sauté the mushrooms and add them to the sieve. Reserve the bacon strips, small onions and mushrooms for the garnish.

Add the coarsely chopped onions and carrots to the same pan and sauté them, over a medium-low heat, for about 30 minutes until they are lightly coloured. Remove them from the pan and set them aside. Over a medium heat, sear the meat on all sides for about 30 minutes, or until evenly browned. Put the sautéed carrots and onions back in the pan, lower the heat, sprinkle the flour over the meat and turn the meat until the flour has browned.

Turn up the heat, pour the cognac into the pan, add the reserved marinade liquid and the stock. Scrape the bottom of the pan with a wooden spoon to dislodge all the deposits and dissolve them in the liquid. Add the bouquet garni, cover the pan, lower the heat and simmer for about 2½ hours. Alternatively, put the covered pan in a preheated 150°C (300°F or Mark 2) oven for 2½ hours.

When the meat is tender, remove it and put it in another pan, add the garnish and keep the pan warm. Pour the remaining contents of the braising pan into a fine-meshed sieve set over a small pan. Remove the carrots and the bouquet garni and press the onions through the sieve into the pan. Place the small pan half on the heat and allow the cooking liquid to simmer. Remove and discard the skin that forms on the side of the pan that is off the heat, repeating this procedure four or five times over a period of 30 minutes or so, until the liquid is free of fat and impurities and slightly thickened. Pour the sauce over the meat and garnish, and simmer for 15 minutes, gently shaking the pan from time to time so that the flavours are thoroughly intermingled and the meat and garnish are evenly heated.

RICHARD OLNEY
SIMPLE FRENCH FOOD

Stuffed Shoulder of Veal Gourmet

This is excellent as a cold plate, sliced thin and garnished with its own jelly, pickled walnuts and watercress. If the veal is served hot, use the liquid hot as the sauce, but add no thickening unless it be a little cream mixed with the yolk of an egg.

	To serve 6	
3 kg	shoulder of veal, boned	6 lb
250 g	calf's liver	8 oz
250 g	ham	8 oz
45 g	fresh white breadcrumbs	1½ oz
½ tbsp	chopped basil	½ tbsp
½ tbsp	chopped thyme	½ tbsp
1 tbsp	chopped chives	1 tbsp
2 tbsp	chopped parsley	2 tbsp
1	medium-sized onion, chopped	1
1	garlic clove, chopped	1
45 g	butter	1½ oz
75 g	salted pistachio nuts	2½ oz
1	egg, beaten with 1 egg yolk	1
	salt and pepper	
60 cl	Chablis or other dry white wine	1 pint
½ litre	gelatinous veal stock (*page 166*)	16 fl oz
2	carrots, sliced	2
1	bay leaf	1
2	sprigs parsley	2

Put the calf's liver and ham through the medium disc of a meat grinder, being careful to save all the juices. Put the liver and ham and their juices into a bowl. Add the breadcrumbs, basil, thyme, chives and parsley. Fry the onion and garlic in 15 g (½ oz) of the butter for 5 minutes; add to the stuffing with the butter; then add the nuts. Pour in the beaten egg and egg yolk and mix thoroughly with the rest of the stuffing. Season. Fill the boned shoulder, reshape it and sew it securely with strong thread. Sear the meat in the rest of the butter in a skillet until it is well browned on all sides—about 5 minutes.

Put the wine, stock, carrot slices, bay leaf and the sprigs of parsley in a large pot. Heat the liquid and add the meat, pouring over the butter in which it was seared. Season; cover securely and simmer for 4 hours or until tender, turning the meat occasionally for even cooking. Cool the meat in its own juice, then remove it from the pot and place it on a plate. Pour the liquid into a bowl and store it and the meat in a refrigerator; the liquid will turn into a clear, golden, deliciously flavoured jelly with a hard layer of fat over the top. Next day, slice the meat thinly and remove the fat from the meat jelly.

JEANNE OWEN
A WINE LOVER'S COOK BOOK

Peasant-Style Mutton Stew

Spezzato di Montone Allacontadina

This dish can also be made with lamb instead of mutton.

	To serve 4	
1 kg	shoulder of mutton, cut into 4 pieces	2 to 2½ lb
	salt and pepper	
2 tbsp	flour	2 tbsp
15 cl	oil	¼ pint
2	onions, thinly sliced	2
1	garlic clove, crushed	1
6	allspice berries, coarsely crushed	6
4	cloves, coarsely crushed	4
½ litre	red wine	¾ pint
500 g	potatoes, cut into 5 mm (¼ inch) slices	1 lb
45 cl	stock (*page 166*)	¾ pint

Season the mutton pieces and roll them in the flour. Heat the oil in a frying pan and brown the meat in it. Put the meat in a fireproof casserole and add the onions, garlic and spices. Pour in the red wine, cover the casserole and stew over a low heat for about 1 hour. Brown the potatoes in the oil and add them to the meat. Cook over a low heat for a further 30 minutes or until the potatoes are cooked and the mutton is tender, moistening from time to time with the stock to replace the liquid lost during cooking.

ANDREAS HELLRIGL
LA CUCINA DELL'ALTO ADIGE

157

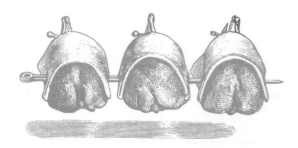

Sautéed Pork with Prunes

Sauté de Porc aux Pruneaux

To serve 6

About 1.5 kg	boned spare rib (neck end) or shoulder of pork, cut into 80 g (3 oz) pieces	About 3 lb
40	prunes, soaked overnight in cold water	40
10 cl	groundnut oil	3½ fl oz
4	large onions, halved and thinly sliced	4
1	lemon, rind pared	1
1	garlic clove, halved and crushed	1
5 cm	stick cinnamon	2 inch
2 tbsp	flour	2 tbsp
20 cl	port	7 fl oz
40 cl	full-bodied red wine	¾ pint
	salt and pepper	

Heat the groundnut oil in a heavy casserole over a high heat. When the oil is hot, add half the meat and brown it all over—this will take about 6 minutes; remove the meat and put it on a plate to drain. Repeat this process with the rest of the meat. Put the sliced onions into the casserole, lower the heat, stir the onions and cook until they are translucent, about 7 minutes.

In the meantime, place the lemon rind, the crushed garlic halves and the cinnamon stick in the middle of a square of muslin. Fold the corners of the muslin over to form a small bundle, tie up the bundle with string, leaving quite a long piece of the string trailing.

Put all the meat and its juices into the casserole, add the flour and stir well with a wooden spoon for 3 minutes. Raise the heat, add the port, the red wine, 1½ teaspoons of salt and a generous amount of pepper. As soon as the mixture comes to the boil, slip the muslin bundle into the casserole and tie the trailing length of string to one of the casserole handles. Lower the heat, cover the casserole and simmer gently for 1 hour.

Drain the prunes, dry them on a towel and add them to the casserole. Cover the casserole again and cook for 1 hour more. Remove the muslin bundle and serve the meat and prunes straight from the casserole.

MICHEL OLIVER
MES RECETTES À LA TÉLÉ

Leg of Pork with Garden Herbs

Varkensfricandeau met Tuinkruiden

To serve 4

750 g	leg of pork	1½ lb
6	rosemary leaves	6
1 tsp	finely chopped tarragon	1 tsp
1 tbsp	finely chopped parsley	1 tbsp
1 tbsp	finely chopped chervil	1 tbsp
	salt and freshly ground white pepper	
1	lemon, juice strained, rind grated	1
50 g	pork back fat or green bacon, chopped	2 oz
100 g	butter	3½ oz
¼ litre	white wine	8 fl oz
¼ litre	veal or chicken stock (*page 166*)	8 fl oz
1	shallot, chopped	1
1	small onion, chopped	1
7 or 8	peppercorns, crushed	7 or 8
1 tbsp	flour	1 tbsp
1 tsp	paprika	1 tsp
10 cl	double cream	3½ fl oz

With a small knife, make incisions in the meat and insert the rosemary leaves. Rub the surface of the meat with salt and pepper and half of the lemon juice. Put the pork back fat or green bacon and 75 g (2½ oz) of the butter in a large pan and heat until the butter has melted. Turn up the heat, add the leg of pork and fry it until it is browned on all sides. Lower the heat, add another 15 g (½ oz) of butter and cook the meat for another 45 minutes, carefully basting it now and then with a few drops of white wine.

In the meantime, reduce the wine and stock with the shallot, onion and peppercorns to 30 cl (½ pint). Remove the meat from the pan. Pour off the fat, add the remaining butter to the pan along with the flour, stir the reduced liquids into the roux, mashing the onion and shallot to a purée, and bring to the boil. Mix the paprika with the cream and add this to the sauce, stirring well. Pour the rest of the lemon juice over the tarragon and leave for a moment. Add the parsley, chervil, grated lemon rind and the tarragon to the sauce. Pour the sauce into a sauceboat and serve it with the pork.

WINA BORN
HERRLIJKE GERECHTEN

Vegetables

Pickled Cabbage with White Wine

Weinkraut

Pickled cabbage is available in delicatessen shops.

Any white wine on the light, dry side, from a modest non-vintage to a fine Riesling, turns sauerkraut into almost a noble dish.

To serve 4

750 g	pickled cabbage (sauerkraut)	1½ lb
20 cl	dry white wine	7 fl oz
30 g	butter	1 oz
30 g	lard	1 oz
1	small onion, finely chopped	1
½ tsp	caraway seeds, crushed	½ tsp
1	small bay leaf	1
	salt and pepper	
20 cl	stock (*page 166*)	7 fl oz
1	potato	1

Drain the pickled cabbage well. Melt the butter and lard in a pan over a moderate heat and cook the onion in it for 2 minutes, taking care not to let the onion brown. Add 2 tablespoons of the wine and let the mixture simmer for a moment or two. Put in the pickled cabbage, crushed caraway seeds, bay leaf and a pinch of salt. Reduce the heat to low and mix all the ingredients well, using a wooden spoon. Add 2 tablespoons each of wine and stock, to allow the pickled cabbage to cook slowly in the liquid, about 1 to 2 hours, with the pan covered. Keep adding the wine and stock at 10-minute intervals until they are used up. Grate the potato and put it in to the pan 20 minutes before the cabbage is cooked. The onion, caraway seeds and potato should all but dissolve during the cooking. Remove the bay leaf before adjusting the seasoning. Pile up the pickled cabbage on a hot serving dish.

ROSL PHILPOT
VIENNESE COOKERY

Red Cabbage in Red Wine

Rotkraut

The author recommends serving this as an accompaniment to baked gammon, roast pork or pork sausages and suggests cooking the dish the morning or the day before it is served and reheating it carefully.

To serve 6 to 8

1 to 1.5 kg	red cabbage, coarse outer leaves removed	2 to 3 lb
30 cl	red wine	½ pint
90 g	lard	3 oz
1	small onion, finely chopped	1
2 tbsp	wine vinegar	2 tbsp
	salt and pepper	
2	cooking apples, peeled, cored and thinly sliced	2
2 tbsp	sugar	2 tbsp
1	bay leaf	1
1	strip lemon rind	1

Shred the cabbage and put it in a colander. Place the colander under the cold tap, wash the cabbage and leave to drain. Melt the lard in a heavy pan over a medium heat and cook the onion in it for 2 minutes without allowing it to brown. Add the wine vinegar and the shredded cabbage. Season with salt and pepper to taste. Cook the cabbage for a few minutes, stirring it well. Add the apple slices to the pan and sprinkle on the sugar. Pour in the wine and add the bay leaf and lemon rind. Lower the heat, cover the pan tightly and stew the cabbage slowly for 1 hour, or cook in a preheated 150°C (300°F or Mark 2) oven for 2 to 3 hours. Before serving, discard the bay leaf and lemon rind and check the seasoning.

ROSL PHILPOT
VIENNESE COOKERY

Broccoli alla Romagna

Cauliflower florets may be cooked in the same way.

To serve 4 to 6		
750 g	broccoli heads	1½ lb
7 tbsp	olive oil	7 tbsp
2	garlic cloves, crushed	2
	salt and freshly ground black pepper	
30 cl	dry white wine	½ pint

Heat the oil over a medium heat and sauté the garlic in it until golden. Add the broccoli heads one by one and sauté them for 4 to 5 minutes, stirring occasionally. Season to taste, then add the wine and enough water to barely cover the vegetables. Bring to the boil, cover and cook for about 25 minutes, until the broccoli is just tender. Drain well.

AUDREY ELLIS
WINE LOVERS COOKBOOK

Potato Stew

Matelote de Pommes de Terre

To serve 4		
750 g	potatoes, sliced into rounds	1½ lb
30 g	butter	1 oz
250 g	small pickling onions	½ lb
1 tbsp	flour	1 tbsp
15 cl	stock (*page 166*)	¼ pint
15 cl	dry white wine	¼ pint
1	bouquet garni	1

Melt the butter in a frying pan and cook the onions over a low heat until they are soft and golden; sprinkle in the flour. Shake and stir the onions, pour in the stock and wine and add the potato slices and the bouquet garni. Cover the pan and simmer for about 25 minutes. Serve immediately.

MAURICE AND GERMAINE CONSTANTIN WEYER
LES SECRETS D'UNE MAÎTRESSE DE MAISON

Courgette Fans

Courgettes en Éventail

The author says that this dish is good hot or cold, but strongly recommends serving it warm, as an hors-d'oeuvre, accompanied by a cold, rustic dry white wine.

To serve 4 to 6		
1 kg	small courgettes	2 lb
3	large, firm, well-ripened tomatoes, unpeeled, conical cores cut out, each tomato halved vertically, then thinly sliced	3
2	large sweet onions, halved and very thinly sliced	2
4 or 5	garlic cloves, sliced paper-thin	4 or 5
3 or 4	sprigs thyme, savory and oregano, or a good pinch of each herb, dried	3 or 4
½ tsp	coriander seeds	½ tsp
	salt and pepper	
6 tbsp	olive oil	6 tbsp
15 cl	dry white wine	¼ pint

Rinse the courgettes, wipe them dry with a towel, trim the tips, and split each in two lengthwise. Place the halves, cut side down, on the chopping board and slice each lengthwise into 5mm (¼ inch) widths without severing the slices from the stem end so that each half, remaining intact, may be spread slightly, fan-like. Slip one or two tomato slices into place between each of the fan sections.

Scatter half the sliced onion and sliced garlic over the bottom of a large, relatively shallow ovenproof dish that has been lightly oiled. Press the courgette fans, cut side down, firmly into place, forcing them slightly, side by side. Slip the sprigs of herbs here and there in the crevices, or sprinkle them over the surface. Scatter the coriander seeds evenly, sprinkle with salt and pepper and scatter the remaining onion and garlic regularly all over. Press the surface firmly with the palm of your hand, dribble olive oil liberally all over and pour over the white wine (the contents of the dish should be slightly more than half immersed in the wine and oil).

Press aluminium foil over the surface and bring to a full boil on top of the oven (protecting the receptacle from direct heat with a fireproof mat if it is earthenware) before transferring it to a preheated 190°C (375°F or Mark 5) oven for about half an hour or until the courgettes are only just tender—they will remain slightly firm, thanks to the acidity of the white wine. Leave for a good half an hour in a warm place (turned-off oven, for instance) before serving from its dish.

RICHARD OLNEY
SIMPLE FRENCH FOOD

Desserts

Baked Fresh Pears Vin

To serve 4

4	pears	4
¼ litre	dry white wine	8 fl oz
2 tbsp	maple syrup	2 tbsp
1 tbsp	sugar	1 tbsp

Cut the pears in half lengthwise, but do not peel them. Remove the cores and place the pears, cut side up, in a casserole. Fill the hollow of each pear with wine, then pour the maple syrup over them. Sprinkle the sugar on top and bake in an oven preheated to 180°C (350°F or Mark 4) for about 20 minutes, or until the pears are tender.

FRANCES D. AND PETER J. ROBOTTI
FRENCH COOKING IN THE NEW WORLD

Pears in Red Wine

Pere al Vino Rosso

To ensure that this dish turns out well, it is essential to use good quality pears that are only just ripe.

To serve 6

6	pears	6
½ litre	red wine	16 fl oz
75 g	sugar	2½ oz
	ground cinnamon	
1	orange, rind pared	1
1	lemon, rind pared	1
4	cloves	4

Put the pears in a deep fireproof casserole. Sprinkle 2 table-spoons of the sugar over the pears, add a pinch of cinnamon, the orange and lemon rinds and the cloves. Pour the wine over the fruit and add the remaining sugar. Cook, uncovered, over a low heat until all the wine has evaporated. Serve hot.

LEONE BOSI
DOLCI PER UN ANNO

Red Fruit Salad with Melon and Port Sorbet

Salade de Fruits Rouges,
Accompagnée de Sorbet Melon au Porto

The author recommends using Cavaillon melons for this recipe; Charentais melons can be substituted.

To serve 6		
600 g	raspberries	1¼ lb
200 g	redcurrants	7 oz
50 g	blackcurrants	2 oz
200 g	strawberries, hulled	7 oz
200 g	wild strawberries, hulled	7 oz
200 g	cherries, stoned	7 oz
800 g	melon, seeds removed, flesh scooped out	1¾ lb
10 cl	port	3½ fl oz
About 200 g sugar		About 7 oz
2	lemons, juice strained	2
	mint leaves	

Purée 300 g (10 oz) of the raspberries, 100 g (3½ oz) of the sugar and the juice of one lemon in a blender. Pass the purée through a fine-meshed sieve into a bowl. Mix the rest of the fruit except the melon into the purée, and put the mixture into the refrigerator.

Put the melon flesh into a pan with 70 to 100 g (2½ to 3½ oz) of sugar—depending on the sweetness of the melon. Add the port and bring the mixture to the boil. Reduce the heat and simmer for 5 minutes. Leave the mixture until it is cold, then blend to a purée with the remaining lemon juice. Freeze the mixture in an ice cream maker or in shallow metal trays, scraping the frozen part from the sides into the rest of the mixture and stirring at regular intervals. To serve, spoon the fruit salad into individual glasses or a large glass bowl and arrange scoops of sorbet on top of the fruit. Garnish each scoop with two mint leaves.

DANIEL BOUCHÉ
INVITATION À LA CUISINE BUISSONIÈRE

Peaches in Recioto

Pesche al Recioto

The Recioto della Valpolicella used in this recipe is a sweet, red dessert wine. Any other sweet wine may be used instead.

	To serve 4	
4	ripe peaches, peeled	4
35 cl	Recioto della Valpolicella	12 fl oz
60 g	castor sugar	5 oz
½	lemon, juice strained	½

Cut the peaches into segments, put them in a serving dish and sprinkle them with the sugar and lemon juice. Put the dish in the refrigerator for 2½ hours. Before serving, pour the wine over the peaches.

GIORGIO GIOCO
LA CUCINA SCALIGERA

Peaches in Red Wine à la Bordelaise

Pêches au Vin Rouge, Dites à la Bordelaise

The technique of peeling peaches and poaching them in red wine is demonstrated on page 76. In the recipe below, the wine and sugar are boiled together before the peaches are poached in the syrup; the same results may be obtained by assembling all the ingredients at the same time. Cinnamon bark is obtainable from Oriental food shops and delicatessens.

Serve with slices of brioche that have been sprinkled with sugar and glazed in a hot oven.

	To serve 4	
4	peaches, peeled and halved	4
30 cl	red Bordeaux	½ pint
100 g	sugar	3½ oz
1 cm	cinnamon bark	½ inch

Sprinkle the peaches with half of the sugar and leave them for 1 hour. Boil the wine with the rest of the sugar and the cinnamon bark in an untinned copper pan. Lower the heat, put the peaches and their juice into the pan and poach until they are tender—about 30 minutes. Remove the peaches from the pan, drain them and arrange them in a glass dish. Reserve the cooking liquid.

Over a high heat, reduce the liquid in which the peaches were cooked to a thick, syrupy consistency. Pour the syrup over the peaches and leave until cold before serving.

PROSPER MONTAGNÉ
NEW LAROUSSE GASTRONOMIQUE

Peaches and Almonds in Brouilly

Pêches et Amandes au Brouilly

Green almonds (amandes fraîches) are young almonds picked whilst their shells are still soft and green. Flaked almonds can be used instead although they are not as good.

The dessert can also be served in ramekins embedded in crushed ice.

	To serve 4	
1 kg	ripe white peaches, peeled	2 to 2½ lb
24	green almonds, hulled, blanched and halved	24
¼ litre	Beaujolais (preferably Brouilly)	8 fl oz
200 g	raspberries, puréed	7 oz
150 g	castor sugar	5 oz

Cut each peach into eight slices and place them in a bowl with the raspberry purée. Mix the wine and sugar together and pour them over the peaches and raspberry purée. Leave the mixture in a cold place for 1 hour. Chill four large burgundy glasses. Put equal amounts of peach slices and sauce into the glasses and scatter the almonds over them.

JEAN AND PIERRE TROISGROS
CUISINIERS À ROANNE

Champagne Water Ice

The technique of making sparkling wine ice is on page 77.

Any kind of wine may be used in the same way.

	To serve 6 to 8	
1 bottle	Champagne, well chilled	1 bottle
6	sugar cubes	6
6	lemons	6
¼ litre	sugar syrup, made with 250 g (8 oz) sugar and 15 cl (¼ pint) water, cooled (*page 166*)	8 fl oz

Rub the sugar cubes on the lemons to extract the oil and flavour from the rinds. Squeeze the lemons, strain their juice into a bowl and dissolve the flavoured sugar cubes in the juice. Add the Champagne, then the cooled sugar syrup to taste. Freeze the mixture in an ice cream churn.

Alternatively, pour the mixture into shallow metal trays and put the trays in a freezer. After about 30 minutes, remove the trays and use a fork or spoon to stir the frozen edges of the mixture into the centre, breaking up any large crystals that have formed. Replace the trays in the freezer and repeat the procedure every hour. After 3 to 4 hours of freezing, scrape the frozen mixture into a bowl and whisk it lightly—the sorbet should be rather mushy in texture. Serve in chilled glasses.

G. A. JARRIN
THE ITALIAN CONFECTIONER

Mercurey and Blackcurrant Sorbet

Sorbet au Mercurey et au Cassis

Crème de cassis is a blackcurrant liqueur. An alternative technique of freezing sorbet is demonstrated on page 77.

To serve 6 to 8

1 bottle	Mercurey or other red Burgundy	1 bottle
330 g	blackcurrants, 20 reserved	11 oz
200 g	castor sugar	7 oz
1	orange, rind thinly pared, juice strained	1
1	lemon, rind thinly pared, juice strained	1
3 to 5	blackcurrant leaves	3 to 5
	crème de cassis (optional)	

Pour the wine into a pan, add the sugar and the orange and lemon rinds; bring to the boil. Add 300 g (10 oz) of the blackcurrants and the blackcurrant leaves to the pan; bring back to the boil and boil for 5 minutes.

Pass the mixture through a food mill, using the medium disc so that the blackcurrant seeds and skins can pass through it. Leave the purée for several hours, then strain it through a very fine sieve into a bowl, pressing it through firmly—only a small lump of skin and pips should be left in the bottom of the sieve. Add the orange and lemon juice. Taste the mixture; if it is too sweet, add a little water. Freeze the mixture in an ice cream churn and, as soon as it has frozen, stir in the reserved blackcurrants. If you like, pour a little *crème de cassis* over the sorbet before serving.

DANIEL BOUCHÉ
INVITATION À LA CUISINE BUISSONIÈRE

Nasturtium Ice

To serve 6

30	nasturtium flowers	30
500 g	sugar	1 lb
1 litre	water	1¾ pints
3	lemons, juice strained	3
4 tbsp	claret or other red wine	4 tbsp

Pound 24 of the nasturtiums to a paste in a mortar with 2 to 3 tablespoons of sugar. Add the rest of the sugar to the water and boil for 5 minutes. Remove the sugar syrup from the heat, stir in the lemon juice and flower paste.

Leave the mixture to cool, strain and put it in the freezer until it is partly frozen. Add the claret and continue freezing, stirring from time to time. Serve in glasses, garnished with the reserved nasturtiums.

CORA, ROSE AND BOB BROWN
THE WINE COOKBOOK

Claret Jelly

To serve 6

¼ litre	claret or other red wine	8 fl oz
250 g	redcurrant jelly	8 oz
125 g	sugar	4 oz
1	strip lemon rind	1
¼ litre	boiling water	8 fl oz
2 tbsp	powdered gelatine, softened in 4 tbsp cold water for 5 minutes	2 tbsp
2 tbsp	brandy	2 tbsp

Put the jelly, sugar, lemon rind and boiling water in a saucepan. Stir over a low heat until the jelly is dissolved. Bring the mixture to the boil, remove it from the heat and add the gelatine, stirring until it is completely dissolved. Strain and add the brandy and claret. Rinse a mould with cold water, pour the mixture into the mould and chill until it has set. Unmould the jelly and serve.

CORA, ROSE AND BOB BROWN
THE WINE COOKBOOK

Cold Zabaglione

Zabaione Freddo

Instead of using vanilla extract, you can replace the sugar with an equal amount of vanilla sugar. Vanilla sugar is made by storing sugar in a closed jar with a vanilla pod.

	To serve 6	
6	egg yolks	6
180 g	sugar	6¼ oz
20 cl	Marsala	7 fl oz
½	lemon, rind grated	½
	ground cinnamon	
	vanilla extract	
30 cl	double cream, whipped	12 fl oz
	sponge fingers or ratafia biscuits	
	strawberries or cherries	

Put the egg yolks, sugar, Marsala, lemon rind, a pinch of cinnamon and a drop of vanilla extract into a pan. Partially immerse the pan in a bain-marie and place on a low heat. Whisk the mixture constantly until it begins to thicken, and continue whisking until it has a thick, creamy consistency—about 10 minutes. Remove the pan from the heat and leave the mixture until it is cold. Fold 20 cl (7 fl oz) of the whipped cream into the cold zabaglione and pour it into cups. Place sponge fingers or ratafia biscuits round the cups, spoon a dollop of whipped cream on top of the zabaglione and put a cherry or strawberry on the cream.

LEONE BOSI
DOLCI PER UN ANNO

Rhenish Wine Cream

	To serve 6	
60 cl	Rhine wine	1 pint
1	stick cinnamon	1
250 g	sugar	8 oz
7	eggs	7
1	lemon, juice strained	1
4 tbsp	orange-flower water	4 tbsp
60 g	candied peel or 2 tbsp castor sugar or 60 g (2 oz) sponge biscuits, crumbled	2 oz

Boil the wine, cinnamon stick and the sugar for 10 minutes. While the mixture is boiling, whisk the eggs well. Take the wine mixture off the heat, let it cool a few moments so that it will not curdle the eggs, and whisk it gradually into the eggs. Continue whisking fast, until the mixture is thick enough to be lifted with the point of a knife, but be sure not to let it curdle. Add the lemon juice and orange-flower water. Pour the wine cream into a serving dish and garnish it with the candied peel, castor sugar or sponge biscuits before serving.

P. LAMB
ROYAL COOKERY: OR THE COMPLEAT COURT COOK BOOK

Sauternes Custard Sauce

Other sweet white Bordeaux wines such as Cérons and Ste. Croix du Mont can be used instead of Sauternes.

	To serve 4	
17.5 cl	Sauternes	6 fl oz
	sugar	
4	egg yolks, beaten	4
6 cl	double cream	2 fl oz
2 tsp	kirsch	2 tsp

Pour the wine into the top of a double boiler and add sugar to taste. Fill the base with hot water. Place the double boiler over a low heat. When the wine is hot, gradually stir in the egg yolks with a wooden spoon. Continue stirring until the custard is thick enough to coat the back of the spoon. Be careful not to let the custard boil as the eggs will curdle. Take the top off the double boiler; keep stirring, adding the cream and then the kirsch. Pour the custard over cooked or preserved fruits.

JEANNE OWEN
A WINE LOVER'S COOK BOOK

Rich Pancakes

The original recipe called for sack, a sweet, rich wine made around the Mediterranean and popular in Britain from the 15th to 17th centuries. Sweet sherry is substituted here.

	To serve 10	
60 cl	double cream	1 pint
30 cl	sweet sherry	½ pint
18	egg yolks	18
250 g	sugar	8 oz
1 tsp	ground cinnamon	1 tsp
¼	nutmeg, grated	¼
¼ tsp	ground mace	¼ tsp
500 g	flour	1 lb
250 g	clarified butter, melted	8 oz

Put the cream, sherry, egg yolks, sugar, cinnamon, nutmeg and mace in a large bowl and beat them well together. Gradually fold in the flour—the batter should be thin and runny. Heat about 15 g (½ oz) of butter in a pancake pan or a heavy frying pan. Put a ladleful of the batter into the pan. Cook for about 2 minutes on each side, until golden-brown. Repeat with the remaining batter.

WILL RABISHA
THE WHOLE BODY OF COOKERY DISSECTED

Tart of the Ananas or Pineapple

This 18th-century recipe called for Canary wine, which was a sweet, fortified wine popular at that time; since it is no longer available, a sweet Madeira has been used instead.

To serve 6

1	large pineapple, peeled, cored and cut into 1 cm (½ inch) slices	1
¼ litre	Madeira	8 fl oz
60 g	sugar	2 oz
20 cl	double cream (optional)	7 fl oz

Sweet dough

250 g	flour	8 oz
40 g	castor sugar	1½ oz
125 g	cold butter, cut into small pieces	4 oz
2 tbsp	milk	2 tbsp
1 tbsp	sweet sherry	1 tbsp
1 tbsp	brandy	1 tbsp

To make the dough, put the flour and sugar into a bowl. Add the butter and rub it into the flour until the mixture resembles fine breadcrumbs. Add the milk, sherry and brandy, and blend them into the mixture with a fork. Wrap the dough in plastic film or wax paper and refrigerate it for at least 1 hour, or put the dough in the freezer for about 20 minutes until the surface has slightly frozen.

Roll out the dough and use it to line a greased 23 cm (9 inch) tart tin. Bake the pastry blind for 15 minutes in a preheated 200°C (400°F or Mark 6) oven.

Stew the pineapple slices, Madeira and sugar in a pan over a low heat for 10 minutes until the pineapple is heated through and has flavoured the wine. Remove from the heat and leave to cool. Pour the cooled pineapple slices and their cooking liquid into the tart tin and bake in a preheated 200°C (400°F or Mark 6) oven for about 20 minutes until the top of the pineapple begins to brown. Remove the pineapple tart from the oven and pour the cream over it, if you wish. Serve the tart either hot or cold.

RICHARD BRADLEY
THE COUNTRY HOUSEWIFE AND LADY'S DIRECTOR

Trifle

The technique of draining the froth from cream through a sieve was used when milk was taken directly from the cow. For a modern alternative which produces a thicker syllabub, macerate the lemon or orange rind and juice in the wine overnight, strain the mixture and mix in the sugar. Pour in the cream slowly, stirring constantly; whisk the mixture with a hand whisk until it thickens and forms soft peaks.

To serve 10 to 12

125 g	macaroons	4 oz
125 g	ratafia biscuits	4 oz
15 cl	sweet white wine or sherry	¼ pint
	redcurrant jelly or crystallized fruit or flowers, and "hundreds and thousands"	

Syllabub

1¼ litre	double cream	2 pints
15 cl	dry white wine	¼ pint
1	lemon or Seville orange, juice strained	1
1	lemon, rind grated	1
250 g	castor sugar	8 oz

Custard

60 cl	milk or single cream	1 pint
100 g	castor sugar	3½ oz
4	egg yolks, beaten	4

To make the syllabub, put the double cream into a large bowl with the dry white wine, lemon or orange juice, grated lemon rind and the sugar. Whisk the mixture well. When a froth forms on top of the mixture, skim it off with a skimmer and put it on a drum-sieve to drain. Continue whisking until all the mixture has been frothed and put to drain. Reserve the syllabub in a cool place.

Arrange the macaroons and ratafia biscuits in the bottom of a deep glass dish and sprinkle the sweet wine or sherry over them. Set the dish aside.

To make the custard, scald the milk or single cream in a pan, then remove the pan from the heat. Add the sugar, mix in the beaten egg yolks and place the pan on a very low heat. Stir the custard until it is thick, 10 to 15 minutes, then pour it over the macaroons and ratafias. Leave until the custard is cold.

Spoon the drained syllabub over the trifle so that it stands as high as possible. Garnish the trifle with redcurrant jelly or crystallized fruit or flowers, and "hundreds and thousands".

RICHARD BRIGGS
THE ENGLISH ART OF COOKERY

Standard Preparations

Veal Stock

For a more gelatinous stock, include a calf's foot, cleaned, split and blanched for 5 minutes in boiling water, then rinsed, and about 250 g (8 oz) of rinsed, blanched pork rinds.

To make 2 to 3 litres (3½ to 5 pints)

1	veal knuckle bone, sawn into 5 cm (2 inch) pieces	1
2 kg	meaty veal trimmings (neck, shank or rib tips)	4 lb
1 kg	chicken back, necks, feet and wing tips	2 to 2½ lb
3 to 5 litres	water	5 to 8 pints
1	bouquet garni, including leek and celery	1
1	garlic head	1
2	medium-sized onions, 1 stuck with 2 cloves	2
4	large carrots	4
	salt	

Place a round grill in the bottom of a large stock-pot to prevent the ingredients from sticking. Fit the meat and bones into the pot and add water to cover by about 5 cm (2 inches). Bring slowly to the boil and, with a spoon, skim off the scum that rises. Keep skimming, occasionally adding a glass of cold water, until no more scum rises—after 10 to 15 minutes. Add the bouquet garni, garlic, onions, carrots and salt, and skim once more as the liquid returns to the boil. Reduce the heat to very low, cover the pot with the lid ajar and simmer for at least 6 hours, skimming at intervals.

Place a colander lined with dampened muslin over a large bowl and pour in the stock. Leave the strained stock to cool completely, then remove the last traces of fat from the surface with a skimmer and kitchen towel; if the stock has been refrigerated, lift off the solidified fat.

Beef stock: Add 2 kg (4 lb) of beef shank, chuck or oxtail to the other meat and simmer the stock for 6 to 7 hours.

Chicken stock: Double the quantity of chicken pieces in the preparation of the veal stock or poach a boiling fowl in veal stock for 1½ to 3 hours, depending on its age.

Fish Fumet

To make about 2 litres (3½ pints)

1 kg	fish heads, bones and trimmings, rinsed and broken or chopped into convenient pieces	2 to 2½ lb
1	large onion, sliced	1
1	carrot, sliced	1
1	leek, sliced	1
1	stick celery, sliced	1
1	sprig thyme	1
1	bay leaf	1
About 2 litres	water	About 3½ pints
	salt	
½ litre	white wine	18 fl oz

Put the vegetables and herbs in the bottom of a large pan and place the fish pieces on top. Add water to cover and season lightly with salt. Bring to the boil over a low heat. With a large, shallow spoon, skim off the scum that rises to the surface as the liquid reaches a simmer. Keep skimming until no more scum rises, then place the lid slightly ajar on the pan and simmer for 15 minutes. Add the wine, return to the boiling point and simmer, lid slightly ajar, for a further 15 minutes. Line a sieve with a layer of dampened muslin, set the sieve over a deep bowl and strain the fumet through it. Leave the fumet to drain well, but do not press the solids when straining in case they cloud the liquid. The fumet is now ready for use as a poaching medium.

Sugar Syrup

The proportions shown here will form a light sugar syrup. For a medium sugar syrup, add 350 g (12 oz) of sugar to each 60 cl (1 pint) of water; for a heavy syrup, the proportions are 500 g (1 lb) of sugar to each 60 cl (1 pint) of water.

To make about ¾ litre (1¼ pints)

250 g	sugar	8 oz
60 cl	water	1 pint

Place the sugar and water in a saucepan and cook over a low heat, stirring occasionally, until the sugar is melted. If any sugar has splashed on to the sides of the pan, brush down the sides with a pastry brush dipped in warm water to remove the crystals. Raise the heat, bring the liquid to the boil and cook for a few seconds without stirring.

The following are a selection of recipes from the suggested menus in Chapter 3 (*pages 49-63*).

Beurre Blanc

To make about 30 to 40 cl (½ to ¾ pint) sauce

6 tbsp	dry white wine	6 tbsp
6 tbsp	white wine vinegar	6 tbsp
3	shallots, very finely chopped	3
	salt	
	pepper	
250 to 400 g	cold unsalted butter, diced	8 to 14 oz

In a heavy stainless steel or enamelled saucepan, boil the wine and vinegar with the shallots and a pinch of salt until only enough liquid remains to moisten the shallots. Remove the pan from the heat and allow it to cool for a few minutes. Season the mixture with pepper. Place the pan on a fireproof mat over a very low heat and whisk in the butter, a handful at a time, until the mixture has a creamy consistency. Remove from the heat as soon as all the butter has been incorporated.

Salt Cod with Potatoes and Eggs

To serve 4

750 g	salt cod, soaked for at least 24 hours in 3 or more changes of water, poached in fresh water with a bay leaf and sprig of thyme, then flaked, bones and skins discarded	1½ lb
1 kg	potatoes, boiled in their skins, peeled and thickly sliced while still hot	2 lb
4	hard-boiled eggs, cut into pieces	4
2 or 3	garlic cloves, pounded to a purée	2 or 3
4 tbsp	chopped parsley	4 tbsp
¼ litre	olive oil	8 fl oz
	pepper	
	salt (optional)	

Mix the garlic purée and parsley together well, add the eggs, and stir gently with half of the olive oil. Add the hot potatoes to the remaining oil over high heat, toss with the flaked cod, and gently stir in the egg mixture; add a generous amount of pepper, and a little salt if the cod is not too salty. Turn out on to a warmed plate and serve.

Crayfish Salad with Fresh Dill

To serve 4 to 6

36	large, live crayfish, washed	36
1 tbsp	finely chopped dill	1 tbsp
	salt and pepper	
1	medium-sized lemon, juice strained	1
¼ litre	double cream	8 fl oz
1	medium-sized lettuce	1

White wine court-bouillon

½ litre	dry white wine	16 fl oz
½ litre	water	16 fl oz
1 tbsp	sea salt	1 tbsp
	cayenne pepper	
½ tsp	mixed herbs	½ tsp
1	bay leaf	1
1	bouquet garni, including parsley and fresh dill	1
1	large onion, thinly sliced	1
1	medium-sized carrot, thinly sliced	1
8 to 10	peppercorns	8 to 10

To make the court-bouillon, bring the wine and water to the boil in a large pan, add the salt, a small pinch of cayenne pepper, the mixed herbs, bay leaf, bouquet garni, onion and carrot. Simmer, covered, over a medium heat for 30 minutes, adding the peppercorns after 20 minutes.

Add half the crayfish to the court-bouillon, cover the pan, hold the lid tightly, and cook for 8 minutes, tossing the pan from time to time. With a wire skimmer, remove the crayfish to a bowl and cook the rest. Combine the two batches and leave to cool in the court-bouillon.

Reserve six of the largest and most perfectly formed crayfish for the garnish, keeping them moist in some court-bouillon. Tear off the tails of the others, remove the tail shell, and put the flesh aside, covered in court-bouillon.

Pound the heads, claws, legs and coral of the crayfish, four or five at a time in a mortar. Pass each pounded batch through the medium disc of a food mill and, once all the juices are thoroughly extracted, discard the débris of shells. When all have been pounded and puréed, pass the purée, a little at a time, through a fine-meshed drum sieve.

Reserve a third of the dill for a garnish and mix the remainder with salt, pepper and the lemon juice; add the cream, mix well and whisk in the crayfish purée. Taste for salt and lemon. Arrange the lettuce leaves on the bottom and round the sides of a deep serving bowl. Drain the reserved crayfish flesh and distribute it on the lettuce. Pour the sauce over the salad, place the unshelled crayfish symmetrically round the border and sprinkle with the remaining dill.

Seafood Sausages

To clean the sausage casings after they have been soaked, attach one end to a funnel and pour cold water through it from a jug; or attach the casing to a cold tap and run water through it. Serve the sausages with *beurre blanc* (*recipe, page 167*).

To serve 4 to 6

1	small sole fillet, diced and sautéed in butter for a few seconds until firm	1
100 g	poached prawn tails, lobster tail or scallops, diced	3½ oz
1 tbsp	green peppercorns	1 tbsp
30 g	pistachio nuts, peeled and coarsely chopped	1 oz
	beef sausage casings, soaked for 2 hours in several changes of tepid water mixed with a splash of lemon juice or vinegar, then cleaned	
	Fish mousseline	
250 g	white fish fillets (whiting, pike, or monkfish), coarsely chopped	8 oz
	salt and pepper	
1	large egg white	1
¼ litre	double cream	8 fl oz

To make the mousseline, pound the fish to a smooth purée with a pestle; season with salt and pepper and add the egg white a little at a time, pounding after each addition until it is completely incorporated. Alternatively, reduce the fish to a purée in a food processor, add the seasoning and egg white and process the mixture again. A little at a time, rub the purée through a fine-meshed sieve. Pack the purée into a metal bowl and press plastic film against the surface. Place the bowl in a larger bowl of crushed ice and refrigerate for at least 1 hour.

Remove the bowls from the refrigerator. Pour off the water from the large bowl and add more crushed ice. Using a wooden spoon, work a little double cream into the mixture, beating well. Return the bowls to the refrigerator for 15 minutes. Continue beating in small quantities of cream, refrigerating for 15 minutes between each addition and replacing the crushed ice as necessary. Beat the mixture vigorously as soon as it becomes soft enough to do so. When about half the cream has been incorporated, refrigerate the mixture for a few minutes. Lightly whip the remaining cream and incorporate it into the purée. Refrigerate until ready for use, but take care not to leave the mousseline too long before using it.

Leave the sole and prawns until cold; remove the mousseline from the refrigerator and place it over a bowl of crushed ice. Toss the sole and prawns into the mousseline, together with the green peppercorns and pistachio nuts and mix all the ingredients together well.

Put some mousseline into a pastry bag and slip a length of

beef casing over the nozzle, leaving 7.5 cm (3 inches) free. Squeeze the stuffing into the casing to make a sausage of the desired length—do not pack it tightly. Pull off another 7.5 cm of empty casing and cut it off. Knot the casing at either end of the sausage. Trim close to the knots.

Prick the sausages all over with a trussing needle and put them in a pan of salted cold water. Partially cover the pan and let the water warm up slowly over a low heat to just below simmering point. Maintain this temperature and poach the sausages for 20 minutes to firm them. Remove the sausages from the pan and slice them diagonally. Serve on hot plates.

Veal Fricandeau

To serve 6 to 8

1.5 kg	rump, loin or leg of veal in one piece, cut lengthwise along the grain and trimmed of fat, gristle or surface membrane	3 lb
200 g	pork fat, cut into lardons and seasoned with salt and pepper	7 oz
1 or 2	onions, chopped	1 or 2
1 or 2	carrots, chopped	1 or 2
¼ litre	dry white wine	8 fl oz
½ litre	hot veal stock (*page 166*)	16 fl oz
	salt	

With a larding needle, lard the veal with the strips of pork fat, drawing the fat through the meat just far enough to make a single stitch. Snip off the surplus fat, leaving the short length in place. Rethread the needle and repeat the process, making one stitch at a time, in neat rows.

Put the onions and carrots in a large braising pan or casserole and place it, covered, in a preheated 220°C (425°F or Mark 7) oven for about 30 minutes or until the vegetables begin to brown. Remove the pan from the oven, add the veal and return the pan, uncovered, to the oven for 10 minutes or until the meat firms a little and takes on a white colour. Transfer the pan to the oven top. Add the wine and reduce it over a high heat before topping up with the hot veal stock.

Cover the veal with buttered greaseproof paper, put a lid on the pan and place it in a preheated 150°C (300°F or Mark 2) oven for 3½ hours. For the last hour, increase the heat to 200°C (400°F or Mark 6) and uncover the meat so it can begin to colour; baste it very frequently with the braising juices. Draw off two-thirds of the braising liquid and reduce it in a sauce-pan to a syrupy consistency. Continue basting with the reduced sauce to give the meat an amber glaze. Remove the meat and keep it warm. Strain the braising liquid into a pan and degrease it, then bring it to a simmer, keeping the pan half off the heat. Remove the skin of impurities that forms on the still side of the surface. Continue simmering and skimming until no more impurities rise to the surface of the sauce. Serve the cleansed sauce with the fricandeau.

Little Cheese Soufflés

Petites Suissesses

The cheese soufflés can be poached in the bain-marie a few hours in advance of baking, if preferred.

To serve 4 to 6

¼ litre	milk	8 fl oz
15 g	flour	½ oz
	salt	
	white pepper	
	grated nutmeg	
60 g	butter	2 oz
125 g	Parmesan cheese, grated	4 oz
3	egg yolks	3
2	egg whites, stiffly beaten	2
35 cl	double cream	12 fl oz

Bring the milk to the boil, leave it until it is lukewarm, and pour it slowly in to the flour, stirring constantly to avoid the mixture becoming lumpy. Season with salt, white pepper and a pinch of nutmeg, and, stirring constantly with a wooden spoon, cook over a medium flame until thickened. Leave to cool for several minutes, add the butter, a little over half of the grated cheese and the three egg yolks, and mix thoroughly. Fold in the egg whites gently but thoroughly.

Butter individual moulds, porcelain ramekins or muffin tins. Spoon in the mixture until they are about two-thirds full, place them in a bain-marie and poach in a preheated 150°C (300°F or Mark 2) oven for 15 to 20 minutes, or until they are firm and spongy to the touch. Run the blade of a knife round the edges of the little soufflés, then unmould them carefully, so as not to damage them, on to a large baking sheet.

Butter a shallow baking or gratin dish of the right size to hold the little soufflés side by side, without—or barely—touching. Sprinkle the bottom with half the remaining cheese, place the soufflés on top and pour in enough cream to immerse them by half. Sprinkle the rest of the cheese over the surface and bake in a preheated 180°C (350°F or Mark 4) oven for another 15 to 20 minutes—or until the cream is nearly all absorbed and a light, golden grain has formed.

Vegetable Stew

Estouffade

Prepare the artichokes at the last moment, add them immediately to the pan, then turn them round instantly in the butter to coat all surfaces and prevent them from blackening. When available, parboiled mange-tout or tender, peeled broad beans can be added to the stew shortly before removing the pan from the heat.

To serve 4 to 6

500 g	large spring onions, white parts only, or very small white onions	1 lb
1	garlic head, cloves cleaned of loose husk but unpeeled	1
6	medium-sized tender artichokes, pared, quartered and chokes removed	6
1	medium-sized tender, leafy lettuce, coarsely shredded	1
500 g	small firm courgettes, thinly sliced	1 lb
125 g	butter	4 oz
1	bouquet garni including stick celery, parsley, bay leaf and thyme	1
	salt and pepper	
2 tbsp	chopped parsley	2 tbsp
1 tsp	finely chopped marjoram (optional)	1 tsp

Melt about 40 g (1½ oz) of the butter in a large, shallow copper saucepan or fireproof casserole and add the onions, garlic cloves and the artichoke quarters. Bury the bouquet garni in the centre of the vegetables, scatter over the lettuce, sprinkle with salt, and cover the pan tightly. Allow the vegetables to sweat by cooking them very gently for about 30 minutes, tossing from time to time (or stirring with a wooden spoon). At intervals, note the moisture in the pan: there should be just the suggestion of a slightly syrupy juice. If the heat is low enough, the lettuce will provide enough liquid without the addition of water. But if the vegetables are cooking in fat only and in danger of colouring, add a couple of tablespoons of water, incorporating it into the vegetables by gently shaking the contents of the pan.

When the onions and artichokes are tender, melt 30 g (1 oz) of the butter in a large omelette pan and sauté the courgettes over a high heat, tossing very often, for 5 to 6 minutes—or until all are just tender and a number lightly coloured. Add the courgettes to the other vegetables, cover the pan and allow the flavours to mingle for 5 to 10 minutes. Taste and season with salt; pepper generously and, away from the heat, add the remaining butter, cut into small pieces. Swirl or gently stir the vegetables until the butter is absorbed into the juices. Discard the bouquet garni. Sprinkle the vegetable stew with parsley and the marjoram, if using, and serve.

Recipe Index

English recipe titles are listed by categories such as "Beef", "Fricassée", "Pears", "Red Wine", "Sauternes" and "Water Ice", and within those categories appear alphabetically. Foreign recipe titles are listed alphabetically without regard to category.

General Index/Glossary

Included in this index are definitions of many of the culinary terms used in this book: definitions are in italics. The recipes in the Anthology are listed in the Recipe Index on page 170.

Recipe Credits

The sources for the recipes in this volume are shown below. Page references in brackets indicate where the recipes appear in the Anthology.

Bize-Leroy, Lalou, Le Nouveau Guide Gault Millau, Connaissance des Voyages. Magazine, September 1981. Copyright by Agence Presse-Loisirs. Published by Jour-Azur S.A., Paris. Translated by permission of Jour-Azur S.A. (pages 144, 152).
Blanch, Lesley, Round the World in Eighty Dishes. Published by John Murray (Publishers) Limited, London 1956. By permission of John Murray (Publishers) Limited (page 155).
Born, Wina, Herrlijke Gerechten. © 1972 by Uitgeverij van Lindonk, Amsterdam. Published by Uitgeverij van Lindonk. Translated by permission of the author, Amsterdam (page 158).
Bosi, Leone, Dolci per un Anno. © 1972 Arnoldo Mondadori Editore, Milano. Published by Arnoldo Mondadori Editore. Translated by permission of Arnoldo Mondadori Editore (pages 161, 164).
Bouché, Daniel, Invitation à la Cuisine Buissonnière. © Atelier Marcel Jullian, 1979. Published by Atelier Marcel Jullian, Paris. Translated by permission of Librairie Hachette, Paris (pages 161, 163).
Bradley, Richard, The Country Housewife and Lady's Director (Parts 1 and 2). Published in 1727 and 1732 respectively. © Prospect Books 1980. Published by Prospect Books, London. By permission of the publisher (page 165).
Briggs, Richard, The English Art of Cookery. 3rd Edition 1794. Printed by G. G. J. and J. Robinson, London (page 165).
Brown, Cora, Rose and Bob, The Wine Cookbook. Copyright 1934, 1941 by Cora, Rose, and Robert Carlton Brown. Published by Little, Brown, and Company, Boston. By permission of Laura P. Brown, Wellfleet, Massachusetts (pages 145, 163).
Buonassisi, Vincenzo and Capogna, Pino, Il Vino in Pentola. © 1977 Arnoldo Mondadori Editore S.p.A., Milano. Published by Arnoldo Mondadori Editore S.p.A. Translated by permission of Arnoldo Mondadori Editore S.p.A. (page 149).
Clément, Gaston, Gastronomie et Folklore. Published by Éditions "Le Sphinx" S.A., Brussels 1957 and 1971. Translated by permission of Éditions "Le Sphinx" S.A. (page 147).
Constantin Weyer, Maurice and Germaine, Les Secrets d'une Maîtresse de Maison. Originally published in 1932. Published by Éditions Jeanne Laffitte, Marseilles 1981. Translated by permission of Éditions Jeanne Laffitte (page 160).

Cùnsolo, Felice, La Cucina del Piemonte. © Copyright by Novedit Milano. Published by Novedit Milano, 1964 (page 154).
Cutler, Carol, The Six-minute Soufflé and other Culinary Delights. Copyright © 1976 by Carol Cutler. Published by Clarkson N. Potter, Inc./Publisher, New York. By permission of Crown Publishers Inc., New York (page 147).
Daguin, André, Le Nouveau Cuisinier Gascon. © 1981, Éditions Stock. Published by Éditions Stock, Paris. Translated by permission of Éditions Stock (pages 150, 153).
Davidson, Alan, Mediterranean Seafood. Copyright © Alan Davidson, 1972, 1981. Published by Penguin Books Ltd., London. By permission of Penguin Books Ltd. (page 148).
Ellis, Audrey, Wine Lovers Cookbook. © Audrey Ellis 1975. Published by Hutchinson & Co. (Publishers) Ltd., London. By permission of Hutchinson Publishing Group (page 160).
Gioco, Giorgio, La Cucina Scaligera. Published by Franco Angeli Editore, Milan 1978 (pages 152, 162).
Gouy, Louis P. De, The Soup Book. Copyright © 1949 by Mrs. Louis P. De Gouy. Published by Dover Publications, Inc., New York. By permission of Jacqueline S. Dooner, New York (page 145).
Hamilton, Ruth Mouton, French Acadian Cook Book. Copyright 1955 The Louisiana Acadian Handicraft Museum, Inc. Published by the Jennings Association of Commerce, Jennings, Louisiana. By permission of the Jennings Association of Commerce (page 148).
Hellrigl, Andreas, La Cucina dell'Alto Adige. Copyright © 1970 by Franco Angeli Editore, Milano. Published by Franco Angeli Editore. Translated by permission of Franco Angeli Editore (page 157).
Jarrin, G. A., The Italian Confectioner. Published by E. S. Ebers and Co., London 1841 (page 162).
Kernmayr, Hans Gustl, So Kochte Meine Mutter. Copyright © 1976 by Mary Hahn's Kochbuchverlag, Berlin-München. Published by Wilhelm Heyne Verlag, Munich. Translated by permission of Mary Hahn's Kochbuchverlag (page 151).
Lallemand, Roger, Le Coq au Vin. © Éditions Goutal-Darly, 1980. Published by Éditions Goutal-Darly, Montrouge. Translated by permission of Éditions Goutal-Darly (pages 150, 151).
Lamb, P., Royal Cookery: or the Compleat Court Cook Book. Printed for E. and R. Nutt and A. Ropper in 1726 (page 164).
Lujan, Nestor and Perucho, Juan, El Libro de la Cocina Española. © Ediciones Danae, S.A. Published by Ediciones Danae, S.A., Barcelona. Translated by permission of Editorial Baber S.A., Barcelona (pages 147, 152).
Montagné, Prosper, New Larousse Gastronomique. Originally pub-

lished under the title "Nouveau Larousse Gastronomique". © Copyright Librairie Larousse, Paris 19, 1960. © Copyright English text The Hamlyn Publishing Group Limited 1977. Published by The Hamlyn Publishing Group Limited, London. By permission of The Hamlyn Publishing Group Limited (page 162).
Oliver, Michel, Mes Recettes à la Télé. © Librairie Plon, 1980. Published by Librairie Plon, Paris. Translated by permission of Librairie Plon (pages 153, 158).
Olney, Richard, Simple French Food. Copyright © Richard Olney 1974. Published by Jill Norman and Hobhouse Ltd., London 1981. By permission of Jill Norman and Hobhouse Ltd. (pages 156, 160).
Owen, Jeanne, A Wine Lover's Cook Book. Copyright 1940 by Jeanne Owen. Published by M. Barrows and Company Inc., New York. By permission of William Morrow Co. Inc., New York (pages 157, 164).
Petits Propos Culinaires 11. July 1982. Copyright © Prospect Books 1982. Published by Prospect Books, London. By permission of the publisher (pages 146, 148).
Philpot, Rosl, Viennese Cookery. Copyright © 1965 by Rosl Philpot. Published by Hodder & Stoughton Limited, London. By permission of Hodder & Stoughton Limited (page 159).
Portinari, Laura Gras, Cucina e Vini del Piemonte e della Valle d'Aosta. © Copyright 1971 U. Mursia & C. Published by Ugo Mursia & C., Mila. Translated by permission of Ugo Mursia Editore (page 154).
Rabisha, Will, The Whole Body of Cookery Dissected. Published London, 1682 (page 164).
Robotti, Frances D. and Peter J., French Cooking in the New World. Copyright © 1967 by Frances Diane Robotti. Published by Doubleday & Company, Inc., New York. By permission of Frances Robotti, New York (page 161).
Senderens, Alain and Eventhia, La Cuisine Réussie. © 1981, Éditions Jean-Claude Lattès. Published by Éditions Jean-Claude Lattès, Paris. Translated by permission of Éditions Jean-Claude Lattès (page 149).
Spoerlin, Marguerite, La Cuisinière du Haut-Rhin. Parts 1 and 2 originally published in Mulhouse in 1842 and 1833 respectively. Reprinted by Éditions Daniel Morcrette, Paris. Translated by permission of Éditions Daniel Morcrette (page 154).
Troisgros, Jean and Pierre, Cuisiniers à Roanne. © Éditions Robert Laffont S.A. 1977. Published by Éditions Robert Laffont S.A., Paris. Translated by permission of Macmillan, London and Basingstoke (page 162).
Vence, Céline, Encyclopédie Hachette de la Cuisine d'Hier et d'Aujourd'hui. © Hachette, 1978. Published by Hachette, Paris. Translated by permission of Hachette (page 155).

Acknowledgements and Picture Credits

The Editors of this book are particularly indebted to Gail Duff, Maidstone, Kent, Berta Julia, Barcelona, Ann Mary O'Sullivan, Deya, Mallorca, David Schwarz, London

They also wish to thank the following: Danielle Adkinson, London; Les Amis du Vin, London; Baccarat, France; Martin Bamford, Château Loudenne, Bordeaux, France; Markie Benet, London; Nicola Blount, London; Jean-Eugène Borie, Château Ducru-Beaucaillou, Bordeaux, France; Judy Brittain, Lumley Employment Company Ltd., London; Mike Brown, London; Martha de la Cal, Lisbon, Cape Wine Centre, London; The Champagne Bureau, London; Windsor Chorlton, London; Emma Codrington, Richmond-upon-Thames, Surrey; Philippe Cottin, Château Mouton-Rothschild, Bordeaux, France; Jean Crété, Château Lafite-Rothschild, Bordeaux, France; Jean Delmas, Château Haut-Brion, Bordeaux, France; June Dowding, Ilford, Essex; Sarah Jane Evans, London; Jay Ferguson, London; Food and Wine from France, London; Neyla Freeman, London; Richard Fyffe, London; Jean-Paul Gardère, Château Latour, Bordeaux, France; Peter

Gordon, London; Maggi Heinz, London; Suzannah Henderson, Lumley Employment Company Ltd., London; Hilary Hockman, London; International Wine and Food Society, London; Italian Institute for Foreign Trade, London; Richard Keele Ltd., London; Anna-Maria Kolkowska, London; Rémi Krug, Krug Champagne, Reims, France; Mr. Lapschies, Swiss Trade Centre, London; Lay & Wheeler Limited, Colchester, Essex; Yves le Canu, Château Lafite-Rothschild, Bordeaux, France; Zelma R. Long, Simi Winery, California; Comte A. de Lur Saluces, Château d'Yquem, Bordeaux, France; Pierre Mackiewicz, Aix-en-Provence, France; Thierry Manoncourt, Château Figeac, Bordeaux, France; Barbara Mayer, London; Pippa Millard, London; Wendy Morris, London; Anders Ousbach, The Winery Limited, London; Lucien Peyraud, Domaine Tempier, (Bandol) Plan du Castellet, France; Jean-Marie Ponsot, Burgundy, France; Alain Querre, Château Monbousquet, Bordeaux, France; R & C Vintners, Carrow, Norwich; Claude Ricard, Domaine de Chevalier, Bordeaux, France; Sylvia Robertson, Surbiton, Surrey; Léon Thienpont, Vieux Château Certan, Bordeaux, France; Stephanie Thompson, London; Fiona Tillett, London; Renato Trestini, London; Aubert de Villaine,

Bouzeron (Chagny), France; Tina Walker, London; Rita Walters, Ilford, Essex; Sally Weston, Richmond-upon-Thames, Surrey; Liz Williams, London.

Photographs by Alan Duns: cover, 4, 22, 32—top, 33—top, 40, 42—top, bottom right, 43, 44—top right, bottom, 50 to 76.

Other photographers (alphabetically):
Tom Belshaw: 28, 29, 46, 47. Pierre Boulat: 6—top, 12 to 14, 16, 18, 19, 38—top right and bottom. John Cook: 34, 35, 38—top left, 42—bottom left, 44—top left, 45. John Elliott: 48, 79. Monique Jacot/Susan Griggs Agency: 7. Louis Klein: 2. Bob Komar: 30, 31, 32—bottom, 33—bottom, 77, 78. Tom Nadeau/Explorer: 17. Pitch: 6—bottom. John Sims/Vision International: 21

Illustrations on pages 18 to 21 by Andrew Riley, The Garden Studio, London. Maps on pages 80 to 89 by Creative Cartography Ltd., London. Line cuts from Mary Evans Picture Library and other private sources.

Colour separations by Scan Studios Ltd.—Dublin, Ireland
Typesetting by Camden Typesetters—London, England
Printed and bound by Brepols S.A.—Tournhout, Belgium.